The Definitive HARTLEPOOL UNITED F.C.

A statistical history to 1998

Gordon Small

Volume 12 in a series of club histories.
A *Soccer Data* Publication from Tony Brown,
on behalf of the Association of Football Statisticians

Published in Great Britain by Tony Brown,
4 Adrian Close, Beeston, Nottingham NG9 6FL.
Telephone 0115 973 6086. E-mail soccer@innotts.co.uk
First published 1998

Other volumes in this series are:

Rochdale
Northampton Town
Chesterfield
Portsmouth
Barnsley
Queen's Park Rangers
Scunthorpe United
Aldershot
Torquay United
Luton Town
Reading

Please write to the publisher for news of future volumes.

ISBN 1 899468 12 9

FOREWORD BY MICK TAIT

The publisher tells me that this is the first book on the club to list all the games and all the players. I'm told that I am one of over 900 men to have appeared in the first team and I am number 32 on the list of managers! I'm grateful for the club for giving me a first taste of management; it is an honour to follow in the footsteps of people like Brian Clough, Len Ashurst and Cyril Knowles.

As a recent player I am well aware of the standards of skill and fitness required in the modern professional game, in the Third Division as well as the Premiership. The task of finding skilful young players and blending them with the experienced pros is a difficult task for the coaching staff and me. The results are visible on the field and our success measured by the League tables.

The book chronicles the ups and downs of my predecessors on the pitch and in the manager's office; what matters now is the next performance.

Mick Tait
October 1998

AUTHOR'S NOTES

Hartlepool United Football Club quietly celebrated its 90th birthday during 1998, so this is an opportune time for a book to appear. It is Volume 12 in a series of "Definitive" club histories published by the AFS, but more importantly it is one of the few books devoted to the history of Hartlepool United. Ed Law's narrative history came out in 1989, and the Hartlepool Mail produced a book to celebrate the 1990/91 promotion, but apart from the odd club publication, that's about it. Hopefully Hartlepool United supporters will not find this book too stale. Essentially it is a strict statistical history, with a limited amount of narrative, but the intention is that readers can dip into it to check on particular matches or to look at the career of a particular player. Perhaps supporters of a nervous disposition may wish to skip certain seasons, but the full ninety years are here in some detail for those fascinated by all things Hartlepool United.

I started supporting Hartlepools United (as they then were) in October 1965 when Brian Clough briefly became the youngest manager in the Football League. Always interested in statistics, I began keeping my own records in 1966/67 which chronicled the club's day-to-day fortunes, and I have continued to keep similar records right up to the present day. As my interest in the club became an obsession, I wanted to find out as much as I could about the club's history. In the early 1970s I first delved back into old newspapers to piece together my own record of the club's fortunes from them entering the Football League in 1921, but it was not until the 1980s that I finally got the opportunity to carry out a fully detailed research of the club back to its formation in 1908. Although I've had the information for this book for many years, it has taken me a long time to get round to having something actually published. It would be nice to think that one day I will produce a Who's Who of Hartlepool United players, and possibly a season-by-season narrative history.

It has to be said that records on Hartlepool United have never been straightforward. For many years Watty Moore's career record for Football League appearances was given as 448, when I always calculated it as 447, and that is the figure which now appears in most record books. Here you will see that Ken Johnson's record Football League goals total is given as 98, but confusion was caused in March 1964 when local newspapers wrongly credited him with having scored his 100th league goal. Even Hartlepool's record attendance of 17,426 against Manchester United is probably wrong, being a transposition of 17,264 which was the figure printed in the newspapers of the day.

Over the years more than 900 players have played first team football for Hartlepool United. There have been many fine club servants, from the club's most prolific goalscorer Joshie Fletcher at the very beginning, right through to Brian Honour in the 1990s. Many players have moved on and made their names elsewhere, while others have arrived at the club with prior reputations to live up to. Almost all players have their place in this book, but unfortunately it has not been possible to give full details on those players who played for Hartlepools only in their North Eastern League days or in the War-time seasons.

I have several "thank yous" to make. To Ray Spiller and the AFS for enabling this book to be published. To Tony Brown, who has done all the organisational and editorial work, and to his helpers Michael Joyce, Leigh Edwards, Steve Emms, and Brian Tabner, who have supplemented my records with their contributions. To Barry Hugman, whose Football League Players Records books have been especially useful, and to anyone who has written a serious statistical football book - it is almost certain I have consulted it in the lengthy build up to this book's appearance. To the Hartlepool Mail, for their kind permission to use the photographs. Finally to Brian Fox, who was my long-time contact in Hartlepool before he emigrated to Mexico, and to Alan Sykes whose generous hospitality allowed me to spend so much time researching this book at the Colindale newspaper library.

Gordon Small

CONTENTS

Joe Allon celebrates

Bobby Cummings signs, with manager Gus McLean

A BRIEF HISTORY

The two towns of the Hartlepools had always been a rugby stronghold, but with West Hartlepool winning the FA Amateur Cup in 1904-05, there was a growing belief that a professional association football club could be supported. The Hartlepools United Football club was duly formed in 1908, with former England international Fred Priest installed as the first manager. The new club took over the Victoria Ground which had previously been used by West Hartlepool RFC, and immediately gained election to the North Eastern League. They got off to a good start, finishing fourth in their inaugural season, and winning the prestigious Durham Senior Cup competition. At the end of the season they undertook a short trip to Germany, easily winning games against Hamburg 4-1 and Bremen 4-2. The following season they were again Durham Senior Cup winners, and in the 1910 close season made an unsuccessful application to join Division Two of the Football League. A second application in 1911 also failed, and with places in Division Two at a premium, Hartlepools were one of the prime movers who tried unsuccessfully to form a Third Division of the Football League that same year.

With their progress effectively halted, Hartlepools settled down as a dependable North Eastern League team until football was suspended in 1915 in respect of the Great War. The Victoria Ground famously suffered damage from a German bombing, but substantial damage was also done by the military authorities who commandeered the ground for their own use. Unfortunately the War years left Hartlepools in severe financial difficulties, and for a time they were forced to play home games at the town's Caledonian Road ground.

Hartlepools United were elected founder members of the new Division Three Northern Section in 1921, and in their first Football League season finished in a creditable fourth place. To celebrate, a second continental tour was arranged, this time to Santander and Oviedo in Spain. Unfortunately this good start did not continue, and as the 1920s progressed their financial problems were greatly increased so that it became a struggle just for the club to keep going. There were real crises in 1924 and 1927, but through the hard work of chairman Bill Yeats and his directors the club was able to continue while others fell by the wayside.

During the 1930's Hartlepools were an average Division Three North side whose achievements were modest. Still under strict financial constraints, they were forced to sell players regularly to pay their way. Their best seasons were 1935-36, when they finished in 8th place also reaching the FA Cup Third Round, and 1936-37, when they finished in 6th place. After these two good years Pools were back struggling at the bottom of the table. In the 1939 close season they reacted to this failure by assembling their most expensive side ever, but with the outbreak of War the players never got a chance to prove themselves.

The club closed down for three years during the Second World War, but in 1943 one of football's characters Fred Westgarth fulfilled his ambition to become manager of Hartlepools United. He held this position for almost 14 years, slowly building up a useful side without having to spend a great deal of money. They had some success in the F.A. Cup, and for three seasons in the mid-1950s they were up with the Division Three North promotion challengers. In 1956-57 they played a memorable home game against Manchester United just losing 4-3, but Fred Westgarth was a sick man and he died the following month. His side continued to do him proud though, and they finished the season in second place behind the promoted Derby County.

After this high, the decline was undeniably quick. They led Division Three North early in 1957-58, but by the end of that season they were in the bottom half of the table which placed them in the new Division Four for 1958-59. Much worse was to follow, and for five seasons in the early 1960's they were "re-election regulars" conceding an average of over

100 goals each season. Serious attempts were made to get the club out of this position, and it was the appointment of Brian Clough as manager in 1965 which was perhaps the most significant. Later to reach the heights of League championships and European Cups, Brian Clough achieved much in his first appointment, but it was his successor Angus McLean who had the honour to take the club to promotion for the first time ever in 1967-68. Hartlepools United became Hartlepool for 1968-69, but their stay in Division Three was brief, lasting just one season, and again the club went into a serious decline.

In the early 1970s, another first-time manager Len Ashurst had assembled a well-balanced side which perhaps should have achieved much more. In both 1971-72 and 1973-74 Hartlepool made terrible starts to the season only to put together a remarkable series of results to escape the bottom four, while in 1974-75 they had their best ever season in the League Cup reaching the Fourth Round.

A familiar pattern began to emerge with Hartlepool again falling back to the lower reaches of Division Four. They made a further name change to Hartlepool United for 1977-78, but there was little improvement in the club's fortunes, although manager Billy Horner's youth policy began to pay dividends in the early 1980's. Never among the best supported clubs, crowds reached an all-time low in 1982-83 and 1983-84 as Pool were again strugglers at the bottom of Division Four. By popular demand, Billy Horner was re-instated as manager, and he was able to get the club back on an even keel with them being promotion candidates in 1985-86.

Fortunes fluctuated, but by the end of the 1980s Hartlepool were back in deep trouble. A strong manager was needed, and the experienced Cyril Knowles proved an inspired appointment to save the club after relegation from the Football League looked inevitable. In 1990-91 the team he had assembled were on the fringes of promotion, but a serious illness meant he had to hand over to Alan Murray as promotion was achieved for only the second time in the club's history.

This time round Hartlepool fared much better in the higher division, and for 18 months they more than held their own. However midway through the 1992-93 season disaster struck with the club's perilous financial situation being revealed. Somehow they hung onto their position in the now re-named Division Two for one more season, but there then followed a difficult three year spell in Division Three as Hartlepool struggled to adjust to their reduced budget. During this period local man Harold Hornsey took over as Chairman, putting a substantial amount of his own money into the club to save it from being wound up. After many years of neglect the Victoria Ground was substantially improved, being re-named Victoria Park. In 1997-98 the ownership of Hartlepool United was taken over by Scandinavian company IOR, and during that season manager Mick Tait was able to introduce overseas players to the side as financial worries were eased.

1956/57. Back: McGuigan, Lumley, Stamper, Guthrie, Anderson, Thompson, Johnson. Front: Robinson, Cameron, Moore, Luke

1976/77. Back: Billy Horner (manager), Endean, Wiggett, Creamer, Richardson, Edgar, Scaife, Poskett, Simpkin, Goad (player-coach). Front: McMaster, Maggiore, Bielby, Scott, McMordie, Elliott, O'Donnell

1985/86. Back: Bird (coach), Little, Walker, Dixon, Blackburn, Alan Stevenson (commercial manager), Robinson, Nobbs, Linighan, Horner (manager). Front: Hogan, Dobson, Shoulder, Taylor, Smith, Newton, Proudlock, Honour, Johnson (physio).

1988/89. Back: Haigh, Baker, Dixon, Grayson, Toman, Tinkler. Centre: Barratt, Doig, Norton, Stokle, Tunks, Borthwick, McKinnon. Front: Honour, Alan Little (assistant manager), Smith, John Bird (manager), Stokes (captain), Hendersdon (physio), Nobbs.

HARTLEPOOL UNITED RECORDS PAGE

PLAYERS:

Most Appearances	Watty Moore, 472 (447 League, 25 F.A. Cup) Ray Thompson, 423 (396 League, 27 F.A. Cup)
Most Goals	Ken Johnson, 106 (98 League, 6 F.A. Cup, 2 F.L. Cup) Johnny Wigham, 106 (95 League, 7 F.A. Cup, 4 others)
Most League Goals in a Season	William Robinson, 28, 1927/28 Joe Allon, 28, 1990/91
Most International Appearances	Ambrose Fogarty, Republic of Ireland, 1 Ken Simpkins, Wales Under-23, 1 Graham Richardson, England Youth, 2

THE CLUB:

Honours:	Durham Senior Cup winners 1908/09, 1909/10 Durham Senior Professional Cup winners 13 times to 1990/91
Best League Performance	2nd Division 3 (North) 1956/57
Best F.A. Cup Performance	4th round 1954/55, 1977/78, 1988/89, 1992/93
Best F.L Cup performance	4th round 1974/75
Most League Points	82, Division Four 1990/91 (3 points for a win) 60, Division Four 1967/68 (2 points for a win)
Most League Goals	90, 1956/57
Most League wins in a season	26, 1955/56
Best League win	10-1 v. Barrow, 4th April 1959
Best League away win	6-1 v. Southport, 4th September 1956
Best F.A. Cup win	10-1 v. St Peters Albion 1923/24
Best League Cup win	5-1 v. Bury, 1994/95
Best League run undefeated	17, from 24th February 1968
Undefeated League games, home	27, from 29th September 1967
Undefeated League games, away	8, from 24th April 1992
Best run of League wins	7, from 4th Sep. 1956 and 1st April 1968
Best run of home League wins	12, from 18th Feb. 1933 and 17th March 1951
Longest run of League draws	4, on 6 occasions, lastly from 28th October 1995

Most appearances:
Watty Moore

Most League goals:
Ken Johnson

HARTLEPOOLS UNITED IN THE NORTH EASTERN LEAGUE

1908/09

1	Sep	5	Hebburn Argyle	2-2	Fletcher 2
2		12	SEAHAM WHITE STAR	0-0	
3		19	Darlington	2-2	Brown 2
4		26	NORTH SHIELDS ATHLETIC	2-0	Edgley, Fletcher
5	Oct	10	WALLSEND PARK VILLA	3-1	Fletcher 2, Hand
6		24	SPENNYMOOR UNITED	2-1	Fletcher 2
7		31	BRADFORD PARK AVENUE 'A'	1-1	Leneghan
8	Nov	7	CARLISLE UNITED	4-1	Edgley 3, Fletcher
9		21	North Shields Athletic	1-3	F Tweddle
10	Dec	19	West Stanley	1-3	F Tweddle
11		25	WEST STANLEY	2-0	Fletcher, T Hegarty
12		28	DARLINGTON	8-1	Hand(p), Swift, Fletcher 2, Roberts, Edgley 3
13	Jan	1	HUDDERSFIELD TOWN	4-1	Fletcher, T Hegarty 2(2p), Roberts
14		2	SUNDERLAND 'A'	4-1	Edgley, F Tweddle, Fletcher, Roberts
15		9	Bradford Park Avenue 'A'	0-4	
16		30	Spennymoor United	3-4	Fletcher 2, Edgley
17	Feb	13	SOUTH SHIELDS ADELAIDE	2-2	Wilson(og), Roberts
18		20	Sunderland 'A'	4-2	Brown, R Hegarty, Smith, Fletcher
19		27	MIDDLESBROUGH 'A'	1-0	T Hegarty(p)
20	Mar	6	Middlesbrough 'A'	0-1	
21		13	Shildon Athletic	2-2	Brown 2
22		20	NEWCASTLE UNITED 'A'	2-4	Fletcher(p), F Tweddle
23		31	SHILDON ATHLETIC	4-1	Fletcher 2, Brown, F Tweddle
24	Apr	3	Sunderland Royal Rovers	1-0	F Tweddle
25		5	Newcastle United 'A'	1-3	Edgley
26		10	South Shields Adelaide	1-1	Hand
27		12	WORKINGTON	5-0	F Tweddle 2, Edgley, Fletcher, Smith(p)
28		13	HEBBURN ARGYLE	5-1	Stevenson(og), Fletcher, T Hegarty(p), Ledger, Ridsdale
29		17	Seaham White Star	5-2	Seal, Edgley, Fletcher 3
30		21	Huddersfield Town	0-0	
31		22	Carlisle United	0-3	
32		24	Wallsend Park Villa	2-2	Brown, Fletcher
33		28	SUNDERLAND ROYAL ROVERS	5-1	Edgley 2, Fletcher 2, Ledger
34		29	Workington	0-1	

		p	w	d	l	f	a	pts
1	Newcastle United 'A'	34	26	4	4	106	48	56
2	South Shields Adelaide	34	22	4	8	80	41	48
3	Bradford Park Avenue 'A'	34	19	5	10	84	49	43
4	HARTLEPOOLS UTD.	34	16	9	9	79	51	41
5	Middlesbrough 'A'	34	17	6	11	82	45	40
6	Sunderland 'A'	34	18	3	13	81	54	39
7	West Stanley	34	18	3	13	73	56	39
8	Darlington	34	15	8	11	76	73	38
9	North Shields Athletic	34	14	6	14	63	48	34
10	Spennymoor United	34	13	7	14	55	63	33
11	Wallsend Park Villa	34	13	6	15	55	66	32
12	Workington	34	12	5	17	50	80	29
13	Seaham White Star	34	10	7	17	55	64	27
14	Hebburn Argyle	34	10	6	18	55	91	26
15	Carlisle United	34	10	4	20	61	84	24
16	Huddersfield Town	34	10	4	20	47	78	24
17	Shildon Athletic	34	7	6	21	51	101	20
18	Sunderland Royal Rovers	34	7	5	22	39	100	19

1909/10

1	Sep	4	Hebburn Argyle	0-1	
2		11	Workington	1-2	Brown
3		25	Sunderland 'A'	1-2	T Hegarty(p)
4	Oct	23	South Shields Adelaide	0-1	
5		30	DARLINGTON	2-1	Hand, Brown
6	Nov	6	West Stanley	2-2	T Hegarty(p), Brown
7		13	CARLISLE UNITED	2-0	Brown, Fletcher
8		20	Sunderland Royal Rovers	0-0	
9		27	WEST STANLEY	2-1	Smith 2
10	Dec	4	Darlington	0-0	
11		18	Shildon Athletic	3-0	Fletcher, F Tweddle 2
12		25	Seaham Harbour	1-1	Edgley
13		27	HEBBURN ARGYLE	10-0	Edgley 4, Fletcher 3, Ledger, Brown, T Hegarty(p)
14		28	NEWCASTLE UNITED 'A'	2-0	F Tweddle, Brown
15	Jan	1	SEAHAM HARBOUR	6-2	Edgley, Brown 2, Fletcher 2, Bennett
16		4	WALLSEND PARK VILLA	8-0	Brown 4, Ledger, Bennett 2, Fletcher
17		8	Wingate Albion	0-0	
18		22	SUNDERLAND ROYAL ROVERS	5-1	Ledger, T Hegarty(p), Fletcher 3
19	Mar	3	Carlisle United	3-1	Fletcher 2, Thompson
20		5	SOUTH SHIELDS ADELAIDE	3-1	Bennett, Ledger, Fletcher
21		12	WINGATE ALBION	2-0	Hogg, Fletcher
22		19	SUNDERLAND 'A'	0-0	
23		25	Middlesbrough 'A'	1-3	Hand
24		28	MIDDLESBROUGH 'A'	2-2	Thompson, Fletcher
25		29	Wallsend Park Villa	3-0	Swift, Fletcher 2
26	Apr	2	Spennymoor United	1-1	Swift
27		4	SPENNYMOOR UNITED	1-1	Thompson
28		9	North Shields Athletic	3-1	Fletcher, Hogg, Hedley(og)
29		16	NORTH SHIELDS ATHLETIC	4-1	Hogg, Fletcher 2, F Tweddle
30		20	WORKINGTON	12-0	Hogg 9, Fletcher 3
31		23	SHILDON ATHLETIC	0-0	
32		27	Newcastle United 'A'	2-0	Fletcher, Swift

		p	w	d	l	f	a	pts
1	Spennymoor United	32	24	3	5	75	39	51
2	Newcastle United 'A'	32	21	6	5	134	31	48
3	Middlesbrough 'A'	32	21	5	6	90	51	47
4	HARTLEPOOLS UTD.	32	18	10	4	82	23	46
5	Darlington	32	16	5	11	60	55	37
6	Sunderland 'A'	32	15	6	11	65	43	36
7	Shildon Athletic	32	13	8	11	61	61	34
8	South Shields Adelaide	32	14	5	13	77	63	33
9	North Shields Athletic	32	12	8	12	60	61	32
10	Seaham Harbour	32	14	3	15	56	57	31
11	Wallsend Park Villa	32	12	6	14	56	67	30
12	Carlisle United	32	11	4	17	52	62	26
13	Wingate Albion	32	8	8	16	43	80	24
14	West Stanley	32	9	5	18	56	85	23
15	Hebburn Argyle	32	8	4	20	33	103	20
16	Workington	32	7	4	21	41	98	18
17	Sunderland Royal Rovers	32	2	5	25	25	83	9

1910/11

1	Sep	3 JARROW	0-3	
2		10 WINGATE ALBION	1-0	Stokoe
3		24 SHILDON ATHLETIC	4-0	Stokoe, Morgan 2, Larkin
4	Oct	8 WALLSEND PARK VILLA	3-1	Featherstone 2, Fletcher
5		15 Newcastle United 'A'	0-4	
6		22 Sunderland 'A'	2-2	Bainbridge, Hedley(p)
7		29 CARLISLE UNITED	4-1	Featherstone, Bainbridge 2, Stokoe
8	Nov	5 West Stanley	3-0	Fletcher, Stokoe, Tomlinson(og)
9		12 WORKINGTON	2-1	Featherstone, Fletcher
10	Dec	3 North Shields Athletic	2-2	Fletcher, Bainbridge
11		10 SPENNYMOOR UNITED	3-1	Ledger, Featherstone, Hedley(p)
12		24 SOUTH SHIELDS	1-1	Featherstone
13		26 Darlington	0-0	
14		31 SUNDERLAND 'A'	2-2	Bainbridge, Featherstone
15	Jan	2 SUNDERLAND ROVERS	5-0	Featherstone 2, Reed(og), Bainbridge, Fletcher
16		7 Seaham Harbour	4-1	Fletcher 2, Featherstone, Bainbridge
17		21 Carlisle United	1-1	Blanthorne
18		28 WEST STANLEY	2-0	Bainbridge, Stokoe
19	Feb	11 HEBBURN ARGYLE	2-0	Bainbridge, Hedley(p)
20		18 Wallsend Park Villa	3-0	Blanthorne 2, MacIntyre
21		25 Shildon Athletic	1-0	MacIntyre
22	Mar	4 NEWCASTLE UNITED 'A'	2-1	Stokoe, MacIntyre
23		11 Spennymoor United	1-2	MacIntyre
24		18 MIDDLESBROUGH 'A'	7-4	Fletcher 4, MacIntyre 2, Bainbridge
25		25 SEAHAM HARBOUR	5-0	Fletcher, Griffin, Featherstone, Stokoe 2
26		27 Wingate Albion	1-1	Hedley(p)
27	Apr	5 Jarrow	0-1	
28		8 Hebburn Argyle	2-4	Griffin, Fletcher
29		14 DARLINGTON	0-1	
30		15 NORTH SHIELDS ATHLETIC	4-2	MacIntyre 3, Fletcher
31		17 South Shields	0-1	
32		18 Sunderland Rovers	0-1	
33		22 Middlesbrough 'A'	2-2	MacIntyre 2
34		29 Workington	2-0	Fletcher, MacIntyre

		p	w	d	l	f	a	pts
1	Newcastle United 'A'	34	25	4	5	88	25	54
2	Sunderland 'A'	34	20	6	8	81	38	46
3	HARTLEPOOLS UTD.	34	18	8	8	71	40	44
4	Darlington	34	19	5	10	79	39	43
5	South Shields	34	18	5	11	56	33	41
6	North Shields Athletic	34	19	3	12	57	56	41
7	Middlesbrough 'A'	34	16	6	12	83	54	38
8	Wingate Albion	34	14	7	13	48	39	35
9	Wallsend Park Villa	34	15	3	16	49	59	33
10	Hebburn Argyle	34	13	6	15	38	62	32
11	Seaham Harbour	34	13	5	16	44	63	31
12	Spennymoor United	32	12	5	15	52	54	29
13	Workington	34	12	3	19	47	72	27
14	Shildon Athletic	34	11	3	20	50	64	25
15	Carlisle United	34	8	8	18	45	52	24
16	Jarrow	34	11	2	21	34	70	24
17	West Stanley	33	10	3	20	39	84	23
18	Sunderland Rovers	34	8	2	24	33	94	18

1911/12

1	Sep	1 Wallsend Park Villa	0-2	
2		2 NEWCASTLE CITY	1-1	Fletcher
3		6 HEBBURN ARGYLE	3-0	Fletcher 2, Mitchell
4		9 Seaham Harbour	1-2	Fletcher(p)
5		13 Hebburn Argyle	2-2	Fletcher 2
6		16 SUNDERLAND 'A'	1-2	Martin
7		23 Wingate Albion	1-1	Stokoe
8		30 MIDDLESBROUGH 'A'	2-2	Martin, Hogg
9	Oct	7 NEWCASTLE UNITED 'A'	0-1	
10		21 Sunderland 'A'	1-1	F Tweddle
11		28 SUNDERLAND ROVERS	4-1	Grierson, Martin 2, Fletcher
12	Nov	4 Carlisle United	1-2	Grierson
13		11 GATESHEAD TOWN	2-1	Stokoe 2
14		25 Jarrow	4-2	Grierson, Stokoe, Hedley, F Tweddle
15	Dec	2 West Stanley	2-2	Fletcher 2
16		9 SOUTH SHIELDS	0-1	
17		23 NORTH SHIELDS ATHLETIC	3-2	Fletcher, Hedley(p), Stokoe
18		25 WALLSEND PARK VILLA	5-0	Grierson, Carr, Griffin, Fletcher, Bennett
19		26 DARLINGTON	0-0	
20		30 Spennymoor United	0-1	
21	Jan	1 SEAHAM HARBOUR	5-0	Grierson, Fletcher 2, Prosser, Griffin
22		6 Shildon	3-2	Grierson 2, Martin
23		13 Sunderland Rovers	3-0	Fletcher 2, Grierson
24	Feb	10 South Shields	0-1	
25		17 SHILDON	5-2	Fletcher, Martin 3, Grierson
26		24 Newcastle City	0-4	
27	Mar	2 JARROW	4-2	Grierson 2, Fletcher, Bennett
28		9 North Shields Athletic	1-0	Fletcher
29		23 Gateshead Town	2-3	Hogg 2
30		30 CARLISLE UNITED	0-0	
31	Apr	5 WEST STANLEY	0-1	
32		6 WINGATE ALBION	0-1	
33		8 Darlington	2-0	Stokoe, Griffin
34		20 Newcastle United 'A'	2-3	Fletcher 2
35		24 SPENNYMOOR UNITED	2-0	Grierson, Fletcher
36		29 Middlesbrough 'A'	0-5	

		p	w	d	l	f	a	pts
1	Middlesbrough 'A'	36	28	5	3	122	33	61
2	Newcastle United 'A'	36	28	2	6	113	33	58
3	Darlington	36	23	8	5	84	34	54
4	Sunderland 'A'	36	21	5	10	99	52	47
5	South Shields	36	21	4	11	73	43	46
6	Spennymoor United	36	18	6	12	62	57	42
7	Newcastle City	36	16	9	11	62	43	41
8	Gateshead Town	36	16	6	14	64	66	38
9	HARTLEPOOLS UTD.	36	14	8	14	62	50	36
10	West Stanley	36	13	10	13	61	58	36
11	North Shields Athletic	36	13	9	14	59	72	35
12	Seaham Harbour	36	15	2	19	52	67	32
13	Hebburn Argyle	36	11	9	16	56	54	31
14	Wingate Albion	36	9	11	16	41	84	29
15	Jarrow	36	10	7	19	52	87	27
16	Shildon Athletic	36	9	6	21	62	97	24
17	Carlisle United	36	7	6	23	27	98	20
18	Wallsend Park Villa	36	8	3	25	43	93	19
19	Sunderland Rovers	36	2	4	30	42	125	8

1912/13

1	Sep	2	Gateshead Town	2-2	Hibbert, Stokoe
2		7	NORTH SHIELDS ATHLETIC	4-2	Stokoe 2, Fletcher, Baker
3		14	HOUGHTON ROVERS	3-2	Mayo, Humphreys, Outhwaite
4		21	SHILDON	3-1	Humphreys 2, Stokoe
5		25	Newcastle City	0-1	
6		28	Newcastle United Reserves	1-1	Humphreys
7	Oct	5	Hebburn Argyle	1-4	Humphreys
8		19	GATESHEAD TOWN	5-0	Humphreys 2, Outhwaite, Mayo, Fletcher
9		26	SPENNYMOOR UNITED	1-1	Fletcher
10	Nov	9	SOUTH SHIELDS	0-4	
11		23	Carlisle United	2-1	Fletcher, Humphreys
12	Dec	25	Middlesbrough Reserves	1-3	Humphreys
13		26	DARLINGTON	0-1	
14		28	HEBBURN ARGYLE	6-0	Butler, Bennett, Fletcher 3, Baker(p)
15	Jan	1	MIDDLESBROUGH RESERVES	0-2	
16		2	Seaham Harbour	0-2	
17		4	Sunderland Rovers	5-3	Baker 2, Marsh 2, Fletcher
18		11	Darlington	2-5	Fletcher, Stokoe
19		18	Wingate Albion	0-1	
20	Feb	1	SUNDERLAND RESERVES	3-3	Brewis, Stokoe 2
21		8	North Shields Athletic	2-3	Baker(p), Rumney
22		15	SUNDERLAND ROVERS	3-1	Fletcher, Baker(p), Brewis
23		22	Houghton Rovers	1-3	Mayo
24	Mar	1	JARROW	5-1	Marsh, Brewis 3, Baker(p)
25		8	South Shields	0-4	
26		15	Shildon	4-0	Stokoe, Brewis, Fletcher 2
27		24	SEAHAM HARBOUR	1-1	Humphreys
28		25	WEST STANLEY	4-0	Marsh, Bennett, Stokoe 2
29		29	Sunderland Reserves	0-1	
30	Apr	2	CARLISLE UNITED	1-2	Humphreys
31		5	WALLSEND	2-2	Fletcher, Marsh
32		9	West Stanley	1-0	Mayo
33		12	NEWCASTLE UNITED RESERVES	1-0	Bennett
34		16	WINGATE ALBION	2-0	Baker(p), Mayo
35		19	Spennymoor United	1-5	Fletcher
36		23	Jarrow	2-1	Stokoe, Mayo
37		26	NEWCASTLE CITY	0-1	
38		30	Wallsend	0-2	

		p	w	d	l	f	a	pts
1	Darlington	38	31	4	3	116	23	66
2	South Shields	38	27	7	4	103	30	61
3	Middlesbrough Reserves	38	26	6	6	102	40	58
4	Sunderland Reserves	38	26	5	7	100	48	57
5	Newcastle United Reserves	38	24	5	9	109	47	53
6	Spennymoor United	38	19	6	13	80	61	44
7	Shildon	38	17	9	12	79	69	43
8	Houghton Rovers	38	15	9	14	53	64	39
9	Wallsend	38	14	10	14	83	71	38
10	North Shields Athletic	38	15	7	16	72	78	37
11	Newcastle City	38	15	7	16	48	62	37
12	HARTLEPOOLS UTD.	38	15	6	17	69	66	36
13	Hebburn Argyle	38	12	6	20	49	75	30
14	Carlisle United	38	12	5	21	61	98	29
15	Seaham Harbour	38	10	7	21	48	77	27
16	Jarrow	38	10	5	23	52	86	25
17	West Stanley	38	7	10	21	54	94	24
18	Sunderland Rovers	38	7	8	23	39	79	22
19	Gateshead Town	38	8	6	24	49	112	22
20	Wingate Albion	38	5	2	31	28	114	12

1913/14

1	Sep	6	SOUTH SHIELDS	1-1	Smith
2		10	Jarrow	2-0	Smith 2
3		13	MIDDLESBROUGH RESERVES	2-1	Smith, Hibbert(p)
4		20	HOUGHTON ROVERS	6-0	Smith, Walker 3, Lowe 2
5	Oct	4	Middlesbrough Reserves	1-2	Bennett
6		18	SHILDON	2-0	Hibbert 2
7		25	Wallsend	3-0	Hibbert(p), Smith 2
8	Nov	8	WEST STANLEY	3-0	Hibbert 2(2p), Smith
9		22	Newcastle United Reserves	1-0	Smith
10	Dec	13	Seaham Harbour	0-0	
11		25	Darlington	1-1	Hibbert
12		26	SUNDERLAND RESERVES	4-0	Bennett, Lowe, Manners, Smith
13	Jan	1	DARLINGTON	1-0	Smith
14		2	HEBBURN ARGYLE	0-0	
15		3	South Shields	2-3	Smith, Young
16		10	Spennymoor United	1-1	Lowe
17		14	Newcastle City	2-1	Bryden, Smith
18		17	SEAHAM HARBOUR	1-1	Flannigan
19		31	West Stanley	1-0	Bryden
20	Feb	14	SPENNYMOOR UNITED	2-0	Smith 2(1p)
21		18	Blyth Spartans	0-2	
22		21	SUNDERLAND ROVERS	2-0	Young, Mitchell
23		28	CARLISLE UNITED	4-0	Young, Mitchell 2, Hibbert(p)
24	Mar	7	WALLSEND	8-0	Walker, Smith 4, Graham, Baker, Hibbert(p)
25		11	North Shields Athletic	2-0	Smith, Baker
26		14	Sunderland Rovers	1-1	Mitchell
27		18	JARROW	1-2	Young
28		21	Shildon	0-2	
29		28	NEWCASTLE UNITED RESERVES	0-3	
30	Apr	4	Hebburn Argyle	1-1	Manners
31		10	Gateshead Town	1-2	Hibbert(p)
32		11	NORTH SHIELDS ATHLETIC	6-2	McGill 2, Wigham, Hibbert(p), Lowe 2
33		13	Sunderland Reserves	1-2	Lowe
34		14	NEWCASTLE CITY	0-1	
35		18	GATESHEAD TOWN	1-1	McGill
36		22	BLYTH SPARTANS	1-1	McGill
37		25	Houghton Rovers	2-4	Brown, Manners
38		30	Carlisle United	1-2	Young

		p	w	d	l	f	a	pts
1	South Shields	38	32	5	1	133	29	69
2	Middlesbrough Reserves	38	23	8	7	99	37	54
3	Newcastle United Reserves	38	24	5	9	91	40	53
4	Darlington	38	20	10	8	72	43	50
5	Sunderland Reserves	38	20	8	10	83	55	48
6	Blyth Spartans	38	19	7	12	71	51	45
7	HARTLEPOOLS UTD.	38	17	10	11	68	37	44
8	Shildon	38	18	3	17	54	60	39
9	Gateshead Town	38	17	5	16	58	76	39
10	Hebburn Argyle	38	14	11	13	55	50	39
11	Jarrow	38	12	10	16	55	63	34
12	North Shields Athletic	38	11	10	17	57	81	32
13	Carlisle United	38	11	10	17	48	84	32
14	Spennymoor United	38	10	11	17	60	63	31
15	Newcastle City	38	7	16	15	34	57	30
16	Sunderland Rovers	38	10	10	18	46	67	30
17	West Stanley	38	13	3	22	54	87	29
18	Houghton Rovers	38	11	2	25	38	81	24
19	Seaham Harbour	38	7	8	23	30	73	22
20	Wallsend	38	5	6	27	44	115	16

1914/15

1	Sep	2 West Stanley	1-2	Smith
2		5 SPENNYMOOR UNITED	1-3	Young
3		9 JARROW	4-1	McGill, Butler 2, Hibbert(p)
4		12 Spennymoor United	4-1	McGill, Hibbert(p), Butler 2
5		19 BLYTH SPARTANS	1-2	Hibbert
6		26 Hebburn Argyle	2-1	Butler, Hibbert(p)
7	Oct	3 NEWCASTLE UNITED RESERVES	1-2	Hibbert
8		10 Middlesbrough Reserves	2-2	McGill 2
9		24 HEBBURN ARGYLE	2-1	Bell, Strugnell
10		31 WEST STANLEY	3-0	Strugnell, Butler, Luke
11	Nov	7 Sunderland Reserves	2-2	Butler, McGill
12		14 SUNDERLAND RESERVES	2-2	Butler, Luke
13		28 Blyth Spartans	1-1	Hibbert
14	Dec	25 South Shields	2-6	Strugnell 2
15		26 DARLINGTON	3-0	Mahon, Butler 2
16		28 NEWCASTLE CITY	5-1	Butler 2, Young, Luke, Hibbert
17	Jan	1 GATESHEAD TOWN	9-0	Luke 4, McGill, Butler 3, Hibbert(p)
18		2 Darlington	0-5	
19		9 Shildon	0-0	
20		16 MIDDLESBROUGH RESERVES	1-0	Luke
21		23 SHILDON	1-1	Strugnell
22	Feb	6 Newcastle City	0-2	
23		13 CARLISLE UNITED	10-0	Butler 3, McGill 3, Strugnell 3, McDougall
24	Mar	6 Sunderland Rovers	2-1	Butler 2
25		10 Wallsend	1-0	Hibbert
26		13 SOUTH SHIELDS	0-3	
27		20 ASHINGTON	0-0	
28		24 Ashington	2-2	Mahon, Opponent(og)
29		27 Houghton Rovers	1-1	Young
30	Apr	2 Gateshead Town	1-1	Butler
31		3 North Shields Athletic	0-1	
32		5 SUNDERLAND ROVERS	3-1	Strugnell 2, Johnson
33		10 Newcastle United Reserves	0-4	
34		17 NORTH SHIELDS ATHLETIC	2-1	McDougall, Johnson
35		21 Jarrow	0-5	
36		24 Carlisle United	0-0	
37		28 WALLSEND	3-2	Young 2, McDougall
38		30 HOUGHTON ROVERS	2-0	Strugnell, Luke

		p	w	d	l	f	a	pts
1	South Shields	38	32	4	3	160	34	66
2	Middlesbrough Reserves	38	28	5	5	151	35	61
3	Newcastle United Reserves	38	26	6	6	138	43	58
4	Darlington	38	25	4	9	109	38	54
5	West Stanley	38	24	4	10	79	44	52
6	Sunderland Reserves	38	18	9	11	86	50	45
7	HARTLEPOOLS UTD.	38	16	11	11	74	57	43
8	North Shields Athletic	38	19	5	14	67	63	43
9	Ashington	38	15	11	12	60	65	41
10	Sunderland Rovers	38	17	4	17	74	79	38
11	Spennymoor United	38	12	9	17	40	82	33
12	Shildon	38	11	9	18	70	58	31
13	Hebburn Argyle	38	12	6	20	50	73	30
14	Jarrow	38	10	10	18	46	85	30
15	Blyth Spartans	38	10	9	19	49	75	29
16	Houghton Rovers	38	11	4	23	43	123	28
17	Carlisle United	38	8	7	23	50	108	23
18	Newcastle City	38	8	5	25	43	87	21
19	Gateshead Town	38	8	3	27	52	121	19
20	Wallsend	38	6	3	29	44	136	15

1919/20

1	Aug	30 ASHINGTON	1-1	Toward(p)
2	Sep	6 Ashington	0-0	
3		13 Darlington	0-1	
4		20 DARLINGTON	0-2	
5		27 WEST STANLEY	1-1	Hewitt(p)
6	Oct	4 West Stanley	0-2	
7		11 South Shields Reserves	0-3	
8		18 Durham City	1-1	Hibbert
9		25 SUNDERLAND RESERVES	1-1	Scott(p)
10	Nov	1 Sunderland Reserves	0-1	
11		15 Houghton Rovers	4-2	Hewitt 4
12	Dec	6 Scotswood	0-2	
13		13 SCOTSWOOD	4-2	Bratt 2, Hewitt 2
14		20 Newcastle United Reserves	1-2	Hewitt
15		25 Middlesbrough Reserves	0-0	
16		26 BLYTH SPARTANS	2-3	Hewitt 2(1p)
17		27 NEWCASTLE UNITED RESERVES	0-2	
18	Jan	1 MIDDLESBROUGH RESERVES	2-3	Hafekost, Toward
19		3 PALMERS JARROW	2-0	Gray, Hafekost(p)
20		17 Wallsend	3-0	Short 2, Dickinson
21		24 WALLSEND	0-0	
22		31 SHILDON	3-0	Bratt 2, Toward
23	Feb	14 CARLISLE UNITED	2-0	Bratt 2
24		21 Carlisle United	0-1	
25		28 LEADGATE PARK	4-0	Short 3, Bratt
26	Mar	6 Leadgate Park	2-0	Bratt 2
27		13 Palmers Jarrow	0-1	
28	Apr	2 Blyth Spartans	2-2	Bratt, Toward
29		3 Spennymoor United	1-1	Toward
30		5 HOUGHTON ROVERS	1-0	Hewitt
31		17 SOUTH SHIELDS RESERVES	4-2	Hewitt 2, Short, Crilly(p)
32		24 SPENNYMOOR UNITED	2-0	Hewitt, Short
33		28 Shildon	0-0	
34	May	1 DURHAM CITY	2-0	Short, Bratt

		p	w	d	l	f	a	pts
1	Middlesbrough Reserves	34	22	7	5	86	30	51
2	Darlington	34	24	1	9	91	44	49
3	Newcastle United Reserves	34	22	5	7	82	41	49
4	Blyth Spartans	34	18	8	8	62	42	44
5	Durham City	34	17	6	11	52	41	40
6	Palmers (Jarrow)	34	16	6	12	55	52	38
7	Ashington	34	14	8	12	51	51	36
8	South Shields Reserves	34	14	7	13	67	57	35
9	HARTLEPOOLS UTD.	34	12	10	12	45	36	34
10	Sunderland Reserves	34	15	4	15	67	49	34
11	Scotswood	34	13	6	15	47	55	32
12	West Stanley	34	12	7	15	45	63	31
13	Carlisle United	34	12	3	19	47	76	27
14	Shildon	34	10	6	18	50	75	26
15	Houghton Rovers	34	8	8	18	28	60	24
16	Spennymoor United	34	10	2	22	52	78	22
17	Leadgate Park	34	8	6	20	51	83	22
18	Wallsend	34	6	6	22	26	71	18

1920/21

1	Aug	28	Durham City	0-1	
2	Sep	1	MIDDLESBROUGH RESERVES	0-0	
3		4	DURHAM CITY	1-0	Hewitt
4		8	Middlesbrough Reserves	0-1	
5		11	Houghton Rovers	1-1	Thoms
6		18	HOUGHTON ROVERS	1-1	Thoms
7		29	Spennymoor United	0-1	
8	Oct	2	LEADGATE PARK	1-1	Hewitt
9		16	Blyth Spartans	1-3	Short
10		30	Ashington	2-2	Lister, Thoms
11	Nov	13	SUNDERLAND RESERVES	2-1	Mulholland, Lister
12		27	Carlisle United	1-4	Crawford(og)
13	Dec	25	Darlington	4-3	Mulholland 2, Lister, Short
14		27	DARLINGTON	0-1	
15	Jan	1	SCOTSWOOD	4-1	Bratt 2, Topping, Mulholland
16		3	SPENNYMOOR UNITED	5-0	Mulholland, Hardy 3, Bratt
17		8	Scotswood	1-0	Kessler
18		15	Leadgate Park	0-1	
19		29	West Stanley	1-3	Hardy
20	Feb	12	SHILDON	3-2	Thoms, Mulholland 2
21		19	Wallsend	0-1	
22		26	BLYTH SPARTANS	2-0	Lister 2
23	Mar	9	South Shields Reserves	3-0	Hardy, Harris, Lister
24		12	SOUTH SHIELDS RESERVES	5-0	Kessler, Mulholland 2, Lister, Short
25		16	Sunderland Reserves	1-2	Bratt
26		19	Newcastle United Reserves	4-1	Hardy 2, Lister 2
27		25	CHESTER-LE-STREET	1-0	Mulholland
28		26	Jarrow	1-3	Mulholland
29		29	JARROW	2-1	Mulholland, Hardy
30	Apr	9	Chester-le-Street	0-2	
31		13	CARLISLE UNITED	0-5	
32		16	Bedlington United	3-1	Kessler, Bratt, Robertson
33		20	WEST STANLEY	1-1	Parkinson
34		23	BEDLINGTON UNITED	3-1	Lister 3
35		27	Shildon	0-2	
36		30	NEWCASTLE UNITED RESERVES	1-0	Harris
37	May	4	ASHINGTON	4-2	Lister 3, Mulholland
38		7	WALLSEND	5-1	Lister 3, Short, Harris

		p	w	d	l	f	a	pts
1	Darlington	38	28	4	6	76	29	60
2	Middlesbrough Reserves	38	27	5	6	93	35	59
3	Newcastle United Reserves	38	23	7	8	96	39	53
4	Sunderland Reserves	38	21	10	7	73	49	52
5	Blyth Spartans	38	19	11	8	69	34	49
6	Carlisle United	38	18	10	10	79	46	46
7	West Stanley	38	14	14	10	54	42	42
8	HARTLEPOOLS UTD.	38	18	6	14	64	50	42
9	Ashington	38	14	13	11	66	52	41
10	Jarrow	38	14	11	13	46	44	39
11	Durham City	38	16	5	17	51	60	37
12	Chester-le-Street	38	13	11	14	50	58	37
13	Leadgate Park	38	13	10	15	57	58	36
14	South Shields Reserves	38	12	11	15	51	66	35
15	Spennymoor United	38	10	10	18	51	79	30
16	Houghton Rovers	38	7	10	21	38	69	24
17	Shildon	38	8	7	23	41	75	23
18	Scotswood	38	8	5	25	35	76	21
19	Wallsend	38	6	8	24	39	96	20
20	Bedlington United	38	4	6	28	32	104	14

1909, with the Durham Senior Cup
Back: Spoors (trainer), T Hegarty, Mearns, R Hegarty, Priest (manager)
Centre: S Tweddle, Hand, Ledger, Smith
Front: F Tweddle, Fletcher, Edgley, Brown, Roberts

INTRODUCTION TO THE STATISTICS PAGES

The season by season grids show the results of games in the Football League, F.A. Cup, Football League Cup, Associate Members' Cup and the Third Division (North) Cup.

Home games are identified by the opponent's name in upper case, away games by the use of lower case. Hartlepool's score is always given first. Attendances for League games are taken from the official Football League records since season 1925/26; before then, estimated attendances based on newspaper reports have been used.

Substitutes have the numbers 12, 13 and 14. 12 is used if only one substitute appeared (no matter what number was on the player's shirt).

A full player list is provided for every player who made a League appearance. Date and place of birth are shown, where known, and the year of death. In 1967 the towns of West Hartlepool and Hartlepool became "united" as Hartlepool. Rather than give West Hartlepool as a player's birthplace, the modern town name has been used. The author conveys his apologies to any players born before the amalgamation who prefer to consider themselves West Hartlepool born and bred!

Players with the same name are given a (1) or (2) after their name to avoid confusion. The next two columns, "seasons played", act as an index to the season by season grids. The years shown are the "first year" of the season; for example, 1971 is season 1971/72. The two columns show the season in which the player made his first team debut; and the final season that he played. However, if he only played in one season, the second column is blank. An entry of "1997" in the second column does not imply that the player has left the club, but means that he appeared in the "final season" (1997/98) of the book.

Note that some players also made F.A. Cup appearances before 1921/22 and in 1945/46. If a player also made a League appearance his F.A. Cup appearances from these seasons are included in the list.

Previous and next clubs show where he was transferred from, and the club he moved to. Non-league club information is included when known.

The appearance columns have separate totals for the League, F.A. Cup, Football League Cup and the miscellaneous cup tournaments listed above. "Goals scored" are also shown under the four headings.

If a player has had more than one spell at the club playing first team football, a consolidated set of appearance and goals are shown on the first line. Subsequent lines show the seasons involved on his return to the club, and his new pair of previous and next clubs.

A full record of meetings against all other League clubs is included. Some clubs have played in the League under different names, but the totals are consolidated under the present day name in this table. Other pages show the club's record in the F.A. Cup in non-League seasons and a list of managers, chairmen and secretaries..

1921/22 4th in Division 3 (North)

						Bratt W	Burn F	Crilly T	Crowther GL	Donald RS	Dougherty J	Franks A	Gill GA	Hardy C	Harris J	Hewitt CW	Hopkins W	Kessler LP	Lee B	Lister J	Mulholland TS	Nicholson BC	Parkinson TO	Parsons D	Robertson P	Rowe GW	Scorgie J	Short W	Summerfield WH	Thompson TR	Thoms H	Towse T	Yews TP
1	Aug 27	Wrexham	2-0	Mulholland, Lister	10000			2		11	4		1				5	7		9	8				10			6			3		
2	Sep 3	WREXHAM	0-1		10000			3		11	4		1				5	7		9	8							6			2		
3	10	Southport	0-3		3570			3		11	4						5	7		9	8				10			6	1		2		
4	17	SOUTHPORT	1-0	Lister	8500			3		11	4	2		10		7	5			9					8			6	1				
5	24	STOCKPORT COUNTY	0-0		9600			3		11	4	2	1	10		7	5								8			6					
6	Oct 1	Stockport County	0-1		10000			3		11	4	2	1	10		7	5								8			9					
7	8	Grimsby Town	0-2					3			4	2	1	10		7	5	11						9	8			6					
8	15	GRIMSBY TOWN	0-0		8500			3		11	4	2	1							9				7				10			5		
9	22	Walsall	1-3	Robertson	8000			3		11	4	2	1				5			9	8				10			6					
10	29	WALSALL	1-0	Scorgie	7000			3				2	1				5			9			10		8		11	6			4		7
11	Nov 5	Halifax Town	0-3					3				2	1				5			9			10		8		11	6			4		7
12	12	HALIFAX TOWN	4-0	Robertson, Lee, Parkinson, Scorgie	6500			3				2	1				5		9			6	10		8		11				4		7
13	19	DURHAM CITY	0-1		6000			3				2	1				5		9			6	10		8		11				4		7
14	26	TRANMERE ROVERS	0-0		7000	6		3				2	1				5	11	9		8				10						4		7
15	Dec 17	WIGAN BOROUGH	0-0		6000		11	3			9	2	1	8			5											6		7	4		
16	24	Wigan Borough	0-1		5000	9	11	3				2	1	10			5						8					6		7	4		
17	26	Stalybridge Celtic	3-1	Hardy 2, Dennis (og)	5000	9	11	3			6	2	1	10			5						8							7	4		
18	27	Tranmere Rovers	2-1	Bratt, Hardy	4000	9		3			6	2	1	10			5						8		11					7	4		
19	31	ROCHDALE	5-3	Parkinson 2, Robertson, Hardy 2	7000	9		3			6	2	1	10			5						8		11					7	4		
20	Jan 2	STALYBRIDGE CELTIC	0-1		8500	9					6	2	1	10			5					4	8		11					7	3		
21	14	Rochdale	1-0	Robertson	6000		11	3	9		6	2	1				5						8		10						4		7
22	21	Nelson	4-0	Parkinson, Yews, Burn, Crowther	4000	10	11	3	9		6	2	1				5						8								4		7
23	28	NELSON	6-1	*see below	5500		11	3	9		6	2			4								8		10				1		5		7
24	Feb 4	Chesterfield	1-2	Robertson	5000		11	3	9		6	2			7								8		10			4	1		5		
25	11	CHESTERFIELD	7-0	Parkinson 2, Crowther 3, Robertson 2	6000			3	9		6	2						11					8		10			4	1	7	5		
26	18	Crewe Alexandra	0-2		6000			3	9		6	2						11					8		10			4	1	7	5		
27	25	CREWE ALEXANDRA	1-0	Robertson	7500			3	9		6	2	1	7			5	11					8		10						4		
28	Mar 4	ACCRINGTON STANLEY	2-1	Crowther, Robertson	7500			3	9		6	2	1	7			5	11					8		10						4		
29	11	Accrington Stanley	1-4	Parkinson	8000			3	9		6	2	1	7			5	11					8		10						4		
30	18	DARLINGTON	0-0		11700			3	9		6	2	1	7			5	11					8		10						4		
31	25	Darlington	0-0		7840			3	9		6	2	1	7			5	11					8					10			4		
32	Apr 1	LINCOLN CITY	1-1	Crowther	6280			3	9		6	2	1	10			5	11					7					8			4		
33	8	Lincoln City	1-1	Parkinson	10000			3	9		6	2	1	10		11	5						8							7	4		
34	15	ASHINGTON	2-1	Hardy 2	5456	8	11	3	9		6	2	1	10			5						7								4		
35	18	Durham City	1-0	Hardy		8	11	3	9		6	2	1	10			5						7								4		
36	22	Ashington	1-4	Crowther	2000			3	9		6		1	10	8	11	5						7								4		
37	29	BARROW	3-1	Hardy 2, Robertson	3000	7		3	9		6	2	1	10			5								8	11					4		
38	May 6	Barrow	1-0	Towse	7000			3			6	2	1	10			5						7		8	11					4	9	
					Apps	10	9	37	17	8	32	34	32	22	3	6	33	13	3	8	5	3	26	2	26	2	4	18	6	9	33	1	8
					Goals	1	1		8					10					1	2	1		10		12		2				1	1	1

One own goal

Scorers in game 23: Parkinson 2, Robertson 2, Thoms, Crowther.
Played in one game: WCS Gregson (game 2, at 10), WM Hick (15, at 10), W Thompson (9, at 7), R Hubery (36, at 2).
Played in games 6 and 8 at 6: L Henderson.
Played in games 5 (at 9) and 8 (at 8): A Butler.

F.A. Cup

						Bratt W	Burn F	Crilly T	Crowther GL	Donald RS	Dougherty J	Franks A	Gill GA	Hardy C	Harris J	Hewitt CW	Hopkins W	Kessler LP	Lee B	Lister J	Mulholland TS	Nicholson BC	Parkinson TO	Parsons D	Robertson P	Rowe GW	Scorgie J	Short W	Summerfield WH	Thompson TR	Thoms H	Towse T	Yews TP
Q5	Dec 3	Stalybridge Celtic	0-2		5300	10		3		11		2	1				5	7		9					8						4		

Played at 6: CB Potter

		P	W	D	L	F	A	W	D	L	F	A	Pts
1	Stockport County	38	13	5	1	36	10	11	3	5	24	11	56
2	Darlington	38	15	2	2	52	7	7	4	8	29	30	50
3	Grimsby Town	38	15	4	0	54	15	6	4	9	18	32	50
4	HARTLEPOOLS UTD.	38	10	6	3	33	11	7	2	10	19	28	42
5	Accrington Stanley	38	15	1	3	50	15	4	2	13	23	42	41
6	Crewe Alexandra	38	13	1	5	39	21	5	4	10	21	35	41
7	Stalybridge Celtic	38	14	3	2	42	15	4	2	13	20	48	41
8	Walsall	38	15	2	2	52	17	3	1	15	14	48	39
9	Southport	38	11	6	2	39	12	3	4	12	16	32	38
10	Ashington	38	13	2	4	42	22	4	2	13	17	44	38
11	Durham City	38	14	0	5	43	20	3	3	13	26	47	37
12	Wrexham	38	12	4	3	40	17	2	5	12	11	39	37
13	Chesterfield	38	12	2	5	33	15	4	1	14	15	52	35
14	Lincoln City	38	11	2	6	32	20	3	4	12	16	39	34
15	Barrow	38	11	2	6	29	18	3	3	13	13	36	33
16	Nelson	38	7	6	6	27	23	6	1	12	21	43	33
17	Wigan Borough	38	9	4	6	32	28	2	5	12	14	44	31
18	Tranmere Rovers	38	7	5	7	41	25	2	6	11	10	36	29
19	Halifax Town	38	9	4	6	37	28	1	5	13	19	48	29
20	Rochdale	38	9	2	8	34	24	2	2	15	18	53	26

1922/23

15th in Division 3 (North)

						Anderson JB	Borthwick JW	Braidford L	Bratt W	Chesser JM	Connell D	Cook JA	Crowther GL	Dixon C	Dowson F	Flanders F	Franks A	Gill GA	Halstead FD	Hampson W	Hardy C	Hopkins W	Longmore SJ	Mitchell T	Mordue WM	Nicholson BC	Parkinson TO	Robertson P	Rowe GW	Summerfield WH	Towse T	Walker JR	Yews TP
1	Aug 26	Walsall	2-2	Robertson, Yews	10000		2								6	3		1		4	10	5						8	11		9		7
2	Sep 2	WALSALL	2-2	Robertson 2	5084		2								6		3	1		4	10	5						8	11		9		7
3	9	SOUTHPORT	1-1	Towse	5768			10							6		2	1		3		5				4		8	11		9		7
4	16	Southport	0-1		5500			10							6		2	1		4		5						8	11		9	3	
5	23	ASHINGTON	3-1	Yews, Robertson(p), Crowther	6084					4			9		6	3		1				5					8	10	11			2	7
6	30	Ashington	2-4	Robertson, Rowe	6000					4			9		6	3		1				5					8	10	11			2	7
7	Oct 7	BARROW	2-0	Towse 2	5480				4						6		3	1				5					8	10	11		9	2	7
8	14	Barrow	0-0		4000				4						6		3	1				5					8		11		9	2	7
9	21	Halifax Town	0-3		10000			8	4						6		3	1			10	5							11		9	2	7
10	28	HALIFAX TOWN	3-2	Hardy 2, Towse	4502			8			4				6		3	1			10	5							11		9	2	7
11	Nov 4	ROCHDALE	0-2		4774			8			4				6		3	1			10	5							11		9	2	7
12	11	Rochdale	0-4		6000			8			4		9		10		3					5				6	7		11	1		2	
13	18	WREXHAM	1-1	Crowther	4050			8			4		9	3	6							5			7			10	11	1		2	
14	25	Wrexham	0-2		4000			8			4		9	3								5			7	6		10	11	1		2	
15	Dec 9	ACCRINGTON STANLEY	0-0		4053				8		4		9	3	6				5						7				11	1	10	2	
16	23	Lincoln City	1-2	Bratt					8		4		9	3			2					5			7	6			11	1	10		
17	25	Darlington	0-4		6000				•		4		9	3	6		2					5					8		11	1	10		7
18	26	DURHAM CITY	2-1	Braidford, Parkinson	3878	4		9						3	6						10	5	2		11		8			1			7
19	30	Nelson	1-4	Braidford		4		9						3	6				5		10		2		11		8			1			7
20	Jan 1	DARLINGTON	1-0	Braidford	6500	4		9						3					5	6	10		2		11		8			1			7
21	2	LINCOLN CITY	2-0	Hardy 2	2800			9			4			3	6					5	10				11		8			1		2	7
22	6	NELSON	5-1	Braidford, Hampson 2(1p), Parkinson, Hardy	5447			9			4			3						6	10	5					8		11	1		2	7
23	20	Stalybridge Celtic	1-1	Parkinson	3000			9			4			3					5	6	10						8		11	1		2	7
24	27	STALYBRIDGE CELTIC	4-0	Hardy 2, Hampson (p), Braidford	4632			9			4			3					5	6	10						8		11	1		2	7
25	Feb 10	BRADFORD PARK AVE.	0-1		4592			9			4			3					5	6	10						8		11	1		2	7
26	17	Tranmere Rovers	1-1	Parkinson	6000			9		6	4			3					5		10						8		11	1		2	7
27	24	TRANMERE ROVERS	0-1		4417			9			4			3					5	6	10						8		11	1		2	7
28	Mar 3	Durham City	2-3	Parkinson, Hardy	3000			9		4				3						6	10	5					8		11	1		2	
29	10	Accrington Stanley	1-2	Hardy	5000	4		9		6				3						5	10		2				8		11	1			7
30	14	Bradford Park Avenue	1-1	Braidford	5000	4		9		6				3						5	10		2	11			8			1			7
31	17	WIGAN BOROUGH	0-0		4200	4		9		6				3						5	10		2	11			8			1			7
32	24	Wigan Borough	0-2		10000	4		9		6				3						5	10		2	11			8			1			7
33	31	CHESTERFIELD	5-0	Braidford 2, Parkinson 2, Hardy	2500	4		9		6				3						5	10		2	11			8			1			7
34	Apr 7	Chesterfield	1-1	Braidford	6000	4		9		6		10		3						5			2	11			8			1			7
35	14	CREWE ALEXANDRA	1-1	Hampson (p)	3633	4		9		6				3						5	10		2	11			8			1			7
36	21	Crewe Alexandra	1-2	Robertson	5000	4		10		6		9		3						5			2	11				8		1			7
37	28	GRIMSBY TOWN	2-0	Hopkins, Hardy	3000	4		9		6				3						2	10	5		11			8			1			7
38	May 5	Grimsby Town	0-1		6000	4		9		6				3						5	10		2				8		11	1			7
					Apps	13	2	29	5	14	15	2	8	26	18	3	11	11	8	22	24	20	12	8	8	4	26	10	26	27	12	20	31
					Goals			9	1				2							4	11	1					7	6	1		4		2

Played in one game: J Harris (game 8, at 10), JT Spencer (4, at 7)
TR Thompson (28, at 7).

F.A. Cup

Q5	Dec 2	Durham City	1-0	Dowson (p)	3000				9		4			3	6							5			7		8	10	11	1		2	
Q6	16	Wrexham	0-1		7000				8		4		9	3	6							5			7				11	1	10	2	

		P	W	D	L	F	A	W	D	L	F	A	Pts
1	Nelson	38	15	2	2	37	10	9	1	9	24	31	51
2	Bradford Park Ave.	38	14	4	1	51	15	5	5	9	16	23	47
3	Walsall	38	13	4	2	32	14	6	4	9	19	30	46
4	Chesterfield	38	13	5	1	49	18	6	2	11	19	34	45
5	Wigan Borough	38	14	3	2	45	11	4	5	10	19	28	44
6	Crewe Alexandra	38	13	3	3	32	9	4	6	9	16	29	43
7	Halifax Town	38	11	4	4	29	14	6	3	10	24	32	41
8	Accrington Stanley	38	14	2	3	40	21	3	5	11	19	44	41
9	Darlington	38	13	3	3	43	14	2	7	10	16	32	40
10	Wrexham	38	13	5	1	29	12	1	5	13	9	36	38
11	Stalybridge Celtic	38	13	2	4	32	18	2	4	13	10	29	36
12	Rochdale	38	8	5	6	29	22	5	5	9	13	31	36
13	Lincoln City	38	9	7	3	21	11	4	3	12	18	44	36
14	Grimsby Town	38	10	3	6	35	18	4	2	13	20	34	33
15	HARTLEPOOLS UTD.	38	10	6	3	34	14	0	6	13	14	40	32
16	Tranmere Rovers	38	11	4	4	41	21	1	4	14	8	38	32
17	Southport	38	11	3	5	21	12	1	4	14	11	34	31
18	Barrow	38	11	2	6	31	17	2	2	15	19	43	30
19	Ashington	38	10	3	6	34	33	1	5	13	17	44	30
20	Durham City	38	7	9	3	31	19	2	1	16	12	40	28

1923/24 — 21st in Division 3 (North)

	Date		Opponent	Score	Scorers	Att.	Abdallah T	Bell JJ	Birnie J	Boulton JWC	Chasser JM	Common J	Cook JA	Dixon C	Duthie JF	Gill GA	Hardy C	Hunt TR	Keenlyside G	Lonie A	Mills WE	Mitchell T	Morris H	Nicholson BC	Parkinson TO	Shaw RA	Smith E	Smith WE	Storey J	Summerfield WH	Sutcliffe P	Walker JR	Walsh W	Young A	Young MS
1	Aug	25	Barrow	2-1	Common, Parkinson	5000				3	6	9		2			10		11						8	4				1	5				7
2	Sep	1	BARROW	1-0	Parkinson	5954				3	6	9		2			10		11						8	4				1	5				7
3		5	Lincoln City	1-1	Hardy	4500				3	6	9		2			10		11						8	4				1	5				7
4		8	Darlington	0-5		5000				3	6	9	8	2			10		11							4				1	5				7
5		15	DARLINGTON	0-1		6569					6	8		2			10		11							4			3	1	5		9		7
6		22	Wigan Borough	1-4	Common	10000					6	8		2			10		11							4			3	1	5		9		7
7		29	WIGAN BOROUGH	0-0		4908			6			8					10	7	11	4								9	3	1		2	5		
8	Oct	6	GRIMSBY TOWN	1-1	Common	4351					6	8					10	7	11	4								9	3	1		2	5		
9		13	Grimsby Town	1-0	W Smith	10000			6			8								4		11				10		9	3	1	5	2			7
10		20	Durham City	0-3		5000			6			8								4		11				10		9	3	1	5	2			7
11		27	DURHAM CITY	0-0		3960			6			9		2					11	4					8			10	3	1	5				7
12	Nov	3	NEW BRIGHTON	0-1		2855			6			8		2			10		7	4		11						9	3	1	5				
13		10	New Brighton	0-0		8000							10	2	8				7	4		11					3	9		1	5		6		
14	Dec	8	WOLVERHAMPTON W.	0-1		5021							11	2			10		8	4							3	9		1	5		6		7
15		22	ACCRINGTON STANLEY	3-0	W Smith, Young, Hardy	3013						4	11	2		1	10		8								3	9			5		6		7
16		25	Halifax Town	0-1								4	11	2		1	10		8								3	9			5		6		7
17		26	HALIFAX TOWN	1-3	W Smith	3200						8	11	2		1	10			4							3	9			5		6		7
18		29	Walsall	0-2		5000						4	7	2	10	1						11				9	3	8			5		6		
19	Jan	1	LINCOLN CITY	1-1	Common (p)	3507						9	7	2	10	1				4		11					3	8			5		6		
20		5	WALSALL	0-1		2959						4	10	2		1			8			11		6			3	9			5				7
21		12	Rochdale	0-1		4000						4	11	2		1			8					5			3	10					6		7
22		19	Tranmere Rovers	0-2		5000						4	11	2		1			8					5			3	10					6		7
23		26	TRANMERE ROVERS	2-1	W Smith, Mitchell	2554					6	4	7	2		1	10		8			11					3	9					5		
24	Feb	2	Bradford Park Avenue	0-4		6000					6	4	7	2		1	10		8			11					3	9					5		
25		9	BRADFORD PARK AVE.	0-0		2485					6	4	9			1						11			8	10	3		2				5		7
26		11	Wolverhampton Wan.	1-2	Hardy	5000					6	4					8					11				9	3		2	1			5		7
27		16	Chesterfield	1-5	Hardy	5909					6	4	9			1	8					11				10	3		2				5		7
28		23	CHESTERFIELD	2-3	Cook, Young	2878					6	4	10				8				9	11					3		2	1			5		7
29	Mar	1	Rotherham County	0-5		6000					6		10			1			8		9	11					3				5		4		7
30		8	ROTHERHAM COUNTY	2-5	W Smith 2	4555		8			6	4		2		1	10					11					3	9					5		7
31		15	WREXHAM	4-0	Bell 2, W Smith, Abdallah	5326	8	9			6			2		1						11	5				3	10					4		7
32		17	Accrington Stanley	0-2		1500	8	11			6			2								10					3		9	1			4	5	7
33		22	Wrexham	0-1		4000	8	9			6	10		2		1						11	5				3							4	7
34		29	DONCASTER ROVERS	1-1	Morris	3970	8	9			11			2		1						10	5				3						4	6	7
35	Apr	5	Doncaster Rovers	1-3	Bell	5000	8	9			6			2		1			7			11	5				3	10					4		
36		12	ROCHDALE	1-2	Morris	4197	8	7			6			2		1			11			9	5				3	10					4		
37		18	Ashington	0-0			8	10			6			2		1						11					3	9					4	5	7
38		21	CREWE ALEXANDRA	2-2	W Smith 2	3945	8	10			6	4		2		1						11					3	9						5	7
39		22	ASHINGTON	0-1			8	10			6	4	9	2		1						11					3	7						5	
40		26	SOUTHPORT	1-0	Bell	1766	8	10			6		9	2					7			11		4			3			1				5	
41		30	Crewe Alexandra	1-2	Young	3000	8				6	4	10	2								11	5				3	9		1					7
42	May	3	Southport	2-2	Keenlyside, Cook	3000		8			6	4	10	2					7			11	5				3	9		1					
						Apps	11	12	5	4	27	32	21	33	3	22	19	2	24	10	2	27	7	4	5	12	30	27	13	20	19	4	27	7	29
						Goals	1	4				4	2				4		1			1	2		2			9							3

Played in one game: J Brown (game 29, at 2), JM Wrightson (26 at 10).
Played in games 21 and 22 at 9: R Carswell.

F.A. Cup

Rd	Date		Opponent	Score	Scorers	Att.	Abdallah T	Bell JJ	Birnie J	Boulton JWC	Chasser JM	Common J	Cook JA	Dixon C	Duthie JF	Gill GA	Hardy C	Hunt TR	Keenlyside G	Lonie A	Mills WE	Mitchell T	Morris H	Nicholson BC	Parkinson TO	Shaw RA	Smith E	Smith WE	Storey J	Summerfield WH	Sutcliffe P	Walker JR	Walsh W	Young A	Young MS
Q4	Nov	17	ST. PETERS ALBION	10-1	W Smith 7(1p), Cook, Lonie, Duthie	2929							11	2	10				8	4							3	9		1	5		6		7
Q5	Dec	1	SHILDON	3-1	W Smith 2(1p), Lonie	4112							11	2			10		8	4							3	9		1	5		6		7
Q6		15	Ashington	1-2	Keenlyside	5000							11	2			10		8	4							3	9		1	5		6		7

		P	W	D	L	F	A	W	D	L	F	A	Pts
1	Wolverhampton Wan.	42	18	3	0	51	10	6	12	3	25	17	63
2	Rochdale	42	17	4	0	40	8	8	8	5	20	18	62
3	Chesterfield	42	16	4	1	54	15	6	6	9	16	24	54
4	Rotherham County	42	16	3	2	46	13	7	3	11	24	30	52
5	Bradford Park Ave.	42	17	3	1	50	12	4	7	10	19	31	52
6	Darlington	42	16	5	0	51	19	4	3	14	19	34	48
7	Southport	42	13	7	1	30	10	3	7	11	14	32	46
8	Ashington	42	14	4	3	41	21	4	4	13	18	40	44
9	Doncaster Rovers	42	13	4	4	41	17	2	8	11	18	36	42
10	Wigan Borough	42	12	5	4	39	15	2	9	10	16	38	42
11	Grimsby Town	42	11	9	1	30	7	3	4	14	19	40	41
12	Tranmere Rovers	42	11	5	5	32	21	2	10	9	19	39	41
13	Accrington Stanley	42	12	5	4	35	21	4	3	14	13	40	40
14	Halifax Town	42	11	4	6	26	17	4	6	11	16	42	40
15	Durham City	42	12	5	4	40	23	3	4	14	19	37	39
16	Wrexham	42	8	11	2	24	12	2	7	12	13	32	38
17	Walsall	42	10	5	6	31	20	4	3	14	13	39	36
18	New Brighton	42	9	9	3	28	10	2	4	15	12	43	35
19	Lincoln City	42	8	8	5	29	22	2	4	15	19	37	32
20	Crewe Alexandra	42	6	7	8	20	24	1	6	14	12	34	27
21	HARTLEPOOLS UTD.	42	5	7	9	22	24	2	4	15	11	46	25
22	Barrow	42	7	7	7	25	24	1	2	18	10	56	25

1924/25 20th in Division 3 (North)

						Allen JT	Best R	Butler E	Carr T	Chape GE	Cook JA	Cowell W	Dixon C	Foster JH	Gray T	Hardy C	Hardy S	Jobson JT	Lee JW	Lilley T	Livingstone AM	Nicholson BC	Osmond JE	Parkinson TO	Reilly P	Richardson GW	Robinson WA	Smith E	Smith TP	Smith WE	Storer C	Summerfield WH	Walsh W	Wayman BO	Young A
1	Aug 30	ROCHDALE	1-1	TP Smith	7739	2	7	11		4								6		3									8	10		1		9	5
2	Sep 1	Grimsby Town	1-2	Richardson		2	7	11		4								6		3						9			8			1		10	5
3	6	Darlington	0-2		5300	2	7	11		4								6		3						9			8			1		10	5
4	10	GRIMSBY TOWN	2-1	Jobson, Richardson	4200	2	7	11										4		3						9		6	8			1		10	5
5	13	BRADFORD PARK AVE.	2-2	Allen 2 (2p)	5430	2	7	11										4		3						9		6	8			1		10	5
6	20	Wrexham	1-3	W Smith	7000	2	7	11										4		3						9		6	8	10		1			5
7	27	ROTHERHAM COUNTY	0-0		5885	2	7	11				1		5				4		3						9		6	8	10					
8	Oct 1	SOUTHPORT	1-2	W Smith	2677	2	7	11				1		4				6								9		3	8	10	5				
9	4	Chesterfield	0-4		9000	2	7	11				1		4				6			8							3	9	10	5				
10	11	ACCRINGTON STANLEY	3-0	TP Smith, C Hardy, Livingstone	4971	2	7	11				1		4		8		6			10							3	9		5				
11	18	Halifax Town	0-2		7000	2	7	11			9	1		4		8					10	6						3			5				
12	25	Tranmere Rovers	3-4	TP Smith, Richardson, S Hardy	4000	2		7		3	8	1		4			11					6				10			9		5				
13	Nov 1	LINCOLN CITY	1-1	S Hardy	4233	2		7				1		4			11					6	3		8	10			9		5				
14	8	Barrow	1-1	S Hardy	4000	2		7				1					11	8				6				10		3	9		5		4		
15	22	Ashington	3-0	S Hardy, Butler 2	4000	2		7	9			1				10	11	4				5						3	8						6
16	Dec 6	Doncaster Rovers	0-1		6000	2		7	9			1				10	11	4										3	8		5				6
17	20	Crewe Alexandra	1-3	TP Smith	6000	2		7	9			1				10	11	4										3	8		5				6
18	25	WIGAN BOROUGH	1-0	Allen (p)	5000	2		7	9			1				10	11	4				5						3	8						6
19	26	Wigan Borough	0-0		6000	2		7	9		8	1				10	11	4		3											5				6
20	27	Rochdale	1-3	Cook	5000	2		7	9		10	1					11	4		3									8		5				6
21	Jan 1	WALSALL	3-1	W Smith 3	3554	2		7				1				10	11	4		3									8	9	5				6
22	3	DARLINGTON	1-1	TP Smith	7431	2		7	9			1					11	4		3							10		8		5				6
23	17	Bradford Park Avenue	0-3		10000	2		7	9		8	1				10	11	4		3											5				6
24	24	WREXHAM	1-1	W Smith	3205	2		7				1				10	11	4										3	8	9	5				6
25	31	Rotherham County	2-1	W Smith 2		2		7				1					11	4						8				3	10	9	5				6
26	Feb 7	CHESTERFIELD	1-0	TP Smith	4443	2		7				1					11	4						8				3	10	9	5				6
27	14	Accrington Stanley	1-4	W Smith	2000	2	7	11				1						4						8			10	3		9	5				6
28	21	HALIFAX TOWN	1-1	Carr	4205		7	11	8			1			2			4									10	3		9	5				6
29	28	TRANMERE ROVERS	2-1	Carr, TP Smith	4771		7	11	8			1			2			4									10	3	9		5				6
30	Mar 7	Lincoln City	1-2	Carr	7000		7	11	8			1			2			4										3	10	9	5				6
31	14	BARROW	1-0	Carr	3522		7	11	9			1			2	10		4										3	8		5				6
32	21	Nelson	0-2		5000		7	11	9			1		5	2	10		4										3	8						6
33	25	NELSON	2-4	S Hardy, Butler	1594			7	9			1		5	2	10	11	4										3	8						6
34	28	ASHINGTON	0-1		3219			7	9			1			2		11	4										3	8	10	5				6
35	Apr 4	Southport	0-2		4000	6		7	9			1			8			4	11	2						10		3			5				
36	10	New Brighton	0-2		6000	5		7	9			1			8			4	11	2						10		3							6
37	11	DONCASTER ROVERS	2-2	Richardson, Carr	3213		7	11	9			1	3		2			4								10			8		5				6
38	13	NEW BRIGHTON	0-2		2465		7	11	8			1	3		2	10		4								9					5				6
39	18	Durham City	1-0	W Smith	1000		7	11	8			1	3			10		4		2										9	5				6
40	22	DURHAM CITY	1-0	W Smith	1975		7	11	8			1	3			10		4		2										9	5				6
41	25	CREWE ALEXANDRA	2-0	C Hardy, W Smith	2857		7	11	8			1	3			10		4		2										9	5				6
42	May 2	Walsall	1-1	C Hardy	1775		7	11	8			1	3	4		10				2										9	5				6
					Apps	29	23	42	23	4	5	36	6	10	11	18	17	38	2	18	3	6	1	3	1	14	4	26	30	17	30	6	1	5	33
					Goals	3		3	5		1					3	5	1			1					4			7	12					

F.A. Cup

Q4	Nov 15	ASHINGTON	0-0		5692	2		7				1					11	8				6				10		3	9		5		4		
rep	19	Ashington	0-2		4000	2		7				1					11	4				6				10		3	9		5		8		
Q5	29	BISHOP AUCKLAND	2-0	TP Smith, Butler	5835	2		7			9	1				10	11	4										3	8		5				6
Q6	Dec 13	ST. ALBANS CITY	4-0	Cook 2, C Hardy, Storer	5852	2		7			9	1				10	11	4										3	8		5				6
R1	Jan 10	Newcastle United	1-4	S Hardy	36632	2		7			9	1				10	11	4		3									8		5				6

R1 replay. Ashington disqualified for fielding an ineligible player. Hartlepools United re-instated.

		P	W	D	L	F	A	W	D	L	F	A	Pts
1	Darlington	42	16	4	1	50	14	8	6	7	28	19	58
2	Nelson	42	18	2	1	58	14	5	5	11	21	36	53
3	New Brighton	42	17	3	1	56	16	6	4	11	19	34	53
4	Southport	42	17	2	2	41	7	5	5	11	18	30	51
5	Bradford Park Ave.	42	15	5	1	59	13	4	7	10	25	29	50
6	Rochdale	42	17	2	2	53	16	4	5	12	22	37	49
7	Chesterfield	42	14	3	4	42	15	3	8	10	18	29	45
8	Lincoln City	42	13	4	4	39	19	5	4	12	14	39	44
9	Halifax Town	42	11	5	5	36	22	5	6	10	20	30	43
10	Ashington	42	13	4	4	41	24	3	6	12	27	52	42
11	Wigan Borough	42	10	7	4	39	16	5	4	12	23	49	41
12	Grimsby Town	42	10	6	5	38	21	5	3	13	22	39	39
13	Durham City	42	11	6	4	38	17	2	7	12	12	51	39
14	Barrow	42	14	4	3	39	22	2	3	16	12	52	39
15	Crewe Alexandra	42	11	7	3	35	24	2	6	13	18	54	39
16	Wrexham	42	11	5	5	37	21	4	3	14	16	40	38
17	Accrington Stanley	42	12	5	4	43	23	3	3	15	17	49	38
18	Doncaster Rovers	42	12	5	4	36	17	2	5	14	18	48	38
19	Walsall	42	10	6	5	27	16	3	5	13	17	37	37
20	HARTLEPOOLS UTD.	42	9	8	4	28	21	3	3	15	17	42	35
21	Tranmere Rovers	42	11	3	7	40	29	3	1	17	19	49	32
22	Rotherham County	42	6	5	10	27	31	1	2	18	15	57	21

1925/26 6th in Division 3 (North)

						Best R	Birtles F	Boland GA	Butler E	Carr T	Cowell W	Craig J	Dixon C	Foster JH	Hardy C	Hardy S	Henderson T	Hunter A	Jobson JT	Kell G	Lilley T	Richardson GW	Robinson WA	Robson FE	Storer C	Wensley H	Young A
1	Aug 29	Rochdale	0-6		9321		8		7		1				10	11			4		2			3	5	9	6
2	Sep 2	Accrington Stanley	2-1	Wensley, C Hardy	5177		8		7		1			5	10	11			4		2			3		9	6
3	5	TRANMERE ROVERS	3-2	S Hardy, C Hardy, Wensley (p)	4832		8		7		1			5	10	11			4		2			3		9	6
4	7	Halifax Town	1-2	Wensley	4169		8		7		1			5	10	11			4		2			3		9	6
5	12	Walsall	2-1	Birtles, C Hardy	5054		8		7		1			5	10	11			4		2			3		9	6
6	16	ACCRINGTON STANLEY	5-1	Wensley 3, Birtles, C Hardy	3698		8		7		1			5	10	11			4		2			3		9	6
7	19	CHESTERFIELD	2-1	Wensley 2	5708		8		7		1			5	10	11			4		2			3		9	6
8	26	Bradford Park Avenue	0-4		9849	7	8				1			5	10	11			4		2			3		9	6
9	Oct 3	GRIMSBY TOWN	1-1	C Hardy	6096	7				8	1			5	10	11			4		2			3		9	6
10	10	Rotherham United	0-1		6015	7	8				1			5	10	11			4		2			3		9	6
11	17	BARROW	2-0	Wensley, Best	4498	7				8	1			5	10	11			4		2			3		9	6
12	24	Nelson	2-5	Wensley, S Hardy	4892	7	8				1		3	5	10	11			4		2					9	6
13	31	NEW BRIGHTON	6-1	Birtles 2, Foster, S Hardy, Wensley, C Hardy	4956	7	8				1			5	10	11			4	3	2	6				9	
14	Nov 7	Wigan Borough	0-1		1829				7	8	1				10	11			5	3	2	6				9	4
15	14	DONCASTER ROVERS	2-1	Wensley, Foster	4221	7			8		1			5	10	11			4	3	2					9	6
16	21	Southport	1-1	S Hardy	3762	7				8	1			5	10	11			4	3	2					9	6
17	Dec 5	Crewe Alexandra	1-2	C Hardy	3781	7				8	1			5	10	11			4	3	2	6				9	
18	12	COVENTRY CITY	3-2	Wensley, Richardson, Best	1956	7					1				10	11		9	4		2	6		3		8	5
19	19	Wrexham	2-2	Carr, C Hardy	4410	7				9	1			5	10	11			4	3	2	6				8	
20	25	DURHAM CITY	1-1	Best	5306	7				8	1			5	10	11			4	3	2	6				9	
21	26	ASHINGTON	2-1	Carr 2	5094	7				8	1				10	11			4	3	2	6				9	5
22	Jan 1	HALIFAX TOWN	1-1	Carr	5036	7				8	1				10	11			4	3	2	6				9	5
23	2	ROCHDALE	4-2	Best, C Hardy 2, Carr	6057	7				8	1			5	10	11			4	3	2	6				9	
24	9	LINCOLN CITY	4-2	S Hardy 2, C Hardy, Wensley	4291	7				8	1			5	10	11			4	3	2	6				9	
25	16	Tranmere Rovers	0-2		4658	7				8	1			5	10	11			4	3	2	6				9	
26	23	WALSALL	9-3	C Hardy 3, Best, Wensley, S Hardy 2, Carr 2	3358	7				8	1			5	10	11			4	3	2	6				9	
27	30	Chesterfield	2-5	Wensley, S Hardy	4316	7				8	1			5	10	11			4	3	2	6				9	
28	Feb 6	BRADFORD PARK AVE.	0-3		7491			11	7	8	1			5	10				4	3	2	6				9	
29	13	Grimsby Town	0-2		7859	7		11			1			5	8				4	3	2	6	10			9	
30	20	ROTHERHAM UNITED	2-1	Richardson 2 (2p)	4408	7	8	11			1			5	10				4	3	2	6				9	
31	27	Barrow	4-1	Boland, Robinson 2, Birtles	1187	7	8	11			1			5						3	2	6	10			9	4
32	Mar 6	NELSON	2-0	Robinson, Wensley	4397	7	8	11			1			5						3	2	6	10			9	4
33	13	New Brighton	2-3	Boland, Birtles	4198	7	8	11			1			5						3	2	6	10			9	4
34	20	WIGAN BOROUGH	0-0		4256	7		11		8	1			5						3	2	6	10			9	4
35	27	Doncaster Rovers	1-2	Best	4694	7			11		1			5	8					3	2	6	10			9	4
36	Apr 2	Ashington	0-2		4596	7			11		1	8		5						3	2	6	10			9	4
37	3	SOUTHPORT	5-0	Wensley, Butler, Robinson, Richardson, C Hardy	3984	7			11		1				8				5	3	2	6	10			9	4
38	5	Durham City	0-0		3886	7			11		1			6	8				5	3	2		10			9	4
39	10	Lincoln City	1-2	Wensley	3627	7			11		1	8							5	3	2	6	10			9	4
40	17	CREWE ALEXANDRA	0-0		2696	7		11			1	8					6		5	3	2		10			9	4
41	24	Coventry City	2-5	Wensley, Richardson	4744	7		11			1	8							5	3	2	6	10			9	4
42	May 1	WREXHAM	5-0	Robinson 3, Wensley, Craig	2171	7			11		1	8							5	3	2	6	10			9	4
					Apps	33	15	9	16	16	42	5	1	32	33	27	1	1	36	29	42	26	13	12	1	42	30
					Goals	6	6	2	1	7		1		2	15	9						5	7			21	

F.A. Cup

						Best R	Birtles F	Boland GA	Butler E	Carr T	Cowell W	Craig J	Dixon C	Foster JH	Hardy C	Hardy S	Henderson T	Hunter A	Jobson JT	Kell G	Lilley T	Richardson GW	Robinson WA	Robson FE	Storer C	Wensley H	Young A
R1	Nov 28	Blyth Spartans	2-2	S Hardy, Best	1819	7				8	1			5	10	11			4	3				2		9	6
rep	Dec 2	BLYTH SPARTANS	1-1	C Hardy	1994	7				8	1			5	10	11			4	3				2		9	6
rep2	7	Blyth Spartans	1-1	Hunter	2000	7					1				10	11		9	4	3	2	6				8	5
rep3	9	Blyth Spartans	1-2	Wensley	3098	7					1				10	11		9	4		2	6		3		8	5

R1 replay and replay 2 a.e.t. Replay 2 at St. James's Park, Newcastle. Replay 3 at Roker Park, Sunderland

		P	W	D	L	F	A	W	D	L	F	A	Pts
1	Grimsby Town	42	20	1	0	61	8	6	8	7	30	32	61
2	Bradford Park Ave.	42	18	2	1	65	10	8	6	7	36	33	60
3	Rochdale	42	16	1	4	55	25	11	4	6	49	33	59
4	Chesterfield	42	18	2	1	70	19	7	3	11	30	35	55
5	Halifax Town	42	12	5	4	34	19	5	6	10	19	31	45
6	HARTLEPOOLS UTD.	42	15	5	1	59	23	3	3	15	23	50	44
7	Tranmere Rovers	42	15	2	4	45	27	4	4	13	28	56	44
8	Nelson	42	12	8	1	67	29	4	3	14	22	42	43
9	Ashington	42	11	6	4	44	23	5	5	11	26	39	43
10	Doncaster Rovers	42	11	7	3	52	25	5	4	12	28	47	43
11	Crewe Alexandra	42	14	3	4	43	23	3	6	12	20	38	43
12	New Brighton	42	13	4	4	51	29	4	4	13	18	38	42
13	Durham City	42	14	5	2	45	19	4	1	16	18	51	42
14	Rotherham United	42	13	3	5	44	28	4	4	13	25	64	41
15	Lincoln City	42	14	2	5	42	28	3	3	15	24	54	39
16	Coventry City	42	13	6	2	47	19	3	0	18	26	63	38
17	Wigan Borough	42	12	5	4	53	22	1	6	14	15	52	37
18	Accrington Stanley	42	14	0	7	49	34	3	3	15	32	71	37
19	Wrexham	42	9	6	6	39	31	2	4	15	24	61	32
20	Southport	42	9	6	6	37	34	2	4	15	25	58	32
21	Walsall	42	9	4	8	40	34	1	2	18	18	73	26
22	Barrow	42	4	2	15	28	49	3	2	16	22	49	18

1926/27 17th in Division 3 (North)

	Date	Opponent	Score	Scorers	Att.	Arch WH	Best R	Boland GA	Carr T	Craig J	Dobell D	Errington A	Foster JH	Hall B	Hardy C	Hardy S	Harrison H	Hickman J	Jobson JT	Kell G	Little RA	McClenn J	Myers EC	Richardson GW	Robinson WA	Telford R	Thompson R (1)	Waite GH	Walton J	Wensley H	Young A
1	Aug 28	BARROW	1-1	Myers	5221	2				8							1		5	3		11	10	6				7		9	4
2	31	Southport	0-1		5758	2				8							1		5	3		11	10	6				7		9	4
3	Sep 4	HALIFAX TOWN	0-1		3671	2	7			10							1		5	3		11		6				8		9	4
4	11	Lincoln City	2-1	Waite 2	5475	2	7	11									1		5	3				6		8		9		10	4
5	13	Stoke City	1-3	Young	8306	2	7	11									1		5	3				6	10			8		9	4
6	18	ACCRINGTON STANLEY	3-1	Wensley 2, Waite	3285	2	7	11									1		5	3				6	10			8		9	4
7	22	STOKE CITY	1-3	Robinson	4348	2	7	11									1		5	3				6	10			8		9	4
8	25	Durham City	1-2	Wensley	2195	2	7	11									1		5	3				6		10		8		9	4
9	Oct 2	TRANMERE ROVERS	2-1	Myers, Thirkell (og)	3242	3	7	11	2				5				1						10	6				8		9	4
10	9	Rochdale	0-3		2596	3	7	11	2				5								1		10	6				8		9	4
11	16	Wigan Borough	0-3		2928	2	7					3	5				1						10	6		9		8		11	4
12	23	DONCASTER ROVERS	3-0	Myers, Thompson, McClenn	2681	2				8			5	4			1			3		7	10	6			9			11	
13	30	Rotherham United	3-5	McClenn, Wensley (p), Thompson	3013	2							5	4			1			3		7	10		8		9		6	11	
14	Nov 6	BRADFORD PARK AVE.	2-4	Wensley (p), Thompson	1278	2				8			5	4						3	1	7			10		9		6	11	
15	13	Walsall	2-2	Craig, Robinson	4276	2				8			5	4					6	3	1	7			10		9			11	
16	20	NELSON	3-2	Richardson 2, McClenn	3171	2				8			5	4		11	1		6	3		7		9	10						
17	Dec 4	ASHINGTON	0-1		2062	2				8			5	4		11	1		6	3		7		9	10						
18	11	New Brighton	1-2	Wensley	4319			11	2	8			5	4			1			3		7	10	6						9	
19	18	WREXHAM	4-0	Myers 2, Craig, Wensley	1625			11	2	8			5	4			1			3		7	10	6						9	
20	25	CREWE ALEXANDRA	1-1	Wensley	3098			11	2	8			5	4			1			3		7	10	6						9	
21	27	Crewe Alexandra	1-0	Boland	5973			11	2					4			1		5	3		7	10	6				8		9	
22	Jan 1	SOUTHPORT	2-0	Robinson, Wensley	3426	2		11						4			1		5	3		7		6	10			8		9	
23	3	STOCKPORT COUNTY	1-2	Boland	4244	2		11		8				4			1		5	3		7		6	10					9	
24	15	Barrow	3-1	Craig, Wensley, Boland	2955	2		11		10				4			1		5	3		7		6				8		9	
25	22	Halifax Town	1-2	Waite	5930	2		11						4			1		5	3		7	10	6				8		9	
26	29	LINCOLN CITY	1-1	Waite	2452	2		11						4			1		5	3		7	10	6				8		9	
27	Feb 5	Accrington Stanley	2-7	Boland, Myers	2877	2		11						4					5	3	1	7	10	6				8		9	
28	12	DURHAM CITY	4-0	Dobell 2, Craig, Myers	2537			11	2	8	9			4				1	5	3			10					7			6
29	19	Tranmere Rovers	0-2		5584			11	2	8	9			4				1	5	3			10					7			6
30	26	ROCHDALE	3-2	Waite, Jobson (p), Craig	4000			11	2	8	9			4				1	5	3			10					7			6
31	Mar 5	WIGAN BOROUGH	2-1	Myers, Waite	2821				2	8	9			4			1		5	3		11	10					7			6
32	12	Doncaster Rovers	0-2		5136				2	8	9			4		11	1		5	3			10					7			6
33	19	ROTHERHAM UNITED	3-1	Carr, S Hardy, Wensley	2766				2					4	10	11	1		5	3			8					7		9	6
34	26	Bradford Park Avenue	1-4	S Hardy	5796				2	8				4		11	1			3			10	6				7		9	5
35	Apr 2	WALSALL	2-2	Wensley 2	2378		7		2	8				4		11	1		5	3			10							9	6
36	9	Nelson	2-6	Kell (p), C Hardy	4369		7		2	8				4	10	11	1			3				6						9	5
37	16	CHESTERFIELD	1-2	Dennis (og)	3122		7		2	8		3		4	10	11	1							6						9	5
38	18	Stockport County	3-3	Wensley 2 (1p), Best	7503		7		2	8		3		4	10	11	1		6											9	5
39	19	Chesterfield	0-1		4405		7		2	8		3		4	10		1		5									11		9	6
40	23	Ashington	0-1		1739			11	2	7		3		4	10		1							6				8		9	5
41	30	NEW BRIGHTON	4-0	Best, Hall, C Hardy, Wensley	1983		7	11	2			3		4	10		1							6	8					9	5
42	May 7	Wrexham	0-4		1536		7	11	2		9	3		4			1		6					10	8						5
					Apps	23	16	23	21	25	6	7	12	31	7	9	35	3	28	33	4	20	22	30	12	3	4	26	2	34	26
					Goals		2	4	1	5	2			1	2	2			1	1		3	8	2	3		3	7		16	1

Two own goals

F.A. Cup

	Date	Opponent	Score	Scorers	Att.	Arch WH	Best R	Boland GA	Carr T	Craig J	Dobell D	Errington A	Foster JH	Hall B	Hardy C	Hardy S	Harrison H	Hickman J	Jobson JT	Kell G	Little RA	McClenn J	Myers EC	Richardson GW	Robinson WA	Telford R	Thompson R (1)	Waite GH	Walton J	Wensley H	Young A
R1	Nov 27	Carlisle United	2-6	Robinson, Craig	7000	2				8			5	4		11	1		6	3		7		9	10						

		P	W	D	L	F	A	W	D	L	F	A	Pts
1	Stoke City	42	17	3	1	57	11	10	6	5	35	29	63
2	Rochdale	42	18	2	1	72	22	8	4	9	33	43	58
3	Bradford Park Ave.	42	18	3	0	74	21	6	4	11	27	38	55
4	Halifax Town	42	13	6	2	46	23	8	5	8	24	30	53
5	Nelson	42	16	2	3	64	20	6	5	10	40	55	51
6	Stockport County	42	13	4	4	60	31	9	3	9	33	38	49
7	Chesterfield	42	15	4	2	65	24	6	1	14	27	44	47
8	Doncaster Rovers	42	13	4	4	58	27	5	7	9	23	38	47
9	Tranmere Rovers	42	13	5	3	54	22	6	3	12	31	45	46
10	New Brighton	42	14	2	5	49	21	4	8	9	30	46	46
11	Lincoln City	42	9	5	7	50	33	6	7	8	40	45	42
12	Southport	42	11	5	5	54	32	4	4	13	26	53	39
13	Wrexham	42	10	5	6	41	26	4	5	12	24	47	38
14	Walsall	42	10	4	7	35	22	4	6	11	33	59	38
15	Crewe Alexandra	42	11	5	5	46	28	3	4	14	25	53	37
16	Ashington	42	9	8	4	42	30	3	4	14	18	60	36
17	HARTLEPOOLS UTD.	42	11	4	6	43	26	3	2	16	23	55	34
18	Wigan Borough	42	10	6	5	44	28	1	4	16	22	55	32
19	Rotherham United	42	8	6	7	41	35	2	6	13	29	57	32
20	Durham City	42	9	4	8	35	35	3	2	16	23	70	30
21	Accrington Stanley	42	9	3	9	45	38	1	4	16	17	60	27
22	Barrow	42	5	6	10	22	40	2	2	17	12	77	22

1927/28

15th in Division 3 (North)

						Boland GA	Brown, Jack	Carr T	Dobell D	Errington A	Hall B	Hardy C	Hardy S	Harris J(2)	Harrison H	Hickman J	Kell G	Liddle I	Mordue J	Mordue WM	Poyntz WI	Rayment J	Richardson GEH	Richardson GW	Robertson T	Robinson WA	Robson C	Williams JT	Young A	Young J
1	Aug 27	Wigan Borough	2-0	Dobell, W Mordue	6385			2	9	3	4		11		1					10	8		7	6					5	
2	Sep 3	DONCASTER ROVERS	1-0	Richardson	5314			2	9	3	4		11		1					10	8		7	6					5	
3	10	Darlington	0-5		6719			2	9	3	4		11		1					10	8		7	6					5	
4	14	Wrexham	2-3	Robinson 2	2927	11		2	9	3					1					8	5			6		10	7		4	
5	17	ASHINGTON	4-1	S Hardy 2, Robson, Robinson	4294			2	9	3			11		1					10	4			6		8	7		5	
6	24	Crewe Alexandra	0-4		3016			2	9	3	5		11		1					10	4			6		8	7			
7	27	Accrington Stanley	2-2	Liddle, W Mordue	6353			2			4		11		1			8		10	9			6	3		7	5		
8	Oct 1	HALIFAX TOWN	0-1		4571			2		3			11		1			8		10	9			6			7	5	4	
9	8	Bradford City	1-2	W Mordue	13762			2			4		11		1		3	8		10	6			9			7		5	
10	15	NEW BRIGHTON	3-3	S Hardy, Richardson, W Mordue	4243			2			4		11		1		3	8		10	6			9			7	5		
11	22	Rotherham United	0-5		2395				9		4			11	1		3	8		10				6	2		7		5	
12	29	ROCHDALE	0-2		4086	11		9			4				1		3	8		10				6	2		7		5	
13	Nov 5	Nelson	2-4	Robinson 2	2001	11		2			4				1		3	8		10	6					9	7		5	
14	12	SOUTHPORT	2-1	W Mordue 2	2429	11		2			4				1		3		8	10	6					9	7		5	
15	19	Durham City	0-1		1580	11		2			4					1				10	8			6	3	9	7		5	
16	Dec 3	Chesterfield	3-1	Robinson, W Mordue, Rayment	2505	11		2			4					1		8		10		7		6	3	9			5	
17	10	DURHAM CITY	2-1	Robinson 2	2497	11		2			4					1		8		10	6	7		5	3	9				
18	17	Tranmere Rovers	2-1	Robinson (p), W Mordue	4878	11		2			4					1		8		10	5	7		6	3	9				
19	24	STOCKPORT COUNTY	2-1	Robinson 2	2033	11		2			4				1			8		10	5	7		6	3	9				
20	26	LINCOLN CITY	1-2	Liddle	3961	11		2			4				1			8		10	5	7		6	3	9				
21	27	Lincoln City	5-1	Robinson 3, J Mordue, W Mordue	9277	11		2			4				1				8	10	5	7		6	3	9				
22	31	WIGAN BOROUGH	1-1	W Mordue	3546	11		2			4				1				8	10	5	7		6	3	9				
23	Jan 2	BARROW	6-2	Robson 2, Robinson 2, J Mordue 2	3377	11		2			4				1				8	10	5				3	9	7		6	
24	7	Doncaster Rovers	1-1	Boland	7641	11		2			4				1				8	10	5	7		6	3	9				
25	14	BRADFORD PARK AVE.	1-1	Robinson (p)	5023	11		2			4				1				8	10	5	7		6	3	9				
26	21	DARLINGTON	0-1		7485	11		2							1				8	10	5	7		6	3	9			4	
27	28	Ashington	1-3	W Mordue	1407	11		2							1					10	5			6	3	9	7		4	8
28	Feb 4	CREWE ALEXANDRA	4-3	Boland, W Mordue, J Young, Robinson	3100	11		2			4				1					10	5				3	9	7		6	8
29	11	Halifax Town	1-4	W Mordue	2424	11					4				1		2		8	10	5				3	9	7		6	
30	18	BRADFORD CITY	2-3	Rayment, Robinson (p)	4475	11				3	4				1		2		8	10	5	7				9			6	
31	25	New Brighton	1-2	Robinson	2861	11					4				1				8	10	5	7		6	2	9		3		
32	Mar 3	ROTHERHAM UNITED	1-3	W Mordue	4190	11					4				1		2		8	10	5	7		6		9		3		
33	10	Rochdale	1-0	Robinson	2582	11	1				4									10	5	7		6	2	9		3		8
34	17	NELSON	4-5	Rigg (og), Robinson 3	2972	11	1				4									10	5	7		6	2	9		3		8
35	24	Southport	2-0	Boland, Dobell	2518	11			9		4				1							7		6	2	10		3	5	8
36	Apr 6	Barrow	0-2		7059	11	1				4									10		7		6	2	9		3	5	8
37	7	Bradford Park Avenue	0-3		12715	11	1	2			4											7		10	3	9		5	6	8
38	9	ACCRINGTON STANLEY	0-2		2245	11	1	2			4	10										7		8	3	9		5	6	
39	14	CHESTERFIELD	1-0	Robinson	1314	11		2			4				1					10				6		9	7	3	5	8
40	21	WREXHAM	4-2	Robinson, Robson, J Young, W Mordue	1542	11		2			4				1					10				6		9	7	3	5	8
41	28	TRANMERE ROVERS	2-0	W Mordue, Robinson	2132	11		2			4				1					10				6		9	7	3	5	8
42	May 5	Stockport County	2-2	Robinson, Robson	4991	11		2			4				1					10				6		9	7	3	5	8
					Apps	32	5	33	8	8	37	1	9	1	33	4	9	12	11	39	31	19	3	36	25	33	20	15	27	11
					Goals	3			2				3					2	3	16		2		2		28	5			2

One own goal

F.A. Cup

						Boland GA	Brown, Jack	Carr T	Dobell D	Errington A	Hall B	Hardy C	Hardy S	Harris J(2)	Harrison H	Hickman J	Kell G	Liddle I	Mordue J	Mordue WM	Poyntz WI	Rayment J	Richardson GEH	Richardson GW	Robertson T	Robinson WA	Robson C	Williams JT	Young A	Young J
R1	Nov 26	Halifax Town	0-3		10341	11		2			4				1					10	8	7		9	3			6	5	

		P	W	D	L	F	A	W	D	L	F	A	Pts
1	Bradford Park Ave.	42	18	2	1	68	22	9	7	5	33	23	63
2	Lincoln City	42	15	4	2	53	20	9	3	9	38	44	55
3	Stockport County	42	16	5	0	62	14	7	3	11	27	37	54
4	Doncaster Rovers	42	15	4	2	59	18	8	3	10	21	26	53
5	Tranmere Rovers	42	14	6	1	68	28	8	3	10	37	44	53
6	Bradford City	42	15	4	2	59	19	3	8	10	26	41	48
7	Darlington	42	15	1	5	63	28	6	4	11	26	46	47
8	Southport	42	15	2	4	55	24	5	3	13	24	46	45
9	Accrington Stanley	42	14	4	3	49	22	4	4	13	27	45	44
10	New Brighton	42	10	7	4	45	22	4	7	10	27	40	42
11	Wrexham	42	15	1	5	48	19	3	5	13	16	48	42
12	Halifax Town	42	11	7	3	47	24	2	8	11	26	47	41
13	Rochdale	42	13	4	4	45	24	4	3	14	29	53	41
14	Rotherham United	42	11	6	4	39	19	3	5	13	26	50	39
15	HARTLEPOOLS UTD.	42	10	3	8	41	35	6	3	12	28	46	38
16	Chesterfield	42	10	4	7	46	29	3	6	12	25	49	36
17	Crewe Alexandra	42	10	6	5	51	28	2	4	15	26	58	34
18	Ashington	42	10	5	6	54	36	1	6	14	23	67	33
19	Barrow	42	10	8	3	41	24	0	3	18	13	78	31
20	Wigan Borough	42	8	5	8	30	32	2	5	14	26	65	30
21	Durham City	42	10	5	6	37	30	1	2	18	16	70	29
22	Nelson	42	8	4	9	50	49	2	2	17	26	87	26

1928/29

21st in Division 3 (North)

							Briggs H	Carr T	Christon L	Coates WA	Dixon RH	Dobell D	Errington A	Fell JW	Hall B	Harland T	Hickman J	Hodgson W	Mackey TS	Mason R	Mordue J	Mordue T	Mordue WM	Richardson W	Rivers JE	Robertson T	Smith G (1)	Spry WH	Williams JT	Young J
1	Aug	25	NELSON	2-2	Young, Spry	5524		2	9			6		11	4					5			10				1	7	3	8
2	Sep	1	Carlisle United	0-8		7346		2	9			6		11	4					5	8		10				1	7	3	
3		5	DARLINGTON	2-0	T Mordue, J Mordue	5271		2		7		6	3	11	4						8	9	10				1		5	
4		8	ROTHERHAM UNITED	1-1	T Mordue	4867		2		7		6	3	11	4						8	9	10				1		5	
5		15	Wigan Borough	0-2		7842		2				6	3	11	4						7	9	10		1				5	8
6		22	CREWE ALEXANDRA	2-1	J Mordue, T Mordue	4015		2				6		11					4		8	9	10	7	1	3			5	
7		25	Accrington Stanley	2-2	J Mordue 2	4488		2			11			7				6	4		8	9	10		1	3			5	
8		29	Tranmere Rovers	0-3		5541					11	6		7	4				5		8	9	10		1	2			3	
9	Oct	6	STOCKPORT COUNTY	1-1	J Mordue	5305		2				6		11	4						8	9	10	7	1	3			5	
10		13	Halifax Town	0-2		3747		2				6		11	4						8	9	10	7	1	3			5	
11		20	SOUTH SHIELDS	0-5		5130	7	2				6		11	4							9	10		1	3			5	8
12		27	Ashington	1-3	T Mordue	1419	7	2				6		11					4	5		9	10		1	3				8
13	Nov	3	DONCASTER ROVERS	2-2	Dobell, T Mordue	3175	7					6		11					4	5		10		9	1	2			3	8
14		10	Barrow	1-2	T Mordue	3988	7	2				4		11						5		10	8	9	1	3			6	
15		17	CHESTERFIELD	0-2		2264	7	2				6		11	4						9	10	8		1	3			5	
16	Dec	1	NEW BRIGHTON	5-2	Briggs, Mackey, T Mordue 2, Dixon	1843	7	2			11							4	6	5	8	10		9	1				3	
17		8	Rochdale	4-7	Mason, Briggs 2, Richardson	3017	7	2			11				4		1			5	8	10	6	9					3	
18		15	SOUTHPORT	4-2	Hall, Richardson 2, T Mordue	1677	7	2			11				4		1			5	8	10	6	9					3	
19		22	Darlington	1-4	Dixon	3080	7	2			11	6			4		1			5	8	10		9					3	
20		25	LINCOLN CITY	3-2	Hall, Richardson, T Mordue	3699	7	2			11	6	3		4		1			5	8	10		9						
21		26	Lincoln City	1-7	Richardson	9668	7	2			11	6	3		4		1			5	8	10		9						
22		29	Nelson	0-1		3507	7	2			11		3		4					5	8	10	6	9	1					
23	Jan	1	BRADFORD CITY	1-3	Richardson	4364	7	2			11	6	3		4					5	8	10		9	1					
24		5	CARLISLE UNITED	1-0	Richardson	3000	7	2				6	3	11							8	10	4	9	1				5	
25		12	Wrexham	1-3	Richardson	5043	7	2				6	3	11							8	10	4	9	1				5	
26		19	Rotherham United	2-3	J Mordue 2	4339	7	2				6	3	11							8	10	4	9	1				5	
27		26	WIGAN BOROUGH	1-3	Hodgson	2848	7	2				6	3	11				9			8	10	4		1				5	
28	Feb	2	Crewe Alexandra	2-4	T Mordue, Richardson	3159		2			11	6					1		5		8	10	4	9				7	3	
29		9	TRANMERE ROVERS	4-1	Dixon 2, Richardson 2	2346		2			11	6					1		5		8	10	4	9				7	3	
30		16	Stockport County	0-3		7468		2			11	6	3				1				8	10	4	9				7	5	
31		23	HALIFAX TOWN	3-1	Richardson 2 (1p), Williams	2867	7	2			11	6	3				1				8	10	4	9					5	
32	Mar	2	South Shields	1-1	Richardson	3728		2			11	6	3	7	4		1		5		8	10		9						
33		9	ASHINGTON	1-3	Richardson (p)	3398		2			11	6	3				1		5		8	10	4	9				7		
34		16	Doncaster Rovers	1-4	T Mordue	5111		2			11	6	3				1		5			10	4	9				7		8
35		23	BARROW	1-0	Young	2314					11	6	3		2		1		5		10	9	4					7		8
36		30	Chesterfield	1-4	Spry	3394		2			11	6	3				1	9	5			10	4					7		8
37	Apr	1	ACCRINGTON STANLEY	1-3	Richardson	2331		2			11	6			3		1		5		8	10	4	9				7		
38		2	Bradford City	1-4	Dixon	24630		2			11	6				3	1		5		8	10	4	9				7		
39		6	WREXHAM	0-2		2492						6	3	11		2	1		5		8	10	4	9				7		
40		13	New Brighton	3-1	Richardson 2, J Mordue	2802		2			11	6	3				1		5		8	10	4	9				7		
41		20	ROCHDALE	0-2		1835		2			11	6	3				1		5		8	10	4	9				7		
42		27	Southport	2-6	Richardson, J Mordue	2056		2			11	6	3				1		5		8	10	4	9				7		
						Apps	18	38	2	2	24	37	22	21	20	2	20	4	19	13	35	40	35	29	18	10	4	15	26	8
						Goals	3				5	1			2			1	1	1	9	12		19				2	1	2

F.A. Cup

							Briggs H	Carr T	Christon L	Coates WA	Dixon RH	Dobell D	Errington A	Fell JW	Hall B	Harland T	Hickman J	Hodgson W	Mackey TS	Mason R	Mordue J	Mordue T	Mordue WM	Richardson W	Rivers JE	Robertson T	Smith G (1)	Spry WH	Williams JT	Young J
R1	Nov	24	Spennymoor United	2-5	T Mordue, Donkin (og)	1836	7	2						11				4	6	5	8	9	10		1				3	

		P	W	D	L	F	A	W	D	L	F	A	Pts
1	Bradford City	42	17	2	2	82	18	10	7	4	46	25	63
2	Stockport County	42	19	2	0	77	23	9	4	8	34	35	62
3	Wrexham	42	17	2	2	59	25	4	8	9	32	44	52
4	Wigan Borough	42	16	4	1	55	16	5	5	11	27	33	51
5	Doncaster Rovers	42	14	3	4	39	20	6	7	8	37	46	50
6	Lincoln City	42	15	3	3	58	18	6	3	12	33	49	48
7	Tranmere Rovers	42	15	3	3	55	21	7	0	14	24	56	47
8	Carlisle United	42	15	3	3	61	27	4	5	12	25	50	46
9	Crewe Alexandra	42	11	6	4	47	23	7	2	12	33	45	44
10	South Shields	42	13	5	3	57	24	5	3	13	26	50	44
11	Chesterfield	42	13	2	6	46	28	5	3	13	25	49	41
12	Southport	42	13	5	3	52	27	3	3	15	23	58	40
13	Halifax Town	42	11	7	3	42	24	2	6	13	21	38	39
14	New Brighton	42	11	3	7	40	28	4	6	11	24	43	39
15	Nelson	42	14	1	6	48	28	3	4	14	29	62	39
16	Rotherham United	42	12	5	4	44	23	3	4	14	16	54	39
17	Rochdale	42	12	4	5	55	34	1	6	14	24	62	36
18	Accrington Stanley	42	11	5	5	42	22	2	3	16	26	60	34
19	Darlington	42	12	6	3	47	26	1	1	19	17	62	33
20	Barrow	42	7	6	8	42	37	3	2	16	22	56	28
21	HARTLEPOOLS UTD.	42	9	4	8	35	38	1	2	18	24	74	26
22	Ashington	42	6	5	10	31	52	2	2	17	14	63	23

1929/30 8th in Division 3 (North)

	Date	Opponent	Score	Scorers	Att	Barson F	Bell ED	Bowron S	Buller J	Dixon RH	Dobell D	Errington A	Harland T	Harrison W	Mackey TS	Mason A	Millar JM	Mordue J	Mordue T	Mordue WM	Nobbs H	Pape AA	Pedwell R	Race W	Rivers JE	Stephenson JR	Thompson JE	Thornton P	Tither J
1	Aug 31	DARLINGTON	2-5	Pape 2	8500	5		3			6					2	11	10		4		9		7	1	8			
2	Sep 2	ACCRINGTON STANLEY	2-2	Pape 2	4953	5		3		11	6					2	7	10		4		9			1	8			
3	7	Southport	1-1	Pape	4107	5		2		11	6	3					7		10	4		9			1	8			
4	9	Accrington Stanley	0-3		4966	5		2		11	6	3					7		10	4		9			1	8			
5	14	Doncaster Rovers	0-0		5194					11	6	3	2		5		7		10	4		9			1	8			
6	21	CHESTERFIELD	0-0		4925				4	11	6	3	2		5				10	7		9			1	8			
7	28	Lincoln City	2-2	T Mordue 2	5792			2		11	6	3			5				10	4		9		7	1	8			
8	Oct 5	TRANMERE ROVERS	2-0	Pape 2	5012			2	4	11		3			5		7		10	6		9			1	8			
9	12	Halifax Town	0-0		4138			2	7		6	3			5		11		10	4		9			1	8			
10	19	NELSON	1-2	Barson	5695	5		2	7	11		3			6				10	4		9			1	8			
11	26	Carlisle United	2-5	W Mordue, Pape	6228			2		11	6	3			5				10	4		9		7	1	8			
12	Nov 2	WIGAN BOROUGH	4-0	Pape, T Mordue, J Mordue, Millar	4725		6	2		11	4	3			5		7	8	10			9			1				
13	9	Wrexham	5-3	Pape, J Mordue, Dixon, Millar 2	3621		6	2		11		3			5		7	8	10	4		9			1				
14	16	BARROW	2-0	Pape 2	4253		6	2							5	3	7	8	10	4		9	11		1				
15	23	Port Vale	1-2	Pape	7166		6	2				3			5		7	8	10	4		9	11		1				
16	Dec 21	Crewe Alexandra	2-5	J Mordue, Jones (og)	3898			5	6			3	2				7	8	10	4		9	11		1				
17	25	SOUTH SHIELDS	2-1	Pedwell, T Mordue	3175			2	4			3					7	8	10	6	5	9	11		1				
18	26	South Shields	5-3	Pape 2, Pedwell, J Mordue, Millar	4118			2	4			3					7	8	10	6	5	9	11		1				
19	28	Darlington	0-0		4197			2	4			3					7	8	10	6	5	9	11		1				
20	Jan 1	ROTHERHAM UNITED	5-1	Thompson (p), Pedwell 2, T Mordue, Millar	4756			2	4							3	7	8	10	6	5		11		1		9		
21	4	SOUTHPORT	1-1	Thompson	5405			2	4			3					7	8	10	6	5		11		1		9		
22	11	NEW BRIGHTON	1-1	Pape	3472			2	4							3	7	8	10	6	5	9	11		1				
23	18	DONCASTER ROVERS	3-0	Race 2, W Mordue	5555			2	4		9					3			10	8			11	7	1			5	6
24	25	Chesterfield	0-2		5888			3	5					8		2			10	6		9	11	7	1			4	
25	Feb 1	LINCOLN CITY	4-0	Pape 2, T Mordue, Harrison	1716			3	4					8		2			10	6		9	11	7	1			5	
26	8	Tranmere Rovers	1-7	Harrison	3500			3	4					8		2			10	6		9	11	7	1			5	
27	15	HALIFAX TOWN	3-0	Pedwell 2, Thompson	3022			3	4							2			10	6		9	11	7	1		8	5	
28	22	Nelson	2-3	T Mordue, Pedwell	2862			3	4				2						10	6		9	11	7	1		8	5	
29	Mar 1	CARLISLE UNITED	1-0	Thompson	4816			3	4				2						10	6		9	11	7	1		8	5	
30	3	Stockport County	1-5	Pedwell	4674			3	4				2						10	6		9	11	7	1		8	5	
31	8	Wigan Borough	3-1	Thompson 3	2709			2	6	10		3									5	9	11	7	1		8	4	
32	15	WREXHAM	5-0	Pedwell 2, Dixon, Pape 2	3200			2	6	10		3						7			5	9	11		1		8	4	
33	22	Barrow	0-3		4312			2	6	10		3						7			5	9	11		1		8	4	
34	29	PORT VALE	2-0	Pedwell, Thompson	7473	5		2	6			3						7	10			9	11		1		8	4	
35	Apr 2	YORK CITY	3-1	Pape, Barson, Thompson	4390	5		2	6			3						7	10			9	11		1		8	4	
36	5	New Brighton	0-0		4415			2	6	11		3		4				7	10		5	9			1		8		
37	12	STOCKPORT COUNTY	0-1		8239	5		2	6			3						7	10			9	11		1		8	4	
38	18	Rochdale	1-1	Pedwell	2441			2	6			3						7	10		5	9	11		1		8	4	
39	19	York City	1-4	J Mordue	2563			2	6	11		3						7	10		5	9			1		8	4	
40	21	ROCHDALE	2-8	Pedwell 2	3655	5		2	6			3						7	10			9	11		1		8	4	
41	26	CREWE ALEXANDRA	5-1	T Mordue 2, J Mordue 2, Pedwell	1944			2	6			3						8	10		5		11	7	1		9	4	
42	May 3	Rotherham United	4-0	Pedwell 2, Thompson, J Mordue	3477			2	6			3						8	10		5		11	7	1		9	4	
					Apps	9	4	40	31	16	11	29	6	4	11	10	18	24	37	29	14	37	27	14	42	11	18	19	1
					Goals	2				2				2			5	8	9	2		21	17	2			10		

One own goal

F.A. Cup

	Date	Opponent	Score	Scorers	Att	Barson F	Bell ED	Bowron S	Buller J	Dixon RH	Dobell D	Errington A	Harland T	Harrison W	Mackey TS	Mason A	Millar JM	Mordue J	Mordue T	Mordue WM	Nobbs H	Pape AA	Pedwell R	Race W	Rivers JE	Stephenson JR	Thompson JE	Thornton P	Tither J
R1	Nov 30	Scunthorpe United	0-1		5305		6	2				3			5		7	8	10	4		9	11		1				

		P	W	D	L	F	A	W	D	L	F	A	Pts
1	Port Vale	42	17	2	2	64	18	13	5	3	39	19	67
2	Stockport County	42	15	3	3	67	20	13	4	4	39	24	63
3	Darlington	42	14	2	5	71	29	8	4	9	37	44	50
4	Chesterfield	42	18	1	2	53	15	4	5	12	23	41	50
5	Lincoln City	42	12	8	1	54	23	5	6	10	29	38	48
6	York City	42	11	7	3	43	20	4	9	8	34	44	46
7	South Shields	42	11	6	4	49	32	7	4	10	28	42	46
8	HARTLEPOOLS UTD.	42	13	4	4	50	24	4	7	10	31	50	45
9	Southport	42	11	5	5	49	31	4	8	9	32	43	43
10	Rochdale	42	14	3	4	57	30	4	4	13	32	61	43
11	Crewe Alexandra	42	12	5	4	55	28	5	3	13	27	43	42
12	Tranmere Rovers	42	12	4	5	57	35	4	5	12	26	51	41
13	New Brighton	42	13	4	4	48	22	3	4	14	21	57	40
14	Doncaster Rovers	42	13	5	3	39	22	2	4	15	23	47	39
15	Carlisle United	42	13	4	4	63	34	3	3	15	27	67	39
16	Accrington Stanley	42	11	4	6	55	30	3	5	13	29	51	37
17	Wrexham	42	10	5	6	42	28	3	3	15	25	60	34
18	Wigan Borough	42	12	4	5	44	26	1	3	17	16	62	33
19	Nelson	42	9	4	8	31	25	4	3	14	20	55	33
20	Rotherham United	42	9	4	8	46	40	2	4	15	21	73	30
21	Halifax Town	42	7	7	7	27	26	3	1	17	17	53	28
22	Barrow	42	9	4	8	31	28	2	1	18	10	70	27

1930/31

20th in Division 3 (North)

	Date	Opponent	Score	Scorers	Att	Bowron S	Buller J	Cowan WD	Dickenson J	Dixon RH	Errington A	Ferguson GC	Harland T	Harrison W	Hewitt JJ	Mason A	Mordue J	Mordue T	Nobbs H	Pedwell R	Race W	Rivers JE	Robinson H	Robson PT	Simmons HR	Swift A	Thayne W	Thompson JE	Thornton P	Tither J	Waller H	Wilson J
1	Aug 30	Halifax Town	1-3	Thornton	8051	3	6								9	2		10	5	11	7	1						8	4			
2	Sep 1	SOUTHPORT	0-2		4123	3	6								9	2		10	5	11	7	1						8	4			
3	6	NEW BRIGHTON	4-1	Thompson, Thornton 2 (1p), Robson	4224	2	6		5		3			4			7			11		1		10				9	8			
4	10	Wigan Borough	2-3	Thompson 2	7852	2	6				3			8			7			11		1		10			5	9	4			
5	13	Stockport County	1-3	Thornton (p)	6372	2	6				3			8			7			11		1		10			5	9	4			
6	20	GATESHEAD	2-3	Pedwell, Cowan	2100	2	6	10			3						8			11	7	1					5	9	4			
7	27	Doncaster Rovers	1-1	J. Mordue	3927	2	6	10							9		7			11		1					5	8	4			3
8	Oct 4	HULL CITY	1-3	Cowan	6991	3	6	10		11			2		9		7					1					5	8	4			
9	11	Lincoln City	0-1		7516	3			6				2	4	9		7	10		11		1					5	8				
10	18	Accrington Stanley	2-0	J. Mordue, Thornton (p)	3344	3			6				2				7	10		11		1			8		5	9	4			
11	25	BARROW	3-2	Simmons, Pedwell 2	3892	3			6				2				7	10		11		1			8		5	9	4			
12	Nov 1	Crewe Alexandra	1-2	Simmons	2697	3			6				2				7		5	11		1			8		9	10	4			
13	8	WREXHAM	2-1	Pedwell, Thompson	4419	3			6				2				7			11		1			8		5	10	4		9	
14	15	Tranmere Rovers	4-5	Waller 2, Thayne, Pedwell	5084	3			6				2				7	10		11		1			8		5		4		9	
15	22	CARLISLE UNITED	3-5	J. Mordue, Simmons, Pedwell	2140	3			6				2				7			11		1			8		5	10	4		9	
16	Dec 6	ROTHERHAM UNITED	4-2	Waller 3, T Mordue	3020	2			6							3	7	10	5	11					8	1			4		9	
17	13	Chesterfield	0-3		4745	2	6									3	7	10	5	11		1			8				4		9	
18	20	ROCHDALE	4-0	Simmons, J. Mordue, T. Mordue, Pedwell	3083	2	6		5							3	7	10		11		1			9			8	4			
19	25	NELSON	4-0	Thompson 2, Thornton, Pedwell	4518	2	3		6								7	10	5	11		1			9			8	4			
20	26	Nelson	1-1	T. Mordue	2267	2	3		6								7	10		11		1			9		5	8	4			
21	27	HALIFAX TOWN	2-1	Thompson, Simmons	3672	2	3		6								7	10	4	11		1			9		5	8				
22	Jan 1	WIGAN BOROUGH	6-1	Simmons 5, J. Mordue	5397	2	3		6	10							7		4	11		1			9		5	8				
23	3	New Brighton	0-1		2892	2	3		6	10							7		4	11		1			9		5	8				
24	17	STOCKPORT COUNTY	1-2	Thayne	4624	2	3		6								7	10	4	11		1			9		5	8				
25	24	Gateshead	0-0		5649	2	3		6								7	10	4	11		1			9		5	8				
26	31	DONCASTER ROVERS	0-2		2835	2	3		6			8					7	10	4	11		1			9		5					
27	Feb 4	York City	2-4	J. Mordue, Simmons	1793	2	3		6								7	10	4	11		1			9		5	8				
28	14	LINCOLN CITY	0-3		3706	2	3		6					4			7	10		11		1			9		5	8				
29	21	ACCRINGTON STANLEY	3-3	T. Mordue 2, Dickinson (p)	2370	2	3		6					4			7	10	5				11		9	1		8				
30	28	Barrow	0-4		6206	2	3			11							7	10							8	1	5	9	4	6		
31	Mar 7	CREWE ALEXANDRA	2-0	Simmons 2	853	2	3			11							7	10				1			8		5	9	4	6		
32	14	Wrexham	0-2		4139	2					3						7	10	4	11		1			8		5	9	6			
33	21	TRANMERE ROVERS	1-2	Thompson	2948		2				3							10	4	11	7	1			8		5	9	6			
34	28	Carlisle United	0-3		3303		2				3							10	4	11	7	1			8		5	9	6			
35	Apr 3	DARLINGTON	1-1	Simmons	2528	2	4				3							10		11		1	7		8		5	9	6			
36	4	YORK CITY	3-0	Pedwell, Simmons, Robinson	3329	2	4		6		3				9				5	11		1	7		10			8				
37	6	Darlington	2-4	Pedwell, Simmons	4478	2	4		6		3				9				5	11		1	7		10			8				
38	11	Rotherham United	1-1	Pedwell	4182		2				3				9		8		4	11		1	7		10		5		6			
39	18	CHESTERFIELD	1-3	Thayne (p)	1434	2	6			10	3				9		7		4	11		1					5	8				
40	20	Hull City	0-5		3221		2			10	3				9				4	11		1	7				5	8	6			
41	25	Rochdale	2-1	Simmons, Thompson	1586		6			11	3					2	7		5			1			10			8	4		9	
42	May 2	Southport	0-2		1986		6			11	3					2	7		5			1			10			8	4		9	
					Apps	36	33	3	23	9	15	1	8	6	10	7	34	24	24	36	5	39	6	3	31	3	30	37	29	2	7	1
					Goals			2	1								6	5		11			1	1	17		3	9	6		5	

F.A. Cup

	Date	Opponent	Score	Scorers	Att	Bowron S	Buller J	Cowan WD	Dickenson J	Dixon RH	Errington A	Ferguson GC	Harland T	Harrison W	Hewitt JJ	Mason A	Mordue J	Mordue T	Nobbs H	Pedwell R	Race W	Rivers JE	Robinson H	Robson PT	Simmons HR	Swift A	Thayne W	Thompson JE	Thornton P	Tither J	Waller H	Wilson J
R1	Nov 29	STOCKPORT COUNTY	2-3	Dickenson, Waller	6038	2			6							3	7	10		11		1			8		5		4		9	

		P	W	D	L	F	A	W	D	L	F	A	Pts
1	Chesterfield	42	19	1	1	66	22	7	5	9	36	35	58
2	Lincoln City	42	16	3	2	60	19	9	4	8	42	40	57
3	Wrexham	42	16	4	1	61	25	5	8	8	33	37	54
4	Tranmere Rovers	42	16	3	2	73	26	8	3	10	38	48	54
5	Southport	42	15	3	3	52	19	7	6	8	36	37	53
6	Hull City	42	12	7	2	64	20	8	3	10	35	35	50
7	Stockport County	42	15	5	1	54	19	5	4	12	23	42	49
8	Carlisle United	42	13	4	4	68	32	7	1	13	30	49	45
9	Gateshead	42	14	4	3	46	22	2	9	10	25	51	45
10	Wigan Borough	42	14	4	3	48	25	5	1	15	28	61	43
11	Darlington	42	9	6	6	44	30	7	4	10	27	29	42
12	York City	42	15	3	3	59	30	3	3	15	26	52	42
13	Accrington Stanley	42	14	2	5	51	31	1	7	13	33	77	39
14	Rotherham United	42	9	6	6	50	34	4	6	11	31	49	38
15	Doncaster Rovers	42	9	8	4	40	18	4	3	14	25	47	37
16	Barrow	42	13	4	4	45	23	2	3	16	23	66	37
17	Halifax Town	42	11	6	4	30	16	2	3	16	25	73	35
18	Crewe Alexandra	42	13	2	6	52	35	1	4	16	14	58	34
19	New Brighton	42	12	4	5	36	25	1	3	17	13	51	33
20	HARTLEPOOLS UTD.	42	10	2	9	47	37	2	4	15	20	49	30
21	Rochdale	42	9	1	11	42	50	3	5	13	20	57	30
22	Nelson	42	6	7	8	28	40	0	0	21	15	73	19

1931/32 13th in Division 3 (North)

						Allen W	Bowron S	Brown W	Buller J	Carr J	Dixon RH	Hamilton J	Hardy LR	Harland T	Hewitt JJ	Jarps J	Lumley S	Mason A	Mordue J	Nobbs H	Owbridge CR	Pedwell R	Rivers JE	Robinson A	Shotton R	Thayne W	Thompson JE	Thornton P	Tither J	Waller H	Wigham J
1	Aug 29	CARLISLE UNITED	2-2	Lumley 2	5295	3	2		6	8	10	5					9		7			11	1					4			
2	31	Lincoln City	0-6		6539		2		6		10	5					9		7			11	1	8	3			4			
3	Sep 9	CHESTER	2-2	Mordue, Thompson	4717		2				11	4					9		7				1		3	5	8	6			10
4	12	DARLINGTON	3-3	Hamilton, Mordue, Lumley	5048		2				11	4					9		7	5			1		3		8	6			10
5	16	Chester	3-2	Lumley 3	8417		2				11	4			8		9		7	5			1		3		10	6			
6	19	Halifax Town	0-2		4396		2		6		11	5			8		9		7				1		3		10	4			
7	23	SOUTHPORT	2-1	Thompson, Mordue	3719		2	10			11	4					9		7	5			1		3		8	6			
8	26	WALSALL	4-3	Carr, Mordue, Thompson, Lumley	4873		2			10	11	4					9		7	5			1		3		8	6			
9	Oct 3	Gateshead	1-3	Dixon	10223		2		4	10	11						9		7	5			1		3		8	6			
10	10	NEW BRIGHTON	1-0	Dixon	5094		2	8	4	10	11							3	7	5			1				9	6			
11	17	WREXHAM	0-1		4600		2			10	11	4			9				7	5			1		3		8	6			
12	24	Accrington Stanley	0-5		2978		2		4	8	11						9		7	5			1		3		10	6			
13	31	STOCKPORT COUNTY	2-2	Buller, Waller	3502		2		7	8	11	6								4			1		3	5				9	10
14	Nov 7	Rotherham United	2-1	Waller, Thornton	3294		2		7	8	11									4			1		3	5		6		9	10
15	14	TRANMERE ROVERS	0-5		3653		2		7	8	11									4			1		3	5		6		9	10
16	21	York City	1-3	Dixon	4113				6	8	11			2	9				7	5			1		3		10	4			
17	Dec 5	Doncaster Rovers	3-1	Mordue, Lumley, Buller	3265		2		4		11				8		9		7	5	1				3			6			10
18	12	ROCHDALE	3-0	Hewitt 2, Dixon	3085		2		4		11				8		9		7	5	1				3			6			10
19	19	Crewe Alexandra	0-6		3815		2		4		11				8		9		7	5	1				3			6			10
20	25	Hull City	1-3	Lumley	13060		2		4		11				8	1	9		7	5					3			6			10
21	26	HULL CITY	2-3	Thornton (p), Lumley	5897		2		4		11				8	1	7			5					3		9	6			10
22	Jan 2	Carlisle United	2-3	Wigham, Lumley	3867		2		4		11				8		9		7	5	1				3			6			10
23	9	CREWE ALEXANDRA	3-1	Wigham 2, Pedwell	2807		2	10			7	5					9			4		11	1		3				6		8
24	23	Darlington	3-6	Lumley, Wigham, Brown (p)	2812		2	10			7	5					9			4		11	1		3				6		8
25	30	HALIFAX TOWN	4-1	Lumley 3, Wigham	2961		2	10				5					9		7	4		11	1		3			6			8
26	Feb 6	Walsall	3-2	Wigham 2, Lumley	2570		2	10			7	5					9			4		11	1		3				6		8
27	13	GATESHEAD	1-2	Wigham	3382		2	10			7	5					9			4		11	1		3				6		8
28	20	New Brighton	1-1	Lumley	2524		2	10			7	5					9		8	4		11	1		3				6		
29	27	Wrexham	3-5	Brown, Lumley, Pedwell	3288		2	10			7	5					9		8	4		11	1		3				6		
30	Mar 5	ACCRINGTON STANLEY	1-0	Hewitt	3051		2	10			7	5			9				8	4		11	1		3				6		
31	12	Stockport County	2-3	Pedwell, Nobbs	4400		2	10			7	5			9				8	4		11	1		3				6		
32	19	ROTHERHAM UNITED	1-4	Brown (p)	2967			10	3		7	5			9				8			11	1		2			4	6		
33	25	BARROW	0-2		4713		2	10				5	8						7	4		11	1		3			6			9
34	26	Tranmere Rovers	0-5		4538		2		4				8				9		7	5		11	1		3			6			10
35	28	Barrow	1-4	Wigham	5632		2		4				8				9		7	5		11	1		3			6			10
36	Apr 2	YORK CITY	7-2	Hewitt 3, Dixon 3, Wigham	2590		3		4		7	5	8	2	9						1	11						6			10
37	9	Southport	2-1	Wigham 2	2414		3		4		7	5	8	2	9						1	11						6			10
38	16	DONCASTER ROVERS	5-0	Hewitt, Pedwell 2, Wigham, Tither(p)	3520		3		4		7	5	8	2	9						1	11							6		10
39	23	Rochdale	3-1	Thornton, Dixon 2	1379		3				7	5	8	2	9						1	11				6		4			10
40	May 7	LINCOLN CITY	4-3	Hewitt 3, Hardy	3723		3				7	5	8	2	9						1	11				6		4			10
					Apps	1	38	13	22	10	36	26	8	6	18	2	25	1	27	30	9	20	29	1	33	6	12	30	10	3	24
					Goals			3	2	1	9	1	1		10		18		5	1		5					3	3	1	2	13

F.A. Cup

						Allen W	Bowron S	Brown W	Buller J	Carr J	Dixon RH	Hamilton J	Hardy LR	Harland T	Hewitt JJ	Jarps J	Lumley S	Mason A	Mordue J	Nobbs H	Owbridge CR	Pedwell R	Rivers JE	Robinson A	Shotton R	Thayne W	Thompson JE	Thornton P	Tither J	Waller H	Wigham J
R1	Nov 28	Chester	1-4	Wigham	9000		2				11	4			8		9		7	5			1		3			6			10

		P	W	D	L	F	A	W	D	L	F	A	Pts
1	Lincoln City	40	16	2	2	65	13	10	3	7	41	34	57
2	Gateshead	40	15	3	2	59	20	10	4	6	35	28	57
3	Chester	40	16	2	2	54	22	5	6	9	24	38	50
4	Tranmere Rovers	40	15	4	1	76	23	4	7	9	31	35	49
5	Barrow	40	16	1	3	59	23	8	0	12	27	36	49
6	Crewe Alexandra	40	15	3	2	64	24	6	3	11	31	42	48
7	Southport	40	14	5	1	44	15	4	5	11	14	38	46
8	Hull City	40	14	1	5	52	21	6	4	10	30	32	45
9	York City	40	14	3	3	49	24	4	4	12	27	57	43
10	Wrexham	40	14	2	4	42	25	4	5	11	22	44	43
11	Darlington	40	12	1	7	41	27	5	3	12	25	42	38
12	Stockport County	40	12	3	5	31	15	1	8	11	24	38	37
13	HARTLEPOOLS UTD.	40	10	4	6	47	37	6	1	13	31	63	37
14	Accrington Stanley	40	14	4	2	56	20	1	2	17	19	60	36
15	Doncaster Rovers	40	12	3	5	38	27	4	1	15	21	53	36
16	Walsall	40	12	3	5	42	30	4	0	16	15	55	35
17	Halifax Town	40	11	6	3	36	18	2	2	16	25	69	34
18	Carlisle United	40	9	7	4	40	23	2	4	14	24	56	33
19	Rotherham United	40	10	3	7	41	23	4	1	15	22	49	32
20	New Brighton	40	8	5	7	25	23	0	3	17	13	53	24
21	Rochdale	40	4	2	14	33	63	0	1	19	15	72	11

1932/33 14th in Division 3 (North)

							Bowron S	Burluraux F	Dixon RH	Hamilton J	Hardy LR	Harland T	Hewitt JJ	Hill R	Makepeace R	O'Donnell J	Owbridge CR	Pedwell R	Proctor MH	Ridley J	Rivers JE	Thayne W	Thornton P	Tither J	Tremain S	Wigham J	Wilks F
1	Aug	27	Tranmere Rovers	3-3	Hewitt, Proctor 2	5392	3		7	5		2	9				1	11	8			6	4			10	
2		31	Halifax Town	0-4		5663	3		7	5	10	2	9				1	11	8			6	4				
3	Sep	3	WREXHAM	3-1	Dixon, Hewitt 2	4757	3		7	5	8	2	9		6		1	11					4			10	
4		7	HALIFAX TOWN	1-1	Dixon	4587	3		7	5	8	2	9		6		1	11				4				10	
5		10	Walsall	1-4	Hardy	6191	3		7	5	8	2	9		6		1	11				4				10	
6		17	GATESHEAD	2-2	Dixon, Hewitt (p)	5735	3		11	5		2	9		6		1		8	7		4				10	
7		24	Stockport County	2-6	Proctor, Hewitt	6725	3		11	5		2	9		6				8	7	1	4				10	
8	Oct	1	DARLINGTON	2-1	Makepeace, Wigham	3894	3		11	5		2	9		6		1		8	7		4				10	
9		8	Doncaster Rovers	1-4	Ridley	3237	3		11			2	9		6		1		8	7		5	4			10	
10		15	HULL CITY	0-1		4553	3		11	5		2	9		6		1		10	7		4				8	
11		22	Accrington Stanley	1-7	Dixon	2927	2		11	5			9		6	3	1		8	7		4				10	
12		29	NEW BRIGHTON	3-2	Makepeace, Wigham, Hewitt	1916	2		11		8		9		5	3				7		4	6			10	1
13	Nov	5	Chester	3-3	Pedwell, Wigham 2	6947	2				8		9		5	3		11		7		4	6			10	1
14		12	BARROW	0-1		3603	2		7		8		9		5	3		11				4	6			10	1
15		19	Carlisle United	1-3	Pedwell	4594	2		7		8					3		11	9			5	4	6		10	1
16	Dec	3	Crewe Alexandra	2-6	Hewitt, Thornton	4641	2		7	5	8		9			3		11				4	6			10	1
17		17	Southport	3-6	Pedwell 2, Dixon	2439	2		7	5	8		9			3		11				4	10	6			1
18		24	MANSFIELD TOWN	6-3	Hewitt 2, Dixon 2, Pedwell, Wigham	3872	2		7	5	8		9			3		11				4	6			10	1
19		26	Barnsley	2-3	Hewitt, Hamilton	9138	2		7	5		3	9					11	8			4	6			10	1
20		27	BARNSLEY	6-4	Hewitt 3, Dixon, Hardy, Wigham	4996	2		7	5	8		9			3		11				4	6			10	1
21		31	TRANMERE ROVERS	2-3	Pedwell 2	3954	2		7	5	8		9			3		11				4	6			10	1
22	Jan	2	ROCHDALE	3-0	Hewitt, Pedwell, Wigham	3359	2		7	5	8	3	9					11				4	6			10	1
23		7	Wrexham	1-8	Wigham	4809	3		7	5	8	2	9					11				4	6			10	1
24		14	YORK CITY	4-2	Pedwell 2, Proctor, Wigham	3105	2		7				9	5	6	3		11	8				4			10	1
25		21	WALSALL	2-0	Proctor, Wigham	4693	2						9	5	6	3		11	8			4	7			10	1
26		28	Gateshead	1-3	Proctor	4171	2				10		9	5	6	3		11	8			4	7				1
27	Feb	4	STOCKPORT COUNTY	1-1	Thayne (p)	4027	2		7		8		9	5	6	3		11				4			1	10	
28		11	Darlington	2-1	Dixon 2	3160	2		7		8		9	5	6	3		11				4			1	10	
29		18	DONCASTER ROVERS	4-0	Dixon, Pedwell, Hewitt, Wigham	1341	2		7		8		9	5	6	3		11				4			1	10	
30		25	Hull City	0-3		5323	2		7		8		9	5	6	3		11				4			1	10	
31	Mar	4	ACCRINGTON STANLEY	3-1	Pedwell, Hewitt (p), Wigham	3410	2				8		9	5	6	3		11	7			4			1	10	
32		11	New Brighton	2-5	Hardy, Proctor	3055	2				8		9	5	6	3		11	7			4			1	10	
33		18	CHESTER	3-1	Hewitt 2, Hardy	5293	2				7		10	5	6	3		11	8			4			1	9	
34		25	Barrow	1-3	O'Donnell (p)	3358	2				7		9	5	6	3		11	8			4			1	10	
35	Apr	1	CARLISLE UNITED	2-1	Wigham, Proctor	3232	2				7		9	5	6	3		11	8			4			1	10	
36		8	York City	1-1	Hewitt	3720	2				7		9	5	6	3		11	8			4			1	10	
37		14	ROTHERHAM UNITED	2-0	Wigham, Pedwell	3682	2		7		8		9	5	6	3		11				4			1	10	
38		15	CREWE ALEXANDRA	3-2	Hardy, Pedwell, O'Donnell (p)	3391	2			4	7		9	5		3		11	8			6			1	10	
39		17	Rotherham United	1-1	Thayne	2659	2		7		6		9	5		3		11	8			4			1	10	
40		22	Rochdale	2-6	Hewitt, Hardy	3249	2			6	7		9	5		3		11	8			4			1	10	
41		29	SOUTHPORT	4-2	Wigham, Pedwell, Hewitt 2	1135	2			6	7		9	5		3		11	8			4			1	10	
42	May	6	Mansfield Town	1-7	Hewitt	2381	3	2		6	7		9	5				11	8			4			1	10	

Apps	42	1	29	22	32	13	41	19	26	28	10	35	24	8	1	40	19	2	16	39	15
Goals			11	1	6		23		2	2		15	8	1		2	1			15	

F.A. Cup

R1	Nov	26	Marine	5-2	Wigham 2, Thornton, Hewitt, Dixon	2347	2		7	5	8		9			3		11				4	6			10	1
R2	Dec	10	Walsall	1-2	Thornton	8841	2		7	5	8		9			3		11				4	6			10	1

		P	W	D	L	F	A	W	D	L	F	A	Pts
1	Hull City	42	18	3	0	69	14	8	4	9	31	31	59
2	Wrexham	42	18	2	1	75	15	6	7	8	31	36	57
3	Stockport County	42	16	2	3	69	30	5	10	6	30	28	54
4	Chester	42	15	4	2	57	25	7	4	10	37	41	52
5	Walsall	42	16	4	1	53	15	3	6	12	22	43	48
6	Doncaster Rovers	42	13	8	0	52	26	4	6	11	25	53	48
7	Gateshead	42	12	5	4	45	25	7	4	10	33	42	47
8	Barnsley	42	14	3	4	60	31	5	5	11	32	49	46
9	Barrow	42	12	3	6	41	24	6	4	11	19	36	43
10	Crewe Alexandra	42	16	3	2	57	16	4	0	17	23	68	43
11	Tranmere Rovers	42	11	4	6	49	31	6	4	11	21	35	42
12	Southport	42	15	3	3	54	20	2	4	15	16	47	41
13	Accrington Stanley	42	12	4	5	55	29	3	6	12	23	47	40
14	HARTLEPOOLS UTD.	42	15	3	3	56	29	1	4	16	31	87	39
15	Halifax Town	42	12	4	5	39	23	3	4	14	32	67	38
16	Mansfield Town	42	13	4	4	57	22	1	3	17	27	78	35
17	Rotherham United	42	14	3	4	42	21	0	3	18	18	63	34
18	Rochdale	42	9	4	8	32	33	4	3	14	26	47	33
19	Carlisle United	42	8	7	6	34	25	5	0	16	17	50	33
20	York City	42	10	4	7	51	38	3	2	16	21	54	32
21	New Brighton	42	8	6	7	42	36	3	4	14	21	52	32
22	Darlington	42	9	6	6	42	32	1	2	18	24	77	28

1933/34

11th in Division 3 (North)

							Bowron S	Brown GA	Catton E	Fairhurst WS	Finnigan J	Hardy LR	Harland T	Hewitt JJ	Hill R	Hird T	Johnson JJ	Johnson MH	Knox T	Makepeace R	Odhams JR	Pedwell R	Proctor MH	Reilly WJ	Strong GJ	Thayne W	Welsh W	Wigham J
1	Aug	26	Mansfield Town	1-1	Pedwell	7101	2			3		8		9	5	7			1			11		6		4		10
2		30	ROCHDALE	2-1	Wigham, Hardy	4580	2			3		8		9	5	7			1			11		6		4		10
3	Sep	2	YORK CITY	2-0	Thayne, Wigham	5310	2			3		8		9	5	7			1			11		6		4		10
4		5	Rochdale	0-3		4766	2			3		8		10	5	7		9	1			11		6		4		
5		9	WREXHAM	4-1	Hardy, Hewitt, Pedwell 2	4951	2			3		8		9	5	7			1			11		6		4		10
6		16	Southport	2-0	Wigham, Hewitt	2946	2			3		8		9	5	7			1			11	6			4		10
7		23	DARLINGTON	6-2	Thayne, Hewitt, Hird, Pedwell 3	5795	2			3		8		9	5	7			1			11	6			4		10
8		30	Gateshead	3-6	Hardy, Hewitt 2	4292	2			3		8		9	5	7			1			11	6			4		10
9	Oct	7	ACCRINGTON STANLEY	3-0	Hewitt 2, Hardy	4605	2			3		8		9		7			1			11	4	6		5		10
10		14	Chesterfield	1-3	Hardy	12341	2			3		8		9		7			1			11	4	6		5		10
11		21	Chester	3-3	Hewitt, Wigham 2	6368	2			3		8		9		7			1	5		11	6			4		10
12		28	DONCASTER ROVERS	2-2	Hewitt, Hardy	2701	2			3		8		9		7			1	5		11	6			4		10
13	Nov	4	Barrow	2-2	Wigham 2	4676	2			3		8		9		7		11	1	5			6			4		10
14		11	CARLISLE UNITED	3-2	Hewitt 2, Wigham	4706	2			3		8		9		7		11	1	5			6			4		10
15		18	Stockport County	2-5	Hewitt 2	7437	2			3		8		9		7		11	1	5			6			4		10
16	Dec	2	Crewe Alexandra	0-1		3247	2	6		3		8		9		7			1	5		11	10			4		
17		16	Rotherham United	2-4	Hird, Wigham	3148	2			3				8	4	7		9	1	5		11	6					10
18		23	WALSALL	0-1		3556	2		8	3				9	4	7			1	5		11	6					10
19		25	BARNSLEY	0-2		5461	2	4		3		8		9		7			1	5		11	6					10
20		26	Barnsley	4-5	Pedwell, Hewitt (p), Catton, Proctor	8559	3		8			4	2	9		7			1	5		11	6					10
21		30	MANSFIELD TOWN	3-1	Hird, Wigham, Proctor	2759	2		8	3				9		7			1	5		11	6			4		10
22	Jan	1	HALIFAX TOWN	5-0	Hird 2, Hewitt (p), Pedwell, Catton	2408	2		8	3		4		9		7			1	5		11	6					10
23		6	York City	3-1	Catton, Hird, Wigham	4118	2		8	3		4		9		7			1	5		11	6					10
24		20	Wrexham	1-3	Hardy	5292	2		10	3		8		9		7			1	5		11	6			4		
25		27	SOUTHPORT	1-2	Pedwell	2592	2		8	3		10		9		7			1	5		11	6			4		
26	Feb	3	Darlington	3-5	Pedwell 2, Hird	3397	2		9	3		10		8		7	1			5		11	6			4		
27		10	GATESHEAD	3-3	Wigham 2, Hewitt	3755				3			2	9	5	7				6		11	4		1		8	10
28		14	NEW BRIGHTON	2-1	Pedwell, Bower (og)	1441	2			3	4	10		9	5	7	1					11	6				8	
29		17	Accrington Stanley	2-2	Hewitt, Corcoran (og)	1977				3	4	8	2	9	5	7	1					11	6					10
30		24	CHESTERFIELD	0-3		5739				3	4		2	9	5	7	1					11	6				8	10
31	Mar	3	CHESTER	1-0	Proctor	2900	2			3		8		9	5	7	1					11	6			4		10
32		10	Doncaster Rovers	0-3		3770	2			3		8		9	5	7	1	11					6			4		10
33		17	BARROW	7-0	Hird, Proctor 3, Hewitt, Pedwell 2	1836	2	4		3				8	5	7	1			6		11	9					10
34		24	Carlisle United	1-4	Wigham	3119		4		3				8	5	7	1			6		11	9			2		10
35		30	TRANMERE ROVERS	1-1	Thayne (p)	4147	2	4		3				8	5	7	1					11	9			6		10
36		31	STOCKPORT COUNTY	3-1	Hird, Hewitt (p), Hardy	4766	2	4		3		9		8	5	7	1					11	6					10
37	Apr	2	Tranmere Rovers	2-3	Hardy 2	3971	2	4		3		9		8	5	7					1	11	6					10
38		7	Halifax Town	2-6	Pedwell, Hird	4849	2	4		3		9		8	5	7	1					11	6					10
39		14	CREWE ALEXANDRA	2-1	Wigham, Pedwell	2332	2	4		3		9		8	5	7	1					11	6					10
40		21	New Brighton	1-4	Pedwell	2878	2	4		3		9		8	5	7	1					11	6					10
41		28	ROTHERHAM UNITED	4-0	Hardy 2, Hewitt, Pedwell	1083	2	4		3		9		8	5	7	1					11	6					10
42	May	5	Walsall	0-5		4616	2	4		3		9			5	7	1					11	8			6		10
						Apps	38	12	8	41	3	34	4	41	26	42	15	6	25	19	1	38	37	7	1	25	3	36
						Goals			3			12		20	1	9						18	6			3		15

Two own goals

F.A. Cup

							Bowron S	Brown GA	Catton E	Fairhurst WS	Finnigan J	Hardy LR	Harland T	Hewitt JJ	Hill R	Hird T	Johnson JJ	Johnson MH	Knox T	Makepeace R	Odhams JR	Pedwell R	Proctor MH	Reilly WJ	Strong GJ	Thayne W	Welsh W	Wigham J
R1	Nov	25	York City	3-2	Hewitt, Pedwell, Wigham	6734	2			3		8		9		7			1	5		11	6			4		10
R2	Dec	9	Halifax Town	1-1	Hardy	13400	2			3		8		9		7			1	5		11	6			4		10
rep		13	HALIFAX TOWN	1-2	Pedwell	9500	2			3		8		9		7			1	5		11	6			4		10

Third Division (North) Cup

							Bowron S	Brown GA	Catton E	Fairhurst WS	Finnigan J	Hardy LR	Harland T	Hewitt JJ	Hill R	Hird T	Johnson JJ	Johnson MH	Knox T	Makepeace R	Odhams JR	Pedwell R	Proctor MH	Reilly WJ	Strong GJ	Thayne W	Welsh W	Wigham J
R1	Jan	13	York City	1-2	Hird	300	2		8	3				9		7			1	5		11	6			4		10

		P	W	D	L	F	A	W	D	L	F	A	Pts
1	Barnsley	42	18	3	0	64	18	9	5	7	54	43	62
2	Chesterfield	42	18	1	2	56	17	9	6	6	30	26	61
3	Stockport County	42	18	3	0	84	23	6	8	7	31	29	59
4	Walsall	42	18	2	1	66	18	5	5	11	31	42	53
5	Doncaster Rovers	42	17	1	3	58	24	5	8	8	25	37	53
6	Wrexham	42	14	1	6	68	35	9	4	8	34	38	51
7	Tranmere Rovers	42	16	2	3	57	21	4	5	12	27	42	47
8	Barrow	42	12	5	4	78	45	7	4	10	38	49	47
9	Halifax Town	42	15	2	4	57	30	5	2	14	23	61	44
10	Chester	42	11	6	4	59	26	6	0	15	30	60	40
11	HARTLEPOOLS UTD.	42	14	3	4	54	24	2	4	15	35	69	39
12	York City	42	11	5	5	44	28	4	3	14	27	46	38
13	Carlisle United	42	11	6	4	43	23	4	2	15	23	58	38
14	Crewe Alexandra	42	12	3	6	54	38	3	3	15	27	59	36
15	New Brighton	42	13	3	5	41	25	1	5	15	21	62	36
16	Darlington	42	11	4	6	47	35	2	5	14	23	66	35
17	Mansfield Town	42	9	7	5	49	29	2	5	14	32	59	34
18	Southport	42	6	11	4	35	29	2	6	13	28	61	33
19	Gateshead	42	10	3	8	46	40	2	6	13	30	70	33
20	Accrington Stanley	42	10	6	5	44	38	3	1	17	21	63	33
21	Rotherham United	42	5	7	9	31	35	5	1	15	22	56	28
22	Rochdale	42	7	5	9	34	30	2	1	18	19	73	24

1934/35 12th in Division 3 (North)

	Date		Opponent	Score	Scorers	Att	Bonass AE	Brown GA	Clough W	Coulthard FR	Dreyer G	Fairhurst R	Fairhurst WS	Graham J	Hardy LR	Hill R	Hird T	Howe JR	Huggins A	Johnson JJ	Lindsay DM	Moses J	Murray J	Park O	Proctor JR	Warren ET	Westmoreland W	Wigham J
1	Aug	25	Walsall	2-1	Bonass, Lindsay	9389	11						3	4			7			1	9			5	2	6	8	10
2		29	CHESTER	0-2		5496	11						3	4			7			1	9			5	2	6	8	10
3	Sep	1	CREWE ALEXANDRA	4-2	Wigham, Lindsay, Hardy, Hird	4206	11							4	8		7			1	9			5	2	6	3	10
4		5	Chester	1-4	Hird	8979	11	4							8		7	3		1	9			5	2	6	10	
5		8	Stockport County	2-3	Hardy, Wigham	9586	11	4							8		7	3		1	9			5	2	6		10
6		15	GATESHEAD	1-2	Wigham	4638	11	4							8		7	3		1	9			5	2	6		10
7		22	Accrington Stanley	4-0	Lindsay 2, Bonass 2	1993	11						3		8	4	7			1	9			5	2	6		10
8		29	DARLINGTON	0-1		3751	11						3		8	4	7			1	9			5	2	6		10
9	Oct	6	York City	1-3	Hird	4387	11						3		8	4	7		10	1	9			5	2	6		
10		13	NEW BRIGHTON	2-2	Hird, Huggins	3208	11						3			4	7		10	1	9			5	2	6	8	
11		20	Chesterfield	0-4		4915				11			3			4	7		10	1	9			5	2	6	8	
12		27	MANSFIELD TOWN	1-1	Lindsay (p)	2206				11					8	4	7	3		1	9			5	2	6		10
13	Nov	3	Barrow	0-2		3979				11		5			8	4	7	3	10	1	9			2		6		
14		10	CARLISLE UNITED	5-2	Hardy, Hird 2, Huggins, Wigham	1586				11		5			8	4	7	3	9	1				2		6		10
15		17	Rochdale	2-3	Lindsay, Bonass	3782	11					5			8	4	7			1	9				2	6	3	10
16	Dec	1	Tranmere Rovers	0-3		5238	11	6					3	8	9	4	7			1				5	2			10
17		15	Halifax Town	1-4	Lindsay	8526	11	6					3		8	4	7			1	9			5	2			10
18		25	DONCASTER ROVERS	2-1	Lindsay, Hird	3616	11				4		3			6	7			1	9	8		5	2			10
19		26	Doncaster Rovers	1-3	Flowers (og)	10904	11	6					3			4	7		9	1		8		5	2			10
20		29	WALSALL	2-1	Bonass, Proctor (p)	2375	11	6					3		8	4	7	9		1				5	2			10
21	Jan	1	WREXHAM	4-3	Lindsay 2, Lewis (og), Bonass	2605	11	6					3		8	4	7			1	9			5	2			10
22		5	Crewe Alexandra	1-1	Lindsay	4100	11	6					3		8	4	7			1	9			5	2			10
23		12	LINCOLN CITY	1-5	Lindsay	2694	11	6					3		8	4	7			1	9			5	2			10
24		19	STOCKPORT COUNTY	4-0	Hird, Bonass, Proctor 2 (2p)	2626	11	6							8	4	7	3		1	9	10		5	2			
25		26	Gateshead	1-2	Hird	1899	11		6						8	4	7	3		1	9	10		5	2			
26	Feb	2	ACCRINGTON STANLEY	4-2	Moses, Lindsay, Bonass 2	2259	11	6					3			4	7			1	9	10		5	2			8
27		9	Darlington	0-3		4898	11	6					3			4	7			1	9	10		5	2			8
28		16	YORK CITY	3-1	Lindsay 2, Bonass	2014	11				4				8	6	7	3		1	9	10		5	2			
29		23	New Brighton	4-1	Hird, Milligan (og), Lindsay, Bonass	2428	11				4				10	6	7	3		1	9			5	2			8
30	Mar	2	CHESTERFIELD	1-1	Lindsay (p)	3895	11	6			4					5	7	3		1	9	10			2			8
31		6	ROTHERHAM UNITED	3-1	Lindsay, Hardy, Hind	2211	11				4				8	6	7	3		1	9	10		5	2			
32		9	Mansfield Town	1-2	Bonass	4006	11				4	3			10	6	7			1	9			5	2			8
33		16	BARROW	5-2	Hird (p), Bonass 3, Wigham	3378	11				4	3				6	7			1	9	10		5	2			8
34		23	Carlisle United	2-2	Wigham, Bonass	4091	11	5			4	3			10	6	7			1	9				2			8
35		30	ROCHDALE	0-0		2955	11	5			4	3				6	7			1	9	10			2			8
36	Apr	6	Lincoln City	1-2	Hill	2847	11	5			4	3			10	6	7			1	9				2			8
37		13	TRANMERE ROVERS	6-1	Wigham 2, Hill, Lindsay, Bonass 2	3960	11				4				10	6	7	3		1	9			5	2			8
38		19	Southport	1-1	Hird	3472	11				4				10	6	7	3			9		1	5	2			8
39		20	Wrexham	2-0	Hill, Hardy	3251	11				4				10	6	7	3			9		1	5	2			8
40		22	SOUTHPORT	4-1	Lindsay 2, Bonass 2	3315	11				4	3			10	6	7				9		1	5	2			8
41		27	HALIFAX TOWN	0-3		2404	11					3		10	4	6	7				9		1	5	2			8
42	May	4	Rotherham United	1-0	Wigham	3231	11				4	3			10	6	7		9				1	5	2			8

	Bonass AE	Brown GA	Clough W	Coulthard FR	Dreyer G	Fairhurst R	Fairhurst WS	Graham J	Hardy LR	Hill R	Hird T	Howe JR	Huggins A	Johnson JJ	Lindsay DM	Moses J	Murray J	Park O	Proctor JR	Warren ET	Westmoreland W	Wigham J
Apps	38	17	1	4	15	11	17	5	31	36	42	16	7	37	37	11	5	37	40	15	7	33
Goals	20								5	3	13		2		21	1			3			9

Three own goals

F.A. Cup

	Date		Opponent	Score	Scorers	Att	Bonass AE	Brown GA	Clough W	Coulthard FR	Dreyer G	Fairhurst R	Fairhurst WS	Graham J	Hardy LR	Hill R	Hird T	Howe JR	Huggins A	Johnson JJ	Lindsay DM	Moses J	Murray J	Park O	Proctor JR	Warren ET	Westmoreland W	Wigham J
R1	Nov	34	Halifax Town	1-1	Bonass	12439	11	6					3		8	4	7			1	9			5	2			10
rep		28	HALIFAX TOWN	2-0	Bonass, Lindsay	8787	11	6					3		8	4	7			1	9			5	2			10
R2	Dec	8	COVENTRY CITY	0-4		13054	11	6					3		8	4	7			1	9			5	2			10

Third Division (North) Cup

	Date		Opponent	Score	Scorers	Att	Bonass AE	Brown GA	Clough W	Coulthard FR	Dreyer G	Fairhurst R	Fairhurst WS	Graham J	Hardy LR	Hill R	Hird T	Howe JR	Huggins A	Johnson JJ	Lindsay DM	Moses J	Murray J	Park O	Proctor JR	Warren ET	Westmoreland W	Wigham J
R1	Jan	23	DARLINGTON	3-1	Hird, Lindsay 2	2509	11	6							8	4	7	3		1	9	10		5	2			
R2	Feb	20	YORK CITY	4-0	Wigham 2, Lindsay, Colquhoun	1700					4					6	7	3		1	9	10		5	2			8
SF	Apr	8	Stockport County	2-6	Bonass, Lindsay	1318	11	5			4	3			8	6	7		10	1	9				2			

Played at 11 on Feb. 20th: DM Colquhoun

		P	W	D	L	F	A	W	D	L	F	A	Pts
1	Doncaster Rovers	42	16	0	5	53	21	10	5	6	34	23	57
2	Halifax Town	42	17	2	2	50	24	8	3	10	26	43	55
3	Chester	42	14	4	3	62	27	6	10	5	29	31	54
4	Lincoln City	42	14	3	4	55	21	8	4	9	32	37	51
5	Darlington	42	15	5	1	50	15	6	4	11	30	44	51
6	Tranmere Rovers	42	15	4	2	53	20	5	7	9	21	35	51
7	Stockport County	42	15	2	4	57	22	7	1	13	33	50	47
8	Mansfield Town	42	16	3	2	55	25	3	6	12	20	37	47
9	Rotherham United	42	14	4	3	56	21	5	3	13	30	52	45
10	Chesterfield	42	13	4	4	46	21	4	6	11	25	31	44
11	Wrexham	42	12	5	4	47	25	4	6	11	29	44	43
12	HARTLEPOOLS UTD.	42	12	4	5	52	34	5	3	13	28	44	41
13	Crewe Alexandra	42	12	6	3	41	25	2	5	14	25	61	39
14	Walsall	42	11	7	3	51	18	2	3	16	30	54	36
15	York City	42	12	5	4	50	20	3	1	17	26	62	36
16	New Brighton	42	9	6	6	32	25	5	2	14	27	51	36
17	Barrow	42	11	5	5	37	31	2	4	15	21	56	35
18	Accrington Stanley	42	11	5	5	44	36	1	5	15	19	53	34
19	Gateshead	42	12	4	5	36	28	1	4	16	22	68	34
20	Rochdale	42	9	5	7	39	35	2	6	13	14	36	33
21	Southport	42	6	6	9	27	36	4	6	11	28	49	32
22	Carlisle United	42	7	6	8	34	36	1	1	19	17	66	23

1935/36 8th in Division 3 (North)

						Aitken AL	Allison WML	Bonass AE	Bradford JR	Brown GA	Chatterton W	Firman JR	Graham JA	Hardy LR	Harris G	Heward HA	Hill R	Howe JR	Huggins A	Hughes J	Mittel JL	Moses J	Murray J	Nobbs W	Owens R	Park O	Pickard F	Proctor JR	Robertson A	Scrimshaw S	Thompson AS	Wigham J
1	Aug 31	HALIFAX TOWN	1-0	Thompson	5615			11								6	4	3	9		1					5		2	10		7	8
2	Sep 4	OLDHAM ATHLETIC	0-1		6582			11								6	4	3	9		1					5		2	10		7	8
3	7	Darlington	2-4	Proctor (p), Thompson	5276			11								6	4	3	8	9	1					5		2	10		7	
4	9	Oldham Athletic	2-2	Bonass, Hughes	6459		3	11		4						6	8			9	1					5		2	10		7	
5	14	GATESHEAD	2-0	Bonass, Thompson	4487		3	11		4						6	8			9	1					5		2	10		7	
6	18	Wrexham	0-1		3555		3	11		4				8			6			9	1					5		2	10		7	
7	21	Tranmere Rovers	1-3	Hughes	6902		3	11		4							6			9	1	10				5		2			7	8
8	28	WALSALL	5-0	Robertson,Hughes,Wigham 2,Thompson	4422		3	11								6	4			9	1					5		2	10		7	8
9	Oct 5	Carlisle United	0-0		7618		3	11								6	4			9	1					5		2	10		7	8
10	12	CREWE ALEXANDRA	1-0	Bonass	4692		3	11								6	4			9	1					5		2	10		7	8
11	19	Accrington Stanley	2-3	Thompson, Graham	2677		3	11					9			6	4				1					5		2	10		7	8
12	26	SOUTHPORT	2-1	Pickard, Hill	3767		3	11					9			6	4				1	10				5	7	2				8
13	Nov 2	Chester	0-4		5503		3	11					9			6	4	2			1	10				5	7					8
14	9	LINCOLN CITY	1-1	Bonass	3560		3	11		4			9				6				1					5		2	10		7	8
15	16	Rochdale	1-0	Bonass	4878		3	11		4			9				6				1					5		2	10		7	8
16	23	YORK CITY	4-2	Wigham 2, Bonass, Thompson	4247		3	11		4			9				6				1					5		2	10		7	8
17	Dec 7	NEW BRIGHTON	4-1	Bonass, Wigham 2, Robertson	3249		3	11		4			9				6						1			5		2	10		7	8
18	21	STOCKPORT COUNTY	1-1	Chatterton	3375		3	11	2	4	9			8		6	5				1	10									7	
19	25	MANSFIELD TOWN	4-1	Wigham 2, Bonass, Proctor (p)	5679		3	11		4						6	8		7		1					5		2	10			9
20	26	Mansfield Town	0-4		2595		3			4			11	8		6					1	10				5	7	2				9
21	28	Halifax Town	1-0	Graham	4624			11		5			9	7		6	8	3			1							2	10	4		
22	Jan 1	WREXHAM	1-1	Wigham	5037		3	11		4				7		6	8				1					5		2	10			9
23	4	DARLINGTON	2-1	Wigham 2	6125			11		4				7		6	8	3			1					5		2	10			9
24	23	Barrow	1-1	Robertson	1568		3	11		4			9	8			6						1			5		2	10		7	
25	29	TRANMERE ROVERS	2-2	Bonass, Thompson	1820		3	11		5			9	8			6				1							2	10	4	7	
26	Feb 1	Walsall	0-6		5970		3	11		4				5			6				1				10			2		8	7	9
27	8	CARLISLE UNITED	1-1	Wigham	4107		3	11		4							6				1					5		2	10	8	7	9
28	12	Gateshead	0-1		1973		3	11		4				9			6				1					5		2	10	8	7	
29	15	Crewe Alexandra	2-3	Moses, Wigham	3808		3	11	2					8		6	4				1	10				5					7	9
30	22	ACCRINGTON STANLEY	2-1	Wigham, Robertson	4056		3	11		4				8		6					1					5		2	10		7	9
31	Mar 7	CHESTER	0-2		4167		3	11		4						6	8				1					5		2	10		7	9
32	14	Southport	1-1	Bonass	1850			11					9	5		6	4	3			1							2		10	7	8
33	18	Lincoln City	0-1		2598			11					9	5		6	4	3			1							2	8	10	7	
34	21	ROCHDALE	1-0	Harris	4110		3	11						5	9	6	4				1	7						2		8		10
35	28	York City	2-2	Thompson, Wigham	2686		3					11				6	8				1			4		5		2		10	7	9
36	Apr 4	BARROW	0-0		2863		3				9	11		8		6					1			4		5		2			7	10
37	10	ROTHERHAM UNITED	5-1	Park, Thompson 2(1p), Wigham, Bonass	4051		3	11								6	8				1			4		5		2	10		7	9
38	11	New Brighton	0-0		2187		3	11					9	6			4				1					5		2	10		7	8
39	13	Rotherham United	0-3		4593		3	11					9	6			4				1					5		2	10		7	8
40	18	CHESTERFIELD	2-1	Nobbs, Graham	4073			11	3	5			9	10			6				1			4				2			7	8
41	25	Stockport County	1-2	Thompson	3008	1	3	11					9	4		6	5											2	10		7	8
42	27	Chesterfield	0-2		7552		3	11					9	8		6	4				1					5		2	10		7	
					Apps	1	34	39	3	22	2	2	18	21	1	28	39	8	4	8	39	7	2	4	1	33	3	39	30	9	34	31
					Goals			11			1		3		1		1			3		1		1		1	1	2	4		11	16

F.A. Cup

						Aitken AL	Allison WML	Bonass AE	Bradford JR	Brown GA	Chatterton W	Firman JR	Graham JA	Hardy LR	Harris G	Heward HA	Hill R	Howe JR	Huggins A	Hughes J	Mittel JL	Moses J	Murray J	Nobbs W	Owens R	Park O	Pickard F	Proctor JR	Robertson A	Scrimshaw S	Thompson AS	Wigham J
R1	Nov 30	Mansfield Town	3-2	Bonass, Robertson, Proctor (p)	4651		3	11		4			9				6				1					5		2	10		7	8
R2	Dec 14	Halifax Town	1-1	Robertson	7698		3	11		4				9			6				1					5		2	10		7	8
rep	18	HALIFAX TOWN	0-0		7713		3	11		4			9				6				1					5		2	10		7	8
rep2	23	Halifax Town	4-1	Wigham 3, Robertson	4900		3	11		4				8			6				1					5		2	10		7	9
R3	Jan 11	GRIMSBY TOWN	0-0		15064		3	11		4				7		6	8				1					5		2	10			9
rep	14	Grimsby Town	1-4	Bonass	11500		3	11		4				7		6	8				1					5		2	10			9

R2 replay a.e.t. Replay two at St. James's Park, Newcastle.

Division 3 (North) Cup

						Aitken AL	Allison WML	Bonass AE	Bradford JR	Brown GA	Chatterton W	Firman JR	Graham JA	Hardy LR	Harris G	Heward HA	Hill R	Howe JR	Huggins A	Hughes J	Mittel JL	Moses J	Murray J	Nobbs W	Owens R	Park O	Pickard F	Proctor JR	Robertson A	Scrimshaw S	Thompson AS	Wigham J
R1	Sep 23	Carlisle United	2-4	Thompson, Lloyd (og)	2400		3	11						4			6		9		1	10				5		2	8		7	

		P	W	D	L	F	A	W	D	L	F	A	Pts
1	Chesterfield	42	15	3	3	60	14	9	9	3	32	25	60
2	Chester	42	14	5	2	69	18	8	6	7	31	27	55
3	Tranmere Rovers	42	17	2	2	75	28	5	9	7	18	30	55
4	Lincoln City	42	18	1	2	64	14	4	8	9	27	37	53
5	Stockport County	42	15	2	4	45	18	5	6	10	20	31	48
6	Crewe Alexandra	42	14	4	3	55	31	5	5	11	25	45	47
7	Oldham Athletic	42	13	5	3	60	25	5	4	12	26	48	45
8	HARTLEPOOLS UTD.	42	13	6	2	41	18	2	6	13	16	43	42
9	Accrington Stanley	42	12	5	4	43	24	5	3	13	20	48	42
10	Walsall	42	15	2	4	58	13	1	7	13	21	46	41
11	Rotherham United	42	14	3	4	52	13	2	6	13	17	53	41
12	Darlington	42	16	3	2	60	26	1	3	17	14	53	40
13	Carlisle United	42	13	5	3	44	19	1	7	13	12	43	40
14	Gateshead	42	11	10	0	37	18	2	4	15	19	58	40
15	Barrow	42	9	9	3	33	16	4	3	14	25	49	38
16	York City	42	10	8	3	41	28	3	4	14	21	67	38
17	Halifax Town	42	12	3	6	34	22	3	4	14	23	39	37
18	Wrexham	42	12	3	6	39	18	3	4	14	27	57	37
19	Mansfield Town	42	13	5	3	55	25	1	4	16	25	66	37
20	Rochdale	42	8	10	3	35	26	2	3	16	23	62	33
21	Southport	42	9	8	4	31	26	2	1	18	17	64	31
22	New Brighton	42	8	5	8	29	33	1	1	19	14	69	24

1936/37 6th in Division 3 (North)

	Date	Opponent	Score	Scorers	Att.	Allison WML	Bradford JR	Dreyer G	English S	Graham SJ	Hardy LR	Hill R	McCambridge J	Middleton CW	Mittel JL	Moore WR	Moses J	Nobbs W	Park O	Proctor JR	Robertson A	Scott J	Scott T	Scrimshaw S	Self ER	Wigham J
1	Aug 29	Southport	1-1	Wigham	5364	3		6	9						1			4	5	2	10	7			11	8
2	Sep 2	ACCRINGTON STANLEY	1-0	English	7342	3		6	9		8				1			4	5	2	10	7			11	
3	5	TRANMERE ROVERS	2-1	Robertson, English	8729	3		4	9						1			6	5	2	10	7			11	8
4	12	Halifax Town	0-2		5798	3		4	9					10	1			6	5	2		7			11	8
5	19	MANSFIELD TOWN	3-0	Self, English, Proctor (p)	7178	3			9			6			1		10	4	5	2		7			11	8
6	26	Crewe Alexandra	1-1	Robertson	4016	3			9			6			1			4	5	2	10	7			11	8
7	29	Accrington Stanley	2-1	Moses, English	3919	3			9			4			1		10	6	5	2			7	8	11	
8	Oct 3	CHESTER	0-1		12220	3			9			4			1			6	5	2	10		7		11	8
9	10	Rochdale	1-1	Scrimshaw	5171	3			9			4			1			6	5	2			7	8	11	10
10	17	OLDHAM ATHLETIC	1-0	English	6138	3			9			4			1			6	5	2			7	8	11	10
11	24	Port Vale	0-1		6659	3			9			4				1		6	5	2	10		7	8		11
12	31	ROTHERHAM UNITED	0-2		5892	3			9			4				1		6	5	2		7	11	10		8
13	Nov 7	Stockport County	1-1	Hardy	8092	3		4	9		7	6				1			5	2	10				11	8
14	14	WREXHAM	2-0	English 2	4683	3		4	9		5	6				1				2	10	7			11	8
15	21	Darlington	5-5	J Scott, Hill, English, Robertson, Wigham	4817	3		4	9		5	6				1				2	10	7			11	8
16	Dec 5	Hull City	0-1		5676	3		4			5	6				1				2	10	7		8	11	9
17	19	Lincoln City	0-3		4032	3		4				6			1				5	2	10	7		8	11	9
18	25	York City	1-4	J Scott	7170	3	2	4			5	6			1			9			10	7			11	8
19	26	SOUTHPORT	2-0	English, J Scott	6574	3	2	4	9		5	6				1					10	7			11	8
20	28	YORK CITY	2-0	English (p), Hardy	2744	3	2	4	9	6	5					1					10	7			11	8
21	Jan 1	BARROW	3-1	Robertson, Wigham, J Scott	6783	3	2	4	9	6	5					1					10	7			11	8
22	2	Tranmere Rovers	0-1		6809	3	2	4		6	5	9				1	8				10	7			11	
23	9	HALIFAX TOWN	5-3	McCambridge 3, Robertson, Self	6154	3		4		6	5		9			1				2	10	7			11	8
24	16	GATESHEAD	6-1	J Scott 3, Robertson 2, McCambridge	7405	3				6	5	4	9			1				2	10	7			11	8
25	23	Mansfield Town	2-8	Proctor (p), Wigham	2696	3				6	5	4	9			1				2	10	7			11	8
26	30	CREWE ALEXANDRA	4-1	Wigham, English, Scott (og), Proctor (p)	2058	3		4	9	6					1				5	2	10	7			11	8
27	Feb 6	Chester	0-3		5444	3		4	9						1			6	5	2	10	7			11	8
28	13	ROCHDALE	4-1	Proctor (p), J Scott, English, Self	4180	3		4	9			6			1				5	2	10	7			11	8
29	20	Oldham Athletic	0-2		4363	3		4		7	6		9		1				5	2	10	8			11	
30	27	PORT VALE	2-0	English 2	2645	3		4	9				6		1				5	2	10	7			11	8
31	Mar 6	Rotherham United	4-2	J Scott 3, Self	2601	3		4	9		8		6		1				5	2	10	7			11	
32	13	STOCKPORT COUNTY	2-4	Wigham, Self	7105	3		4	9				6		1				5	2	10	7			11	8
33	20	Wrexham	1-0	Robertson	3083	3			9		6		8			1		4	5	2	10	7			11	
34	26	Carlisle United	0-2		8366	3			9		6		8			1		4	5	2	10	7			11	
35	27	DARLINGTON	1-3	English	4604	3		4	9				6			1			5	2	10	7		8		11
36	29	CARLISLE UNITED	3-0	Self, Proctor (p), Robertson	4748	3			9	6	4		8		1				5	2	10	7			11	
37	Apr 3	Gateshead	2-2	J Scott, Robertson	2738	3			9	6	4		8		1				5	2	10	7			11	
38	10	HULL CITY	2-2	Annables (og), English	4936	3			9	6	7				1			4	5	2	10	11				8
39	17	New Brighton	0-4		1865	3			9	6	4		8		1				5	2	10	7				11
40	24	LINCOLN CITY	3-1	Robertson, Self, Proctor	5552	3		4	9		5		6		1					2	10	7			11	8
41	28	NEW BRIGHTON	5-0	English 2, Wigham 2, Proctor (p)	2870	3		4	9		5		6		1					2	10	7			11	8
42	May 1	Barrow	1-3	Proctor (p)	3395		3	4	9		5		6		1					2	10	7		8	11	
					Apps	41	6	26	34	12	24	19	16	1	26	16	3	17	28	37	36	36	6	9	37	32
					Goals				18		2	1	4				1			8	11	12		1	7	8

Two own goals

F.A. Cup

	Date	Opponent	Score	Scorers	Att.	Allison WML	Bradford JR	Dreyer G	English S	Graham SJ	Hardy LR	Hill R	McCambridge J	Middleton CW	Mittel JL	Moore WR	Moses J	Nobbs W	Park O	Proctor JR	Robertson A	Scott J	Scott T	Scrimshaw S	Self ER	Wigham J
R1	Nov 28	Rotherham United	4-4	Proctor (p), English, Self, Park	11552	3		4	9			6			1				5	2	10	7			11	8
rep	Dec 2	ROTHERHAM UTD.	2-0	Self, J Scott	8532	3		4			8	6			1				5	2	10	7			11	9
R2	12	Crewe Alexandra	1-1	English	5104	3		4	9			6			1				5	2	10	7			11	8
rep	16	CREWE ALEXANDRA	1-2	Self	7636	3		4			9	6			1				5	2	10	7			11	8

Third Division (North) Cup

	Date	Opponent	Score	Scorers	Att.	Allison WML	Bradford JR	Dreyer G	English S	Graham SJ	Hardy LR	Hill R	McCambridge J	Middleton CW	Mittel JL	Moore WR	Moses J	Nobbs W	Park O	Proctor JR	Robertson A	Scott J	Scott T	Scrimshaw S	Self ER	Wigham J
R1	Oct 7	Lincoln City	2-0	Robertson, Firman	1115	3			9			4			1			6	5	2	10		7	8		
R2	Mar 17	York City	0-5			3		4			5		6		1					2	10	7		8	11	

Played at 11 Oct 7th: JR Firman. Played at 9 Mar 17th: G Oxley

		P	W	D	L	F	A	W	D	L	F	A	Pts
1	Stockport County	42	17	3	1	59	18	6	11	4	25	21	60
2	Lincoln City	42	18	1	2	65	20	7	6	8	38	37	57
3	Chester	42	15	5	1	68	21	7	4	10	19	36	53
4	Oldham Athletic	42	13	7	1	49	25	7	4	10	28	34	51
5	Hull City	42	13	6	2	39	22	4	6	11	29	47	46
6	HARTLEPOOLS UTD.	42	16	1	4	53	21	3	6	12	22	48	45
7	Halifax Town	42	12	4	5	40	20	6	5	10	28	43	45
8	Wrexham	42	12	3	6	41	21	4	9	8	30	36	44
9	Mansfield Town	42	13	1	7	64	35	5	7	9	27	41	44
10	Carlisle United	42	13	6	2	42	19	5	2	14	23	49	44
11	Port Vale	42	12	6	3	39	23	5	4	12	19	41	44
12	York City	42	13	3	5	54	27	3	8	10	25	43	43
13	Accrington Stanley	42	14	2	5	51	26	2	7	12	25	43	41
14	Southport	42	10	8	3	39	28	2	5	14	34	59	37
15	New Brighton	42	10	8	3	36	16	3	3	15	19	54	37
16	Barrow	42	11	5	5	42	25	2	5	14	28	61	36
17	Rotherham United	42	11	7	3	52	28	3	0	18	26	63	35
18	Rochdale	42	12	3	6	44	27	1	6	14	25	59	35
19	Tranmere Rovers	42	10	8	3	52	30	2	1	18	19	58	33
20	Crewe Alexandra	42	6	8	7	31	31	4	4	13	24	52	32
21	Gateshead	42	9	8	4	40	31	2	2	17	23	67	32
22	Darlington	42	6	8	7	42	46	2	6	13	24	50	30

1937/38 20th in Division 3 (North)

No	Date	Opponent	Score	Scorers	Att	Allison WML	Curtis ER	Davidson DL	Embleton E	English S	Hughes, Jack	Johnson TO	Mackie J	McLean R	Nevin W	Oliver HS	Park O	Pickering A	Proctor JR	Reid TS	Robertson A	Rodger JJ	Rutherford J	Scott J	Self ER	Smith W	Taylor A	Telling H	Thomas E	Thompson N	Turner R	West N	Whyte C	Wigham J
1	Aug 26	Lincoln City	1-2	Scott	8779	3	4	5		9	6								2		10			7	11		1							8
2	Sep 1	ACCRINGTON STANLEY	2-0	English, Proctor (p)	7751	3	6	5		9									2		10			7	11		1		4					8
3	4	HULL CITY	2-2	Wigham 2	8173	3	6	5	10	9									2					7	11		1		4					8
4	6	Accrington Stanley	1-2	Embleton	4812	3	10		8		6								2	5					11		1		4	9				
5	11	New Brighton	1-4	Proctor (p)	5419	3	6			9									2	5				7	11		1		4			10		8
6	13	Wrexham	3-6	West, Curtis, English	2752	3	8			9									2	5				7	11		1	6	4			10		
7	18	GATESHEAD	1-3	Proctor (p)	7503	3	4			9									2	5				7	11			6				10		8
8	25	Oldham Athletic	1-3	Wigham	6861	3	8	5	7	9	6								2						11		1		4					10
9	Oct 2	DARLINGTON	2-1	English, Wigham	6867	3	6	5		9									2		10			7	11		1		4					8
10	9	Port Vale	1-5	Scott	7951	3		5		9	4							6	2		10			7	11		1							8
11	16	CHESTER	0-1		5955	3				9	4								2	5	10			7	11	6	1							8
12	23	Rotherham United	1-3	Robertson	4700				8		6								2	5	10		1	7	11	4							3	9
13	30	ROCHDALE	3-3	Wigham 2, Scott	5087					9	6								2	5	10		1	7	11	4							3	8
14	Nov 6	Doncaster Rovers	3-3	Proctor (p), Scott 2	10538	3			8		6						5		2		10		1	7	11	4								9
15	13	SOUTHPORT	1-2	Wigham	4384	3				9	6		11				5		2		10			7		4	1							8
16	20	Bradford City	1-4	Self	5202	3			8	9	6						5		2		10			7	11	4	1							
17	Dec 4	Tranmere Rovers	0-4		5128	3			8	10	6						5						1	7	11	4					2			9
18	18	Carlisle United	1-3	Smith	3855	3			7		6						5		2						11	9	1		4			10		8
19	25	CREWE ALEXANDRA	2-2	Embleton, Wigham	6267	3			10	9	6						2							7	11	4	1		5					8
20	27	Crewe Alexandra	0-2		5167	3	8				6			9							10			7	11	4	1		5				2	
21	Jan 1	LINCOLN CITY	2-0	English, Scott	5126	3	8			9	6								2		10			7	11	4	1		5					
22	12	YORK CITY	0-0		2665	3	8			9	6								2		10			7	11	4	1		5					
23	15	Hull City	0-4		8607	3			10	9	6													7	11	4	1		5					8
24	29	Gateshead	1-2	Self	7308	3			8	9	6								2			5			11	10	1		4					7
25	Feb 2	NEW BRIGHTON	1-0	Proctor (p)	1911	3	8		10	9	6	1							2			5		7	11	4								
26	5	OLDHAM ATHLETIC	2-0	Embleton, English	5310	3			10	9	6	1							2			5		7	11	4								8
27	12	Darlington	0-2		4610	3			10	9	6	1							2			5		7	11	4								8
28	19	PORT VALE	2-1	English, Scott	4483	3			10	9	6	1										2		7	11	4			5					8
29	26	Chester	0-6		3723	3			10	9	6	1										5		7	11	2			4					8
30	Mar 5	ROTHERHAM UNITED	4-0	Nevin, Mackie 2, English	5639	2				10	6	1	11		9										7	4			5				3	8
31	12	Rochdale	2-2	Nevin, Self	5615	2				10	6		11		9										7	4	1		5				3	8
32	19	DONCASTER ROVERS	0-0		5547					10	6		11		9	3			2						7	4	1		5					8
33	26	Southport	0-2		3140					10	6		11		9	3						2			7	4	1		5					8
34	Apr 2	BRADFORD CITY	1-1	Proctor (p)	3801	3	10			9	6					5			2					7	11	8	1		4					
35	9	York City	0-1		3565		8			10	6					3			2					7	11	4	1		5					9
36	15	BARROW	1-1	Wigham	5449	3	8			10	6								2					7	11	4	1		5					9
37	16	TRANMERE ROVERS	2-2	Proctor, English	4826	3			10	9	6	1							2					7	11	4			5					8
38	18	Barrow	0-0		3991				10	9	6	1				3			2			4		7	11				5					8
39	23	Halifax Town	0-0		2821				10	9	6	1				3			2			4		7	11				5					8
40	30	CARLISLE UNITED	4-1	English,Scott,Embleton,Hughes	2766				10	9	6	1				3			2			4		7	11				5					8
41	May 4	HALIFAX TOWN	2-0	Embleton, West	4940				10		6	1				3			2			4		7	11	8			5			9		
42	7	WREXHAM	2-0	West, Embleton	5135				10		6	1				3			2			4		7	11				5			9		8
					Apps	32	16	6	22	35	36	12	5	1	4	9	6	1	33	7	13	12	4	34	41	28	25	2	29	1	1	6	5	33
					Goals		1		6	9	1		2		2				7		1			8	3	1						3		9

Played in one game: JH Brown (7, at 1), R Copeman (23 at 2), I Fenton (4, at 7)

F.A. Cup

Rd	Date	Opponent	Score	Scorers	Att	Allison WML	Curtis ER	Davidson DL	Embleton E	English S	Hughes, Jack	Johnson TO	Mackie J	McLean R	Nevin W	Oliver HS	Park O	Pickering A	Proctor JR	Reid TS	Robertson A	Rodger JJ	Rutherford J	Scott J	Self ER	Smith W	Taylor A	Telling H	Thomas E	Thompson N	Turner R	West N	Whyte C	Wigham J
R1	Nov 27	SOUTHPORT	3-1	Scott, English, Embleton	7415	3			8	10	6						5							7	11	4	1				2			9
R2	Dec 11	Tranmere Rovers	1-3	Self	7994	3			8		6						5				10		1	7	11	4							2	9

Third Division (North) Cup

Rd	Date	Opponent	Score	Scorers	Att	Allison WML	Curtis ER	Davidson DL	Embleton E	English S	Hughes, Jack	Johnson TO	Mackie J	McLean R	Nevin W	Oliver HS	Park O	Pickering A	Proctor JR	Reid TS	Robertson A	Rodger JJ	Rutherford J	Scott J	Self ER	Smith W	Taylor A	Telling H	Thomas E	Thompson N	Turner R	West N	Whyte C	Wigham J
R1	Oct 21	Hull City	1-1	Wigham	4000				7		6				9				2	5	10		1		11	4							3	8
rep	27	HULL CITY	3-0	English, Embleton, Proctor (p)	1900				8	9	6								2	5	10		1	7	11	4							3	
R2	Feb 15	Southport	0-6		1000					9			10						2		8	5			11	7	1		4				3	

Played in R2 at 6: G Mathison

		P	W	D	L	F	A	W	D	L	F	A	Pts
1	Tranmere Rovers	42	15	4	2	57	21	8	6	7	24	20	56
2	Doncaster Rovers	42	15	4	2	48	16	6	8	7	26	33	54
3	Hull City	42	11	8	2	51	19	9	5	7	29	24	53
4	Oldham Athletic	42	16	4	1	48	18	3	9	9	19	28	51
5	Gateshead	42	15	5	1	53	20	5	6	10	31	39	51
6	Rotherham United	42	13	6	2	45	21	7	4	10	23	35	50
7	Lincoln City	42	14	3	4	48	17	5	5	11	18	33	46
8	Crewe Alexandra	42	14	3	4	47	17	4	6	11	24	36	45
9	Chester	42	13	4	4	54	31	3	8	10	23	41	44
10	Wrexham	42	14	4	3	37	15	2	7	12	21	48	43
11	York City	42	11	4	6	40	25	5	6	10	30	43	42
12	Carlisle United	42	11	5	5	35	19	4	4	13	22	48	39
13	New Brighton	42	12	5	4	43	18	3	3	15	17	43	38
14	Bradford City	42	12	6	3	46	21	2	4	15	20	48	38
15	Port Vale	42	11	8	2	45	27	1	6	14	20	46	38
16	Southport	42	8	8	5	30	26	4	6	11	23	56	38
17	Rochdale	42	7	10	4	38	27	6	1	14	29	51	37
18	Halifax Town	42	9	7	5	24	19	3	5	13	20	47	36
19	Darlington	42	10	4	7	37	31	1	6	14	17	48	32
20	HARTLEPOOLS UTD.	42	10	8	3	36	20	0	4	17	17	60	32
21	Barrow	42	9	6	6	28	20	2	4	15	13	51	32
22	Accrington Stanley	42	9	2	10	31	32	2	5	14	14	43	29

1938/39 21st in Division 3 (North)

	Date	Opponent	Score	Scorers	Att	Brown CM	Calder JH	Chapman J	Diamond JJ	Don RP	Douglas JS	Johnson H	Lealman F	Love RW	Mackie J	McGarry T	Musgrave JW	Peart R	Price J	Race H	Robbins P	Robinson J	Rose LER	Self ER	Thomas E	Wallace J	West N	Wigham J	Wilson JB	Woffinden RS	Woods C	Wright J
1	Aug 27	Carlisle United	0-2		7014					4		3		9			6		7		10			11	5	1		8				2
2	29	Wrexham	0-3		4908					4		3					6		7	8	10			11	5	1					9	2
3	Sep 3	CREWE ALEXANDRA	0-1		5863					4		3	7				6			8	10			11	5	1					9	2
4	7	Darlington	0-3		3125					4		3		9			6		7			1		11	5			10			8	2
5	10	Southport	0-2		5053						5		7			9	6			8		1		11	4			10	3			2
6	14	DARLINGTON	3-0	Wigham, Lealman, McGarry	3942						5		7			9	6				10			11	4	1		8	3			2
7	17	DONCASTER ROVERS	1-3	Musgrave	5722						5		7			9	6				10			11	4	1		8	3			2
8	24	Rotherham United	1-5	West	7698							3					4		7		10		6	11	5	1	9	8				2
9	Oct 1	ROCHDALE	4-2	Woods, Wigham 2, Self	4446			4				3				9			7				6	11	5	1		10			8	2
10	8	York City	0-2		6208			4				2				9			7				6	11	5	1		10	3		8	
11	15	Bradford City	1-0	McGarry	6552			4				2	7			9							6	11	5	1		10	3		8	
12	22	HULL CITY	3-3	Woods, Wigham, McGarry	6189			4				2	7			9							6	11	5	1		10	3		8	
13	29	Lincoln City	2-2	McGarry, Self	4682			4				2				9			7				6	11	5	1		10	3		8	
14	Nov 5	STOCKPORT COUNTY	4-2	McGarry 3, Wigham	6519			4				2				9			7				6	11	5	1		10	3		8	
15	12	Accrington Stanley	0-0		5063			4				2				9			7				6	11	5	1		10	3		8	
16	19	BARNSLEY	0-1		8582			4				2			11	9			7				6		5	1		10	3		8	
17	Dec 3	HALIFAX TOWN	1-0	Love	4603							2		9			4		7		8		6	11	5	1		10	3			
18	17	BARROW	1-2	Woods	2926			4						10					7				6	11	5	1		8	3		9	2
19	24	CARLISLE UNITED	2-1	Price, Musgrave (p)	2435												4		7		8		6	11	5	1	10	9	3			2
20	26	CHESTER	2-5	Musgrave (p), Robbins	5177	6	3									9	4		7		8			11	5	1		10				2
21	27	Chester	2-8	Self 2	7748	6	5					3				9	8		7		10			11	4	1						2
22	31	Crewe Alexandra	2-3	Self, Lealman	4969							2	7			9	6				8			11	5	1		10	3			4
23	Jan 7	Oldham Athletic	2-4	Price, Robbins	2708							2				9	6		7		8	1		11	5			10	3			4
24	14	SOUTHPORT	0-2		3985				9		5	2					6		7		8			11	4	1	10					3
25	18	New Brighton	2-5	Woods 2	1453		3		9			2					6		7					11	5	1	10				8	4
26	26	Doncaster Rovers	1-3	Price	2675				9			2					6		7					11	5	1	10		3		8	4
27	28	ROTHERHAM UNITED	1-1	Wigham	2604	2			9								6		7					11	5	1		10	3		8	4
28	Feb 4	Rochdale	4-3	Robbins 2, Wigham, McGarry	5557							3				9			4		11			7	5	1		10		6	8	2
29	11	YORK CITY	3-2	Wigham, McGarry 2	3105							3				9			4		11			7	5	1		10		6	8	2
30	18	BRADFORD CITY	1-3	Wigham	4344							3				9			4		11			7	5	1		10		6	8	2
31	25	Hull City	1-4	McGarry	4565		3							9		7			4		11	1			5			10		6	8	2
32	Mar 4	LINCOLN CITY	2-1	McGarry, Wigham	2393									9		7			4		11				5	1	10	8	3	6		2
33	11	Stockport County	0-5		5198									9					4		11			7	5	1	10	8	3	6		2
34	18	ACCRINGTON STANLEY	2-1	Diamond, Love	2463				9					10				5	4		11					1		8	3	6	7	2
35	25	Barnsley	0-2		11611				9					10				5	4		11					1		8	3	6	7	2
36	Apr 1	OLDHAM ATHLETIC	0-0		3147				9					10				5	4		11	1		7				8	3	6		2
37	7	GATESHEAD	3-1	West 2, Robbins	3992				9								7	5	4		11	1					10	8	3	6		2
38	8	Halifax Town	0-2		3379				9								4	5	7			1		11			10	8	3	6		2
39	10	Gateshead	0-2		4593													5	4		11	1		7			10	8	3	6	9	2
40	15	NEW BRIGHTON	3-2	Woffinden, Woods, West	1554							3		7				5	4			1		11			10	8		6	9	2
41	22	Barrow	1-1	Self	4356	3								8				5	4			1		11			10	7		6	9	2
42	May 6	WREXHAM	0-0		3455	3					5			8					4			1		11			10	7		6	9	2
					Apps	5	4	9	9	4	5	24	7	13	1	20	20	8	35	3	24	11	12	36	33	31	13	36	25	15	25	34
					Goals				1				2	2		12	3		3		5			6			4	10		1	6	

F.A. Cup

	Date	Opponent	Score	Scorers	Att	Brown CM	Calder JH	Chapman J	Diamond JJ	Don RP	Douglas JS	Johnson H	Lealman F	Love RW	Mackie J	McGarry T	Musgrave JW	Peart R	Price J	Race H	Robbins P	Robinson J	Rose LER	Self ER	Thomas E	Wallace J	West N	Wigham J	Wilson JB	Woffinden RS	Woods C	Wright J
R1	Nov 26	ACCRINGTON STANLEY	2-1	Woods, Self	7068			4				2				9			7				6	11	5	1		10	3		8	
R2	Dec 10	QUEEN'S PARK RANGERS	0-2		11924			4				2				9			7		8		6	11	5	1		10	3			

Third Division (North) Cup

	Date	Opponent	Score	Scorers	Att	Brown CM	Calder JH	Chapman J	Diamond JJ	Don RP	Douglas JS	Johnson H	Lealman F	Love RW	Mackie J	McGarry T	Musgrave JW	Peart R	Price J	Race H	Robbins P	Robinson J	Rose LER	Self ER	Thomas E	Wallace J	West N	Wigham J	Wilson JB	Woffinden RS	Woods C	Wright J
R1	Jan 2	DARLINGTON	4-1	McGarry 2, Wigham, Robbins	2000							2	7			9	6				8			11	5	1		10	3			4
R2	Mar 8	Gateshead	0-0		290									9		8		5	4		11					1	10		3			2
rep	15	GATESHEAD	5-1	Diamond 4, Price	700				9									5	8		11			7	4	1			3			2
SF	29	Bradford City	2-5	Love, Spencer (p)	1125									9				5	4		8			11		1			3			2

Played in R2 and SF at 7: E Copeland. Played in R2 replay and SF at 10: R Halliday.
T Spencer played at 6 in R2, R2 replay and SF.

		P	W	D	L	F	A	W	D	L	F	A	Pts
1	Barnsley	42	18	2	1	60	12	12	5	4	34	22	67
2	Doncaster Rovers	42	12	5	4	47	21	9	9	3	40	26	56
3	Bradford City	42	16	2	3	59	21	6	6	9	30	35	52
4	Southport	42	14	5	2	47	16	6	5	10	28	38	50
5	Oldham Athletic	42	16	1	4	51	21	6	4	11	25	38	49
6	Chester	42	12	5	4	54	31	8	4	9	34	39	49
7	Hull City	42	13	5	3	57	25	5	5	11	26	49	46
8	Crewe Alexandra	42	12	5	4	54	23	7	1	13	28	47	44
9	Stockport County	42	13	6	2	57	24	4	3	14	34	53	43
10	Gateshead	42	11	6	4	45	24	3	8	10	29	43	42
11	Rotherham United	42	12	4	5	45	21	5	4	12	19	43	42
12	Halifax Town	42	9	10	2	33	22	4	6	11	19	32	42
13	Barrow	42	11	5	5	46	22	5	4	12	20	43	41
14	Wrexham	42	15	2	4	46	28	2	5	14	20	51	41
15	Rochdale	42	10	5	6	58	29	5	4	12	34	53	39
16	New Brighton	42	11	2	8	46	32	4	7	10	22	41	39
17	Lincoln City	42	9	6	6	40	33	3	3	15	26	59	33
18	Darlington	42	12	2	7	43	30	1	5	15	19	62	33
19	Carlisle United	42	10	5	6	44	33	3	2	16	22	78	33
20	York City	42	8	5	8	37	34	4	3	14	27	58	32
21	HARTLEPOOLS UTD.	42	10	4	7	36	33	2	3	16	19	61	31
22	Accrington Stanley	42	6	5	10	30	39	1	1	19	19	64	20

1946/47 — 13th in Division 3(N)

No	Date	Opponent	Score	Scorers	Att	Allison JJ	Anderson C	Brown WH	Copeland E	Gregory CF	Harden LJ	Heywood AE	Hughes WH	Jones H	Lambert EV	Mason TWM	McMahon HJ	Mitchell JG	Morris D	Moses G	Newton JL	Parkes S	Porter W	Price J	Russell WH	Scott S	Sloan J	Spelman I	Thompson R	Wilkinson K	Willetts J
1	Aug 31	BARROW	1-1	Harden	7259			2	7	3	11	1		6	5		10			8				9				4			
2	Sep 4	Gateshead	1-0	Price	3740			2	7	3		1		6	5		11			8				9	10			4			
3	7	Crewe Alexandra	1-1	Moses	7385			2	7	3		1		6	5		11			10				9	8			4			
4	11	Darlington	1-2	Copeland	7201			2	7	3		1		6	5		11			10				9	8			4			
5	14	LINCOLN CITY	2-0	Scott, Moses	8027			2	7	3		1		6	5		11			10				9		8		4			
6	16	DARLINGTON	4-1	Copeland, Jones, Scott, Moses	9546			2	7	3		1		6	5		11			10				9		8		4			
7	21	Southport	3-3	Price, McMahon (p), Copeland	5000	8	4	2	7	3		1		6	5		11			10				9							
8	28	ROTHERHAM UNITED	2-1	Scott. Moses	12800			2	7	3		1		6	5		11			10				9		8		4			
9	Oct 5	Chester	1-2	Harden	8323	8		2	7	3	11	1		6	5					10				9				4			
10	12	YORK CITY	1-1	McMahon (p)	9238			2	7	3		1		6	5		11			10				9		8		4			
11	19	ACCRINGTON STANLEY	0-2		8945	9		2	7		11	1	5	6			10						3			8		4			
12	26	Carlisle United	1-5	Scott	10775			2				1		6	5		11		7	10				9		8		4			3
13	Nov 2	HALIFAX TOWN	1-4	Copeland	6709	10		2	7	3		1			5		11			9	6					8		4			
14	9	New Brighton	1-2	Sloan	4857			2	7	3		1			5		11			10	6			4		8	9				
15	16	ROCHDALE	0-3		7323			2	7	3		1			5		11				6			10	8		9	4			
16	23	Doncaster Rovers	1-5	Sloan	13093			2	7	3		1		4	5		11				6			10	8		9				
17	Dec 7	Stockport County	2-1	Sloan, McMahon (p)	6928			2		3		1		6	5		11			10				8		7	9	4			
18	21	Bradford City	2-1	Sloan, Copeland	6445			2	7			1	5	6			11			3				8	10		9	4			
19	25	HULL CITY	0-0		8130			2	7	3		1	5	6			11							8	10		9	4			
20	26	Hull City	1-1	Sloan	30064			2	7	3		1	5	6			11							8		10	9	4			
21	28	Barrow	0-2		7701			2	7	3		1	5	6			11							8		10	9	4			
22	Jan 1	WREXHAM	1-3	Copeland	8931	10		2	7			1	5	6			11						3	8			9	4			
23	4	CREWE ALEXANDRA	5-2	Copeland, Sloan, Scott 2, Price	6877		5	2	7	3				6			11					1		8		10	9	4			
24	11	OLDHAM ATHLETIC	1-1	Sloan	4818			2	7	3			5	6			11					1		8		10	9	4			
25	18	Lincoln City	2-5	McMahon 2	7414			2	7	3			5	6			11					1		8		10	9	4			
26	25	SOUTHPORT	3-0	Copeland, McMahon 2	5869			2	7			1	5	6			11			10				9	8			4	3		
27	Feb 1	Rotherham United	0-4		9354			2	7			1	5	6			11							10	8		9	4	3		
28	8	CHESTER	5-1	Mitchell 2, Harden, Price 2	4462			2	7		11	1	5	6				9			6			10		8			3		
29	22	Accrington Stanley	1-2	Price	3560			2	7			1	5	6				9		11	6			10		8			3		
30	Mar 1	CARLISLE UNITED	4-1	Harden, Scott, Sloan, Price	4372			2	7		11	1	5	6										10		8	9	4	3		
31	15	NEW BRIGHTON	3-0	Copeland, Sloan, Harden	5874			2	7		11	1	5	6						4				10		8	9		3		
32	22	Rochdale	0-1		7504			2	7		11	1	5	6		4								10		8	9		3		
33	29	DONCASTER ROVERS	0-2		8310			2	7		11	1	5	6		4		9						10		8			3		
34	Apr 4	TRANMERE ROVERS	1-0	Harden	9679			2	7		11	1	5	6		4								10		8	9		3		
35	5	Wrexham	1-4	Harden	4877	6		2	7		11	1	5			4								10		8	9		3		
36	7	Tranmere Rovers	1-4	Scott	10690	6		2			11	1	5			4			7					10	8	9			3		
37	12	STOCKPORT COUNTY	1-0	Russell	8002	6		2	7		11	1	5											10	8	9			3	4	
38	19	Oldham Athletic	0-0		8714	4		2	7		11	1	5	6										10	8	9			3		
39	26	BRADFORD CITY	0-0		6623	4		2	7		11	1	5	6										10		8			3	9	
40	May 10	York City	4-1	Wilkinson, Morris, Scott, Harden	4514	4		2			11	1	5						7	6				10		8			3	9	
41	24	Halifax Town	4-1	Scott 2, Harden, Morris	3949	4		2			11	1	5						7					10		8			3	9	6
42	26	GATESHEAD	1-3	Scott	7000	4		2			11	1	5						7					10		8			3	9	6
					Apps	13	2	42	36	21	17	39	25	33	16	5	26	3	5	19	6	3	2	40	12	29	18	25	17	5	3
					Goals				9		9			1			7	2	2	4				7	1	12	9			1	

F.A. Cup

Rd	Date	Opponent	Score	Scorers	Att	Allison JJ	Anderson C	Brown WH	Copeland E	Gregory CF	Harden LJ	Heywood AE	Hughes WH	Jones H	Lambert EV	Mason TWM	McMahon HJ	Mitchell JG	Morris D	Moses G	Newton JL	Parkes S	Porter W	Price J	Russell WH	Scott S	Sloan J	Spelman I	Thompson R	Wilkinson K	Willetts J
R1	Nov 30	NORTH SHIELDS	6-0	Sloan 4, Scott 2	8000			2		3		1		6	5		11			10				8		7	9	4			
R2	Dec 12	ROCHDALE	1-6	McMahon	7000			2		3		1		6	5		11			10				8		7	9	4			

		P	W	D	L	F	A	W	D	L	F	A	Pts
1	Doncaster Rovers	42	15	5	1	67	16	18	1	2	56	24	72
2	Rotherham United	42	20	1	0	81	19	9	5	7	33	34	64
3	Chester	42	17	2	2	63	13	8	4	9	42	38	56
4	Stockport County	42	17	0	4	50	19	7	2	12	28	34	50
5	Bradford City	42	12	5	4	40	20	8	5	8	22	27	50
6	Rochdale	42	9	5	7	39	25	10	5	6	41	39	48
7	Wrexham	42	13	5	3	43	21	4	7	10	22	30	46
8	Crewe Alexandra	42	12	4	5	39	26	5	5	11	31	48	43
9	Barrow	42	10	2	9	28	24	7	5	9	26	38	41
10	Tranmere Rovers	42	11	5	5	43	33	6	2	13	23	44	41
11	Hull City	42	9	5	7	25	19	7	3	11	24	34	40
12	Lincoln City	42	12	3	6	52	32	5	2	14	34	55	39
13	HARTLEPOOLS UTD.	42	10	5	6	36	26	5	4	12	28	47	39
14	Gateshead	42	10	3	8	39	33	6	3	12	23	39	38
15	York City	42	6	4	11	35	42	8	5	8	32	39	37
16	Carlisle United	42	10	5	6	45	38	4	4	13	26	55	37
17	Darlington	42	12	4	5	48	26	3	2	16	20	54	36
18	New Brighton	42	11	3	7	37	30	3	5	13	20	47	36
19	Oldham Athletic	42	6	5	10	29	31	6	3	12	26	49	32
20	Accrington Stanley	42	8	3	10	37	38	6	1	14	19	54	32
21	Southport	42	6	5	10	35	41	1	6	14	18	44	25
22	Halifax Town	42	6	3	12	28	36	2	3	16	15	56	22

1947/48 19th in Division 3(N)

							Baines PC	Brown WH	Cairns JG	Copeland E	Donaldson RS	Harden LJ	Hawkins H	Hooper HR	Hughes WH	Isaac J	Jarrie F	Jones H	McMahon HJ	Morris D	Nevins L	Newton JL	Parkes S	Price J	Richardson F	Rimmington N	Russell WH	Scott S	Simpson R	Sloan J	Theaker CA	Thompson R	Tootill GA	Underwood WK	Wildon LE	Wilkinson K
1	Aug	23	Accrington Stanley	2-4	Wilkinson 2	6104	7	2							4	8		6	11				1	10									3	5			9
2		27	TRANMERE ROVERS	1-1	Isaac	9133		2				11			4	8	1	6						10					7			3	5			9
3		30	ROTHERHAM UNITED	2-2	Price, Wilkinson	9798		2				11			4			6						10				8	7		1	3	5			9
4	Sep	2	Tranmere Rovers	0-1		7985	10	2							4			6	11									8	7		1	3	5			9
5		6	Carlisle United	1-1	Simpson	14223	10	2							4	7		6										8	11		1	3	5			9
6		13	CREWE ALEXANDRA	0-1		8406	10	2		7					4			6										8	11		1	3	5			9
7		16	Oldham Athletic	2-0	Baines, Isaac	7819	10	2						3	4	7						6						8	11		1		5			9
8		20	Chester	0-2		7146	8	2						3	4	7		6						10					11		1		5			9
9		27	MANSFIELD TOWN	1-0	Isaac	7497	9	2				11		3	4	8		6										10	7		1		5			
10	Oct	4	York City	0-4		9219	10	2				11		3	4	8		6											7		1		5			9
11		11	Hull City	0-5		25414	10	2						3	4	7		8				6							11		1		5			9
12		18	STOCKPORT COUNTY	0-0		6903		2						8	4					7		6			9				11	10	1	3	5			
13		25	Bradford City	1-3	Richardson	11544		2				11			4			6		7			1	10	9					8		3	5			
14	Nov	1	BARROW	0-3		6761		2				11		5	4	7		6						10	9					8	1	3				
15		8	Wrexham	1-3	Harden	9223		2	10		4	11		5											9				7	8	1	3				6
16		15	HALIFAX TOWN	1-1	Harden	5461		2			4	11				10									9				7	8	1	3	5			6
17		22	Rochdale	2-0	Sloan 2	4502		2		7	4	11			5	10									9					8	1	3				6
18	Dec	25	Gateshead	0-7		6329					4	11			5	10							1		9		7			8		3	2			6
19		27	GATESHEAD	3-2	Scott 2, Harden	6608		2			4	11		3	5	10									9	1		7		8						6
20	Jan	1	OLDHAM ATHLETIC	3-1	Hayes (og), Richardson, Harden	8097		2			4	11		3	5	10									9	1		7		8						6
21		3	Rotherham United	2-3	Hooper (p), Harden	13765					4	11		3	5	10									9	1		7		8			2			6
22		10	NEW BRIGHTON	1-0	Wilkinson	6927					4	11		3	5	10									9	1		7		8			2			6
23		17	CARLISLE UNITED	1-1	Isaac	7522					4	11		2	5	10									9	1		7		8		3				6
24		24	LINCOLN CITY	1-2	Sloan	8090		2			4	11		3	5	10									9	1		7		8						6
25		31	Crewe Alexandra	0-2		5343		2			4	11		3	5	10									9	1				8				7		6
26	Feb	7	CHESTER	2-1	Scott 2	6353		2			4	11		3	5	10									9	1		7		8						6
27		14	Mansfield Town	2-3	Isaac, Scott	12326		2			4	11		3	5	10									9	1		7		8						6
28		21	YORK CITY	2-2	Sloan, Harden	4890		2			4	11		3		10									9	1		7		8			5			6
29		28	HULL CITY	3-1	Richardson, Sloan 2	8333		2			10	11		3	5	7		4							9	1				8						6
30	Mar	6	Stockport County	0-2		9991		2			10				5	7		4			11				9	1				8		3				6
31		13	BRADFORD CITY	0-2		8330		2			4		10		5	7					11				9	1				8		3				6
32		20	Barrow	2-1	Nevins 2	7484		2	10		4	7			5	8		6			11				9	1						3				
33		26	Darlington	0-1		10294		2	10		4	11			5	8		6		7					9	1						3				
34		27	WREXHAM	0-2		9389		2	10		4	11			5	7		6							8	1						3			9	
35		29	DARLINGTON	3-0	Hooper (p), Isaac, Richardson	8713		2			8	11		3	5	10		4							9	1		7								6
36	Apr	3	Halifax Town	0-0		5920		2			8	11		3	5	10		4							9	1		7								6
37		10	ROCHDALE	4-1	Donaldson 2, Richardson 2	7907		2			8	11		3	5	10		4							9	1		7								6
38		17	New Brighton	2-1	Richardson, Hooper (p)	2810		2			8	11		3	5	10		4							9	1		7								6
39		19	Southport	0-2		9991		2			8	11		3	5	10		4							9	1				7						6
40		24	SOUTHPORT	2-0	Nevins 2	5941		2			8				5	10		4			11				9	1				7		3				6
41		28	ACCRINGTON STANLEY	4-0	Nevins 2, Sloan, Isaac	6126		2			8				5	10		4			11				9	1				7		3				6
42	May	1	Lincoln City	0-5		20024		2			8				5	10		4			11				9	1		7				3				6

	Baines PC	Brown WH	Cairns JG	Copeland E	Donaldson RS	Harden LJ	Hawkins H	Hooper HR	Hughes WH	Isaac J	Jarrie F	Jones H	McMahon HJ	Morris D	Nevins L	Newton JL	Parkes S	Price J	Richardson F	Rimmington N	Russell WH	Scott S	Simpson R	Sloan J	Theaker CA	Thompson R	Tootill GA	Underwood WK	Wildon LE	Wilkinson K
Apps	9	38	4	2	28	29	1	24	39	36	1	25	2	3	6	3	3	6	31	24	1	20	13	23	14	22	18	1	1	35
Goals	1				2	6		3		7					6			1	7			5	1	7						4

One own goal

F.A. Cup

							Baines PC	Brown WH	Cairns JG	Copeland E	Donaldson RS	Harden LJ	Hawkins H	Hooper HR	Hughes WH	Isaac J	Jarrie F	Jones H	McMahon HJ	Morris D	Nevins L	Newton JL	Parkes S	Price J	Richardson F	Rimmington N	Russell WH	Scott S	Simpson R	Sloan J	Theaker CA	Thompson R	Tootill GA	Underwood WK	Wildon LE	Wilkinson K
R1	Nov	29	DARLINGTON	1-0	Isaac	11290		2		7	4	11			5	10							1		9					8		3				6
R2	Dec	13	BRIGHTON & HOVE ALB.	1-1	Isaac	11000		2		7	4	11			5	10									9					8	1	3				6
rep		20	Brighton & Hove Albion	1-2	Harden	15000		2			4	11			5	10							1		9				7	8		3				6

Extra time played in first R2 game.

		P	W	D	L	F	A	W	D	L	F	A	Pts
1	Lincoln City	42	14	3	4	47	18	12	5	4	34	22	60
2	Rotherham United	42	15	4	2	56	18	10	5	6	39	31	59
3	Wrexham	42	14	3	4	49	23	7	5	9	25	31	50
4	Gateshead	42	11	5	5	48	28	8	6	7	27	29	49
5	Hull City	42	12	5	4	38	21	6	6	9	21	27	47
6	Accrington Stanley	42	13	1	7	36	24	7	5	9	26	35	46
7	Barrow	42	9	4	8	24	19	7	9	5	25	21	45
8	Mansfield Town	42	11	4	6	37	24	6	7	8	20	27	45
9	Carlisle United	42	10	4	7	50	35	8	3	10	38	42	43
10	Crewe Alexandra	42	12	4	5	41	24	6	3	12	20	39	43
11	Oldham Athletic	42	6	10	5	25	25	8	3	10	38	39	41
12	Rochdale	42	12	4	5	32	23	3	7	11	16	49	41
13	York City	42	8	7	6	38	25	5	7	9	27	35	40
14	Bradford City	42	10	4	7	38	27	5	6	10	27	39	40
15	Southport	42	10	4	7	34	27	4	7	10	26	36	39
16	Darlington	42	7	8	6	30	31	6	5	10	24	39	39
17	Stockport County	42	9	6	6	42	28	4	6	11	21	39	38
18	Tranmere Rovers	42	10	1	10	30	28	6	3	12	24	44	36
19	HARTLEPOOLS UTD.	42	10	6	5	34	23	4	2	15	17	50	36
20	Chester	42	11	6	4	44	25	2	3	16	20	42	35
21	Halifax Town	42	4	10	7	25	27	3	3	15	18	49	27
22	New Brighton	42	5	6	10	20	28	3	3	15	18	53	25

1948/49 16th in Division 3(N)

						Brownlow JM	Burnett WJ	Cairns JG	Donaldson RS	Douglas JS	Harden LJ	Hawkins H	Hooper HR	Hughes WH	Isaac J	Jones H	Leonard H	Moore W	Morris D	Nevins L	Newton JL	O'Connor VJ	Price J	Richardson F	Rimmington N	Sherratt JA	Sloan J	Thompson R	Wildon LE	Wilkinson K	Willetts J
1	Aug 21	ROCHDALE	6-1	Price,Hawkins 2,Richardson 2,Watson(og)	10383				4			8		5	7	6				11			10	9	1			3		2	
2	25	Darlington	0-2		12393				4			8		5	7	6				11			10	9	1			3		2	
3	28	New Brighton	1-1	Richardson	9093				4			8		5	7	6				11			10	9	1			3		2	
4	30	DARLINGTON	0-1		14585				4			8		5	7	6				11			10	9	1			3		2	
5	Sep 4	CHESTER	2-1	Hooper (p), Hawkins	9181				4			10	2	5	7	6				11			8	9	1			3			
6	6	Rotherham United	1-2	Richardson	15468							10	2	5	7	6				11			8	9	1			3		4	
7	11	Southport	2-1	Isaac, Richardson	7801				4			10	2	5	7	6				11				9	1			3	8		
8	13	ROTHERHAM UNITED	1-4	Richardson	12777				4			10	2	5	7	6				11				9	1		8	3			
9	18	CREWE ALEXANDRA	4-1	Nevins, Richardson 3	9279				4			10	2	5	7	6				11				9	1		8	3			
10	25	York City	0-4		10706				4		11	10	2	5								7		9	1		8	3		6	
11	Oct 2	STOCKPORT COUNTY	0-0		9298				4		11	10	2	5		6							8	9	1			3	7		
12	9	HULL CITY	0-2		17118				4		11	10	2	5	8	6								9	1			3	7		
13	16	Doncaster Rovers	0-0		14766	7			4		11	10		5	8	6									1			3	9	2	
14	23	BRADFORD CITY	1-0	Wildon	8516	7			4		11	10		5	8	6									1			3	9	2	
15	30	Halifax Town	0-2		9735	7			4		11	10		5	8	6									1			3	9	2	
16	Nov 6	WREXHAM	2-2	Moore, Harden	8789		7		4		11	10		5	8	6		9							1			3		2	
17	13	Barrow	0-2		5788		7		4		11			5	8	6	2	9							1		10	3			
18	20	MANSFIELD TOWN	1-1	Isaac	7394		7		4			9		5	8	6	2			11			10		1			3			
19	Dec 4	OLDHAM ATHLETIC	1-2	Harden	6892		7		2	5	11			4	8						6				1		10	3	9		
20	11	Accrington Stanley	2-1	Sherratt 2	3408		7		4		11	10	2	5							6				1	9	8	3			
21	18	Rochdale	1-0	Sloan	5803		7		4		11	10	2	5							6				1	9	8	3			
22	25	Gateshead	1-2	Sherratt	7146		7		4		11	10		5							6				1	9	8	3		2	
23	27	GATESHEAD	1-3	Burnett	9035		7		2	6		10		5								11			1	9	8	3		4	
24	Jan 1	NEW BRIGHTON	3-1	Hughes (p), Sloan 2	7891		7	4		6	11	10		5											1	9	8	3			2
25	8	ACCRINGTON STANLEY	1-0	Hawkins	5724		7		4	6	11	10	2	5											1	9	8	3			
26	15	Chester	0-0		3215		7		4	6	11	10	2	5											1	9	8	3			
27	22	SOUTHPORT	2-2	Sloan 2	7192		7		4	6	11	10	2	5											1	9	8	3			
28	29	Tranmere Rovers	2-0	Sherratt, Burnett	8577		7		4	6	11	10	2	5											1	9	8	3			
29	Feb 5	Crewe Alexandra	0-3		6187		7		4	6	11	10	2	5											1	9	8	3			
30	19	YORK CITY	2-3	Donaldson, Douglas	8148		7		4	6	11	10	2	5											1	9	8	3			
31	26	Stockport County	0-4		6954		7	10	4	2		11		5							6				1	9	8			3	
32	Mar 5	Hull City	0-2		35357		7	10	4	6	11		2	5											1		8	3	9		
33	12	DONCASTER ROVERS	2-1	Hughes, Sloan	6925				10	4	11		2	5					7		6				1	9	8	3			
34	19	Bradford City	0-0		7452				10	4	11		2	5					7		6				1	9	8	3			
35	26	HALIFAX TOWN	0-0		4756				4		11		2	5	10				7		6				1	9	8	3			
36	Apr 2	Wrexham	0-1		4538		7		4	10	11		2	5							6				1	9	8	3			
37	9	BARROW	1-0	Summerbee (og)	5435		7		4	10	11		2	5	8						6				1			3	9		
38	15	CARLISLE UNITED	1-0	Nevins	8874		7		4	10			2	5	8					11	6				1			3	9		
39	16	Mansfield Town	0-1		9017		7		4	6			2	5						11	10				1	8		3	9		
40	18	Carlisle United	0-0		7055				4	6	11		2	5				10	7						1	8		3	9		
41	23	TRANMERE ROVERS	3-0	Wildon 2, Burnett	6527		7		10	4	11		2	5							6				1	8		3	9		
42	30	Oldham Athletic	1-5	Sloan	12898		7		4		11		2	5							6				1	8	10	3	9		
					Apps	3	23	3	40	19	28	29	27	42	20	17	2	3	4	12	14	2	8	12	42	20	23	41	14	13	1
					Goals		3		1	1	2	4	1	2	2			1		2			1	9		4	7		3		

Two own goals

F.A. Cup

						Brownlow JM	Burnett WJ	Cairns JG	Donaldson RS	Douglas JS	Harden LJ	Hawkins H	Hooper HR	Hughes WH	Isaac J	Jones H	Leonard H	Moore W	Morris D	Nevins L	Newton JL	O'Connor VJ	Price J	Richardson F	Rimmington N	Sherratt JA	Sloan J	Thompson R	Wildon LE	Wilkinson K	Willetts J
R1	Nov 27	CHESTER	1-3	Price	8563		7		4			9		5	8		2			11	6		10		1			3			

		P	W	D	L	F	A	W	D	L	F	A	Pts
1	Hull City	42	17	1	3	65	14	10	10	1	28	14	65
2	Rotherham United	42	16	4	1	47	17	12	2	7	43	29	62
3	Doncaster Rovers	42	10	8	3	26	12	10	2	9	27	28	50
4	Darlington	42	10	3	8	42	36	10	3	8	41	38	46
5	Gateshead	42	10	6	5	41	28	6	7	8	28	30	45
6	Oldham Athletic	42	12	4	5	49	28	6	5	10	26	39	45
7	Rochdale	42	14	3	4	37	16	4	6	11	18	37	45
8	Stockport County	42	13	5	3	44	16	3	6	12	17	40	43
9	Wrexham	42	12	6	3	35	22	5	3	13	21	40	43
10	Mansfield Town	42	13	6	2	39	15	1	8	12	13	33	42
11	Tranmere Rovers	42	8	9	4	23	19	5	6	10	23	38	41
12	Crewe Alexandra	42	13	4	4	31	18	3	5	13	21	56	41
13	Barrow	42	10	8	3	27	13	4	4	13	14	35	40
14	York City	42	11	3	7	49	28	4	6	11	25	46	39
15	Carlisle United	42	12	7	2	46	32	2	4	15	14	45	39
16	HARTLEPOOLS UTD.	42	10	5	6	34	25	4	5	12	11	33	38
17	New Brighton	42	10	4	7	25	19	4	4	13	21	39	36
18	Chester	42	10	7	4	36	19	1	6	14	21	37	35
19	Halifax Town	42	8	4	9	26	27	4	7	10	19	35	35
20	Accrington Stanley	42	11	4	6	39	23	1	6	14	16	41	34
21	Southport	42	6	5	10	24	29	5	4	12	21	35	31
22	Bradford City	42	7	6	8	29	31	3	3	15	19	46	29

1949/50 18th in Division 3(N)

	Date	Opponent	Score	Scorers	Att.	Briggs W	Burnett WJ	Cairns JG	Clarke JH	Denham JW	Donaldson RS	Douglas JS	Dunn R	Harden LJ	Holmes S	Hooper HR	Hughes WH	Johnson K	Kerr P	McCready TS	Miller W	Moore W	Morris D	Newton JL	Owens TL	Ramsden B	Rimmington N	Sloan J	Stamper FFT	Sykes K	Thompson R	Vitty R	Wildon LE	Willetts J
1	Aug 20	Halifax Town	2-1	Burnett, Mycock (og)	9002		7				4		8	11		2	5			10				6	9		1				3			
2	22	NEW BRIGHTON	2-0	Owens, Dunn	9738		7				4	5	8	11		2				10				6	9		1				3			
3	27	ROCHDALE	1-2	Owens	10519		7				4	5	8	11		2				10				6	9		1				3			
4	31	New Brighton	0-1		6225		7				8	5		11					4	10				6	9		1				3	2		
5	Sep 3	Bradford City	3-1	Newton, McCready, Owens (p)	10463		7				4	5		11						10				6	9		1		8		3	2		
6	5	GATESHEAD	3-5	Harden 2, Burnett	12078		7				4	5		11						10				6	9		1		8		3	2		
7	10	CHESTER	5-1	Owens 4, Harden	9341	1	7				4		8	11			5			10				6	9						3	2		
8	17	Southport	1-2	Dunn	7663	1	7				4		8	11			5			10				6	9						3	2		
9	24	STOCKPORT COUNTY	1-0	Owens	10036	1					4			11		2	5		7	10				6	9						3		8	
10	Oct 1	Doncaster Rovers	0-0		16155	1	7				4			11		2	5			10				6	9						3		8	
11	8	LINCOLN CITY	2-1	Wildon, Harden	10871	1	7				4			11		2	5			8				6	9						3		10	
12	15	Rotherham United	1-5	Wildon	10721		7				4			11		2	5			8				6			1	9			3		10	
13	22	CARLISLE UNITED	1-5	Moore	10145	1					4			11		2	5			8		9	7	6							3		10	
14	29	Mansfield Town	1-7	McCready	13166	1	7			3	4		10	11		2	5			8				6	9									
15	Nov 5	ACCRINGTON STANLEY	0-0		6689	1	7				4			11		2	5			8				6	9						3		10	
16	12	Wrexham	0-1		7836		7				4			11			5			8				6	9		1				3		10	2
17	19	OLDHAM ATHLETIC	0-2		6669		7				4	6		11			5			8					9		1				3		10	2
18	Dec 3	TRANMERE ROVERS	2-0	Wildon 2	6423		7		9		4			11			5							6	8		1				3		10	2
19	17	HALIFAX TOWN	3-3	Burnett, Owens 2	3896		7							11			5							6	9		1	8	4		3		10	2
20	24	Rochdale	0-4		7439	1					7	4		11		3	5			8				6	9								10	2
21	26	Barrow	0-0		8476	1	7		9		4					3	5			10				6	8								11	2
22	27	BARROW	2-3	Sloan, Willetts (p)	6910	1			7		4			11		3	5							6	9			8					10	2
23	31	BRADFORD CITY	3-0	Owens, Burnett, Johnson	7283	1	7						10			3		8				5		6	9				4				11	2
24	Jan 2	Gateshead	0-2		9813	1	7						10			3						5		6	9			8	4				11	2
25	14	Chester	0-3		5138	1	7						8	11	2					10		5		4	9				6					3
26	21	SOUTHPORT	1-0	Harrison (og)	5789	1							8							10		5	7	4	9	2			6				11	3
27	28	York City	2-0	Clarke, Cairns	5913	1	7	10	9				8									5		4		2			6				11	3
28	Feb 4	Stockport County	0-1		20873	1	7	10	9				8									5		4		2			6				11	3
29	11	Crewe Alexandra	0-1		6552	1		10	9				8									5	7	4		2			6				11	3
30	18	DONCASTER ROVERS	1-1	Wildon	9523	1	7	10												8		5		4	9	2			6				11	3
31	25	Oldham Athletic	1-3	Cairns	8041	1	7	8												10		5		4	9	2			6				11	3
32	Mar 4	YORK CITY	2-0	Owens, McCready	6134	1	7	8												10	4	5		6	9	2							11	3
33	11	Carlisle United	1-2	Wildon	8219	1	7	8			2									10		5		4	9				6				11	3
34	18	MANSFIELD TOWN	1-3	Wildon	5555	1	7	8	9											10		5		4		2			6				11	3
35	25	Accrington Stanley	2-1	Harden, Webster (og)	4771		7				4			11						10		5		6		2	1	8					9	3
36	Apr 1	WREXHAM	3-1	Sloan, Newton, Burnett	5200		7				4			11						10		5		6		2	1	8					9	3
37	7	DARLINGTON	2-0	Burnett, Sloan	9383		7				4			11						10		5		6		2	1	8					9	3
38	8	Lincoln City	0-6		9116		7				4			11				8		10		5				2	1	9	6					3
39	10	Darlington	0-1		4480		7				4			11			6			10		5					1	8		3			9	2
40	15	ROTHERHAM UNITED	1-2	Morris	5951						4			11						10		5	7			2	1	8	6				9	3
41	22	Tranmere Rovers	1-2	Harden	6194						4	6		11						10		5	7				1	8				2	9	3
42	29	CREWE ALEXANDRA	1-6	Wildon	3662			6			4			11						10		5	7				1	8				2	9	3
					Apps	23	33	9	7	1	30	8	13	30	1	15	18	2	2	34	1	21	6	36	28	13	19	12	16	1	18	7	31	27
					Goals		6	2	1				2	6				1		3		1	1	2	12			3					8	1

Three own goals

F.A. Cup

	Date	Opponent	Score	Scorers	Att.	Briggs W	Burnett WJ	Cairns JG	Clarke JH	Denham JW	Donaldson RS	Douglas JS	Dunn R	Harden LJ	Holmes S	Hooper HR	Hughes WH	Johnson K	Kerr P	McCready TS	Miller W	Moore W	Morris D	Newton JL	Owens TL	Ramsden B	Rimmington N	Sloan J	Stamper FFT	Sykes K	Thompson R	Vitty R	Wildon LE	Willetts J
R1	Nov 26	Accrington Stanley	1-0	Owens	8000		7				4			11			5			8				6	9		1				3		10	2
R2	Dec 10	NORWICH CITY	1-1	Clarke	11144				9		4			11			5			7				6	8		1				3		10	2
rep	15	Norwich City	1-5	Harden	18064		7		9		4			11			5							6	8		1				3		10	2

		P	W	D	L	F	A	W	D	L	F	A	Pts
1	Doncaster Rovers	42	9	9	3	30	15	10	8	3	36	23	55
2	Gateshead	42	13	5	3	51	23	10	2	9	36	31	53
3	Rochdale	42	15	3	3	42	13	6	6	9	26	28	51
4	Lincoln City	42	14	5	2	35	9	7	4	10	25	30	51
5	Tranmere Rovers	42	15	3	3	35	21	4	8	9	16	27	49
6	Rotherham United	42	10	6	5	46	28	9	4	8	34	31	48
7	Crewe Alexandra	42	10	6	5	38	27	7	8	6	30	28	48
8	Mansfield Town	42	12	4	5	37	20	6	8	7	29	34	48
9	Carlisle United	42	12	6	3	39	20	4	9	8	29	31	47
10	Stockport County	42	14	2	5	33	21	5	5	11	22	31	45
11	Oldham Athletic	42	10	4	7	32	31	6	7	8	26	32	43
12	Chester	42	12	3	6	47	33	5	3	13	23	46	40
13	Accrington Stanley	42	12	5	4	41	21	4	2	15	16	41	39
14	New Brighton	42	10	5	6	27	25	4	5	12	18	38	38
15	Barrow	42	9	6	6	27	20	5	3	13	20	33	37
16	Southport	42	7	10	4	29	26	5	3	13	22	45	37
17	Darlington	42	9	8	4	35	27	2	5	14	21	42	35
18	HARTLEPOOLS UTD.	42	10	3	8	37	35	4	2	15	15	44	33
19	Bradford City	42	11	1	9	38	32	1	7	13	23	44	32
20	Wrexham	42	8	7	6	24	17	2	5	14	15	37	32
21	Halifax Town	42	9	5	7	35	31	3	3	15	23	54	32
22	York City	42	6	7	8	29	33	3	6	12	23	37	31

1950/51 16th in Division 3(N)

No.	Month	Date	Opponent	Score	Scorers	Att.	Bain WC	Ballantyne JD	Briggs W	Burnett WJ	Derbyshire T	Donaldson RS	Harden LJ	McClure W	McGuigan T	McKeown J	Moore W	Morris D	Newton JL	Ollerenshaw J	Rimmington N	Sales RD	Sloan J	Stamper FFT	Thompson R	Whitelock A	Wildon LE	Willetts J
1	Aug	19	CREWE ALEXANDRA	0-2		10359	9		1	7				11	8	4			6	2		5			3		10	
2		21	York City	0-3		10522	9		1	7				11	8	4			6	2		5			3		10	
3		26	New Brighton	0-1		6079			1	7		4		11	10	8	5		6						3		9	2
4		28	YORK CITY	4-1	McGuigan 2, Wildon, Willetts (p)	8648			1	7		4		11	10	8	5		6						3		9	2
5	Sep	2	BRADFORD CITY	1-1	Wildon	9107			1	7		4		11	10	8	5		6						3		9	2
6		7	Carlisle United	0-1		14780			1	7		4		11	10	8	5							6	3		9	2
7		9	Rochdale	1-3	McGuigan	9146			1	7		4		11	10	8	5							6	3		9	2
8		11	CARLISLE UNITED	3-3	Willetts (p), McKeown, Wildon	8654			1	7		4		11	10	8	5							6	3		9	2
9		16	CHESTER	1-2	McKeown	8773			1	7		4		11	10	8	5							6	3		9	2
10		23	Shrewsbury Town	0-1		9268				7		4		11	10	8	5		6		1		9		3			2
11		30	LINCOLN CITY	2-2	Wildon 2	6729				7		4		11	10	8	5		6		1				3		9	2
12	Oct	7	WREXHAM	4-1	Wildon 4	8386				7		4		11	10	8	5		6		1				3		9	2
13		14	Oldham Athletic	1-5	McGuigan	11831				7				11	10	8	5		6		1			4	3		9	2
14		21	MANSFIELD TOWN	1-1	Wildon	8524				7				11	10	8	5		4		1			6	3		9	2
15		28	Scunthorpe United	0-0		10576				7				11	10	8	5		4		1			6	3		9	2
16	Nov	4	BARROW	6-1	Wildon 3, McClure 2, McGuigan	5783				7				11	10	8	5		4		1			6	3		9	2
17		11	Rotherham United	1-2	Noble (og)	10440				7				11	10	8	5		4		1			6	3		9	2
18		18	BRADFORD PARK AVE.	3-1	Wildon 3	7536				7				11	10	8	5		4		1			6	3		9	2
19	Dec	2	SOUTHPORT	3-2	Wildon 2, Burnett	7868				7				11	10	8	5		4		1			6	3		9	2
20		16	Crewe Alexandra	1-3	Donaldson	3741				7		9		11	10	8	5		4		1			6	3			2
21		23	NEW BRIGHTON	0-1		4520				7				11	10	8	5		4		1			6	3		9	2
22		25	Gateshead	1-0	Wildon	8595				7		4		11	10	6	5				1		8		3		9	2
23		26	GATESHEAD	3-0	Burnett, McGuigan, McKeown	9269				7		4		11	10	8	5		6		1				3		9	2
24		30	Bradford City	1-3	Wildon	7772				7		4		11	10	8	5		6		1				3		9	2
25	Jan	6	HALIFAX TOWN	5-2	McClure 3, Wildon 2	2987				7		2		11	10	8	5		4		1			6			9	3
26		13	ROCHDALE	0-0		7585				7				11	10	8	5		4		1	3		6			9	2
27		20	Chester	1-2	McClure	4809				7		4		11	10	8	5		6		1			3			9	2
28		27	Halifax Town	0-1		6674				7		4		11	10	8	5		6		1			3			9	2
29	Feb	3	SHREWSBURY TOWN	1-0	Fisher (og)	7081				7				11	10	8	5		4		1			6	3		9	2
30		10	STOCKPORT COUNTY	2-0	McKeown, McClure	7162				7				11	10	8	5		4		1			6	3		9	2
31		17	Lincoln City	0-1		10336				7		4		11	10	8			6		1			5	3		9	2
32		24	Wrexham	0-1		7386				7		4		11		8	5		6		1			9	3		10	2
33	Mar	3	OLDHAM ATHLETIC	0-1		8075				7		4		11	8	3	5		6		1			10			9	2
34		10	Mansfield Town	0-1		7282						7		11	10	8	5		4		1			6		2	9	3
35		17	SCUNTHORPE UNITED	4-2	McKeown 2, McClure, Wildon	5365			1	7				11	10	8	5		4					6		2	9	3
36		23	DARLINGTON	6-1	Willetts 3(3p),McKeown,McClure,Wildon	10003			1	7				11	10	8	5		4					6		2	9	3
37		24	Barrow	0-3		6289			1	7				11	10	8	5		4					6		2	9	3
38		26	Darlington	1-0	McClure	4498			1	7				11	10	8	5		4					6	3		9	2
39		31	ROTHERHAM UNITED	3-1	Wildon, Harden, Noble (og)	8706			1	7			11		10	8	5		4					6	3		9	2
40	Apr	7	Bradford Park Avenue	1-1	Newton	6910			1	7			11		10	8	5		4					6	3		9	2
41		14	TRANMERE ROVERS	2-1	Newton, McGuigan	7626			1	7		4		11	10	8			6					5	3		9	2
42		17	Tranmere Rovers	0-1		7999			1	7		4		11	10	8			6					5	3		9	2
43		21	Southport	0-3		3990			1	7		4		11	10	8			6					5		2	9	3
44		25	Accrington Stanley	0-2		4091		2	1	8				11		4	5	7					9	6			10	3
45		28	ACCRINGTON STANLEY	1-0	Wildon	3568		4	1	7				11		8	5						9	6		2	10	3
46	May	5	Stockport County	0-2		6005		3		7	1			11		8	5		4				9	6			10	2
						Apps	2	3	20	45	1	24	2	44	42	46	40	1	39	2	25	3	5	35	33	6	44	44
						Goals				2		1	1	10	7	7			2								26	5

Three own goals

F.A. Cup

Rd	Month	Date	Opponent	Score	Scorers	Att.	Bain WC	Ballantyne JD	Briggs W	Burnett WJ	Derbyshire T	Donaldson RS	Harden LJ	McClure W	McGuigan T	McKeown J	Moore W	Morris D	Newton JL	Ollerenshaw J	Rimmington N	Sales RD	Sloan J	Stamper FFT	Thompson R	Whitelock A	Wildon LE	Willetts J
R1	Nov	25	Worcester City	4-1	McGuigan 2, Burnett, Wildon	10000				7				11	10	8	5		4		1			6	3		9	2
R2	Dec	9	OLDHAM ATHLETIC	1-2	Stamper	15360				7				11	10	8	5		4		1			6	3		9	2

		P	W	D	L	F	A	W	D	L	F	A	Pts
1	Rotherham United	46	16	3	4	55	16	15	6	2	48	25	71
2	Mansfield Town	46	17	6	0	54	19	9	6	8	24	29	64
3	Carlisle United	46	18	4	1	44	17	7	8	8	35	33	62
4	Tranmere Rovers	46	15	5	3	51	26	9	6	8	32	36	59
5	Lincoln City	46	18	1	4	62	23	7	7	9	27	35	58
6	Bradford Park Ave.	46	15	3	5	46	23	8	5	10	44	49	54
7	Bradford City	46	13	4	6	55	30	8	6	9	35	33	52
8	Gateshead	46	17	1	5	60	21	4	7	12	24	41	50
9	Crewe Alexandra	46	11	5	7	38	26	8	5	10	23	34	48
10	Stockport County	46	15	3	5	45	26	5	5	13	18	37	48
11	Rochdale	46	11	6	6	38	18	6	5	12	31	44	45
12	Scunthorpe United	46	10	12	1	32	9	3	6	14	26	48	44
13	Chester	46	11	6	6	42	30	6	3	14	20	34	43
14	Wrexham	46	12	6	5	37	28	3	6	14	18	43	42
15	Oldham Athletic	46	10	5	8	47	36	6	3	14	26	37	40
16	HARTLEPOOLS UTD.	46	14	5	4	55	26	2	2	19	9	40	39
17	York City	46	7	12	4	37	24	5	3	15	29	53	39
18	Darlington	46	10	8	5	35	29	3	5	15	24	48	39
19	Barrow	46	12	3	8	38	27	4	3	16	13	49	38
20	Shrewsbury Town	46	11	3	9	28	30	4	4	15	15	44	37
21	Southport	46	9	4	10	29	25	4	6	13	27	47	36
22	Halifax Town	46	11	6	6	36	24	0	6	17	14	45	34
23	Accrington Stanley	46	10	4	9	28	29	1	6	16	14	72	32
24	New Brighton	46	7	6	10	22	32	4	2	17	18	58	30

1951/52 9th in Division 3(N)

No	Month	Day	Opponent	Score	Scorers	Att	Ballantyne JD	Briggs W	Brown RB	Burnett WJ	Donaldson RS	Elder AYP	Harden LJ	McClure W	McGuigan T	Moore W	Morrison GC	Newton JL	Richley L	Rimmington N	Sloan J	Stamper FFT	Thompson R	Wildon LE	Willetts J	Willox A
1	Aug	18	Tranmere Rovers	1-4	McGuigan	10406		1		7				11	10	5		4				6	3	8	2	9
2		20	CREWE ALEXANDRA	3-0	Wildon, McGuigan, McClure	11394			1	7		8		11	10	5		4				6	3	9	2	
3		25	SCUNTHORPE UNITED	3-1	Wildon, Willetts(p), Elder	9028			1	7		8		11	10	5		4				6	3	9	2	
4		29	Crewe Alexandra	2-4	Willetts (p), McClure	4804			1	7		8		11	10	5		4				6	3	9	2	
5	Sep	1	Lincoln City	3-4	Wildon, Elder 2	11888			1	7		8		11	10	5		4				6	3	9	2	
6		3	GATESHEAD	1-0	Wildon	12225				7		8		11	10	5		4		1		6	3	9	2	
7		8	CHESTER	2-1	Harden 2	11053				7		8	11		10	5		4		1		6	3	9	2	
8		10	Gateshead	0-2		9367				7		8	11		10	5		4		1		6	3	9	2	
9		15	York City	1-3	Wildon	5935				7	4	8	11		10	2	5			1		6		9	3	
10		19	Darlington	1-2	Moore	5082	3			7	4	8	11		10	5				1		6		9	2	
11		22	BRADFORD CITY	2-1	Wildon, McClure	8483	3			7	4	8		11	10	5				1		6		9	2	
12		29	HALIFAX TOWN	6-1	Sloan 2, McGuigan 3, McClure	8979	3			7	4	8		11	10	5				1	9	6			2	
13	Oct	6	Rochdale	0-3		5574	3			7	4	8		11	10	5				1	9	6			2	
14		13	ACCRINGTON STANLEY	4-2	Elder 2, McClure, Burnett	8617	3			7	4	8		11	10	5				1		6		9	2	
15		20	Carlisle United	1-2	Wildon	8893	3			7	4	8		11	10	5				1		6		9	2	
16		27	STOCKPORT COUNTY	0-1		9280	3			7	4	8		11	10	5				1		6		9	2	
17	Nov	3	Workington	1-1	Elder	6152	3			7		8	11		10	5		4		1		6		9	2	
18		10	BARROW	3-1	Wildon, Elder, Willetts (p)	8372	3			7		8		11	10	5		4		1		6		9	2	
19		17	Grimsby Town	0-2		12296	3			7		8		11	10	5		4		1		6		9	2	
20	Dec	1	Chesterfield	2-2	Elder, Wildon	9552			1	7		8			10	5	9	4	6				3	11	2	
21		8	BRADFORD PARK AVE.	2-1	Wildon 2	5973			1	7		8		11	10	5		4	6				3	9	2	
22		22	Scunthorpe United	0-2		7320			1	7			11	10	8	5		4	6				3	9	2	
23		25	MANSFIELD TOWN	2-0	Wildon, Newton	10542			1	7			11	10	8	5		4	6				3	9	2	
24		26	Mansfield Town	1-0	McClure	9185			1	7				11	10	5		4	6				3	8	2	9
25		29	LINCOLN CITY	1-1	Wildon	11420			1	7				11	10	5		4	6				3	8	2	9
26	Jan	1	WREXHAM	1-0	Newton	8910			1	7		8		11	10	5		4	6				3	9	2	
27		5	Chester	3-3	McGuigan, Willetts (p), Wildon	4902			1	7				11	10	5		4	6			8	3	9	2	
28		16	SOUTHPORT	3-1	Stamper, Willetts (p), McGuigan	5844			1	7				11	10	5		4	6			8	3	9	2	
29		19	YORK CITY	3-2	Stamper 2, Wildon	9168			1	7				11	10	5		4	6			8	3	9	2	
30		26	Bradford City	2-0	McClure, Stamper	13717			1	7				11	10	5		4	6			8	3	9	2	
31	Feb	2	Southport	0-2		4107			1	7				11	10	5		4	6			8	3	9	2	
32		9	Halifax Town	0-2		5503			1	7				11	10	5		4	6			8	3		2	9
33		16	ROCHDALE	1-1	Elder	8403			1	7		8		11	10	5		4	6				3	9	2	
34		23	DARLINGTON	2-0	Howe (og), Wildon	9516			1			8		11	10	5		4	6				3	9	2	7
35	Mar	1	Accrington Stanley	0-0		4755			1	8		9		11	10	5		4	6				3		2	7
36		8	CARLISLE UNITED	1-0	Stamper	9233			1	7		8		11		5		4	6			10	3	9	2	
37		15	Stockport County	1-0	Wildon	11020			1	7		8		11	10	5		4	6				3	9	2	
38		22	WORKINGTON	0-1		8175			1	7		8		11	10	5		4	6				3	9	2	
39		29	Barrow	1-2	McGuigan	2264			1	7		8		11	10	5		4	6			9	3		2	
40	Apr	5	GRIMSBY TOWN	2-1	Stamper, Burnett	9063			1	7		8		11	10	5		4	6			9	3		2	
41		11	Oldham Athletic	2-5	Willetts (p), McClure	15972			1	7		8		11	10	5		4	6			9	3		2	
42		12	Wrexham	0-0		7788			1	7				11	10	5		4	6			9	3	8	2	
43		14	OLDHAM ATHLETIC	1-1	Newton	12013			1	7				11	10	5		4	6			9	3	8	2	
44		19	CHESTERFIELD	4-1	Elder, Burnett, Wildon, Willetts (p)	8665			1	7	4	8		11		5			6			9	3	10	2	
45		26	Bradford Park Avenue	2-1	Wildon, McClure	7415			1	7		8		11	10	5			6			4	3	9	2	
46		30	TRANMERE ROVERS	0-1		8342			1	7		8		11	10	5			6			4	3	9	2	
						Apps	10	1	31	45	9	33	7	40	44	46	2	35	27	14	2	34	35	39	46	6
						Goals				3		10	2	9	8	1		3			2	6		19	7	

One own goal

F.A. Cup

Rd	Month	Day	Opponent	Score	Scorers	Att	Ballantyne JD	Briggs W	Brown RB	Burnett WJ	Donaldson RS	Elder AYP	Harden LJ	McClure W	McGuigan T	Moore W	Morrison GC	Newton JL	Richley L	Rimmington N	Sloan J	Stamper FFT	Thompson R	Wildon LE	Willetts J	Willox A
R1	Nov	24	RHYL	2-0	Elder, Harden	13037				7		8	11		10	5		4		1		6	3	9	2	
R2	Dec	15	Watford	2-1	McClure, Burnett	15108			1	7		8		11	10	5		4	6				3	9	2	
R3	Jan	12	Burnley	0-1		38608			1	7				11	10	5		4	6			8	3	9	2	

		P	W	D	L	F	A	W	D	L	F	A	Pts
1	Lincoln City	46	19	2	2	80	23	11	7	5	41	29	69
2	Grimsby Town	46	19	2	2	59	14	10	6	7	37	31	66
3	Stockport County	46	12	9	2	47	17	11	4	8	27	23	59
4	Oldham Athletic	46	19	2	2	65	22	5	7	11	25	39	57
5	Gateshead	46	14	7	2	41	17	7	4	12	25	32	53
6	Mansfield Town	46	17	3	3	50	23	5	5	13	23	37	52
7	Carlisle United	46	10	7	6	31	24	9	6	8	31	33	51
8	Bradford Park Ave.	46	13	6	4	51	28	6	6	11	23	36	50
9	HARTLEPOOLS UTD.	46	17	3	3	47	19	4	5	14	24	46	50
10	York City	46	16	4	3	53	19	2	9	12	20	33	49
11	Tranmere Rovers	46	17	2	4	59	29	4	4	15	17	42	48
12	Barrow	46	13	5	5	33	19	4	7	12	24	42	46
13	Chesterfield	46	15	7	1	47	16	2	4	17	18	50	45
14	Scunthorpe United	46	10	11	2	39	23	4	5	14	26	51	44
15	Bradford City	46	12	5	6	40	32	4	5	14	21	36	42
16	Crewe Alexandra	46	12	6	5	42	28	5	2	16	21	54	42
17	Southport	46	12	6	5	36	22	3	5	15	17	49	41
18	Wrexham	46	14	5	4	41	22	1	4	18	22	51	39
19	Chester	46	13	4	6	46	30	2	5	16	26	55	39
20	Halifax Town	46	11	4	8	31	23	3	3	17	30	74	35
21	Rochdale	46	10	5	8	32	34	1	8	14	15	45	35
22	Accrington Stanley	46	6	8	9	30	34	4	4	15	31	58	32
23	Darlington	46	10	5	8	39	34	1	4	18	25	69	31
24	Workington	46	8	4	11	33	34	3	3	17	17	57	29

1952/53 17th in Division 3(N)

						Brown RB	Burnett WJ	Elder AYP	Harden LJ	Johnson K	McClure W	McGuigan T	Moore W	Newton JL	Pearson JG	Powton B	Richardson F	Richley L	Stamper FFT	Thompson R	Todd A	Weatherspoon C	Wildon LE	Willetts J
1	Aug 23	ACCRINGTON STANLEY	4-1	McGuigan, Elder, Weatherspoon, McClure	10765	1	7	8			11	10	5					6	4	3		9		2
2	25	Halifax Town	2-3	McGuigan, Willetts (p)	9246	1	7	8			11	10	5					6	4	3		9		2
3	30	Carlisle United	1-4	Weatherspoon	10876	1	7	8			11	10	5					6	4	3		9		2
4	Sep 1	HALIFAX TOWN	0-0		10826	1				7	11	10	5	4				6	8	3			9	2
5	6	SOUTHPORT	3-0	Willetts(p), Elder, Wildon	8452	1	7	8			11	10	5	4					6	3			9	2
6	8	Gateshead	1-1	Elder	3147	1	7	8			11	10	5	4					6	3			9	2
7	13	Crewe Alexandra	0-2		5581	1	7	8			11	10	5	4					6	3			9	2
8	15	GATESHEAD	0-0		8370	1	7	8			11	10	5	4					6	3			9	2
9	20	PORT VALE	2-0	McClure, Wildon	9945	1	7	8			11	10	5	4					6	3			9	2
10	22	YORK CITY	2-1	Wildon, Willetts (p)	9626	1	7	8			11	10	5	4					6	3			9	2
11	27	Chester	1-0	Elder	4110	1	7	8			11	10	5					4	6	3			9	2
12	Oct 1	Bradford City	1-1	Wildon	2265	1	7	8			11	10	5	4					6	3			9	2
13	4	SCUNTHORPE UNITED	1-1	Elder	9060	1	7	8			11	10	5	4					6	3			9	2
14	11	MANSFIELD TOWN	2-0	Wildon, Elder	8554	1	7	8			11	10	5					4	6	3			9	2
15	18	Oldham Athletic	2-4	Wildon 2	17833	1	7	8			11	10	5					4	6	3			9	2
16	25	BRADFORD PARK AVE.	0-1		9554		7	8			11	10	5			1		4	6	3			9	2
17	Nov 1	Wrexham	2-3	Elder, McClure	9243		7	8			11	10	5	4		1		6	3				9	2
18	8	BARROW	2-0	Wildon, Stamper	7396			8			11	7	5	4		1		6	10	3			9	2
19	15	Grimsby Town	0-7		13096			8			11	7	5	4		1		6	10	3			9	2
20	29	Tranmere Rovers	2-0	Elder, McGuigan	5473	1	7	8				10		4			9	6	5	3			11	2
21	Dec 13	Workington	1-1	McGuigan	4083	1		8			11	10	5	4			9	6	3				7	2
22	20	Accrington Stanley	1-1	Elder	3195	1		8			11	10	5	4			9	6	3				7	2
23	25	Stockport County	1-1	McGuigan	8891	1	7	8			11	10	5	4			9	6	3					2
24	27	STOCKPORT COUNTY	0-2		7387	1	7	8			11	10	5	4			9	6	3					2
25	Jan 1	BRADFORD CITY	0-0		5999	1		8			11	10	5	4			9	6		3			7	2
26	3	CARLISLE UNITED	1-0	Willetts (p)	5773	1	7				11	10	5	4			9		6	3			8	2
27	10	DARLINGTON	1-0	Howe (og)	7787	1	7				11	10	5	4			9		6	3			8	2
28	17	Southport	0-0		4592	1	7				11	10	5	4			9		6	3			8	2
29	24	CREWE ALEXANDRA	2-1	Richardson, McClure	7209	1	7				11	10	5	4			9		6	3			8	2
30	31	Darlington	0-3		4879	1	7				11	10	5	4			9		6	3			8	2
31	Feb 7	Port Vale	0-3		13919	1	7	8			11	10	5	4			9		6	3				2
32	14	CHESTER	2-2	Harden, Wildon	6499	1	7		11			10	5	4			9		6	3			8	2
33	21	Scunthorpe United	0-0		7076	1	7		11			8	5	4			9		6	3			10	2
34	28	Mansfield Town	0-2		6720	1	7		11			8	5	4			9		6	3			10	2
35	Mar 7	OLDHAM ATHLETIC	4-1	Burnett, Newton, Richardson, McClure	9421	1	7	8			11	10	5	4			9		6	3				2
36	14	Bradford Park Avenue	1-1	McGuigan	6006	1	7	8			11	10	5	4			9		6	3				2
37	21	WREXHAM	1-2	Richardson	7919	1	7	8			11	10	5	4			9		6	3				2
38	28	Barrow	1-2	Elder	4061	1	7	8			11		5	4			9		6	3	10			2
39	Apr 3	ROCHDALE	2-1	Harden, Newton	8777	1	7	8	11			10	5	4			9	6		3				2
40	4	GRIMSBY TOWN	2-0	Harden 2	8714	1	7	8	11			10	5	4			9	6		3				2
41	6	Rochdale	1-3	Richardson	3378	1	7	8	11			10	5	4			9	6		3				2
42	11	York City	0-1		7939	1	7		11	8		10	5	4	2		9	6						3
43	18	TRANMERE ROVERS	4-1	Johnson, McGuigan, Harden, Steele (og)	6357	1	7		11	8		10	5	4			9	6		3				2
44	20	CHESTERFIELD	2-0	McGuigan, Wildon	6996	1			11	8		10	5	4			9	6		3			7	2
45	25	Chesterfield	0-2		6511	1			11	8		10	5	4			9	6		3			7	2
46	29	WORKINGTON	2-2	Wildon, McGuigan	4327	1			11	8		10	5	4			9	6		3			7	2
					Apps	42	37	32	11	6	34	45	45	39	1	4	27	25	37	40	1	3	31	46
					Goals		1	10	5	1	5	9		2			4		1			2	11	4

Two own goals

F.A. Cup

						Brown RB	Burnett WJ	Elder AYP	Harden LJ	Johnson K	McClure W	McGuigan T	Moore W	Newton JL	Pearson JG	Powton B	Richardson F	Richley L	Stamper FFT	Thompson R	Todd A	Weatherspoon C	Wildon LE	Willetts J
R1	Nov 22	Chester	1-0	McClure	6778	1	7	8			11	10	5	4				6	3				9	2
R2	Dec 6	Tranmere Rovers	1-2	Elder	11297	1	7	8			11	10		4				6	5	3			9	2

		P	W	D	L	F	A	W	D	L	F	A	Pts
1	Oldham Athletic	46	15	4	4	48	21	7	11	5	29	24	59
2	Port Vale	46	13	9	1	41	10	7	9	7	26	25	58
3	Wrexham	46	18	3	2	59	24	6	5	12	27	42	56
4	York City	46	14	5	4	35	16	6	8	9	25	29	53
5	Grimsby Town	46	15	5	3	47	19	6	5	12	28	40	52
6	Southport	46	16	4	3	42	18	4	7	12	21	42	51
7	Bradford Park Ave.	46	10	8	5	37	23	9	4	10	38	38	50
8	Gateshead	46	13	6	4	51	24	4	9	10	25	36	49
9	Carlisle United	46	13	7	3	57	24	5	6	12	25	44	49
10	Crewe Alexandra	46	13	5	5	46	28	7	3	13	24	40	48
11	Stockport County	46	13	8	2	61	26	4	5	14	21	43	47
12	Tranmere Rovers	46	16	4	3	45	16	5	1	17	20	47	47
12	Chesterfield	46	13	6	4	40	23	5	5	13	25	40	47
14	Halifax Town	46	13	5	5	47	31	3	10	10	21	37	47
15	Scunthorpe United	46	10	6	7	38	21	6	8	9	24	35	46
16	Bradford City	46	14	7	2	54	29	0	11	12	21	51	46
17	HARTLEPOOLS UTD.	46	14	6	3	39	16	2	8	13	18	45	46
18	Mansfield Town	46	11	9	3	34	25	5	5	13	21	37	46
19	Barrow	46	15	6	2	48	20	1	6	16	18	51	44
20	Chester	46	10	7	6	39	27	1	8	14	25	58	37
21	Darlington	46	13	4	6	33	27	1	2	20	25	69	34
22	Rochdale	46	12	5	6	41	27	2	0	21	21	56	33
23	Workington	46	9	5	9	40	33	2	5	16	15	58	32
24	Accrington Stanley	46	7	9	7	25	29	1	2	20	14	60	27

1953/54 — 18th in Division 3(N)

	Date	Opponent	Score	Scorers	Att.	Brown RB	Burnett WJ	Cameron J	Clarke N	Corbett AM	Davison E	Desmond P	Harden LJ	Johnson K	Linacre W	Luke GT	MacGregor JP	McGuigan T	McLaughlin J	Moore W	Newton JL	Richardson F	Richley L	Smith J	Stamper FFT	Taylor GL	Thompson R	Todd A	Wildon LE	Wilkinson T	Willetts J
1	Aug 22	Chester	1-1	Johnson	6695				6	1				8	7			10	11		4	9			5		3				2
2	24	YORK CITY	2-2	McLaughlin, McGuigan	11854				6	1				8	7			10	11		4	9			5		3				2
3	29	CREWE ALEXANDRA	0-0		9701					1					7			10	11		4	9	6		5		3		8		2
4	31	York City	0-5		3645					1				8	7			10	11		4	9	6		5		3				2
5	Sep 5	Port Vale	1-3	Burnett	20052		7			1				8				10	11	5		9	6		4		3				2
6	7	SOUTHPORT	1-1	McGuigan	8925		7			1				8				10	11	5		9	4		6		3				2
7	12	BRADFORD PARK AVE.	0-2		8409		7			1					8			10	11	5		9	6		4		3				2
8	15	Southport	1-2	McGuigan	4566	1							11		7			10		5		8			6		3		9	4	2
9	19	Barnsley	2-3	McGuigan, Harden	10757	1							11		7			10		5		8			6		3		9	4	2
10	21	SCUNTHORPE UNITED	3-2	Harden, Johnson, Wildon	6174	1						10	11	8	7					5					6		3		9	4	2
11	26	DARLINGTON	1-0	Wildon	7865	1							11	8	7			10		5					6		3		9	4	2
12	Oct 1	Scunthorpe United	0-0		9102	1							11	8	7			10		5					6		3		9	4	2
13	3	HALIFAX TOWN	2-0	Harden, Wildon	8255	1							11	8	7			10		5					6		3		9	4	2
14	10	Accrington Stanley	0-2		7729	1							11	8	7			10		5					6		3		9	4	2
15	17	GRIMSBY TOWN	3-0	Stamper, Wildon 2	9039	1								8	7	11		10		5					6		3		9	4	2
16	24	Stockport County	0-1		8867	1								8	7	11		10		5					6		3		9	4	2
17	31	ROCHDALE	6-0	Harden 4, Linacre, Johnson	6763	1							11	8	7			10		5					6		3		9	4	2
18	Nov 7	Wrexham	0-2		7106	1							11	8	7			10		5	4	9			6		3				2
19	14	MANSFIELD TOWN	3-1	Wildon, Linacre, Johnson	7128	1							11	8	7			10		5					6		3		9	4	2
20	28	BRADFORD CITY	1-1	Wildon	8353	1							11		7			10		5	4	8			6		3		9		2
21	Dec 5	Chesterfield	1-2	Wildon	7038	1									7			10	11	5	4	8			6		3		9		2
22	19	CHESTER	2-0	Richardson, Wildon	5481	1								9	7			10		5	4	8					3		11	6	2
23	25	Workington	0-0		9103	1							11	7				10		5	4	8					3		9	6	2
24	26	WORKINGTON	2-2	Wildon, Willetts (p)	6731	1							11		7			10		5	4	8	6				3		9		2
25	Jan 1	Tranmere Rovers	2-3	Willetts (p), Wildon	6973	1	7						11					10		5	4	8					3		9	6	2
26	2	Crewe Alexandra	0-3		2938	1	7						11	8				6		5	4	10					3		9		2
27	16	PORT VALE	2-1	McGuigan 2	8554	1							11		7			10		5		8	4				3		9	6	2
28	23	Bradford Park Avenue	0-5		5998	1							11		7			10		5		8	6				3		9	4	2
29	30	Carlisle United	3-2	McGuigan, Richardson 2	5024									8	7			10	11	5	4	9				1	3	6			2
30	Feb 6	BARNSLEY	0-1		7276									8	7			10	11	5	4	9				1	3	6			2
31	20	Halifax Town	0-1		4861									8	7			10	11	5	4	9				1	3	6			2
32	27	ACCRINGTON STANLEY	0-1		7518								11		7			10		5	4	8	6	9		1	3				2
33	Mar 6	Grimsby Town	0-3		5628									8	7			10		5	4	9				1	3		11	6	2
34	13	STOCKPORT COUNTY	6-0	McGuigan 3, Willetts (p), Johnson, Linacre	5879									8	7	11		10		5	4	9	6			1	3				2
35	20	Rochdale	2-2	Johnson, McLaughlin	6583									8	7			10	11	5	4	9	6			1	3				2
36	24	Darlington	1-0	Richardson	3516		7							8		11		10		5	4	9	6			1	3				2
37	27	WREXHAM	1-1	Burnett	6209		7							8				10	11	5	4	9	6			1	3				2
38	Apr 3	Mansfield Town	0-1		5948		7							8	11			10		5	4	9	6			1	3				2
39	5	TRANMERE ROVERS	1-2	Richardson	5010		7				5			8	11			10			4	9	6			1	3				2
40	10	BARROW	2-2	Thompson, Johnson	5328		7						11	8				10		5	4	9	6			1	3				2
41	12	CARLISLE UNITED	1-1	Wildon	5398		7						11	8				10		5	4		6			1	3		9		2
42	16	GATESHEAD	1-0	Wildon	8701								11		7			10		5	4	8	6			1	3		9		2
43	17	Bradford City	1-1	Richardson	7150								11		7		6	10		5	4	8				1	3		9		2
44	19	Gateshead	3-1	Wildon 2, Harden	3962								11		7			10		5	4	8	6			1	3		9		2
45	24	CHESTERFIELD	0-1		6238								11		7			10		5	4	8	6			1	3		9		2
46	26	Barrow	1-1	Johnson	3915			2						10	7					5	4	8			6	1	11		9		3
					Apps	21	11	1	2	7	1	1	24	31	37	4	1	44	13	41	30	36	20	1	22	18	46	3	28	17	46
					Goals		2						8	8	3			10	2			6			1		1		15		3

F.A. Cup

	Date	Opponent	Score	Scorers	Att.	Brown RB	Burnett WJ	Cameron J	Clarke N	Corbett AM	Davison E	Desmond P	Harden LJ	Johnson K	Linacre W	Luke GT	MacGregor JP	McGuigan T	McLaughlin J	Moore W	Newton JL	Richardson F	Richley L	Smith J	Stamper FFT	Taylor GL	Thompson R	Todd A	Wildon LE	Wilkinson T	Willetts J
R1	Nov 21	MANSFIELD TOWN	1-1	Willetts (p)	11779	1								8	7	11		10		5	4				6		3		9		2
rep	25	Mansfield Town	3-0	Wildon, Linacre, Richardson	6237	1									7	11		10		5	4	8			6		3		9		2
R2	Dec 12	Northampton Town	1-1	Harden	18772	1							11		7			10		5	4	8			6		3		9		2
rep	16	NORTHAMPTON T	1-0	Linacre	12169	1								9	7			10		5	4	8			6		3		11		2
R3	Jan 9	Stoke City	2-6	Richardson 2	23927	1							11		7			10		5	4	8					3		9	6	2

		P	W	D	L	F	A	W	D	L	F	A	Pts
1	Port Vale	46	16	7	0	48	5	10	10	3	26	16	69
2	Barnsley	46	16	3	4	54	24	8	7	8	23	33	58
3	Scunthorpe United	46	14	7	2	49	24	7	8	8	28	32	57
4	Gateshead	46	15	4	4	49	22	6	9	8	25	33	55
5	Bradford City	46	15	6	2	40	14	7	3	13	20	41	53
6	Chesterfield	46	13	6	4	41	19	6	8	9	35	45	52
7	Mansfield Town	46	15	5	3	59	22	5	6	12	29	45	51
8	Wrexham	46	16	4	3	59	19	5	5	13	22	49	51
9	Bradford Park Ave.	46	13	6	4	57	31	5	8	10	20	37	50
10	Stockport County	46	14	6	3	57	20	4	5	14	20	47	47
11	Southport	46	12	5	6	41	26	5	7	11	22	34	46
12	Barrow	46	12	7	4	46	26	4	5	14	26	45	44
13	Carlisle United	46	10	8	5	53	27	4	7	12	30	44	43
14	Tranmere Rovers	46	11	4	8	40	34	7	3	13	19	36	43
15	Accrington Stanley	46	12	7	4	41	22	4	3	16	25	52	42
16	Crewe Alexandra	46	9	8	6	30	26	5	5	13	19	41	41
17	Grimsby Town	46	14	5	4	31	15	2	4	17	20	62	41
18	HARTLEPOOLS UTD.	46	10	8	5	40	21	3	6	14	19	44	40
19	Rochdale	46	12	5	6	40	20	3	5	15	19	57	40
20	Workington	46	10	9	4	36	22	3	5	15	23	58	40
21	Darlington	46	11	3	9	31	27	1	11	11	19	44	38
22	York City	46	8	7	8	39	32	4	6	13	25	54	37
23	Halifax Town	46	9	6	8	26	21	3	4	16	18	52	34
24	Chester	46	10	7	6	39	22	1	3	19	9	45	32

1954/55 5th in Division 3(N)

							Brown RB	Cameron J	Dyson J	Harden LJ	Johnson K	Linacre W	Luke GT	Lumley R	MacGregor JP	McGuigan T	Moore W	Newton JL	Richardson F	Stamper FFT	Taylor GL	Thompson R	Wildon LE	Willetts J	Willis JG
1	Aug	21	CREWE ALEXANDRA	2-1	Wildon, McGuigan	7390		2			8	7				10	5	4		6	1	11	9	3	
2		23	York City	0-1		10156		2			8	7				10	5	4		6	1	11	9	3	
3		28	Carlisle United	2-3	Wildon 2	7425		2		11	8	7				10	5	4		6	1	3	9		
4		30	YORK CITY	1-0	Harden	8103		2		11	8	7				10	5	4		6	1	3	9		
5	Sep	4	CHESTER	3-1	Wildon, McGuigan, Harden	7909		2		11	8	7				10	5	4		6	1	3	9		
6		6	Gateshead	0-3		4577		2		11	8	7				10	5	4		6	1	3	9		
7		11	Grimsby Town	0-1		10117		2		11	8	7				10	5	4		6	1	3	9		
8		13	GATESHEAD	0-0		8628		2			8	7				10	5	4	11	6	1	3	9		
9		18	BRADFORD PARK AVE.	0-1		8279	1	2		11	8	7				10	5	4		6		3	9		
10		20	Stockport County	2-0	Richardson, Harden	5152	1	2		11	8	7				10	5	4	9	6		3			
11		25	Rochdale	1-2	Johnson	6222	1	2		11	8	7				10	5	4	9	6				3	
12		27	STOCKPORT COUNTY	2-1	Richardson, McGuigan	6604	1	2		11	8	7				10	5	4	9	6				3	
13	Oct	2	TRANMERE ROVERS	4-0	Harden, McGuigan 2, Johnson	7610	1	2		11	8	7				10	5	4	9	6				3	
14		9	HALIFAX TOWN	1-0	Harden	7422	1	2		11	8	7				10	5	4	9	6				3	
15		16	Oldham Athletic	1-0	Richardson	6925	1	2		11	8	7				6	5	4	9				10	3	
16		23	BRADFORD CITY	0-0		7140	1	2		11	8	7				10	5	4	9	6				3	
17		30	Barnsley	0-0		10377	1	2			8	7	11			10	5	4	9	6				3	
18	Nov	6	SCUNTHORPE UNITED	4-2	Richardson, McGuigan 2, Luke	7621	1	2			8	7	11			10	5	4	9	6				3	
19		13	Wrexham	4-1	McGuigan 2, Johnson 2	5362	1	2			8	7	11			10	5	4	9	6				3	
20		27	Mansfield Town	2-0	Richardson, Linacre	7855	1	2			8	7	11			10	5	4	9	6				3	
21	Dec	4	WORKINGTON	3-2	Richardson, McGuigan, Luke	8290	1	2			8	7	11			10	5	4	9	6				3	
22		18	Crewe Alexandra	1-1	McGuigan	3384	1	2			8	7	11			10	5	4	9	6				3	
23		25	DARLINGTON	1-0	Harden	12430	1	2		11	8		7			10	5	4	9	6				3	
24		27	Darlington	1-0	Harden	17576	1	2		11	8					10	5	4	9	6				3	7
25	Jan	1	CARLISLE UNITED	1-0	Richardson	12445	1	2		11	8	7				10	5	4	9	6				3	
26		15	Chester	0-1		1723		2		11	8		7			10	5	4	9	6	1			3	
27	Feb	5	Bradford Park Avenue	0-1		7373		2			8	7	11		10		5			6	1	3		4	9
28		12	ROCHDALE	3-1	McGuigan, Lumley 2	6611		2			9	7	11	8		10	5	4		6	1	3			
29		19	Tranmere Rovers	1-3	McGuigan	4250		2			9	7	11	8		10	5	4		6	1	3			
30	Mar	5	OLDHAM ATHLETIC	2-0	Johnson, McGuigan	7195	1	2			9	7	11	8		10	5	4		6		3			
31		12	Bradford City	1-0	Johnson	6839	1	2			9	7	11	8		10	5	4		6		3			
32		19	BARNSLEY	0-3		8411	1	2			9	7	11	8		10	5	4		6		3			
33		23	GRIMSBY TOWN	3-2	Linacre, McGuigan, Luke	4134	1	2			8	7	11			10	5	4	9	6		3			
34		26	Scunthorpe United	1-5	Linacre	4155	1	2			8	7	11			10	5	4	9	6		3			
35		28	Halifax Town	0-1		3693	1	2			8	7	11			10	5	4	9	6		3			
36		30	SOUTHPORT	2-1	Richardson, Thompson	5417	1	2		11	8	7				10	5	4	9	6		3			
37	Apr	2	WREXHAM	3-0	McGuigan, Linacre, Johnson	6373	1	2		11	8	7				10	5	4	9	6		3			
38		8	Chesterfield	0-3		10886		2		11	8	7				10	5	4	9	6	1	3			
39		9	Accrington Stanley	5-2	Johnson, Wildon, Stamper 2, Linacre	11267	1	2			9	7		8		10	5	4		6		3	11		
40		11	CHESTERFIELD	2-0	Linacre, Newton (p)	9551	1	2			9	7	11	8		10	5	4		6		3			
41		16	MANSFIELD TOWN	1-2	Johnson	7484	1	2			9	7	11	8			5	4		6		3	10		
42		18	Barrow	2-0	McGuigan, Lumley	3378		2				7	11	8		10	5	4	9	6	1	3			
43		23	Workington	1-0	McGuigan	5161						7	11	8		10	5	4	9	6	1	3		2	
44		25	ACCRINGTON STANLEY	1-3	Luke	9371						7	11	8		10	5	4	9	6	1	3		2	
45		30	BARROW	0-0		5708			1		9	7	11	8		10	5	4		6		3		2	
46	May	2	Southport	0-1		2200			1			7	11	8		10	5	4	9	6		3		2	
						Apps	28	42	2	20	42	43	24	13	1	44	46	45	28	45	16	30	12	23	2
						Goals				7	9	6	4	3		18		1	8	2		1	5		

F.A. Cup

							Brown RB	Cameron J	Dyson J	Harden LJ	Johnson K	Linacre W	Luke GT	Lumley R	MacGregor JP	McGuigan T	Moore W	Newton JL	Richardson F	Stamper FFT	Taylor GL	Thompson R	Wildon LE	Willetts J	Willis JG
R1	Nov	20	CHESTERFIELD	1-0	Richardson	12643	1	2			8	7	11			10	5	4	9	6				3	
R2	Dec	11	ALDERSHOT	4-0	McGuigan 2, Richardson, Willetts (p)	14813	1	2			8	7	11			10	5	4	9	6				3	
R3	Jan	8	DARLINGTON	1-1	Harden	12450	1	2		11	8	7				10	5	4	9	6				3	
rep		12	Darlington	2-2	Richardson 2	10598	1	2		11	8	7				10	5	4	9	6				3	
rep2		17	Darlington	2-0	Richardson, Newton (p)	10891		2			8	7	11			10	5	4	9	6	1	3			
R4		29	NOTTM FOREST	1-1	Newton (p)	17200		2			8	7	11			10	5	4	9	6	1	3			
rep	Feb	2	Nottingham Forest	1-2	Stamper	20479		2			8	7	11			10	5	4	9	6	1	3			

R3 and R4 replays a.e.t.

		P	W	D	L	F	A	W	D	L	F	A	Pts
1	Barnsley	46	18	3	2	51	17	12	2	9	35	29	65
2	Accrington Stanley	46	18	2	3	65	32	7	9	7	31	35	61
3	Scunthorpe United	46	14	6	3	45	18	9	6	8	36	35	58
4	York City	46	13	5	5	43	27	11	5	7	49	36	58
5	HARTLEPOOLS UTD.	46	16	3	4	39	20	9	2	12	25	29	55
6	Chesterfield	46	17	1	5	54	33	7	5	11	27	37	54
7	Gateshead	46	11	7	5	38	26	9	5	9	27	43	52
8	Workington	46	11	7	5	39	23	7	7	9	29	32	50
9	Stockport County	46	13	4	6	50	27	5	8	10	34	43	48
10	Oldham Athletic	46	14	5	4	47	22	5	5	13	27	46	48
11	Southport	46	10	9	4	28	18	6	7	10	19	26	48
12	Rochdale	46	13	7	3	39	20	4	7	12	30	46	48
13	Mansfield Town	46	14	4	5	40	28	4	5	14	25	43	45
14	Halifax Town	46	9	9	5	41	27	6	4	13	22	40	43
15	Darlington	46	10	7	6	41	28	4	7	12	21	45	42
16	Bradford Park Ave.	46	11	7	5	29	21	4	4	15	27	49	41
17	Barrow	46	12	4	7	39	34	5	2	16	31	55	40
18	Wrexham	46	9	6	8	40	35	4	6	13	25	42	38
19	Tranmere Rovers	46	9	6	8	37	30	4	5	14	18	40	37
20	Carlisle United	46	12	1	10	53	39	3	5	15	25	50	36
21	Bradford City	46	9	5	9	30	26	4	5	14	17	29	36
22	Crewe Alexandra	46	8	10	5	45	35	2	4	17	23	56	34
23	Grimsby Town	46	10	4	9	28	32	3	4	16	19	46	34
24	Chester	46	10	3	10	23	25	2	6	15	21	52	33

1955/56 4th in Division 3(N)

							Anderson WB	Brown RB	Cameron J	Dyson J	Harden LJ	Healey WR	Johnson K	Linacre W	Luke GT	Lumley R	McGuigan T	Moore W	Newton JL	Rayment JW	Richardson F	Robinson JW	Smith J	Stamper FFT	Thompson R	Wilkinson T	Willetts J
1	Aug	20	DARLINGTON	3-0	Smith, Rayment, Luke	10194			2	1					11	8	10	5	4	7			9	6	3		
2		24	Workington	1-5	Stamper	5553			2	1			9	7	11	8	10	5	4					6	3		
3		27	Stockport County	0-4		5942				1			9		11	8	10	5	4	7				6	3		2
4		29	WORKINGTON	1-0	Luke	8761			2	1					11	8	10	5	4	7			9	6	3		
5	Sep	3	MANSFIELD TOWN	4-2	Smith 3, Luke	7714			2	1		6			11	8	10	5	4	7			9		3		
6		5	YORK CITY	0-1		9184			2	1		6			11	8	10	5	4	7	9				3		
7		10	Wrexham	3-1	McGuigan, Lumley, Luke	13702		1	2			4		7	11	8	10	5			9			6	3		
8		12	York City	0-3		10171		1	2			4		7	11	8	10	5			9			6	3		
9		17	HALIFAX TOWN	3-2	Richardson, Lumley, Luke	7348			2	1		4		7	11	8	10	5			9			6	3		
10		19	DERBY COUNTY	2-0	Linacre, Luke	9170			2	1				7	11	8	10	5			9			6	3		4
11		24	Bradford City	0-2		13418			2	1				7	11	8	10	5	4		9			6	3		
12		27	Oldham Athletic	2-3	Luke, Lumley	3097			2	1					11	8	10	5	4	7	9			6	3		
13	Oct	1	SCUNTHORPE UNITED	0-2		8170			2	1				7	11	8	10	5	4		9			6	3		
14		8	SOUTHPORT	1-0	Smith	5650			2	1		6		7	11	8	10	5	4				9		3		
15		15	Accrington Stanley	0-1		8824			2	1				7	11	8	10	5	4				9	6	3		
16		22	CHESTERFIELD	3-0	Robinson, Smith 2	5479			2	1					11	8	10	5	4			7	9	6	3		
17		29	Rochdale	4-1	Luke 2, Lumley, Robinson	4388			2	1					11	8	10	5	4			7	9	6	3		
18	Nov	5	BRADFORD PARK AVE.	3-1	Smith, McGuigan 2	6383			2	1					11	8	10	5	4			7	9	6	3		
19		12	Grimsby Town	0-1		14481			2	1			9		11	8	10	5	4			7		6	3		
20		26	Chester	1-0	Johnson	5876			2	1			9		11	8		5	4		10	7		6	3		
21	Dec	3	BARROW	1-0	Robinson	5853			2	1			9		11	8		5	4		10	7		6	3		
22		17	Darlington	0-0		5578			2	1			9		11	8		5	4		10	7		6	3		
23		24	STOCKPORT COUNTY	0-0		9299			2	1			9		11	8		5	4		10	7		6	3		
24		26	CREWE ALEXANDRA	6-1	Johnson 4, Luke, Lumley	6959			2	1			9		11	8	10	5	4	7				6	3		
25		27	Crewe Alexandra	3-1	Stamper, Johnson, Luke	3948			2	1			9		11	8		5	4	7	10			6	3		
26		31	Mansfield Town	1-5	Luke	7294			2	1			9		11	8		5	4		10	7		6	3		
27	Jan	2	OLDHAM ATHLETIC	1-0	Luke	8646			2	1			9		11	8	10	5	4		7			6	3		
28		14	WREXHAM	3-2	McGuigan, Robinson, Johnson	3851			2	1			9		11	8	10	5	4			7		6	3		
29		21	Halifax Town	2-0	Johnson 2	7346			2	1			9		11	8	10	5	4	7				6	3		
30		28	Tranmere Rovers	2-2	Johnson, Lumley	6788			2	1			9		11	8	10	5	4	7				6	3		
31	Feb	4	BRADFORD CITY	1-0	Rayment	5169			2	1			9		11	8	10	5	4	7				6	3		
32		11	Scunthorpe United	1-5	Johnson	5614			2	1			9		11	8	10	5	4	7				6	3		
33		18	Southport	0-0		6219			2	1			9		11	8	10	5	4	7				6	3		
34	Mar	3	Chesterfield	3-2	Rayment, Johnson 2	9161	6		2	1			9		11	8	10	5	4	7					3		
35		10	ROCHDALE	1-0	Luke (p)	8150	6		2	1			9		11	8	10	5	4	7					3		
36		17	Carlisle United	3-0	Lumley, Johnson 2	4118	6		2	1			9		11	8	10	5	4	7					3		
37		24	GRIMSBY TOWN	1-2	Rayment	10360	6		2	1			9		11	8	10	5	4	7					3		
38		30	Gateshead	1-2	McGuigan	5757	6		2	1			9		11	8	10	5	4	7					3		
39		31	Bradford Park Avenue	3-1	Luke, Johnson 2	6579	6		2	1			9		11	8	10	5	4	7					3		
40	Apr	2	GATESHEAD	3-1	Harden, McGuigan, March (og)	8450	6		2	1	11		9			8	10	5	4	7					3		
41		7	CHESTER	3-1	Johnson, McGuigan, Luke	6646	6		2	1			9		11	8	10	5	4	7					3		
42		14	Barrow	2-3	McGuigan, Johnson	4734	6			1			9		11	8	10	5	4	7					3		2
43		21	TRANMERE ROVERS	4-0	Lumley, Luke, Johnson 2	6262	6		2	1			9		11	8	10	5		7					3	4	
44		28	Derby County	2-3	Luke, Rayment	10794	6		2	1			9		11	8	10	5		7					3	4	
45		30	CARLISLE UNITED	3-0	Robinson, Waters (og), Luke	5445	6	1	2				9		11	8	10	5				7			3	4	
46	May	3	ACCRINGTON STANLEY	0-0		7331	6	1	2				9		11	8	10	5				7			3	4	
						Apps	13	4	44	42	1	6	30	9	45	46	40	46	38	24	15	12	8	30	46	4	3
						Goals					1		21	1	19	8	8			5	1	5	8	2			

Two own goals

F.A. Cup

							Anderson WB	Brown RB	Cameron J	Dyson J	Harden LJ	Healey WR	Johnson K	Linacre W	Luke GT	Lumley R	McGuigan T	Moore W	Newton JL	Rayment JW	Richardson F	Robinson JW	Smith J	Stamper FFT	Thompson R	Wilkinson T	Willetts J
R1	Nov	19	GATESHEAD	3-0	Luke 2, Lumley	10890			2	1			9		11	8		5	4		10	7		6	3		
R2	Dec	10	Chesterfield	2-1	Luke 2	10280			2	1			9		11	8		5	4		10	7		6	3		
R3	Jan	7	CHELSEA	0-1		16862			2	1			9		11	8	10	5	4	7				6	3		

		P	W	D	L	F	A	W	D	L	F	A	Pts
1	Grimsby Town	46	20	1	2	54	10	11	5	7	22	19	68
2	Derby County	46	18	4	1	67	23	10	3	10	43	32	63
3	Accrington Stanley	46	17	4	2	61	19	8	5	10	31	38	59
4	HARTLEPOOLS UTD.	46	18	2	3	47	15	8	3	12	34	45	57
5	Southport	46	12	9	2	39	18	11	2	10	27	35	57
6	Chesterfield	46	18	1	4	61	21	7	3	13	33	45	54
7	Stockport County	46	16	4	3	65	22	5	5	13	25	39	51
8	Bradford City	46	16	5	2	57	25	2	8	13	21	39	49
9	Scunthorpe United	46	12	4	7	40	26	8	4	11	35	37	48
10	Workington	46	13	4	6	47	20	6	5	12	28	43	47
11	York City	46	12	4	7	44	24	7	5	11	41	48	47
12	Rochdale	46	13	5	5	46	39	4	8	11	20	45	47
13	Gateshead	46	15	4	4	56	32	2	7	14	21	52	45
14	Wrexham	46	11	5	7	37	28	5	5	13	29	45	42
15	Darlington	46	11	6	6	41	28	5	3	15	19	45	41
16	Tranmere Rovers	46	11	4	8	33	25	5	5	13	26	59	41
17	Chester	46	10	8	5	35	33	3	6	14	17	49	40
18	Mansfield Town	46	13	6	4	59	21	1	5	17	25	60	39
19	Halifax Town	46	10	6	7	40	27	4	5	14	26	49	39
20	Oldham Athletic	46	7	12	4	48	36	3	6	14	28	50	38
21	Carlisle United	46	11	3	9	45	36	4	5	14	26	59	38
22	Barrow	46	11	6	6	44	25	1	3	19	17	58	33
23	Bradford Park Ave.	46	13	4	6	47	38	0	3	20	14	84	33
24	Crewe Alexandra	46	9	4	10	32	35	0	6	17	18	70	28

1956/57 2nd in Division 3(N)

							Anderson WB	Cameron J	Guthrie R	Howells P	Johnson K	Luke GT	Lumley R	MacCallum S	MacGregor TJ	McGuigan T	Moore W	Newton JL	Rayment JW	Robinson JW	Smith J	Stamper FFT	Thompson R	Waugh K	Willis JG
1	Aug	18	CHESTERFIELD	5-1	Lumley, Rayment, Johnson, McGuigan, Stamper	5444	4	2	1		9	11	8			10	5		7			6	3		
2		22	Wrexham	2-2	Newton, Rayment	9936	4	2	1		9		8			10	5	11	7			6	3		
3		25	Chester	1-0	Rayment	8374	4	2	1		9		8			10	5	11	7			6	3		
4		27	WREXHAM	2-1	McGuigan, Johnson	3973	4	2	1		9	11	8			10	5		7			6	3		
5	Sep	1	Gateshead	3-4	Lumley 2 (2p), McGuigan	7246	4	2	1		9	11	8			10	5		7			6	3		
6		4	Southport	6-1	Robinson 2, Johnson 4	5037	4	2	1		9	11	8			10	5			7		6	3		
7		8	BRADFORD CITY	2-0	Johnson, McGuigan	10821	4	2	1		9	11	8			10	5			7		6	3		
8		10	SOUTHPORT	5-2	Lumley, Rankin (og), Stamper, Johnson, Luke	10474	4	2	1		9	11	8			10	5			7		6	3		
9		15	Stockport County	4-2	Stamper, McGuigan, Johnson, Luke	13577	4	2	1		9	11	8			10	5			7		6	3		
10		18	Tranmere Rovers	1-0	Robinson	5763	4	2	1		9	11	8			10	5			7		6	3		
11		22	CARLISLE UNITED	2-1	Robinson, Luke	12267	4	2	1		9	11	8			10	5			7		6	3		
12		24	TRANMERE ROVERS	5-1	Johnson 4, Luke	10219	4	2	1		9	11	8			10	5			7		6	3		
13		29	Accrington Stanley	1-2	Johnson	10969	4	2	1		9	11	8			10	5			7		6	3		
14	Oct	6	DERBY COUNTY	2-1	Anderson, Johnson	12072	4	2	1		9		8			10	5		7	11		6	3		
15		13	Crewe Alexandra	2-1	Rayment, Stamper	5676	4		1		9		8			10	5	2	7	11		6	3		
16		20	DARLINGTON	2-1	McGuigan, Devlin (og)	13202	4	2	1		8	11				10	5			7	9	6	3		
17		27	Rochdale	0-1		12237	8	2	1		9	11		4		10	5			7		6	3		
18	Nov	3	HALIFAX TOWN	0-1		10273	4	2	1		9	11				10	5			7		6	3		8
19		10	Workington	1-1	Luke	7658	4	2	1		9	11	8			10	5			7		6	3		
20		24	Barrow	1-3	Luke	6033	4	2	1		9	11	8			10	5			7		6	3		
21	Dec	1	SCUNTHORPE UNITED	0-0		7881		2	1		9	11	10				5	4	7			6	3		8
22		15	Chesterfield	1-5	Luke	9257	6	2	1		9	11			8	10	5	4	7				3		
23		22	CHESTER	2-2	Newton (p), Johnson	6515		2	1		9	11			8	10	5	4	7			6	3		
24		25	York City	3-3	Robinson, Luke, Johnson	8663	6		1		9	11				10	5	4		7		8	3	2	
25		26	YORK CITY	2-0	Stamper, Johnson	6954	6		1		9	11			8		5	4		7		10	3	2	
26		29	GATESHEAD	4-1	Stamper 2, Luke 2	9254	6		1		9	11				10	5	4		7		8	3	2	
27	Jan	1	HULL CITY	3-3	Stamper, Newton (p), Johnson	9768	6		1	11	9					10	5	4		7		8	3	2	
28		12	Bradford City	1-1	Smith	22126	6		1			11				8	5	4		7	9	10	3	2	
29		19	STOCKPORT COUNTY	4-1	Stamper 2, Luke, Rayment	8155	6		1			11		4		8	5		7		9	10	3	2	
30		26	OLDHAM ATHLETIC	4-1	Smith 2, Luke, Rayment	9127	6		1			11				8	5	4	7		9	10	3	2	
31	Feb	2	Carlisle United	1-2	Stamper	12121	6		1			11			8		5	4	7		9	10	3	2	
32		9	ACCRINGTON STANLEY	2-1	Johnson, Smith	12518	6		1		8	11					5	4	7		9	10	3	2	
33		16	Derby County	0-2		24644	6		1		8	11					5	4	7		9	10	3	2	
34		23	CREWE ALEXANDRA	2-0	Johnson, Luke	8164	6		1		8	11	10				5	4	7		9		3	2	
35	Mar	2	Darlington	1-3	Smith	14051	6		1		8	11	10				5	4	7		9		3	2	
36		9	ROCHDALE	0-0		9339	6		1		9	11	8				5	4	7			10	3	2	
37		16	Halifax Town	0-2		5652	6		1		9	11	8				5	4	7			10	3	2	
38		23	WORKINGTON	2-1	Rayment, Johnson	11794			1		9	11	8				5	4	7		10	6	3	2	
39		30	Hull City	0-2		13310			1		9	11	8				5	4	7		10	6	3	2	
40	Apr	6	BARROW	2-0	Luke, Rayment	6878			1		9	11	8				5	4	7		10	6	3	2	
41		13	Scunthorpe United	2-1	Luke, Johnson	4599			1		9	11	8				5	4	7		10	6	3	2	
42		16	Oldham Athletic	0-0		4956			1		9	11	8				5	4			10	6	3	2	7
43		19	MANSFIELD TOWN	2-1	Rushby (og), Luke	8984			1		9	11	8			10	5	4	7			6	3	2	
44		20	BRADFORD PARK AVE.	2-1	Luke 2	8102			1		9	11	8			10	5	4	7			6	3	2	
45		23	Mansfield Town	1-4	Johnson	10963	4		1		9	11	8			10	5		7			6	3	2	
46		27	Bradford Park Avenue	2-0	Rayment, Luke	6193			1		9	11	8			10	5	4	7			6	3	2	
						Apps	36	22	46	1	42	41	31	2	4	32	46	27	27	20	14	43	46	23	3
						Goals	1				24	19	4			6		3	9	5	5	11			

Three own goals

F.A. Cup

							Anderson WB	Cameron J	Guthrie R	Howells P	Johnson K	Luke GT	Lumley R	MacCallum S	MacGregor TJ	McGuigan T	Moore W	Newton JL	Rayment JW	Robinson JW	Smith J	Stamper FFT	Thompson R	Waugh K	Willis JG
R1	Nov	17	SELBY TOWN	3-1	Luke, Stamper, Robinson	11227	4	2	1		9	11	8			10	5			7		6	3		
R2	Dec	8	Blyth Spartans	1-0	Johnson	10168		2	1		9	11	8			10	5	4	7			6	3		
R3	Jan	5	MANCHESTER UTD.	3-4	Stamper, Johnson, Newton	17264	6		1		9	11				8	5	4		7		10	3	2	

		P	W	D	L	F	A	W	D	L	F	A	Pts
1	Derby County	46	18	3	2	69	18	8	8	7	42	35	63
2	HARTLEPOOLS UTD.	46	18	4	1	56	21	7	5	11	34	42	59
3	Accrington Stanley	46	15	4	4	54	22	10	4	9	41	42	58
4	Workington	46	16	4	3	60	25	8	6	9	33	38	58
5	Stockport County	46	16	3	4	51	26	7	5	11	40	49	54
6	Chesterfield	46	17	5	1	60	22	5	4	14	36	57	53
7	York City	46	14	4	5	43	21	7	6	10	32	40	52
8	Hull City	46	14	6	3	45	24	7	4	12	39	45	52
9	Bradford City	46	14	3	6	47	31	8	5	10	31	37	52
10	Barrow	46	16	2	5	51	22	5	7	11	25	40	51
11	Halifax Town	46	16	2	5	40	24	5	5	13	25	46	49
12	Wrexham	46	12	7	4	63	33	7	3	13	34	41	48
13	Rochdale	46	14	6	3	38	19	4	6	13	27	46	48
14	Scunthorpe United	46	9	5	9	44	36	6	10	7	27	33	45
15	Carlisle United	46	9	9	5	44	36	7	4	12	32	49	45
16	Mansfield Town	46	13	3	7	58	38	4	7	12	33	52	44
17	Gateshead	46	9	6	8	42	40	8	4	11	30	50	44
18	Darlington	46	11	5	7	47	36	6	3	14	35	59	42
19	Oldham Athletic	46	9	7	7	35	31	3	8	12	31	43	39
20	Bradford Park Ave.	46	11	2	10	41	40	5	1	17	25	53	35
21	Chester	46	8	7	8	40	35	2	6	15	15	49	33
22	Southport	46	7	8	8	31	34	3	4	16	21	60	32
23	Tranmere Rovers	46	5	9	9	33	38	2	4	17	18	53	27
24	Crewe Alexandra	46	5	7	11	31	46	1	2	20	12	64	21

1957/58 17th in Division 3(N)

							Anderson WB	Burlison TH	Cameron J	Dyson J	Edwards E	Guthrie R	Hartnett JB	Hogan T	Johnson D	Johnson K	Luke GT	Lumley R	McGuigan T	Mitchell N	Moore W	Newton JL	Rayment JW	Robinson JW	Smith J	Stamper FFT	Thompson P	Thompson R	Waugh K	Wilkinson T	Willis JG
1	Aug	24	Accrington Stanley	2-1	McGuigan, Smith	9678						1					11	8	10		5	4			9	6		3	2		7
2		26	DARLINGTON	5-1	Lumley 2, Willis 2, Smith	15176						1					11	8	10		5	4			9	6		3	2		7
3		31	CHESTER	2-1	P Thompson, Smith	11629						1					11	8			5	4			9	6	10	3	2		7
4	Sep	4	Darlington	3-1	P Thompson 2, Newton (p)	9509						1					11	8			5	4			9	6	10	3	2		7
5		7	Chesterfield	1-2	Willis	11511						1					11	8			5	4			9	6	10	3	2		7
6		9	OLDHAM ATHLETIC	4-1	Luke 2, Smith 2	11084						1					11	8	7		5	4			9	6	10	3	2		
7		14	TRANMERE ROVERS	1-1	Smith	10823						1					11	8	10		5	4		7	9	6		3	2		
8		17	Oldham Athletic	0-4		5566						1				7	11	8	10		5	4			9	6		3	2		
9		21	Gateshead	0-0		5976						1				9	11	10	7		5	4			8	6		3	2		
10		23	BARROW	4-1	K Johnson 3, Smith	6112						1				9	11	10			5	4			8	6		3	2		7
11		28	Bradford Park Avenue	3-2	Lumley 2, Stamper	9220						1				9	11	10			5	4			8	6		3	2		7
12		30	Barrow	3-3	Willis, Luke, K Johnson	4896						1				9	11	10			5	4			8	6		3	2		7
13	Oct	5	CARLISLE UNITED	0-1		10119						1				9	11	10			5	4			8	6		3	2		7
14		12	WORKINGTON	1-0	Newton (p)	8469		4				1		8					10		5	7		11		6	9	3	2		
15		19	Wrexham	1-3	Smith	8962	6				3	1		8			11		10		5	4			7		9		2		
16		26	CREWE ALEXANDRA	1-1	P Thompson	8326		4				1					11	8			5			7	9	6	10	3	2		
17	Nov	2	Rochdale	0-7		5508		4				1					11	10			5			7	8	6	9	3	2		
18		9	HALIFAX TOWN	5-0	Luke 2, McGuigan 2, P Thompson	6195		4	3	1							11	7	10			6			8	5	9		2		
19		23	HULL CITY	5-1	K Johnson 2, P Thompson 2, McGuigan	8754		4	3	1						7	11		10		5				8	6	9		2		
20		30	Bradford City	1-0	K Johnson	11417		4	3	1						7	11		10		5				8	6	9		2		
21	Dec	14	Mansfield Town	1-5	Hogan	8097		4	3	1				8		9		7	10		5				11	6			2		
22		21	ACCRINGTON STANLEY	1-1	Stamper	7179		4	3	1						9	11		10		5			7	8	6			2		
23		25	YORK CITY	2-2	Wragg (og), McGuigan (p)	6837	4		3	1			11		10	9			8		5			7		6			2		
24		26	York City	2-2	McGuigan 2	10785	4		3			1	11		10	9			8		5			7		6			2		
25		28	Chester	1-2	Hartnett	7725	4		3			1	11			9			8		5			7	10	6			2		
26	Jan	1	SOUTHPORT	2-1	K Johnson, Willis	7582	4		3			1	11			9			8		5					10			2	6	7
27		4	Southport	0-0		2639	8	4	3			1	11			9			10		5					6			2		7
28		11	CHESTERFIELD	0-2		8129	4		3			1				8	11		10		5		7		9	6			2		
29		18	Tranmere Rovers	2-3	P Thompson, Rayment	8338	4		3	1						8	11		10		5		7			6	9		2		
30	Feb	1	GATESHEAD	2-2	P Thompson, McGuigan	6183	4		3	1						8	11		10		5		7			6	9		2		
31		8	BRADFORD PARK AVE.	0-0		4805				1						4	11		10		5		7		8	6	9	3	2		
32		15	Carlisle United	2-1	K Johnson, Rayment	7670				1						8	11		10		5	4	7			6	9	3	2		
33		22	Hull City	1-1	Rayment	11926				1						8			10		5	4	7	11		6	9	3	2		
34	Mar	1	WREXHAM	1-2	P Thompson	6749	4			1				10		8					5		7	11		6	9	3	2		
35		8	Crewe Alexandra	1-2	Robinson	3771	10			1						8					5	4		7		6	9	3	2		11
36		15	ROCHDALE	1-3	P Thompson	5862				1			11			9			10	7	5	4				6	8	3	2		
37		22	Workington	0-1		4055		4	3			1	11			9			10	7	5					6	8		2		
38		29	STOCKPORT COUNTY	1-2	Mitchell	3070		4	3			1				9			10	11	5		7			6	8		2		
39	Apr	4	BURY	2-1	P Thompson, McGuigan (p)	7824	6	4	3			1		8					10	11	5		7				9		2		
40		5	Scunthorpe United	0-2		8684	6	4	3			1		8					10	11	5		7				9		2		
41		7	Bury	3-3	Stamper, P Thompson, Mitchell	6987	6	4	2			1		8						11	5		7			10	9		3		
42		12	BRADFORD CITY	2-0	P Thompson 2	6628	6	4	3			1		8					10	11	5		7				9		2		
43		14	Stockport County	1-2	Mitchell	8046	6	4	3			1		8					10	11	5						9		2		7
44		19	Halifax Town	0-3		7368	6	4	3			1							10	11	5					8	9		2		7
45		26	MANSFIELD TOWN	2-0	Smith, Thomas (og)	4922	6	4	3			1							10	11	5				8		9		2		7
46		28	SCUNTHORPE UNITED	1-2	P Thompson	8159	6	4	3			1							10	11	5				8		9		2		7
						Apps	19	19	23	14	1	32	7	9	2	26	25	17	34	11	45	20	12	11	26	39	29	22	46	1	16
						Goals							1	1		9	5	4	9	3		2	3	1	9	3	16				5

Two own goals

F.A. Cup

R1	Nov	16	PRESCOT CABLES	5-0	Newton, P Thompson 4	9424		4	3	1							11	7	10			6			8	5	9		2		
R2	Dec	7	Stockport County	1-2	K Johnson	12500		4	3	1						7	11		10		5				8	6	9		2		

		P	W	D	L	F	A	W	D	L	F	A	Pts
1	Scunthorpe United	46	16	5	2	46	19	13	3	7	42	31	66
2	Accrington Stanley	46	16	4	3	53	28	9	5	9	30	33	59
3	Bradford City	46	13	7	3	42	19	8	8	7	31	30	57
4	Bury	46	17	4	2	61	18	6	6	11	33	44	56
5	Hull City	46	15	6	2	49	20	4	9	10	29	47	53
6	Mansfield Town	46	16	3	4	68	42	6	5	12	32	50	52
7	Halifax Town	46	15	5	3	52	20	5	6	12	31	49	51
8	Chesterfield	46	12	8	3	39	28	6	7	10	32	41	51
9	Stockport County	46	15	4	4	54	28	3	7	13	20	39	47
10	Rochdale	46	14	4	5	50	25	5	4	14	29	42	46
11	Tranmere Rovers	46	12	6	5	51	32	6	4	13	31	44	46
12	Wrexham	46	13	8	2	39	18	4	4	15	22	45	46
13	York City	46	11	8	4	40	26	6	4	13	28	50	46
14	Gateshead	46	12	5	6	41	27	3	10	10	27	49	45
15	Oldham Athletic	46	11	7	5	44	32	3	10	10	28	52	45
16	Carlisle United	46	13	3	7	56	35	6	3	14	24	43	44
17	HARTLEPOOLS UTD.	46	11	6	6	45	26	5	6	12	28	50	44
18	Barrow	46	9	7	7	36	32	4	8	11	30	42	41
19	Workington	46	11	6	6	46	33	3	7	13	26	48	41
20	Darlington	46	15	3	5	53	25	2	4	17	25	64	41
21	Chester	46	7	10	6	38	26	6	3	14	35	55	39
22	Bradford Park Ave.	46	8	6	9	41	41	5	5	13	27	54	37
23	Southport	46	8	3	12	29	40	3	3	17	23	48	28
24	Crewe Alexandra	46	6	5	12	29	41	2	2	19	18	52	23

1958/59

19th in Division 4

	Date		Opponent	Score	Scorers	Att.	Anderson WB	Burlison TH	Cameron J	Clark HM	Denham CH	Dixon JW	Dunn BJ	Dyson J	Gibbon AT	Herring H	Johnson K	Langland JR	Luke GT	MacGregor TJ	Mitchell N	Moore W	Nicholson S	Oakley N	Roberts W	Scott JC	Smith J	Thompson P	Waugh K	Walford W	Willis JG
1	Aug	23	SHREWSBURY TOWN	0-2		7344	6	4	3				11	1								5	10				8	9	2		7
2		25	BRADFORD PARK AVE.	3-0	Anderson (p), Willis, Dunn	6994	6	4	3				11	1								5	10				8	9	2		7
3		30	Southport	1-1	Willis	3642	6	4	3				11	1								5	10				8	9	2		7
4	Sep	1	Bradford Park Avenue	1-4	Smith	7688	6	4	3	10			11	1							7	5					8	9	2		
5		6	TORQUAY UNITED	2-4	Clark, Nicholson	6472	6	4	3	8			11	1							7	5	10					9	2		
6		8	PORT VALE	1-5	Anderson (p)	6158	4			8		2	11		3	7	6					5	10	1				9			
7		13	Crewe Alexandra	2-0	Langland, Thompson	7106	4			8					3	7	6	9	11			5		1				10	2		
8		15	Port Vale	1-1	Mitchell	9313	4			8					3		6	9	11		7	5		1				10	2		
9		20	NORTHAMPTON T	3-0	Thompson 2, Luke	7463	4			8					3		6	9	11		7	5		1				10	2		
10		22	CRYSTAL PALACE	4-1	Mitchell 2, Thompson, Luke	8368	4			8					3		6	9	11		7	5		1				10	2		
11		27	Workington	0-3		5085	4			8					3		6	9	11		7	5		1				10	2		
12	Oct	1	Crystal Palace	2-1	Thompson, Luke	16596	4			8					3		6	9	11		7	5		1				10	2		
13		4	YORK CITY	1-5	Clark	9799	4			8					3		6	9	11			5		1			7	10	2		
14		8	Chester	1-1	Thompson	3220	4			8		5	11		3		6	9			7			1				10	2		
15		11	WALSALL	1-1	Clark	6434	4			10		5			3		6	9	11		7			1				8	2		
16		18	Millwall	2-3	Smith 2	14157	4					5			3		6	8	11		7			1			9	10	2		
17		25	ALDERSHOT	0-3		6158		4		8		5			3		6	7	11					1			9	10	2		
18	Nov	1	Gateshead	0-3		3927		4		8					3		6		11		7	5		1				10	2		9
19		8	OLDHAM ATHLETIC	4-0	Langland 2, Johnson, Anderson (p)	4329	6		2	7		5					8	9	11					1	10				3	4	
20		22	CARLISLE UNITED	1-2	Clark	4064	6		2	7		5					8	9	11					1	10				3	4	
21		29	Gillingham	1-4	Johnson	6121	6		2	8		5	11				10				7			1			9		3	4	
22	Dec	13	Coventry City	1-4	Johnson	11118	6		2	7		5					8		11				10	1			9		3	4	
23		20	Shrewsbury Town	0-3		4783	6	10	2	7		5					8		11					1			9		3	4	
24		26	DARLINGTON	1-0	Anderson (p)	5689	6	9	2	7							8	10	11			5		1					3	4	
25		27	Darlington	1-3	Anderson	6861	6	9	2	7							8	10	11			5		1					3	4	
26	Jan	1	CHESTER	1-3	Langland	3952	6	9	2	7							8	10	11			5		1					3	4	
27		3	SOUTHPORT	1-1	Clark	4137	6	4	2	7							8		11			5		1		10	9		3		
28		17	Torquay United	3-1	Denham 2, Smith	3990	6		2	10	7						4		11			5		1		8	9		3		
29		24	EXETER CITY	3-3	Luke, Scott, Denham	4413	6		2	10	7						4		11			5		1		8	9		3		
30		31	CREWE ALEXANDRA	2-1	Luke, Smith	5118	6		2	10	7						4		11			5		1		8	9		3		
31	Feb	7	Northampton Town	1-2	Clark	6055	6	11	2	10	7						4					5		1		8	9		3		
32		14	WORKINGTON	0-3		3641	6	9	2	10	7						4		11			5		1		8			3		
33		21	York City	1-1	Anderson (p)	5339	6	7	2	10							4	9	11			5		1		8			3		
34		28	Walsall	0-0		7285	6		2	10			11				4	9	7			5	8	1					3		
35	Mar	7	MILLWALL	3-1	Clark, Scott, Luke	3489	6	7	2	10							4	9	11			5		1		8			3		
36		14	Aldershot	4-2	Langland 3, Scott	3932	6	7	2	10							4	9	11			5		1		8			3		
37		21	GATESHEAD	0-0		4156	6	7	2	10							4	9	11			5		1		8			3		
38		27	WATFORD	4-3	Luke 2 (1p), Smith, Burlison	6716	6	7	2								4		11			5		1	10	8	9		3		
39		28	Oldham Athletic	0-1		5154	6	7	2	10							4		11			5		1		8	9		3		
40		30	Watford	1-4	Anderson	6480	6		2	10							4	7	11			5		1		8	9		3		
41	Apr	4	BARROW	10-1	*see below	4126	6		2	10							4	8	11			5		1		7	9		3		
42		11	Carlisle United	0-1		4828	6		2	10			11				4	8				5		1		7	9		3		
43		18	GILLINGHAM	3-1	Clark, Langland, Smith	3169	6	11	2	10							4	8				5		1		7	9		3		
44		21	Barrow	1-1	Clark	3101	6	11	2	10							4	8				5		1		7	9		3		
45		25	Exeter City	0-3		6561	6	11	2	10							4	8				5		1		7	9		3		
46		27	COVENTRY CITY	2-1	MacGregor, Clark	4288	6	11	2	10							4			8		5		1		7	9		3		
						Apps	44	24	33	41	5	10	10	5	13	2	41	27	32	1	12	37	7	41	3	19	24	18	45	8	4
						Goals	7	1		12	3		1				3	9	10	1	3		1			4	10	6			2

Scorers in game 41: Smith 3, Luke 2, Clark 2, Scott, Langland, Marsden (og)

One own goal

F.A. Cup

	Date		Opponent	Score	Scorers	Att.	Anderson WB	Burlison TH	Cameron J	Clark HM	Denham CH	Dixon JW	Dunn BJ	Dyson J	Gibbon AT	Herring H	Johnson K	Langland JR	Luke GT	MacGregor TJ	Mitchell N	Moore W	Nicholson S	Oakley N	Roberts W	Scott JC	Smith J	Thompson P	Waugh K	Walford W	Willis JG
R1	Nov	15	ROCHDALE	1-1	Luke	7154	6		2	7		5					8	9	11					1	10				3	4	
rep		19	Rochdale	3-3	Luke 2, Johnson	8763	6		2	7		5					8	9	11					1	10				3	4	
rep2		27	Rochdale	2-1	Smith, Johnson	6126	6		2	7		5					8		11					1	10		9		3	4	
R2	Dec	6	Barrow	0-2		5718	6		2	7		5					8		11				10	1			9		3	4	

R1 replay a.e.t.. Second replay at Old Trafford.

		P	W	D	L	F	A	W	D	L	F	A	Pts
1	Port Vale	46	14	6	3	62	30	12	6	5	48	28	64
2	Coventry City	46	18	4	1	50	11	6	8	9	34	36	60
3	York City	46	12	10	1	37	17	9	8	6	36	35	60
4	Shrewsbury Town	46	15	5	3	59	24	9	5	9	42	39	58
5	Exeter City	46	16	4	3	55	24	7	7	9	32	37	57
6	Walsall	46	13	5	5	56	25	8	5	10	39	39	52
7	Crystal Palace	46	12	8	3	54	27	8	4	11	36	44	52
8	Northampton Town	46	14	5	4	48	25	7	4	12	37	53	51
9	Millwall	46	13	6	4	46	23	7	4	12	30	46	50
10	Carlisle United	46	11	6	6	37	30	8	6	9	25	35	50
11	Gillingham	46	14	6	3	53	27	6	3	14	29	50	49
12	Torquay United	46	11	5	7	45	32	5	7	11	33	45	44
13	Chester	46	10	5	8	39	33	6	7	10	33	51	44
14	Bradford Park Ave.	46	15	1	7	51	29	3	6	14	24	48	43
15	Watford	46	10	6	7	46	36	6	4	13	35	43	42
16	Darlington	46	7	8	8	37	36	6	8	9	29	32	42
17	Workington	46	9	10	4	40	32	3	7	13	23	46	41
18	Crewe Alexandra	46	11	5	7	52	32	4	5	14	18	50	40
19	HARTLEPOOLS UTD.	46	11	4	8	50	41	4	6	13	24	47	40
20	Gateshead	46	11	3	9	33	30	5	5	13	23	55	40
21	Oldham Athletic	46	15	0	8	39	29	1	4	18	20	55	36
22	Aldershot	46	8	4	11	37	45	6	3	14	26	52	35
23	Barrow	46	6	6	11	34	45	3	4	16	17	59	28
24	Southport	46	7	8	8	26	25	0	4	19	15	61	26

1959/60 Bottom of Division 4

							Anderson WB	Atkinson CBC	Bircham WC	Burlison TH	Butler K	Cameron J	Clark HM	Dixon JW	Dunn BJ	Folland R	Johnson K	Langland JR	Luke GT	MacGregor TJ	McKenna F	Moore W	Oakley N	Oldham E	Peek J	Robinson JN	Scott JC	Smith J	Waugh K	Wilkinson J
1	Aug	22	ALDERSHOT	3-0	Smith 2, Clark	6016	6	5				3	10				4		11		7		1				8	9	2	
2		25	Walsall	2-2	Smith, Luke	11244	6	5				2	10				4		11		7		1	3			8	9		
3		29	Crewe Alexandra	0-1		8005	6	5				2	10				4		11		7		1	3			8	9		
4		31	WALSALL	1-2	Smith	6877	6	5				2	10				4		11		7		1	3			8	9		
5	Sep	5	CHESTER	2-3	Clark, Smith	5112	6	5				3	10				4		11		7		1			10		9	2	
6		7	OLDHAM ATHLETIC	2-2	Langland, Clark	4404		6		7		3	10				4	8	11			5	1					9	2	
7		12	Crystal Palace	2-5	Smith, Langland	14722	4	6				3	10				7	8	11			5	1					9	2	
8		15	Oldham Athletic	2-1	Smith, McGill (og)	5697	2	6					10				4		11		7	5	1				8	9	3	
9		19	BRADFORD PARK AVE.	3-0	Clark 2, Scott	4109	2	6					10				4		11		7	5	1				8	9	3	
10		21	NOTTS COUNTY	2-4	Smith 2	3926	2	6					10				4		11	7		5	1				8	9	3	
11		26	Stockport County	1-2	Clark	5931	2	6					10				4		11	7		5	1				8	9	3	
12	Oct	1	Notts County	0-4		10732	2	5					10	3			4		11		7		1			6	8	9		
13		3	EXETER CITY	4-3	Anderson (p), Luke, Clark 2	3804	2	5					10	3			4		11		7		1			6	8	9		
14		10	GATESHEAD	3-0	Clark, Smith, McKenna	3832	2	5				3	10				4		11		7		1			6	8	9		
15		13	Watford	2-7	McKenna, Luke	11183	2	5					10	3			4		11		7		1			6	8	9		
16		17	Rochdale	0-2		4856	2	5				3	10		11		4				7		1			6	8	9		
17		24	WORKINGTON	1-4	Smith	2717	2	5				3	10		11		4				7		1			6	8	9		
18		31	Doncaster Rovers	1-5	Clark	4149	6						10	3	11		8			4		5	1				7	9	2	
19	Nov	7	NORTHAMPTON T	1-4	Scott	1953	2	5		4			10		11		6				7		1				8	9	3	
20		21	MILLWALL	0-2		2677	6	3									4	11		10	7	5	1				8	9	2	
21		28	Southport	1-2	Smith	3208	6	3									4	11		10	7	5	1				8	9	2	
22	Dec	12	Barrow	2-2	Clark, Clark (og)	4445	6	3					10				4	11			7	5	1				8	9	2	
23		19	Aldershot	0-3		2857	6						10	3			4	11			7	5	1				8	9	2	
24		26	DARLINGTON	1-2	Smith	5018	6						10	3			4	11			7	5	1				8	9	2	
25		28	Darlington	0-2		5109	6						10	3	11		4				7	5	1				8	9	2	
26	Jan	2	CREWE ALEXANDRA	2-0	Smith, Clark	3398	6						7	3	11		4	10				5	1				8	9	2	
27		9	Torquay United	0-3		5082	6						7				4	10			11	5	1	3			8	9	2	
28		16	Chester	1-1	McKenna	4653	6				11		10				4				7	5	1	3			8	9	2	
29		23	CRYSTAL PALACE	0-1		3981	6				11		10				4				7	5	1	3			8	9	2	
30		30	GILLINGHAM	3-1	Clark 2, Smith	2659	6				11		10				4				7	5	1	3			8	9	2	
31	Feb	6	Bradford Park Avenue	2-6	Scott, Johnson	6921	6		7		11		10				4					5	1	3			8	9	2	
32		13	STOCKPORT COUNTY	2-1	Smith, Clark	2870	6		7		11		10				4					5	1	3			8	9	2	
33		20	Exeter City	0-5		6996	6		7		11		10				4					5	1	3			8	9	2	
34		27	Gateshead	1-1	Clark	2652	6		7		11		10				4					5	1	3			8	9	2	
35	Mar	5	ROCHDALE	0-1		3286	6		7		11		10				4					5	1	3			8	9	2	
36		12	Workington	0-3		3663	4		7				11			9						5	1		2	6	8	10	3	
37		19	DONCASTER ROVERS	2-6	Bircham, Clark	2893	4		7				11								9	5	1		2	6	8	10	3	
38		23	WATFORD	0-0		2189	6		7				11							4	9	5			3		8	10	2	1
39		26	Northampton Town	0-3		5954	6		7				11							4	9	5			3		8	10	2	1
40	Apr	2	TORQUAY UNITED	4-0	McKenna 2, Smith, Clark	2754	6						11					8		4	9	5			3		7	10	2	1
41		9	Millwall	0-4		11356	6						11				4	8			9	5			3		7	10	2	1
42		15	Carlisle United	1-1	Clark	3164	6						11				8			4	9	5			2		7	10	3	1
43		16	SOUTHPORT	3-2	Clark, Scott (p), Bircham	3249	3	5	7		11		10				4			6							8	9	2	1
44		18	CARLISLE UNITED	1-2	Clark	3603	3				11		10				4			6	7	5					8	9	2	1
45		23	Gillingham	1-3	Butler	5373	3	5			11		10	6						4	7						8	9	2	1
46		30	BARROW	0-1		2533	3	5			11		10	6		9				4							7	8	2	1
						Apps	45	24	10	2	12	10	44	10	6	2	39	11	15	13	32	31	37	12	7	9	43	46	37	9
						Goals	1		2		1		21				1	2	3		5						4	17		

Two own goals

F.A. Cup

							Anderson WB	Atkinson CBC	Bircham WC	Burlison TH	Butler K	Cameron J	Clark HM	Dixon JW	Dunn BJ	Folland R	Johnson K	Langland JR	Luke GT	MacGregor TJ	McKenna F	Moore W	Oakley N	Oldham E	Peek J	Robinson JN	Scott JC	Smith J	Waugh K	Wilkinson J
R1	Nov	14	Bury	0-5		9694	2	5		4					11		6	10			7		1				8	9	3	

		P	W	D	L	F	A	W	D	L	F	A	Pts
1	Walsall	46	14	5	4	57	33	14	4	5	45	27	65
2	Notts County	46	19	1	3	66	27	7	7	9	41	42	60
3	Torquay United	46	17	3	3	56	27	9	5	9	28	31	60
4	Watford	46	17	2	4	62	28	7	7	9	30	39	57
5	Millwall	46	12	8	3	54	28	6	9	8	30	33	53
6	Northampton Town	46	13	6	4	50	22	9	3	11	35	41	53
7	Gillingham	46	17	4	2	47	21	4	6	13	27	48	52
8	Crystal Palace	46	12	6	5	61	27	7	6	10	23	37	50
9	Exeter City	46	13	7	3	50	30	6	4	13	30	40	49
10	Stockport County	46	15	6	2	35	10	4	5	14	23	44	49
11	Bradford Park Ave.	46	12	10	1	48	25	5	5	13	22	43	49
12	Rochdale	46	15	4	4	46	19	3	6	14	19	41	46
13	Aldershot	46	14	5	4	50	22	4	4	15	27	52	45
14	Crewe Alexandra	46	14	3	6	51	31	4	6	13	28	57	45
15	Darlington	46	11	6	6	40	30	6	3	14	23	43	43
16	Workington	46	10	8	5	41	20	4	6	13	27	40	42
17	Doncaster Rovers	46	13	3	7	40	23	3	7	13	29	53	42
18	Barrow	46	11	8	4	52	29	4	3	16	25	58	41
19	Carlisle United	46	9	6	8	28	28	6	5	12	23	38	41
20	Chester	46	10	8	5	37	26	4	4	15	22	51	40
21	Southport	46	9	7	7	30	32	1	7	15	18	60	34
22	Gateshead	46	12	3	8	37	27	0	6	17	21	59	33
23	Oldham Athletic	46	5	7	11	20	30	3	5	15	21	53	28
24	HARTLEPOOLS UTD.	46	9	2	12	40	41	1	5	17	19	68	27

1960/61

23rd in Division 4

No.	Month	Day	Opponents	Score	Scorers	Att.	Anderson WB	Atkinson CBC	Bilcliff R	Bircham WC	Burlison TH	Butler K	Cain JP	Clark HM	Clydesdale W	Cooper D	Dixon JW	Dunn BJ	Folland R	Godbold H	Johnson K	Jones K	Lackenby G	Lithgo G	Lonsdale JS	Lumley R	MacGregor TJ	Melville AA	Oakley N	Parkes BJ	Patterson GT	Waugh K	Wilkinson J
1	Aug	20	Southport	0-2		4062	3			7		11		10		9					4		5			8					6	2	1
2		22	PETERBOROUGH UTD.	0-2		10784	3			7		11		10		9					4		5			8					6	2	1
3		27	DARLINGTON	5-0	Clark,Anderson 2(2p),Folland,Johnson	5852	6					11		7	3				9		8		5			10					4	2	1
4		29	Peterborough United	2-3	Johnson 2	15245	6					11		7	3				9		8		5			10					4	2	1
5	Sep	3	Crystal Palace	2-2	MacGregor, Folland	19099	3							7				11	9		8		5			10	4				6	2	1
6		5	STOCKPORT COUNTY	0-2		7937	3							7				11	9		8		5			10	4				6	2	1
7		10	DONCASTER ROVERS	2-1	Lumley, Folland	4711	6						4	7	3			11	9		8		5			10						2	1
8		12	Stockport County	1-1	Clark	8958	6						4	7	3		9	11			8		5			10						2	1
9		17	Crewe Alexandra	0-3		5535	6							7	3			11	9		8		5			10					4	2	1
10		19	EXETER CITY	0-0		3156	6							7	3	9		11			8		5			10					4	2	1
11		24	Wrexham	0-1		6340	6			7				10	3			11			9		5			8					4	2	1
12		26	Exeter City	1-2	Patterson	4376	6			7			4		3			11			9		5			10					8	2	1
13	Oct	1	CARLISLE UNITED	0-1		3259	6			7			4		3			11			9		5			10					8	2	1
14		3	Rochdale	0-4		3852				7		11	4	10	3						9		5			8					6	2	1
15		8	ACCRINGTON STANLEY	4-1	Johnson 3(1p), Clark	2525				7		11	6	10	3						9		5			8					4	2	1
16		15	Millwall	2-5	Butler, Bircham	7855	6			7		11		10	3						9		5			8	4					2	1
17		22	BARROW	0-2		2939				7	6	11		10	3						9		5			8	4					2	1
18		29	Gillingham	1-5	Bircham	3816	3			7				11		8	6				9		5			10	4					2	1
19	Nov	12	Northampton Town	3-3	Cooper 2, Lumley	9484	6	3		7				11		8	5				9		2			10	4		1				
20		19	ALDERSHOT	3-1	Cooper, Lumley, Clark	2767	6			7				10		9	2	11					5		3	8	4		1				
21	Dec	3	WORKINGTON	4-1	Johnson, Cooper, Clark, Dixon (p)	2662	6			7				11		9	2				8		5		3	10	4		1				
22		10	Chester	2-1	Clark, Johnson	2644	6			7				10		9	2				11		5		3	8	4		1				
23		17	SOUTHPORT	1-5	Johnson	3735	6			7				10		9	2				11		5		3	8	4		1				
24		26	Mansfield Town	1-2	Cooper	6283	6			7				10		9	2				11		5		3	8	4		1				
25		27	MANSFIELD TOWN	3-2	Bradley (og), Cooper, Clark	4094	3			7				10		9	2				11					8	4	5	1		6		
26		31	Darlington	0-4		7994				7				10		9	2				11		5		3	8	4		1		6		
27	Jan	2	YORK CITY	1-3	Dixon (p)	5337		3		7				10		9	2	11			4		5			8	6		1				
28		7	Oldham Athletic	1-2	Johnson	13551				7				10		9	3				11		5			8	4		1		6	2	
29		14	CRYSTAL PALACE	2-4	Bircham, McNichol (og)	4430				7						9	3			11	10		5			8	4		1		6	2	
30		21	Doncaster Rovers	3-5	Clark, Lumley, Lunn (og)	2771				7				10			2			11	9		5		3	8	4		1		6		
31		28	BRADFORD PARK AVE.	2-4	Lumley, Clark	3207			2	7				10					9	11	6	3	5			8	4		1				
32	Feb	4	CREWE ALEXANDRA	1-2	Godbold	3317			2	7						9	6			11	8	3	4					5		10			1
33		11	WREXHAM	0-0		2672			2	7	6			10						11	9	3	5			8	4						1
34		18	Carlisle United	2-2	Godbold, Clark	3667			2	7	6			10						11	9	3	5			8	4						1
35		25	Accrington Stanley	0-3		2059			2	7	6			10						11	9	3	5			8	4						1
36	Mar	4	MILLWALL	2-2	Godbold, Lumley	2698			2		6			10						11	9	3	5		7	8	4						1
37		11	Barrow	1-2	Parkes	3083			2		6		4	9						11		3	5		7	8				10			1
38		18	GILLINGHAM	1-0	Godbold	2332			2	7	6		4						9	11		3	5			8				10			1
39		25	Bradford Park Avenue	3-1	Johnson 2, Folland	8975				7	6		4						9	11	8	3	5							10		2	1
40		31	York City	0-4		8933				7	6		4		3				9		8		5			11				10		2	1
41	Apr	1	NORTHAMPTON T	4-2	Parkes 3 (2p), Folland	3460			2	7	6		4						9	11	8	3	5							10			1
42		8	Aldershot	0-4		5153			2	7	6		4						9	11	8	3	5							10			1
43		15	OLDHAM ATHLETIC	5-1	Folland 5	4078				7	6		4						9	11	8	3	5							10		2	1
44		22	Workington	0-2		2246			4	7			6						9	11	8	3	5							10		2	1
45		24	ROCHDALE	2-0	Parkes 2	3771			2	7			4						9	11	6	3	5	8						10			1
46		29	CHESTER	4-4	Folland 2, Lithgo, Parkes (p)	4381			2	7			4						9	11	6	3	5	8						10			1
						Apps	22	2	13	36	12	8	16	33	14	16	15	11	16	17	43	15	45	2	9	38	22	2	13	11	18	24	33
						Goals	2			3		1		10		6	2		12	4	12			1		6	1			7	1		

Three own goals

F.A. Cup

Rd	Month	Day	Opponents	Score	Scorers	Att.	Anderson WB	Atkinson CBC	Bilcliff R	Bircham WC	Burlison TH	Butler K	Cain JP	Clark HM	Clydesdale W	Cooper D	Dixon JW	Dunn BJ	Folland R	Godbold H	Johnson K	Jones K	Lackenby G	Lithgo G	Lonsdale JS	Lumley R	MacGregor TJ	Melville AA	Oakley N	Parkes BJ	Patterson GT	Waugh K	Wilkinson J
R1	Nov	5	Halifax Town	1-5	Cooper	6402	3			7				11		8	6				9		5			10	4		1			2	

F.L. Cup

Rd	Month	Day	Opponents	Score	Scorers	Att.	Anderson WB	Atkinson CBC	Bilcliff R	Bircham WC	Burlison TH	Butler K	Cain JP	Clark HM	Clydesdale W	Cooper D	Dixon JW	Dunn BJ	Folland R	Godbold H	Johnson K	Jones K	Lackenby G	Lithgo G	Lonsdale JS	Lumley R	MacGregor TJ	Melville AA	Oakley N	Parkes BJ	Patterson GT	Waugh K	Wilkinson J
R1	Oct	11	Oldham Athletic	1-2	Johnson	3630				7		11	6	10	3						9		5			8					4	2	1

		P	W	D	L	F	A	W	D	L	F	A	Pts
1	Peterborough Utd.	46	18	3	2	85	30	10	7	6	49	35	66
2	Crystal Palace	46	16	4	3	64	28	13	2	8	46	41	64
3	Northampton Town	46	16	4	3	53	25	9	6	8	37	37	60
4	Bradford Park Ave.	46	16	5	2	49	22	10	3	10	35	52	60
5	York City	46	17	3	3	50	14	4	6	13	30	46	51
6	Millwall	46	13	3	7	56	33	8	5	10	41	53	50
7	Darlington	46	11	7	5	41	24	7	6	10	37	46	49
8	Workington	46	14	3	6	38	28	7	4	12	36	48	49
9	Crewe Alexandra	46	11	4	8	40	29	9	5	9	21	38	49
10	Aldershot	46	16	4	3	55	19	2	5	16	24	50	45
11	Doncaster Rovers	46	15	0	8	52	33	4	7	12	24	45	45
12	Oldham Athletic	46	13	4	6	57	38	6	3	14	22	50	45
13	Stockport County	46	14	4	5	31	21	4	5	14	26	45	45
14	Southport	46	12	6	5	47	27	7	0	16	22	40	44
15	Gillingham	46	9	7	7	45	34	6	6	11	19	32	43
16	Wrexham	46	12	4	7	38	22	5	4	14	24	34	42
17	Rochdale	46	13	7	3	43	19	4	1	18	17	47	42
18	Accrington Stanley	46	12	4	7	44	32	4	4	15	30	56	40
19	Carlisle United	46	10	7	6	43	37	3	6	14	18	42	39
20	Mansfield Town	46	10	3	10	39	34	6	3	14	32	44	38
21	Exeter City	46	12	3	8	39	32	2	7	14	27	62	38
22	Barrow	46	10	6	7	33	28	3	5	15	19	51	37
23	HARTLEPOOLS UTD.	46	10	4	9	46	40	2	4	17	25	63	32
24	Chester	46	9	7	7	38	35	2	2	19	23	69	31

1961/62

22nd in Division 4

#	Month	Day	Opponent	Score	Scorers	Att	Bilcliff R	Bircham WC	Burlison TH	Cain JP	Edgar J	Folland R	Fraser AM	Godbold H	Hawkes B	Hinchliffe J	Johnson K	Jones K	Lackenby G	Lithgo G	MacGregor TJ	McLean JD	Melville AA	Oakley N	Parkes BJ	Price KE	Waugh K	Wilkie D	Wilkinson J
1	Aug	19	Rochdale	1-3	Milburn (og)	2400	2	7	6		8			11			4	3	5						10	9			1
2		21	OLDHAM ATHLETIC	1-1	Folland	6167			6		8	9		11			4	3	5						10	7	2		1
3		26	SOUTHPORT	4-2	Folland 2, Edgar, Price	4804			6		8	9		11			4	3	5						10	7	2		1
4		30	Oldham Athletic	2-5	Godbold, Edgar	12777			6		8	9		11	10		4	3	5							7	2		1
5	Sep	1	Tranmere Rovers	2-3	Edgar, Folland	9728		7	6		8	9		11			4	3	5						10		2		1
6		4	STOCKPORT COUNTY	2-2	Folland, Godbold	6313		7	6		8	9		11			4	3	5						10		2		1
7		9	CHESTER	1-3	Folland	4838		7	6		8	9		11			4	3		10			5				2		1
8		16	Colchester United	1-6	Edgar	5036		7		6	8	9		11			4	3		10			5				2		1
9		20	Crewe Alexandra	0-3		5948	3			6	8	9		11			4			10			5	1		7	2		
10		23	CARLISLE UNITED	0-3		3831	3	7		6	8	9			11		4			10				1			2	5	
11		25	CREWE ALEXANDRA	2-1	Edgar, Folland	2904	3			6	8	9			11		4			7					10		2	5	1
12		30	Bradford City	1-5	Lithgo	4347	3			6	8	9			11		4			7					10		2	5	1
13	Oct	2	ALDERSHOT	0-2		3374	3			6	8	9			11		10		4	7							2	5	1
14		7	Exeter City	1-1	Edgar	4173	3			6	8	9		11			7		4						10		2	5	1
15		9	Aldershot	1-1	Edgar	7671	3			6	8	9		11			7		4						10		2	5	1
16		14	WREXHAM	1-4	Edgar	6798	3				8	9				4	11		6			7			10		2	5	1
17		21	DONCASTER ROVERS	3-0	Malloy (og), Folland 2	4621	3			6	8	9		11		4			2			7			10			5	1
18		28	WORKINGTON	0-1		5076	3			6	8	9		11		4			2			7			10			5	1
19	Nov	11	CHESTERFIELD	1-2	Johnson	4116	3			6		9		11	10	4	8		2			7						5	1
20		18	Gillingham	0-4		6562	3			6	8	9		11	10	4	7		2									5	1
21	Dec	2	Mansfield Town	1-3	Hinchliffe	6619	3			6		9		11		4	8		2			7			10			5	1
22		9	BARROW	2-3	Johnson, McLean	3206	3	11		6		9	4			10	8		2			7						5	1
23		16	ROCHDALE	3-1	Edgar 2, Folland	2387	2	7	6		10	9		11		4		3				8						5	1
24		23	Southport	1-0	Bircham	3850	2	7	6		10	9		11		4		3				8						5	1
25	Jan	13	TRANMERE ROVERS	0-0		4121	2	7	6		10	9		11		4		3				8						5	1
26		20	Chester	4-4	Bircham, Edgar 3	2602	2	7	6		10	9		11		4		3				8						5	1
27		27	MILLWALL	2-0	Bircham, Johnson	5008		7	6		10				11	4	9	3	2			8						5	1
28	Feb	3	COLCHESTER UNITED	1-1	Bircham	6918		7	6		10			11		4	9	3	2			8						5	1
29		10	Carlisle United	0-1		4208	2	7	6		10			11		4	9	3				8						5	1
30		17	BRADFORD CITY	1-3	Edgar	4757	2	7	6		10		5		11	4	9	3				8							1
31		24	EXETER CITY	0-0		3113	2	7	6		10	9		11				3	4			8						5	1
32	Mar	3	Wrexham	1-10	Folland	6546	2	7	6		10	9		11		4		3	5			8							1
33		10	Doncaster Rovers	2-2	Price 2	2291	2	7	6		10					4	11					8				9	3	5	1
34		17	Workington	1-1	McLean	2355	2	7	6		10					4	11		3			8				9		5	1
35		19	York City	0-2		6613	2	7			10		6			4	11		3			8		1		9		5	
36		24	YORK CITY	0-2		3130	2	7	6			9	4	11			8		3					1	10			5	
37		31	Chesterfield	0-2		2701	2	7	6		9		4	11			8		3	10				1				5	
38	Apr	7	GILLINGHAM	1-3	Edgar	2434	2	7	6		9		4	11					3	10		8		1				5	
39		9	Stockport County	1-1	Johnson	4024	2	7	11		9		4				10		3		6	8		1				5	
40		14	Millwall	2-3	Burlison, Edgar	10709	2	7	11		9		4				10		3		6	8		1				5	
41		20	DARLINGTON	2-0	Edgar 2	4899		7	11		9		4				10		3		6	8		1			2	5	
42		21	MANSFIELD TOWN	0-1		2239		7	11		9		4				10		3		6	8		1			2	5	
43		23	Darlington	2-1	Edgar 2	3380		7	11		9		4				10		3		6	8		1			2	5	
44		28	Barrow	1-5	Johnson	3811		7	11		9		4				10		3		6	8		1			2	5	
						Apps	31	29	28	14	40	28	12	27	9	19	35	18	31	9	6	26	3	12	14	8	20	33	32
						Goals		4	1		20	11		2		1	5			1		2				3			

Two own goals

F.A. Cup

Rd	Month	Day	Opponent	Score	Scorers	Att	Bilcliff R	Bircham WC	Burlison TH	Cain JP	Edgar J	Folland R	Fraser AM	Godbold H	Hawkes B	Hinchliffe J	Johnson K	Jones K	Lackenby G	Lithgo G	MacGregor TJ	McLean JD	Melville AA	Oakley N	Parkes BJ	Price KE	Waugh K	Wilkie D	Wilkinson J
R1	Nov	4	BLYTH SPARTANS	5-1	Folland 3, Johnson, Parkes	5416	3			6		9		11		4	8		2			7			10			5	1
R2	Nov	25	ACCRINGTON STANLEY	2-1	Folland, McLean	5227	3			6		9		11		4	8		2			7			10			5	1
R3	Jan	6	Fulham	1-3	Burlison	18044	2	7	6		10	9		11		4		3				8						5	1

F.L. Cup

Rd	Month	Day	Opponent	Score	Scorers	Att	Bilcliff R	Bircham WC	Burlison TH	Cain JP	Edgar J	Folland R	Fraser AM	Godbold H	Hawkes B	Hinchliffe J	Johnson K	Jones K	Lackenby G	Lithgo G	MacGregor TJ	McLean JD	Melville AA	Oakley N	Parkes BJ	Price KE	Waugh K	Wilkie D	Wilkinson J
R1	Sep	11	Bristol Rovers	1-2	Lithgo	8469		7		6	8	9		11			4	3		10			5				2		1

		P	W	D	L	F	A	W	D	L	F	A	Pts
1	Millwall	44	16	3	3	47	18	7	7	8	40	44	56
2	Colchester United	44	17	4	1	78	24	6	5	11	26	47	55
3	Wrexham	44	12	6	4	56	23	10	3	9	40	33	53
4	Carlisle United	44	15	3	4	35	22	7	5	10	29	41	52
5	Bradford City	44	14	5	3	58	32	7	4	11	36	54	51
6	York City	44	17	2	3	62	19	3	8	11	22	34	50
7	Aldershot	44	16	4	2	56	20	6	1	15	25	40	49
8	Workington	44	12	6	4	40	23	7	5	10	29	47	49
9	Barrow	44	12	7	3	49	20	5	7	10	25	38	48
10	Crewe Alexandra	44	16	3	3	53	24	4	3	15	26	46	46
11	Oldham Athletic	44	12	7	3	47	26	5	5	12	30	44	46
12	Rochdale	44	14	3	5	47	28	5	4	13	24	43	45
13	Darlington	44	13	5	4	37	24	5	4	13	24	49	45
14	Mansfield Town	44	14	3	5	51	19	5	3	14	26	47	44
15	Tranmere Rovers	44	15	2	5	53	37	5	2	15	17	44	44
16	Stockport County	44	13	3	6	42	27	4	6	12	28	42	43
17	Southport	44	13	5	4	36	25	4	4	14	25	46	43
18	Exeter City	44	11	5	6	43	32	2	6	14	19	45	37
19	Chesterfield	44	11	3	8	43	38	3	6	13	27	49	37
20	Gillingham	44	10	6	6	48	30	3	5	14	25	64	37
21	Doncaster Rovers	44	8	5	9	34	29	3	2	17	26	56	29
22	HARTLEPOOLS UTD.	44	6	5	11	27	35	2	6	14	25	66	27
23	Chester	44	5	9	8	36	37	2	3	17	18	59	26

1962/63 Bottom of Division 4

No			Opponent	Score	Scorers	Att	Atkinson CBC	Bilcliff R	Bircham WC	Brown JT	Burlison TH	Douglas JS(2)	Edgar J	Folland R	Fraser AM	Godbold H	Hinchliffe J	Johnson K	Lackenby G	Lithgo G	MacGregor TJ	McLean JD	Miller LR	Oakley N	Parkes BJ	Thomson KG	Wilkie D	Younger W
1	Aug	18	NEWPORT COUNTY	2-3	Edgar (p), Bircham	5391		2	7	3			9		6		4					8		1	10		5	11
2		20	Southport	1-1	Edgar	4520		2	7	3			9		6		4					8		1	10		5	11
3		25	Oxford United	2-6	McLean, Edgar (p)	9099		2	7	3			9		6		4					8		1	10		5	11
4		27	SOUTHPORT	4-0	Bircham 2, McLean 2	5172		2	7	3	6			9		11	4					8		1			5	10
5	Sep	1	BRADFORD CITY	2-2	McLean, Edgar	6450		2	7	3	6		9			11	4					8		1			5	10
6		3	DARLINGTON	0-2		8690		2	7	3	6		9			11	4					8		1			5	10
7		8	Tranmere Rovers	1-6	Manning (og)	6143	5	2	7	3	6		10	9			4					8		1				11
8		10	Darlington	2-0	McLean, Younger	6888		2	7	3	6		9			11	4					8		1			5	10
9		15	TORQUAY UNITED	0-3		5248		2	7	3	6		9			11	4					8		1			5	10
10		19	Aldershot	2-3	Bircham 2	5849		2	7	3	6		9			11		4		8				1			5	10
11		22	Lincoln City	1-4	Edgar	5014		2	7	3	6		9			11		4		8				1			5	10
12		24	ALDERSHOT	1-2	Younger	3250		2	7	3	11		9				4	6				8		1			5	10
13		29	OLDHAM ATHLETIC	0-1		4129		2	7	3	11		9				4	6				8		1			5	10
14	Oct	2	Brentford	0-4		10729		2	7	3	11		9				4	6				8		1			5	10
15		6	ROCHDALE	4-0	McLean 2, Edgar 2	3850		2	7	3	11		9				4	6				8		1			5	10
16		13	Chesterfield	2-2	Burlison, McLean	6540		2	7	3	11		9				4	6				8		1		5		10
17		20	EXETER CITY	0-2		5143			7	3	11		9					6	2		4	8		1		5		10
18		27	Workington	0-0		2442		2	7	3	11			9	4			6				8		1		5		10
19	Nov	10	Doncaster Rovers	3-2	Douglas, Burlison, McLean	7640		2		3	11	9			4			6				7	8	1		5		10
20		17	STOCKPORT COUNTY	3-0	McLean 2, Miller	3856		2		3	11	9			4			6				7	8	1		5		10
21	Dec	1	CREWE ALEXANDRA	1-5	Thomson	5180		2		3	11	9			4			6				7	8	1		5		10
22		7	Chester	0-1		4441				3	11		8		4			6	2			7	9	1		5		10
23		15	Newport County	1-2	Younger	2388				3	11	9	8		4			6	2			7		1		5		10
24		22	OXFORD UNITED	1-2	Edgar	3308			7	3	11	9	8		4			6	2					1		5		10
25	Feb	2	Torquay United	0-2		2736		2		3			8		4			9	6			7	11	1		5		10
26	Mar	9	Exeter City	1-3	Edgar	2815		2		3	11		8		4			6		9		7		1		5		10
27		12	Rochdale	1-2	Godbold	2857		2		3			8		4	11		6	9			7		1		5		10
28		16	WORKINGTON	2-2	Johnson, Folland	2602		2		3			8	9	4	11		6				7		1		5		10
29		23	Mansfield Town	1-3	Douglas	7554		2		3	6	8		9	4	11						7		1		5		10
30		25	York City	0-2		4558				3	6	8		9	4	11			2			7		1		5		10
31		30	Gillingham	1-5	Miller	5330		2		3	6			9	4	11						8	7	1	10	5		
32	Apr	1	GILLINGHAM	1-1	Douglas	2629				3	6	8		9	4	11							7	1		5	2	10
33		6	Stockport County	1-4	Hinchliffe (p)	2619				3		8		9	4	11	6	10					7	1		5	2	
34		8	CHESTERFIELD	1-1	Hinchliffe (p)	2565				3		8		9	4	11	6	10					7	1		5	2	
35		12	BARROW	1-1	Godbold	3494	5			3		8		9	4	11	6	10				7		1			2	
36		13	DONCASTER ROVERS	1-1	Douglas	2666	5		7	3		9		10	4	11	6					8		1			2	
37		15	Barrow	0-2		4010			7	3		9	10		4	11	6					8		1		5	2	
38		20	Crewe Alexandra	1-4	Edgar	5002			7	3			10		4	11	6		9			8		1		5	2	
39		22	BRENTFORD	2-1	Edgar, Lackenby	3465			7	3			10		4	11	6		9			8		1		5	2	
40		27	CHESTER	0-3		2728			7	3			10		4	11	6		9			8		1		5	2	
41		29	YORK CITY	1-1	Thomson	2659		2	7	3	6		10				4	9				8		1		5		11
42	May	4	LINCOLN CITY	3-0	Jones (og), Brown, Bircham	2683		2	7	9	6		10				4					8		1		5	3	11
43		8	Oldham Athletic	1-6	Brown	12283		2	7	9	6		10				4					8		1		5	3	11
44		11	Bradford City	1-1	Brown	2095		2	7	9	6		10				4					8		1		5	3	11
45		13	MANSFIELD TOWN	3-4	Brown 2, Younger	2735	5	2	7	9	6		10				4					8		1			3	11
46		18	TRANMERE ROVERS	0-2		2028		2	7	9	6						4	10				8		1		5	3	11
						Apps	4	32	30	46	32	13	32	12	26	21	28	24	10	3	1	40	9	46	4	28	28	37
						Goals			6	5	2	4	11	1		2	2	1	1			11	2			2		4

Two own goals

F.A. Cup

Rd			Opponent	Score	Scorers	Att	Atkinson CBC	Bilcliff R	Bircham WC	Brown JT	Burlison TH	Douglas JS(2)	Edgar J	Folland R	Fraser AM	Godbold H	Hinchliffe J	Johnson K	Lackenby G	Lithgo G	MacGregor TJ	McLean JD	Miller LR	Oakley N	Parkes BJ	Thomson KG	Wilkie D	Younger W
R1	Nov	3	Carlisle United	1-2	O'Connell (og)	6627		2	7	3	11			9	4			6				8		1		5		10

F.L. Cup

Rd			Opponent	Score	Scorers	Att	Atkinson CBC	Bilcliff R	Bircham WC	Brown JT	Burlison TH	Douglas JS(2)	Edgar J	Folland R	Fraser AM	Godbold H	Hinchliffe J	Johnson K	Lackenby G	Lithgo G	MacGregor TJ	McLean JD	Miller LR	Oakley N	Parkes BJ	Thomson KG	Wilkie D	Younger W
R1	Sep	6	BARNSLEY	1-1	Younger	2393	5	2	7	3	6		10	9			4					8		1				11
rep		13	Barnsley	1-2	Bircham	5130		2	7	3	6		9			11	4					8		1			5	10

		P	W	D	L	F	A	W	D	L	F	A	Pts
1	Brentford	46	18	2	3	59	31	9	6	8	39	33	62
2	Oldham Athletic	46	18	4	1	65	23	6	7	10	30	37	59
3	Crewe Alexandra	46	15	4	4	50	21	9	7	7	36	37	59
4	Mansfield Town	46	16	4	3	61	20	8	5	10	47	49	57
5	Gillingham	46	17	3	3	49	23	5	10	8	22	26	57
6	Torquay United	46	14	8	1	45	20	6	8	9	30	36	56
7	Rochdale	46	16	6	1	48	21	4	5	14	19	38	51
8	Tranmere Rovers	46	15	3	5	57	25	5	7	11	24	42	50
9	Barrow	46	14	7	2	52	26	5	5	13	30	54	50
10	Workington	46	13	4	6	42	20	4	9	10	34	48	47
11	Aldershot	46	9	9	5	42	32	6	8	9	31	37	47
12	Darlington	46	13	3	7	44	33	6	3	14	28	54	44
13	Southport	46	11	9	3	47	35	4	5	14	25	71	44
14	York City	46	12	6	5	42	25	4	5	14	25	37	43
15	Chesterfield	46	7	10	6	43	29	6	6	11	27	35	42
16	Doncaster Rovers	46	9	10	4	36	26	5	4	14	28	51	42
17	Exeter City	46	9	6	8	27	32	7	4	12	30	45	42
18	Oxford United	46	10	10	3	44	27	3	5	15	26	44	41
19	Stockport County	46	9	7	7	34	29	6	4	13	22	41	41
20	Newport County	46	11	6	6	44	29	3	5	15	32	61	39
21	Chester	46	11	5	7	31	23	4	4	15	20	43	39
22	Lincoln City	46	11	1	11	48	46	2	8	13	20	43	35
23	Bradford City	46	8	5	10	37	40	3	5	15	27	63	32
24	HARTLEPOOLS UTD.	46	5	7	11	33	39	2	4	17	23	65	25

1963/64 23rd in Division 4

No.	Date		Opponent	Score	Scorers	Att.	Atkinson CBC	Bilcliff R	Bradley W	Brown JT	Burlison TH	Cunningham KH	Fogarty AG	Francis T	Fraser AM	Hamilton H	Hinchliffe J	Hinshelwood W	Johnson K	Lithgo G	McCubbin R	McLean JD	Morrell RI	Oakley N	Simpkins K	Stonehouse D	Thompson P	Wallis DR	Wilkie D
1	Aug	24	Aldershot	1-4	Devereux (og)	5666	5		10	9					6	7	4	3		11		8		1					2
2		26	TORQUAY UNITED	1-4	Hinshelwood	5415	5		10	3		9				7	4	6		11		8		1					2
3		31	BRADFORD CITY	1-0	Hinchliffe	3749	5	2	10	3		9				7	4	6		11		8		1					
4	Sep	7	Lincoln City	2-4	Hinchliffe, Hinshelwood	6110		2	10	3	4				5	7	8	6	9	11				1					
5		11	Torquay United	2-4	Lithgo 2	4942	5	2	10	3					4	7	8	6	9	11				1					
6		14	GILLINGHAM	0-0		3022	5	2	10	3	8				4	7		6		11				1				9	
7		16	CARLISLE UNITED	0-6		3815	5	2		3	8				4	7	10	6		11				1				9	
8		21	Southport	1-2	Hinshelwood	3242	5	2		3	10				8	9	4	6		11	7			1					
9		28	EXETER CITY	1-1	Brown	2821	5	2	10	9	6				8		4			11	7			1					3
10	Oct	1	Carlisle United	1-7	Lithgo	7075	5	2	10		6				8	7	4			11				1		3	9		
11		5	BRIGHTON & HOVE ALB	2-2	Hinchliffe (p), Lithgo	3552		2	7	10	6				5		4		8	11				1		3	9		
12		7	Tranmere Rovers	3-2	Johnson, Thompson, Brown	6008		2	7	10	6				5		4		8	11				1			9		3
13		12	York City	1-0	Thompson	5460		2	7	10	6				5		4		8	11				1			9		3
14		19	BARROW	0-0		5267		2	7	10	6				5		4		8	11				1			9		3
15		21	Darlington	0-0		6376		2	7	9	6				5		4		8	11		10		1		3			
16		26	Rochdale	0-2		2764		2	7	9	6				5		4		8	11		10		1		3			
17	Nov	2	OXFORD UNITED	2-1	McLean, Brown	4096		2	11	10	6				5		4		8			7		1		3	9		
18		9	Workington	0-2		4117		2	11	10	6				5		4		8			7		1		3	9		
19		23	Stockport County	0-1		3216		2	11	9	6		8		5		4	10				7		1		3			
20		30	BRADFORD PARK AVE.	4-2	Burlison, Francis 3	5632		2	11		6		8	10	5		4					7		1		3	9		
21	Dec	14	ALDERSHOT	1-4	Fogarty	5116		2	11		6		8	10	5		4					7		1		3	9		
22		21	Bradford City	0-2		3534		2	11		6		8	10	5		4					7		1		3	9		
23		26	CHESTER	2-0	Thompson, Hinchliffe (p)	5531		2	11		6		8	10	5		4					7		1		3	9		
24		28	Chester	1-2	Hamilton	6317		2	11		6		8	9	5	7	4	10						1		3			
25	Jan	1	DARLINGTON	0-2		8642			7		6		8	10	5		4			11				1		3	9		2
26		11	LINCOLN CITY	1-2	Bradley	4330		4	11	9			8	10	5		7	6						1		2			3
27		18	Gillingham	0-2		7536		2	9		11		8		5		7	6	4			10		1		3			
28		25	Chesterfield	2-0	Fogarty 2	3689		2	9		11		8		5		7	6	4			10		1		3			
29	Feb	1	SOUTHPORT	2-3	Thompson 2	3869		2	11				8		5		7	6	4			10		1		3	9		
30		8	Exeter City	1-2	Thompson	6077		2	10		11		8		5		7	6	4					1		3	9		
31		15	Brighton & Hove Albion	1-4	Fogarty	8664		2	10		11		8		5		7	6	4					1		3	9		
32		22	YORK CITY	0-1		3278		2	10				8	11	5		4	6				7		1		3	9		
33		28	Barrow	2-1	Fraser, Thompson	2834	5	2	11				8		10		4		6			7		1		3	9		
34	Mar	7	ROCHDALE	1-1	Fraser	2836	5	2	10		11		8		9		4		6			7			1	3			
35		14	Oxford United	1-5	McLean	4300	5	2	11		6		8		10		4		9			7			1				3
36		21	WORKINGTON	1-2	Bradley	1805	5	2	11				8		9		10		6			7	4		1	3			
37		23	TRANMERE ROVERS	3-2	Bradley, Brown 2	2587	5	2	7	9	11		8	10	6								4		1				3
38		27	HALIFAX TOWN	1-1	Bradley	4841	5	2	7	9	11		8	10	6								4		1				3
39		28	Doncaster Rovers	2-2	Lithgo (p), Johnson	5816	2				6		8	10	5	7			9	11			4		1				3
40		30	Halifax Town	1-4	Hamilton	4860	2				6		8	10	5	7			9	11			4		1				3
41	Apr	4	STOCKPORT COUNTY	3-0	Johnson, Lithgo, Hamilton	2641		2					8	10	5	7	6		9	11			4		1	3			
42		6	NEWPORT COUNTY	1-1	Thompson	4266		2					8		5	7	6		9	11			4		1	3	10		
43		11	Bradford Park Avenue	1-3	McLean	5104		2					8	10	5		6			11		7	4		1	3	9		
44		17	CHESTERFIELD	1-0	Hamilton	4401		2		9			8		5	7	6			11			4		1	3	10		
45		20	DONCASTER ROVERS	2-1	Hinchliffe (p), Fogarty	4385		2	11				8		5	7	6					10	4		1	3	9		
46		25	Newport County	1-2	Bradley	2521		2	11				8		5	7	6					10	4		1	3	9		

	Atkinson CBC	Bilcliff R	Bradley W	Brown JT	Burlison TH	Cunningham KH	Fogarty AG	Francis T	Fraser AM	Hamilton H	Hinchliffe J	Hinshelwood W	Johnson K	Lithgo G	McCubbin R	McLean JD	Morrell RI	Oakley N	Simpkins K	Stonehouse D	Thompson P	Wallis DR	Wilkie D
Apps	17	41	38	22	31	2	28	14	44	17	41	17	23	23	2	23	11	33	13	29	22	2	13
Goals			5	5	1		5	3	2	4	5	3	3	6		3					8		

One own goal

F.A. Cup

Rd	Date		Opponent	Score	Scorers	Att.	Atkinson CBC	Bilcliff R	Bradley W	Brown JT	Burlison TH	Cunningham KH	Fogarty AG	Francis T	Fraser AM	Hamilton H	Hinchliffe J	Hinshelwood W	Johnson K	Lithgo G	McCubbin R	McLean JD	Morrell RI	Oakley N	Simpkins K	Stonehouse D	Thompson P	Wallis DR	Wilkie D
R1	Nov	16	LINCOLN CITY	0-1		5698		2	11	9	6				5		4	10	8			7		1		3			

F.L. Cup

Rd	Date		Opponent	Score	Scorers	Att.	Atkinson CBC	Bilcliff R	Bradley W	Brown JT	Burlison TH	Cunningham KH	Fogarty AG	Francis T	Fraser AM	Hamilton H	Hinchliffe J	Hinshelwood W	Johnson K	Lithgo G	McCubbin R	McLean JD	Morrell RI	Oakley N	Simpkins K	Stonehouse D	Thompson P	Wallis DR	Wilkie D
R1	Sep	4	Lincoln City	2-3	Johnson, Hinchliffe	4748		2		3	10	9			5	7	4	6	8	11				1					

		P	W	D	L	F	A	W	D	L	F	A	Pts
1	Gillingham	46	16	7	0	37	10	7	7	9	22	20	60
2	Carlisle United	46	17	3	3	70	20	8	7	8	43	38	60
3	Workington	46	15	6	2	46	19	9	5	9	30	33	59
4	Exeter City	46	12	9	2	39	14	8	9	6	23	23	58
5	Bradford City	46	15	3	5	45	24	10	3	10	31	38	56
6	Torquay United	46	16	6	1	60	20	4	5	14	20	34	51
7	Tranmere Rovers	46	12	4	7	46	30	8	7	8	39	43	51
8	Brighton & Hove A.	46	13	3	7	45	22	6	9	8	26	30	50
9	Aldershot	46	15	3	5	58	28	4	7	12	25	50	48
10	Halifax Town	46	14	4	5	47	28	3	10	10	30	49	48
11	Lincoln City	46	15	2	6	49	31	4	7	12	18	44	47
12	Chester	46	17	3	3	47	18	2	5	16	18	42	46
13	Bradford Park Ave.	46	13	5	5	50	34	5	4	14	25	47	45
14	Doncaster Rovers	46	11	8	4	46	23	4	4	15	24	52	42
15	Newport County	46	12	3	8	35	24	5	5	13	29	49	42
16	Chesterfield	46	8	9	6	29	27	7	3	13	28	44	42
17	Stockport County	46	12	7	4	32	19	3	5	15	18	49	42
18	Oxford United	46	10	7	6	37	27	4	6	13	22	36	41
19	Darlington	46	8	9	6	40	37	6	3	14	26	56	40
20	Rochdale	46	9	8	6	36	24	3	7	13	20	35	39
21	Southport	46	12	6	5	42	29	3	3	17	21	59	39
22	York City	46	9	3	11	29	26	5	4	14	23	40	35
23	HARTLEPOOLS UTD.	46	8	7	8	30	36	4	2	17	24	57	33
24	Barrow	46	4	10	9	30	36	2	8	13	21	57	30

1964/65

15th in Division 4

	Date	Opponent	Score	Scorers	Att	Ashworth B	Bannister N	Bradley W	Brass RA	Entwistle RP	Fogarty AG	Fox A	Francis T	Hamilton H	Harrison EG	Hodgson M	Marshall WF	Morrell RI	Scott MR	Simpkins K	Stonehouse D	Storton SE	Thompson P	Wright GC
1	Aug 22	Lincoln City	2-4	Bradley, Harrison	5222		7	11			8	5			6		3	4		1		2	9	10
2	24	YORK CITY	2-2	Francis, Bradley	6473			11				5	10	7	6		3	4		1		2	9	8
3	29	BRIGHTON & HOVE ALB	1-1	Thompson	6708			11				5	10	7	6		3	4		1		2	9	8
4	31	York City	0-0		5601			11				5	10	7	6		3	4		1		2	9	8
5	Sep 5	Oxford United	0-3		7990		7	10				5			6		3	4	11	1		2	9	8
6	7	STOCKPORT COUNTY	4-3	Thompson 2, Bradley, Bannister	6619		7	11			8	5			6		3	4		1		2	9	10
7	12	BARROW	3-0	Thompson, Fogarty 2	7128		7	11			8	5			6		3	4		1		2	9	10
8	14	Stockport County	1-0	Fogarty	5259			11			8	5		7	6		3	4		1		2	9	10
9	18	Tranmere Rovers	1-5	Wright	11861		7	11			8	5			6		3	4		1		2	9	10
10	21	TORQUAY UNITED	1-0	Thompson	8563		7	11			8	5			6		3	4		1		2	9	10
11	26	Rochdale	0-3		3736		7	11			8	5			6		3	4		1		2	9	10
12	28	CHESTER	1-1	Fogarty (p)	8822		7	11			8	5			6		3	4		1		2	9	10
13	Oct 3	MILLWALL	1-0	Thompson	10734		7	11			8	5			6		3	4		1		2	9	10
14	7	Chester	0-4		7796		7	11			8	5			6		3	4		1		2	9	10
15	10	CREWE ALEXANDRA	2-4	Bradley, Fogarty	7276		9	11			8	5		7	6		3	4		1		2		10
16	17	Newport County	0-2		3587		9	10			8	5		7	6		3	4	11	1		2		
17	19	Torquay United	1-2	Entwistle	4409		11	10		9	8	5		7	6		3	4		1		2		
18	24	HALIFAX TOWN	4-0	Entwistle, Wright, Bradley, Bannister	4525		7	11		9	10	5			6		3	4		1		2		8
19	28	Wrexham	0-3		7766		7	11		9	10	5			6		3	4		1		2		8
20	31	Notts County	0-1		4924		11			9			10	7	6		3	4		1	2	5		8
21	Nov 7	CHESTERFIELD	1-1	Entwistle	4433		7	11		9	10	5			6		3	4		1		2		8
22	21	ALDERSHOT	1-1	Harrison	5165		7	11		8	10	5			6			4		1	3	2	9	
23	28	Bradford Park Avenue	0-4		5721		7	11		9	10	5			6			4		1	3	2	8	
24	Dec 12	LINCOLN CITY	3-0	Bannister 2, Fogarty	3102		11		4		8	5			6	7				1	3	2	9	10
25	19	Brighton & Hove Albion	0-5		12267		11		4		8	5		7	6		2			1	3	9		10
26	26	DARLINGTON	4-3	Fogarty, Hamilton, Bradley, Harrison	3166		11	10	4		8	5		7	6		3			1		2	9	
27	Jan 2	OXFORD UNITED	1-1	Bannister	4955		11	10	4		8	5		7	6		3			1		2	9	
28	16	Barrow	2-4	Thompson, Hamilton	1781		11	10	4		8	5		7	6		3			1		2	9	
29	23	TRANMERE ROVERS	2-0	Fogarty, Thompson	4578		11	10	4		8	5		7	6		3			1		2	9	
30	30	Doncaster Rovers	1-0	Hamilton	6383		11	10	4		8	5		7	6		3			1		2	9	
31	Feb 6	ROCHDALE	1-1	Bradley	5049		11	10	4		8	5		7	6		3			1		2	9	
32	13	Millwall	0-0		7142		11	10	4		8	5		7	6		3			1		2	9	
33	20	Crewe Alexandra	3-2	Thompson 2, Bannister	5625		11	10	4		8	5		7	6		3			1		2	9	
34	22	Darlington	3-2	Bradley, Atkinson (og), Fogarty (p)	4869		7	11	4	10	8	5			6		3			1		2	9	
35	27	NEWPORT COUNTY	2-4	Thompson, Fogarty	6461		7	11	4	10	8	5			6		3			1		2	9	
36	Mar 13	NOTTS COUNTY	2-2	Bradley, Thompson	5031	10	7	11	4		8	5			6		3			1		2	9	
37	16	Halifax Town	1-2	Thompson	1916	4		11		10	8	5		7	6		3			1		2	9	
38	20	Chesterfield	1-3	Ashworth	3806	4	7	11		10		5			6		3			1		2	9	8
39	29	DONCASTER ROVERS	1-1	Thompson	5935	4	7	11	6	10	8	5					3			1		2	9	
40	Apr 3	Aldershot	0-3		3234	4	7	11	6	9	8	5					3			1		2	10	
41	5	SOUTHPORT	2-1	Bannister 2	5192	4	7	11	6	9	8	5					3			1		2	10	
42	10	BRADFORD PARK AVE.	2-0	Wright, Bradley	4697	4	7	11			8	5			6		3			1		2	9	10
43	16	BRADFORD CITY	2-2	Wright, Ingle (og)	6791	4	7	11			8	5			6		3			1		2	9	10
44	17	Southport	1-1	Thompson	1872	4	7	11			8	5			6		3			1		2	9	10
45	19	Bradford City	0-4		2888	4	7	11			8	5			6		3			1		2	9	10
46	24	WREXHAM	1-0	Thompson	3923	8	7	11	4			5			6		3			1		2	9	10
					Apps	11	41	43	17	14	39	45	4	18	43	1	43	23	2	46	5	46	38	27
					Goals	1	8	10		3	10		1	3	3								16	4

Two own goals

F.A. Cup

	Date	Opponent	Score	Scorers	Att	Ashworth B	Bannister N	Bradley W	Brass RA	Entwistle RP	Fogarty AG	Fox A	Francis T	Hamilton H	Harrison EG	Hodgson M	Marshall WF	Morrell RI	Scott MR	Simpkins K	Stonehouse D	Storton SE	Thompson P	Wright GC
R1	Nov 14	Corby Town	3-1	Entwistle 2, Fogarty (p)	4511		7	11		8	10	5			6			4		1	3	2	9	
R2	Dec 5	DARLINGTON	0-0		9027		7	11			10	5			6			4		1	3	2	9	8
rep	9	Darlington	1-4	Fogarty	14566			11		9	7	5			6			4		1	3	2	8	10

F.L. Cup

	Date	Opponent	Score	Scorers	Att	Ashworth B	Bannister N	Bradley W	Brass RA	Entwistle RP	Fogarty AG	Fox A	Francis T	Hamilton H	Harrison EG	Hodgson M	Marshall WF	Morrell RI	Scott MR	Simpkins K	Stonehouse D	Storton SE	Thompson P	Wright GC
R1	Sep 2	Chesterfield	0-3		4513			10				5	9	7	6		3	4	11	1		2		8

		P	W	D	L	F	A	W	D	L	F	A	Pts
1	Brighton & Hove A.	46	18	5	0	68	20	8	6	9	34	37	63
2	Millwall	46	13	10	0	45	15	10	6	7	33	30	62
3	York City	46	20	1	2	63	21	8	5	10	28	35	62
4	Oxford United	46	18	4	1	54	13	5	11	7	33	31	61
5	Tranmere Rovers	46	20	2	1	72	20	7	4	12	27	36	60
6	Rochdale	46	15	4	4	46	22	7	10	6	28	31	58
7	Bradford Park Ave.	46	14	8	1	52	22	6	9	8	34	40	57
8	Chester	46	19	1	3	75	26	6	5	12	44	55	56
9	Doncaster Rovers	46	13	6	4	46	25	7	5	11	38	47	51
10	Crewe Alexandra	46	11	8	4	55	34	7	5	11	35	47	49
11	Torquay United	46	11	5	7	41	33	10	2	11	29	37	49
12	Chesterfield	46	13	5	5	36	22	7	3	13	22	48	48
13	Notts County	46	12	7	4	43	23	3	7	13	18	50	44
14	Wrexham	46	12	5	6	59	37	5	4	14	25	55	43
15	HARTLEPOOLS UTD.	46	11	10	2	44	28	4	3	16	17	57	43
16	Newport County	46	14	5	4	54	26	3	3	17	31	55	42
17	Darlington	46	14	2	7	52	30	4	4	15	32	57	42
18	Aldershot	46	14	3	6	46	25	1	4	18	18	59	37
19	Bradford City	46	9	2	12	37	36	3	6	14	33	52	32
20	Southport	46	5	9	9	35	45	3	7	13	23	44	32
21	Barrow	46	9	4	10	30	38	3	2	18	29	67	30
22	Lincoln City	46	8	4	11	35	33	3	2	18	23	66	28
23	Halifax Town	46	9	4	10	37	37	2	2	19	17	66	28
24	Stockport County	46	8	4	11	30	34	2	3	18	14	63	27

1965/66 18th in Division 4

						Ashworth B	Bates JW	Bradley W	Brass RA	Cooper JT	Drysdale B	Fogarty AG	Fox A	Gill JBA	Grant BP	Green L	Hamilton H	Harrison EG	Livingstone J	Marshall WF	McGovern JP	McLeod RA	McPheat W	Mulvaney J	Parry AJ	Phythian ER	Simpkins K	Small JH	Storton SE	Thompson P	Wright GC
1	Aug 21	SOUTHPORT	3-1	Mulvaney, Ashworth, Phythian	5756	4				7		8	5					6		3				11		10	1		2	9	
2	24	Doncaster Rovers	0-4		10851	4				7		8	5					6		3				11		10	1		2	9	
3	28	Wrexham	1-1	Mulvaney	6437	4				7		8	5					6		3				11		10	1		2	9	
4	Sep 4	BRADFORD PARK AVE.	2-3	Thompson, Phythian	4205	4				7		8	5					6		3				11		10	1		2	9	
5	11	Aldershot	0-5		5001	4				7	12		5					6		3				11		10	1		2	9	8
6	13	DONCASTER ROVERS	2-0	Cooper, Wright	5324	4		11		7		6	5							3			10			9	1		2		8
7	18	NEWPORT COUNTY	5-2	Phythian 3, Ashworth, Wright	4949	4		11		7		6	5							3			10			9	1		2		8
8	25	Torquay United	0-2		4423	4				7		6	5							3			10	11		9	1		2		8
9	Oct 2	CHESTERFIELD	1-2	Phythian	5184	4		11		7		8	5					6		3			10			9	1		2		
10	4	Barrow	0-2		4581	4		11		7		10	5					6		3						9	1		2		8
11	9	TRANMERE ROVERS	0-0		4245	4		11		7		10	5					6		3						8	1		2	9	
12	16	Colchester United	0-2		4421	4		11		7		10	5					6		3						8		1	2	9	12
13	23	BARNSLEY	1-2	Harrison	4194			10	12	7	3	4	5					6						11		9		1	2		8
14	30	Bradford City	3-1	Wright, Mulvaney 2	2373	6				7	3	4						5		2			10	11		9	1				8
15	Nov 6	CREWE ALEXANDRA	4-1	Phythian 2, Wright 2	4302				6	7	3	4						5		2			10	11		9	1				8
16	20	HALIFAX TOWN	1-2	Wright	4282				6		3	4					7	5					10	11		9	1		2		8
17	27	Chester	0-2		6547	4		11	6		3					1	7	5					10			9			2		8
18	Dec 11	Lincoln City	1-2	McPheat	3332	4			6	7	3	11				1		5					10			9			2		8
19	18	COLCHESTER UNITED	0-1		4067				6		3	4				1		5					10	11	7	9			2		8
20	27	DARLINGTON	1-1	Thompson	9290				6	7	3	4				1		5						12	8	9			2	10	11
21	28	Darlington	1-1	Phythian	8316	4			6	7	3	2				1		5							8	9				10	11
22	Jan 1	Tranmere Rovers	1-6	Wright	5479	4		7	6		3	2				1		5							8	9				10	11
23	8	PORT VALE	2-0	Thompson, Phythian	4284	4		7	6		3	10			2	1		5								9				8	11
24	15	Barnsley	2-2	Thompson 2	3471	4		7		11	3	10			2	1		5								9			6	8	
25	29	Southport	1-4	Wright	4983	4		7			3	10			2	1		5					12			9			6	8	11
26	Feb 5	WREXHAM	4-2	Phythian 2, Fogarty, Thompson	3959	4		11	6		3	10				1						5				9			2	8	7
27	12	Luton Town	1-2	Thompson	6131	4		11			3	10		5	2	1										9			6	8	7
28	26	ALDERSHOT	3-0	Phythian, Fogarty (p), Thompson	4410	4		11			3	10		5	2	1										9			6	8	7
29	Mar 5	LUTON TOWN	2-0	Phythian, Wright	4896	4		11			3	10		5	2	1										9			6	8	7
30	12	Newport County	0-3		2285	4		11			3			5	2	1							10			9			6	8	7
31	19	TORQUAY UNITED	0-2		4789	4	7				3			5				6							8	9	1		2	10	11
32	21	Port Vale	0-0		4908		7				3	4		5	2			6						11	12	9	1			8	10
33	25	Chesterfield	3-1	Mulvaney, Phythian, Parry	2653		7				3			5	2			6						11	8	9	1			4	10
34	Apr 1	Crewe Alexandra	1-3	Wright	3148		7				3			5	2			6						11	8	9	1			4	10
35	8	STOCKPORT COUNTY	2-1	Phythian, Mulvaney	4393		7				3	4		5	2			6						11		9	1			8	10
36	9	NOTTS COUNTY	2-0	Fogarty, Thompson	4001	4					3	10		5	2			6						11		9	1			8	7
37	11	Stockport County	2-1	Thompson, Mulvaney	5453		7				3	4		5	2			6						11		9	1			8	10
38	15	Halifax Town	0-1		1533		7				3	4		5	2			6						11		9	1			8	10
39	19	Bradford Park Avenue	1-4	Gill	3755		7				3	4		5	2			6						11		9	1			8	10
40	23	CHESTER	2-0	Phythian, Fogarty	4138	4	7				3	10		5	2			6								9	1			8	11
41	26	Rochdale	1-3	McPheat	1964	4					3	10		5	2			6					7			9	1			8	11
42	30	Notts County	0-1		4448	4	7				3			5	2	1		6					10			9				8	11
43	May 7	LINCOLN CITY	3-1	Mulvaney 2, Fogarty	4904	4					3	10		5	2	1	12	6						11		9				8	7
44	9	BARROW	3-0	Ashworth, Wright, Mulvaney	5236	4					3	10		5	2	1	7	6					12	8		9					11
45	16	ROCHDALE	0-0		5779	4	7				3	10		5	2	1		6						8		9					11
46	21	BRADFORD CITY	1-1	Livingstone	4776	4					3	10		5	2	1		6	8		7					9					11
					Apps	34	11	17	11	19	35	39	13	20	22	19	4	38	1	14	1	1	15	23	8	46	25	2	26	31	39
					Goals	3				1		5		1				1	1				2	10	1	17				10	11

F.A. Cup

						Ashworth B	Bates JW	Bradley W	Brass RA	Cooper JT	Drysdale B	Fogarty AG	Fox A	Gill JBA	Grant BP	Green L	Hamilton H	Harrison EG	Livingstone J	Marshall WF	McGovern JP	McLeod RA	McPheat W	Mulvaney J	Parry AJ	Phythian ER	Simpkins K	Small JH	Storton SE	Thompson P	Wright GC
R1	Nov 13	WORKINGTON	3-1	McPheat 2, Brass	7466				6	7	3	4						5					10	11		9	1		2		8
R2	Dec 4	WREXHAM	2-0	Wright, Mulvaney	6897	4			6		3	7						5					10	11		9	1		2		8
R3	Jan 25	Huddersfield Town	1-3	Thompson	24505	4		7			3	10			2			5								9	1		6	8	11

F.L. Cup

						Ashworth B	Bates JW	Bradley W	Brass RA	Cooper JT	Drysdale B	Fogarty AG	Fox A	Gill JBA	Grant BP	Green L	Hamilton H	Harrison EG	Livingstone J	Marshall WF	McGovern JP	McLeod RA	McPheat W	Mulvaney J	Parry AJ	Phythian ER	Simpkins K	Small JH	Storton SE	Thompson P	Wright GC
R1	Sep 1	BRADFORD CITY	1-0	Mulvaney	3515	4				7		8	5					6		3				11		10	1		2	9	
R2	22	Leeds United	2-4	Cooper, Wright	11081	4		11		7		10	5					6		3						9	1		2		8

		P	W	D	L	F	A	W	D	L	F	A	Pts
1	Doncaster Rovers	46	15	6	2	49	21	9	5	9	36	33	59
2	Darlington	46	16	3	4	41	17	9	6	8	31	36	59
3	Torquay United	46	17	2	4	43	20	7	8	8	29	29	58
4	Colchester United	46	13	7	3	45	21	10	3	10	25	26	56
5	Tranmere Rovers	46	15	1	7	56	32	9	7	7	37	34	56
6	Luton Town	46	19	2	2	65	27	5	6	12	25	43	56
7	Chester	46	15	5	3	52	27	5	7	11	27	43	52
8	Notts County	46	9	8	6	32	25	10	4	9	29	28	50
9	Newport County	46	14	6	3	46	24	4	6	13	29	51	48
10	Southport	46	15	6	2	47	20	3	8	14	21	49	48
11	Bradford Park Ave.	46	14	2	7	59	31	7	3	13	43	61	47
12	Barrow	46	12	8	3	48	31	4	7	12	24	45	47
13	Stockport County	46	12	4	7	42	29	6	2	15	29	41	42
14	Crewe Alexandra	46	12	4	7	42	23	4	5	14	19	40	41
15	Halifax Town	46	11	6	6	46	31	4	5	14	21	44	41
16	Barnsley	46	11	6	6	43	24	4	4	15	31	54	40
17	Aldershot	46	12	6	5	47	27	3	4	16	28	57	40
18	HARTLEPOOLS UTD.	46	13	4	6	44	22	3	4	16	19	53	40
19	Port Vale	46	12	7	4	38	18	3	2	18	10	41	39
20	Chesterfield	46	8	9	6	37	35	5	4	14	25	43	39
21	Rochdale	46	12	1	10	46	27	4	4	15	25	60	37
22	Lincoln City	46	9	7	7	37	29	4	4	15	20	53	37
23	Bradford City	46	10	5	8	37	34	2	8	13	26	60	37
24	Wrexham	46	10	4	9	43	43	3	5	15	29	61	35

1966/67 8th in Division 4

	Date	Opponent	Score	Scorers	Att	Aston S	Bell TJ	Beresford JT	Bircumshaw A	Broadbent AH	Drysdale B	Fogarty AG	Gill JBA	Grant BP	Green L	Joyce J	Livingstone J	McGovern JP	McLeod RA	Mulvaney J	Parry AJ	Phythian ER	Sheridan J	Simpkins K	Somers MR	Wright GC
1	Aug 20	Aldershot	1-1	Livingstone	3590						3	8	5	2	1		10				6	9	4		11	7
2	27	WREXHAM	2-1	Livingstone, Phythian	5664						3	8	5	2			10				6	9	4	1	11	7
3	Sep 2	Southend United	0-2		6689						3	8	5	2			10				6	9	4	1	11	7
4	5	BARROW	2-1	Fogarty (p), Livingstone	5463						3	8	5	2			10	7			6	9	4	1	11	12
5	10	TRANMERE ROVERS	0-2		5903						3	8	5	2			10	7			6	9	4	1	11	
6	17	Bradford City	0-3		3727		12		2		3	6	5				10	7				9	4	1	11	8
7	19	NEWPORT COUNTY	0-1		4096		10		2		3		5				9	7				6	4	1	11	8
8	24	EXETER CITY	3-1	Phythian 2, Mulvaney	4227				2		3	6	5					7		10		9	4	1	11	8
9	26	Barrow	3-2	Mulvaney, Phythian 2	5662				2		3	6	5					7		10		9	4	1	11	8
10	Oct 1	CREWE ALEXANDRA	1-2	Phythian	4394				2		3	6	5					7		10		9	4	1	11	8
11	7	York City	1-1	Mulvaney	5203				2		3	6	5					7		10		9	4	1	11	8
12	15	LINCOLN CITY	5-0	*see below	3987				2		3	6	5					7		10		9	4	1	11	8
13	17	Newport County	2-0	Phythian, Sheridan	5463		7	6	2		3		5							10		9	4	1	11	8
14	22	Chesterfield	0-1		5275		7	6	2		3		5							10		9	4	1	11	8
15	29	STOCKPORT COUNTY	1-0	Phythian	5976		8		2		3		5					7		10		9	4	1	6	11
16	Nov 5	Rochdale	2-3	Mulvaney, Phythian	2005		8	6	2		3	7	5							10		9	4	1	11	
17	12	SOUTHPORT	1-1	Mulvaney	5516		8		2		3	6	5							10		9	4	1	11	7
18	19	Notts County	0-0		3922		8		2		3	6	5							10		9	4	1	11	7
19	Dec 3	Bradford Park Avenue	2-1	Wright, Taylor (og)	4309				2		3	6			1			7	5	10	8	9	4			11
20	10	PORT VALE	2-1	Wright, Phythian	5342				2		3	6	5		1			7		10	12	9	4		11	8
21	17	ALDERSHOT	3-2	Mulvaney 2, Wright	5159		8		2		3	6	5		1			7		10		9	4			11
22	26	BRENTFORD	2-2	Phythian (p), Livingstone	8420		8		2		3		5		1		9	7		10		6	4			11
23	27	Brentford	2-1	Phythian 2	5775	5			2		3				1		8	7		10	6	9	4			11
24	31	Wrexham	1-4	Mulvaney	12005	5			2		3				1		8	7		10	6	9	4			11
25	Jan 6	SOUTHEND UNITED	1-2	Phythian	9586	5	12		2		3				1		8	7		10		9	4		6	11
26	13	Tranmere Rovers	0-2		6149	5			2		3				1			7		10	6	9	4		11	8
27	21	BRADFORD CITY	1-0	Phythian	6109	5	6		2		3						8	12		10		9	4	1	11	7
28	30	CHESTER	3-2	Phythian, Wright, Mulvaney	7988	5	8		2		3	6						7		10		9	4	1		11
29	Feb 4	Exeter City	0-1		3702	5	12		2		3	8	6					7		10		9	4	1		11
30	11	Crewe Alexandra	2-1	Mulvaney, Wright	6331	5	8				3			2					6	10	7	9	4	1		11
31	18	BARNSLEY	1-1	Bell	6715	5	8				3			2				7	6	10		9	4	1		11
32	25	YORK CITY	4-2	Mulvaney 3, Wright	6638	5				8	3	6		2				7		10		9	4	1		11
33	Mar 4	Lincoln City	0-3		4667	5			3	8		6		2	1			12		10	7	9	4			11
34	11	Barnsley	2-1	Phythian 2	6479	5				8	3			2	1			7	4	10	6	9				11
35	18	CHESTERFIELD	3-2	Mulvaney, Phythian 2	5604	5				8	3			2	1			7	4	10	6	9				11
36	24	LUTON TOWN	2-1	Phythian, Mulvaney	8442	5	12			8	3			2	1			7	4	10	6	9				11
37	25	Chester	0-1		3126	5	11			8	3			2	1			7	4	10	6	9				
38	27	Luton Town	2-0	Parry, McGovern	7370	5			2	8	3				1			7	4	10	6	9			11	
39	Apr 1	ROCHDALE	2-1	Somers, Broadbent	5952	5			2	8	3							7	4	10	6	9		1	11	
40	8	Southport	1-3	Broadbent	4277				2	8	3		5				10		4		6	9		1	11	7
41	11	Halifax Town	1-2	Broadbent	3252				2	8	3		5				10		4		6	9		1	11	7
42	15	NOTTS COUNTY	2-1	Mulvaney 2	4674				2	8	3		5					7	6	10		9	4	1	11	
43	21	Stockport County	0-2		8865	5			2	8	3							7	4	10	6	9		1	11	
44	24	HALIFAX TOWN	1-3	Parry	3479	5			2	8	3							7	4	10	6	9		1	12	11
45	29	BRADFORD PARK AVE.	2-0	Somers, Phythian	3567				2	8	3		5			7				10	6	9	4	1	11	
46	May 6	Port Vale	0-0		3178				2	8	3		5							10	6	9	4	1	11	7
					Apps	19	18	3	34	15	45	21	27	13	15	1	14	33	14	37	24	46	36	31	31	38
					Goals		1			3		2					4	1		19	2	23	1		2	7

Scorers in game 12: Phythian, Mulvaney 2, Fogarty (p), Wright (p).

One own goal

F.A. Cup

	Date	Opponent	Score	Scorers	Att	Aston S	Bell TJ	Beresford JT	Bircumshaw A	Broadbent AH	Drysdale B	Fogarty AG	Gill JBA	Grant BP	Green L	Joyce J	Livingstone J	McGovern JP	McLeod RA	Mulvaney J	Parry AJ	Phythian ER	Sheridan J	Simpkins K	Somers MR	Wright GC
R1	Nov 26	Shrewsbury Town	2-5	Phythian, Fogarty	6515		8		2		3	6	5					7		10		9	4	1		11

F.L. Cup

	Date	Opponent	Score	Scorers	Att	Aston S	Bell TJ	Beresford JT	Bircumshaw A	Broadbent AH	Drysdale B	Fogarty AG	Gill JBA	Grant BP	Green L	Joyce J	Livingstone J	McGovern JP	McLeod RA	Mulvaney J	Parry AJ	Phythian ER	Sheridan J	Simpkins K	Somers MR	Wright GC
R1	Aug 23	Bradford Park Avenue	2-2	Phythian, Livingstone	4128						3	8	5	2			10				6	9	4	1	11	7
rep	31	BRADFORD PARK AVE.	1-2	Phythian	4835						3	8	5	2			10				6	9	4	1	11	7

		P	W	D	L	F	A	W	D	L	F	A	Pts
1	Stockport County	46	16	5	2	41	18	10	7	6	28	24	64
2	Southport	46	19	2	2	47	15	4	11	8	22	27	59
3	Barrow	46	12	8	3	35	18	12	3	8	41	36	59
4	Tranmere Rovers	46	14	6	3	42	20	8	8	7	24	23	58
5	Crewe Alexandra	46	14	5	4	42	26	7	7	9	28	29	54
6	Southend United	46	15	5	3	44	12	7	4	12	26	37	53
7	Wrexham	46	11	12	0	46	20	5	8	10	30	42	52
8	HARTLEPOOLS UTD.	46	15	3	5	44	29	7	4	12	22	35	51
9	Brentford	46	13	7	3	36	19	5	6	12	22	37	49
10	Aldershot	46	14	4	5	48	19	4	8	11	24	38	48
11	Bradford City	46	13	4	6	48	31	6	6	11	26	31	48
12	Halifax Town	46	10	11	2	37	27	5	3	15	22	41	44
13	Port Vale	46	9	7	7	33	27	5	8	10	22	31	43
14	Exeter City	46	11	6	6	30	24	3	9	11	20	36	43
15	Chesterfield	46	13	6	4	33	16	4	2	17	27	47	42
16	Barnsley	46	8	7	8	30	28	5	8	10	30	36	41
17	Luton Town	46	15	5	3	47	23	1	4	18	12	50	41
18	Newport County	46	9	9	5	35	23	3	7	13	21	40	40
19	Chester	46	8	5	10	24	32	7	5	11	30	46	40
20	Notts County	46	10	7	6	31	25	3	4	16	22	47	37
21	Rochdale	46	10	4	9	30	27	3	7	13	23	48	37
22	York City	46	11	5	7	45	31	1	6	16	20	48	35
23	Bradford Park Ave.	46	7	6	10	30	34	4	7	12	22	45	35
24	Lincoln City	46	7	8	8	39	39	2	5	16	19	43	31

1967/68 3rd in Division 4: Promoted

No	Month	Day	Opponent	Score	Scorers	Att	Adamson T	Aston S	Bell TJ	Bircumshaw A	Blowman P	Broadbent AH	Cummings RD	Drysdale B	Gill JBA	Goad AM	Hepplewhite W	King A	McGovern JP	McLeod RA	Mulvaney J	Parry AJ	Phythian ER	Sheridan J	Simpkins K	Smith A (1)	Smith GH	Somers MR	White D	Wright GC
1	Aug	19	BRENTFORD	2-0	Phythian, Mulvaney	5372						10		3	5	2	6				8		9	4			1	11		7
2		26	Bradford Park Avenue	1-0	Wright	3780						10		3	5	2	6				8		9	4			1	11		7
3	Sep	1	DONCASTER ROVERS	0-0		7669						10		3	5	2	6				8		9	4			1	11		7
4		4	ROCHDALE	1-1	McGovern	8361		12	8			10		3	5	2	6		7				9	4			1	11		
5		9	Luton Town	0-1		8347						10		3	5	2	6		7		8		9	4			1	11		
6		16	SOUTHEND UNITED	0-1		5946		4						3	5	2	10		7		12	6	9				1	11		8
7		23	Wrexham	0-6		7381				2		10		3	5		6		7	4	8		9				1	11		12
8		25	Rochdale	1-1	Bell	2041	4		8			10		3	5	2	6		7			12	9				1			11
9		29	BARNSLEY	2-1	Phythian 2	5002			8	2		10		3	5		6		7				9	4			1			11
10	Oct	3	Newport County	0-2		2781			8	2				3	5		6		7			10	9	4			1	11		
11		7	Workington	1-2	Phythian (p)	2500			8					3	5	2	6	12			7	10	9	4			1	11		
12		13	LINCOLN CITY	1-1	Smith	5031				2		10			5		6		7				9	4		8	1	11	3	
13		21	Halifax Town	0-3		4865				2		10		3	5		6		7			12	9	4		8	1	11		
14		23	NEWPORT COUNTY	2-0	Mulvaney, Phythian	4942				2				11	5		3				10	6	7	4	9		1			8
15		27	BRADFORD CITY	1-0	Bell	5476			9	2				11	5		3				10	6	7	4			1			8
16	Nov	4	Crewe Alexandra	1-2	Bradshaw (og)	5604			9	2				3	5		6		11			10	7	4			1			8
17		10	NOTTS COUNTY	3-1	Blowman 2, Wright	4141			10	2	8			3	5							6	7	4	9		1			11
18		14	Doncaster Rovers	1-0	Bell	7818			10	2	8			3	5		6					4	7		9		1	12		11
19		18	Port Vale	3-2	Bell, Blowman, Simpkins	3875			10	2	8			3	5		6					4	7		9		1	12		11
20		24	CHESTER	0-0		4638			10	2	8			3	5		6					4	7		9		1			11
21	Dec	2	Chesterfield	1-3	Bircumshaw	10800			9	2	8			3	5		6					4	7	10			1	11	12	
22		16	Brentford	1-0	Phythian	6210			10		8			3	5	2	6		7			4	9				1	11		
23		22	BRADFORD PARK AVE.	2-0	Blowman, Phythian	4268			10	2	8			3	5		6		7			4	9				1	11		
24		26	DARLINGTON	1-0	Bell	9488			10	2	8			3			6		7			5	9	4			1	11		
25		30	Darlington	3-2	Bell, Phythian 2	5715			10	2	8			3			6		7			5	9	4			1	11		
26	Jan	13	LUTON TOWN	2-1	Phythian, Bell	4766			10	2	8			3	5		6		7			4	9				1	11		
27		20	Southend United	1-2	Blowman	8452			10	2	8			3	5		6		7			4	9	12			1	11		
28		27	Aldershot	0-2		4425			10		8			3	5	2	6		7			4	9	12			1	11		
29	Feb	3	WREXHAM	3-0	Blowman 2, Phythian (p)	4726			10		8		9	3	5		6					2	7	4			1	11		
30		10	Barnsley	0-4		12896			10		8		9	3	5		6		12			2	7	4			1	11		
31		24	PORT VALE	2-2	Cummings, McGovern	4388				2	8		9	3	5		6		7			4	10	12			1	11		
32	Mar	2	Lincoln City	2-1	Somers, Bell	4363			8	2			9	3	5				7			6		4			1	11		10
33		9	ALDERSHOT	1-0	Bell	4943			8	2			9	3			6		7			5		4			1	11		10
34		15	HALIFAX TOWN	0-0		5158			10	2	8		9	3	5				7			6		4			1			11
35		23	Bradford City	1-1	Cummings	6196			8	2			9	3	5				7			6		4			1	11		10
36		30	CREWE ALEXANDRA	1-1	Wright	5944			8	2			9	3	5							6	7	4			1	11		10
37	Apr	1	EXETER CITY	3-1	McGovern, Bell, Cummings	4502			8	2			9	3	5				7			6		4	1			11		10
38		6	Notts County	3-0	Bell, Cummings (p), Wright	4976			8	2			9	3	5				7			6		4			1	11		10
39		12	YORK CITY	1-0	Cummings	9128			8	2			9	3	5				7			6		4			1	11		10
40		13	WORKINGTON	2-1	Cummings 2 (1p)	6063			8	2			9	3	5				7			6		4			1	11		10
41		15	York City	2-0	Bell 2	5916			8	2			9	3	5		4		7			6					1	11		10
42		20	Chester	2-0	Bell, Wright	3990			8	2			9	3	5	4	11		7			6					1			10
43		26	CHESTERFIELD	2-1	Hepplewhite, Cummings	11399			8	2			9	3	5		11		7			6		4			1			10
44	May	4	Exeter City	0-0		3693			8	2	12		9	3	5		4		7			6					1	11		10
45		6	Swansea Town	2-0	Cummings, Hepplewhite	3491			8	2			9	3	5		11		7			6		4			1			10
46		11	SWANSEA TOWN	2-0	Wright, McGovern	11011			8	2			9	3	5		11		7			6		4			1			10
						Apps	1	2	36	34	17	10	18	45	43	11	37	1	33	1	9	38	32	34	6	2	45	34	2	29
						Goals			14	1	7		9				2		4		2		11		1	1		1		6

One own goal

F.A. Cup

Rd	Month	Day	Opponent	Score	Scorers	Att	Adamson T	Aston S	Bell TJ	Bircumshaw A	Blowman P	Broadbent AH	Cummings RD	Drysdale B	Gill JBA	Goad AM	Hepplewhite W	King A	McGovern JP	McLeod RA	Mulvaney J	Parry AJ	Phythian ER	Sheridan J	Simpkins K	Smith A (1)	Smith GH	Somers MR	White D	Wright GC
R1	Dec	9	BURY	2-3	Bell, Wright	4830			10	2				3	5		6		7			4	8		9		1			11

F.L. Cup

Rd	Month	Day	Opponent	Score	Scorers	Att	Adamson T	Aston S	Bell TJ	Bircumshaw A	Blowman P	Broadbent AH	Cummings RD	Drysdale B	Gill JBA	Goad AM	Hepplewhite W	King A	McGovern JP	McLeod RA	Mulvaney J	Parry AJ	Phythian ER	Sheridan J	Simpkins K	Smith A (1)	Smith GH	Somers MR	White D	Wright GC
R1	Aug	23	BRADFORD CITY	2-0	Broadbent, Phythian	4946						10		3	5	2	6				8		9	4			1	11		7
R2	Sep	13	Derby County	0-4		17810						10		3	5	2	8		7			6	9	4			1	11		12

		P	W	D	L	F	A	W	D	L	F	A	Pts
1	Luton Town	46	19	3	1	55	16	8	9	6	32	28	66
2	Barnsley	46	17	6	0	43	14	7	7	9	25	32	61
3	HARTLEPOOLS UTD.	46	15	7	1	34	12	10	3	10	26	34	60
4	Crewe Alexandra	46	13	10	0	44	18	7	8	8	30	31	58
5	Bradford City	46	14	5	4	41	22	9	6	8	31	29	57
6	Southend United	46	12	8	3	45	21	8	6	9	32	37	54
7	Chesterfield	46	15	4	4	47	20	6	7	10	24	30	53
8	Wrexham	46	17	3	3	47	12	3	10	10	25	41	53
9	Aldershot	46	10	11	2	36	19	8	6	9	34	36	53
10	Doncaster Rovers	46	12	8	3	36	16	6	7	10	30	40	51
11	Halifax Town	46	10	6	7	34	24	5	10	8	18	25	46
12	Newport County	46	11	7	5	32	22	5	6	12	26	41	45
13	Lincoln City	46	11	3	9	41	31	6	6	11	30	37	43
14	Brentford	46	13	4	6	41	24	5	3	15	20	40	43
15	Swansea Town	46	11	8	4	38	25	5	2	16	25	52	42
16	Darlington	46	6	11	6	31	27	6	6	11	16	26	41
17	Notts County	46	10	7	6	27	27	5	4	14	26	52	41
18	Port Vale	46	10	5	8	41	31	2	10	11	20	41	39
19	Rochdale	46	9	8	6	35	32	3	6	14	16	40	38
20	Exeter City	46	9	7	7	30	30	2	9	12	15	35	38
21	York City	46	9	6	8	44	30	2	8	13	21	38	36
22	Chester	46	6	6	11	35	38	3	8	12	22	40	32
23	Workington	46	8	8	7	35	29	2	3	18	19	58	31
24	Bradford Park Ave.	46	3	7	13	18	35	1	8	14	12	47	23

1968/69 22nd in Division 3: Relegated

No	Date	Opponent	Score	Scorers	Att	Allen KR	Atkinson DJ	Bell TJ	Bircumshaw A	Blowman P	Cummings RD	Drysdale B	Gate KB	Gill J	Gill JBA	Goad AM	Hepplewhite W	Joyce J	McGovern JP	McLeod RA	Oliver HD	Parry AJ	Pearson J	Sheridan J	Smith GH	Solan K	Somers MR	Thompson MG	Tunstall EW	Wright GC	Young JD	Young R
1	Aug 10	BOURNEMOUTH	1-1	Bell	6791			8	2	10	9	3			5		11		7			6		4	1							
2	17	Crewe Alexandra	0-1		5564			8			9	3			5	2			7			6		4	1		11			10		
3	24	SWINDON TOWN	0-0		5732			8			9	3			5	2	11		7			6		4	1					10		
4	30	Reading	0-7		8969			8	2	12	9	3			5	6	11		7					4	1					10		
5	Sep 6	Bristol Rovers	1-2	Wright	7284		7	8		12	9	3			5	2	6		11					4	1					10		
6	13	SHREWSBURY TOWN	0-0		5348			8	2		9	3			5		11	7		6				4	1					10		
7	16	WATFORD	2-1	R Young, Cummings (p)	5140				2	8	9	3			5		6	7						4	1					10		11
8	21	Northampton Town	0-0		6749				2	8	9	3			5		6	7		12				4	1					10		11
9	28	STOCKPORT COUNTY	0-0		5336		7		2	8	9	3			5		6							4	1					10		11
10	Oct 4	MANSFIELD TOWN	1-1	R Young	5776		7		2	8	9	3			5		6							4	1					10		11
11	9	Plymouth Argyle	0-3		7565		7		2		9	3			5		6				12	11		4	1					8		10
12	12	Luton Town	0-3		13145			10	2		9	3			5	6	11							4	1					8		7
13	14	PLYMOUTH ARGYLE	1-1	Bircumshaw	4748		7	10	2		9	3			5	6				12				4	1					8		11
14	18	BARNSLEY	2-1	R Young, Blowman	4658		7	10	2	8	9	3			5	6								4	1							11
15	26	Orient	1-0	Solan	6134		7	9	2	8	12	3			5	6								4	1	10						11
16	Nov 1	BARROW	1-4	Blowman	3086			8	2	7	9	3			5	6								4	1	10						11
17	6	SOUTHPORT	2-2	Blowman 2	3625			9	2	8		3			5	6	11			12				4	1	10						7
18	9	Rotherham United	1-1	Hague (og)	8970				2	8		3			9	6	11			5				4	1	10						7
19	23	Oldham Athletic	2-1	Blowman 2	2849				2	8	9	3			5		12					6		4	1	10				11		7
20	29	TRANMERE ROVERS	2-4	R Young, Cummings	4355					8	9	3			5	2						6		4	1	10				11		7
21	Dec 14	LUTON TOWN	1-0	Blowman	3887				2	7	8				5	3						6		4	1			9		10		11
22	21	Barnsley	1-2	R Young	7701				2	7	8	3			5							6		4	1			9	12	10		11
23	26	Mansfield Town	0-2		6683			8	2	7		3			5	6						4			1			9		10		11
24	Jan 4	TORQUAY UNITED	2-2	Thompson, Atkinson	3695	1	7	8	2			3								5		6		4				9		10		11
25	11	Barrow	2-1	Bircumshaw, Drysdale	4622			8	2			3		1	5	6	12					4						9		10	7	11
26	18	ROTHERHAM UNITED	0-3		3677			8	2			3		1	5	6						4						9		10	7	11
27	24	Southport	0-3		4150			12	2	7		3		1		6				5		4	8					9		10		11
28	Feb 1	Gillingham	2-2	Thompson, Cummings	4885				2	8	10	3		1	5	6						7		4				9				11
29	4	Swindon Town	1-1	Thompson	19124	1			2	8	10	3			5	6						7		4				9				11
30	22	BRIGHTON & HOVE ALB	2-5	Thompson, Bell	2924	1		8		7		3	2		5	4				12		6						9		10		11
31	24	OLDHAM ATHLETIC	0-2		2535	1		8	2	7		3			5	4				12		6						9		10		11
32	Mar 1	Bournemouth	0-4		6246	1		12		7	8	3			5	2						6						9		10	4	11
33	3	Torquay United	0-3		5903	1		7			8	3			5	2				6		4						9		10		11
34	10	GILLINGHAM	1-1	Bell	2401	1		7			8	3			5	2				6		4						9		10		11
35	19	Brighton & Hove Albion	1-1	Bell	11334			8	2		10	3			5	6						7		4	1			9				11
36	22	READING	2-0	Bell 2	2754			8	2		10	3			5	6						7		4	1			9				11
37	28	BRISTOL ROVERS	1-0	Parry	3447			8	2		10	3			5	6						7		4	1			9				11
38	Apr 4	WALSALL	1-1	R Young	6695			8	2		10	3			5	6						7		4	1			9		12		11
39	5	Stockport County	0-1		4375			8	2	12	10	3				6				5		7		4	1			9		11		
40	7	Watford	0-0		20771				2	8	10	3			5	6						7		4	1			9				11
41	11	NORTHAMPTON T	3-0	Thompson, Bell, Drysdale	3729			8	2	10		3			5	6						7		4	1			9				11
42	15	Walsall	2-1	Thompson, Blowman	5003			8	2	10		3			5	6						7		4	1			9				11
43	19	Shrewsbury Town	1-1	Thompson	7793			8	2	10	12	3			5	6						7		4	1			9				11
44	21	ORIENT	0-0		4237			8	2	10	12	3			5	6						7		4	1			9				11
45	24	Tranmere Rovers	0-1		2861			8	2		12	3			5	6						7		4	1			9		10		11
46	May 5	CREWE ALEXANDRA	0-0		2035			8	2			3			5	6						7		4	1			9		10		11
					Apps	7	8	33	38	29	34	45	1	4	43	36	15	3	5	12	1	32	1	37	35	6	1	26	1	30	3	39
					Goals		1	7	2	8	3	2										1				1		7		1		6

One own goal

F.A. Cup

Rd	Date	Opponent	Score	Scorers	Att	Allen KR	Atkinson DJ	Bell TJ	Bircumshaw A	Blowman P	Cummings RD	Drysdale B	Gate KB	Gill J	Gill JBA	Goad AM	Hepplewhite W	Joyce J	McGovern JP	McLeod RA	Oliver HD	Parry AJ	Pearson J	Sheridan J	Smith GH	Solan K	Somers MR	Thompson MG	Tunstall EW	Wright GC	Young JD	Young R
R1	Nov 16	ROTHERHAM UNITED	1-1	R Young	6579				2	8		3			5	6	11							4	1	10						7
rep	19	Rotherham United	0-3		11518				2	8	9	3			5		11			4		6			1	10						7

Played at 9 in game 1: R Hold

F.L. Cup

Rd	Date	Opponent	Score	Scorers	Att	Allen KR	Atkinson DJ	Bell TJ	Bircumshaw A	Blowman P	Cummings RD	Drysdale B	Gate KB	Gill J	Gill JBA	Goad AM	Hepplewhite W	Joyce J	McGovern JP	McLeod RA	Oliver HD	Parry AJ	Pearson J	Sheridan J	Smith GH	Solan K	Somers MR	Thompson MG	Tunstall EW	Wright GC	Young JD	Young R
R1	Aug 14	Bradford City	2-3	McGovern 2	4183			8	2		9	3			5		12		7			6		4	1		11			10		

		P	W	D	L	F	A	W	D	L	F	A	Pts
1	Watford	46	16	5	2	35	7	11	5	7	39	27	64
2	Swindon Town	46	18	4	1	38	7	9	6	8	33	28	64
3	Luton Town	46	20	3	0	57	14	5	8	10	17	24	61
4	Bournemouth	46	16	2	5	41	17	5	7	11	19	28	51
5	Plymouth Argyle	46	10	8	5	34	25	7	7	9	19	24	49
6	Torquay United	46	13	4	6	35	18	5	8	10	19	28	48
7	Tranmere Rovers	46	12	3	8	36	31	7	7	9	34	37	48
8	Southport	46	14	8	1	52	20	3	5	15	19	44	47
9	Stockport County	46	14	5	4	49	25	2	9	12	18	43	46
10	Barnsley	46	13	6	4	37	21	3	8	12	21	42	46
11	Rotherham United	46	12	6	5	40	21	4	7	12	16	29	45
12	Brighton & Hove A.	46	12	7	4	49	21	4	6	13	23	44	45
13	Walsall	46	10	9	4	34	18	4	7	12	16	31	44
14	Reading	46	13	3	7	41	25	2	10	11	26	41	43
15	Mansfield Town	46	14	5	4	37	18	2	6	15	21	44	43
16	Bristol Rovers	46	12	6	5	41	27	4	5	14	22	44	43
17	Shrewsbury Town	46	11	8	4	28	17	5	3	15	23	50	43
18	Orient	46	10	8	5	31	19	4	6	13	20	39	42
19	Barrow	46	11	6	6	30	23	6	2	15	26	52	42
20	Gillingham	46	10	10	3	35	20	3	5	15	19	43	41
21	Northampton Town	46	9	8	6	37	30	5	4	14	17	31	40
22	HARTLEPOOL	46	6	12	5	25	29	4	7	12	15	41	39
23	Crewe Alexandra	46	11	4	8	40	31	2	5	16	12	45	35
24	Oldham Athletic	46	9	6	8	33	27	4	3	16	17	56	35

1969/70 23rd in Division 4

No	Date		Opponent	Score	Scorers	Att	Bell TJ	Bircumshaw A	Blowman P	Blythe JD	Boylan A	Dobbing R	Forrest K	Gill JBA	Goad AM	Green W	Humphreys DJB	Hunter P	Kirk HJ	Lee TJ	McCluskey A	McPartland D	Parry AJ	Robson L	Sheridan J	Smith GH	Thompson KJ	Thompson MG	Trail DJF	Walker JM	White D	Wright GC	Young R
1	Aug	9	BRENTFORD	0-0		3020			12			3			6					8			5		4	1		9	11		2	10	7
2		16	Grimsby Town	0-2		3507			8			3	12		6					9			5		4	1			11		2	10	7
3		23	YORK CITY	2-2	Bell, Dobbing	2990	8					3		5	6										4	1		9	11		2	10	7
4		25	SWANSEA CITY	3-0	Bell 2, Young	3540	9	2				3		5	6					8			12		4	1			11			10	7
5		30	Chesterfield	0-3		3997	9	2				3		5	6					8			12		4	1			11			10	7
6	Sep	6	NORTHAMPTON T	1-1	Bell	3090	9	2	8			3		5	6								7		4	1		12				10	11
7		13	Southend United	2-0	Young, Thompson	8271	9	2				3		5	6										4	1		8	11			10	7
8		15	Newport County	1-1	Bell	2950	9	2				3		5	6	12									4	1		8	11			10	7
9		20	COLCHESTER UNITED	0-0		3627	9	2				3		5	6	12									4	1		8	11			10	7
10		27	Peterborough United	0-4		6872	9	2	12			3		5	6								7		4	1		8	11			10	
11	Oct	1	Aldershot	1-4	Wright	5172	9	2	7					5	3	12							6		4	1		8	11			10	
12		4	OLDHAM ATHLETIC	1-1	Goad	2744	9	2				3		5	6								7		4	1		8	11		12	10	
13		6	GRIMSBY TOWN	0-1		2758	9	2				3	8	5	6								7		4	1			11		12	10	
14		11	Chester	1-2	Bell	4175	9					3	8	5	4		1	7					6						11		2	10	
15		18	BRADFORD PARK AVE.	5-2	Kirk 2, Bell 3	2816	9					3	8	5	4		1		11				6						7		2	10	
16		25	Scunthorpe United	1-3	Kirk	3600	9	2					8	5			1		11				6				4		7		3	10	
17	Nov	1	WREXHAM	1-3	Thompson	3024	9	2				3		12	6	5	1		11				4					8	7				10
18		8	Workington	3-1	Trail, Young, Parry	1351	9	2	8			3			6	5			11				4			1			7				10
19		22	CREWE ALEXANDRA	1-1	Young	2613	9	2	12			3		5	6				11				4			1			7			10	8
20		24	DARLINGTON	1-3	Young	2353	9	2	8			3		5	6	4			11							1		12	10				7
21	Dec	13	SOUTHEND UNITED	2-1	Bell, Bircumshaw (p)	1824	9	2	8					5	6				11		4					1			10		3		7
22		20	Northampton Town	1-0	Bell	2979	9	2	8			3		5	6				11		12					1			10		4		7
23		26	York City	0-0		4581	9	2	8			3		5	6				11							1			10		4		7
24		27	CHESTERFIELD	0-0		3248	9	2	8			3		5	6				11							1			10		4		7
25	Jan	10	Colchester United	1-1	Kirk	3200	9	2	8			3		5	6				11		12					1			10		4		7
26		17	PETERBOROUGH UTD.	4-2	Trail, Bell, Young, Goad	2382	9	2	8			3		5	6				11							1			10		4		7
27		24	Exeter City	0-6		4241	9	2	8			3		5	6				11							1			10		4		7
28		31	Oldham Athletic	0-1		3026	9	2	8	12				5	6				11		4					1			10		3		7
29	Feb	2	ALDERSHOT	1-3	Bircumshaw (p)	2245	9	2		8				5	6				11				4			1			12		3	10	7
30		7	CHESTER	1-2	Young	2233	9	2	8					5	3				11				6			1			10		4	12	7
31		20	SCUNTHORPE UNITED	1-2	Wright	1555	9	2			12			5	3				11				6			1			7		4	10	8
32		23	Brentford	0-3		7352	9	2			4			5	3				11				6			1		12	7			10	8
33		28	Wrexham	0-1		7071		2			6	3		5	8				11				4	9		1			10				7
34	Mar	2	NOTTS COUNTY	4-0	Young, Goad 2, Needham (og)	1797		2			6	3		5	8				11				4	9		1			10				7
35		9	Port Vale	0-3		5456		2			6	3		5	8				11				4	9		1				10			7
36		14	LINCOLN CITY	0-3		2555		2			4	3		5	8				11				6	9		1			12	10			7
37		16	EXETER CITY	2-0	Robson 2	1980		2				3		5	6							1	4	9				8	7	10			11
38		21	Notts County	0-1		5313		2				3		5	6				12			1	4	9				8	7	10			11
39		27	WORKINGTON	1-0	Young	2852		2	12			3		5	6				11			1	4	8				9		10			7
40		28	PORT VALE	0-2		2227		2				3		5	6				11			1		8				9	10	4			7
41		31	Bradford Park Avenue	0-3		2294		2			4	3		5	8	6			11			1						9	12	10			7
42	Apr	4	Swansea City	0-3		7691					4	3		5		6			11		10	1						9		8	2		7
43		10	Crewe Alexandra	0-3		2477		2			8			5	4				11		10	1	6					9		7	3		
44		13	NEWPORT COUNTY	0-1		1473		2			9			5	8	4			11			1	6						7	10	3		
45		18	Lincoln City	0-3		3772		2	8					5	6	4			11	9		1	10								3		7
46		22	Darlington	0-4		2259		2	12					5	6	4			11	8		1	10					9			3		7
						Apps	30	40	20	2	10	34	5	43	44	11	4	1	31	6	6	10	30	8	13	32	1	20	39	10	24	21	37
						Goals	12	2				1			4				4				1	2				2	2			2	9

One own goal

F.A. Cup

Rd	Date		Opponent	Score	Scorers	Att	Bell TJ	Bircumshaw A	Blowman P	Blythe JD	Boylan A	Dobbing R	Forrest K	Gill JBA	Goad AM	Green W	Humphreys DJB	Hunter P	Kirk HJ	Lee TJ	McCluskey A	McPartland D	Parry AJ	Robson L	Sheridan J	Smith GH	Thompson KJ	Thompson MG	Trail DJF	Walker JM	White D	Wright GC	Young R
R1	Nov	15	NORTH SHIELDS	3-0	Bell 2, Kirk	2713	9	2				3		5	6	12			11				4			1			7			10	8
R2	Dec	6	WREXHAM	0-1		2989	9	2	8			3		5	6				11				4			1		12	10				7

F.L. Cup

Rd	Date		Opponent	Score	Scorers	Att	Bell TJ	Bircumshaw A	Blowman P	Blythe JD	Boylan A	Dobbing R	Forrest K	Gill JBA	Goad AM	Green W	Humphreys DJB	Hunter P	Kirk HJ	Lee TJ	McCluskey A	McPartland D	Parry AJ	Robson L	Sheridan J	Smith GH	Thompson KJ	Thompson MG	Trail DJF	Walker JM	White D	Wright GC	Young R
R1	Aug	12	Scunthorpe United	2-0	R Young 2	2800			12			3			6					8			5		4	1		9			2	10	7
R2	Sep	3	DERBY COUNTY	1-3	Bell	7700	9	2				3		5	6								7		4	1		8				10	11

Played at 11 in R1: Roy Young

		P	W	D	L	F	A	W	D	L	F	A	Pts
1	Chesterfield	46	19	1	3	55	12	8	9	6	22	20	64
2	Wrexham	46	17	6	0	56	16	9	3	11	28	33	61
3	Swansea City	46	14	8	1	43	14	7	10	6	23	31	60
4	Port Vale	46	13	9	1	39	10	7	10	6	22	23	59
5	Brentford	46	14	8	1	36	11	6	8	9	22	28	56
6	Aldershot	46	16	5	2	52	22	4	8	11	26	43	53
7	Notts County	46	14	4	5	44	21	8	4	11	29	41	52
8	Lincoln City	46	11	8	4	38	20	6	8	9	28	32	50
9	Peterborough Utd.	46	13	8	2	51	21	4	6	13	26	48	48
10	Colchester United	46	14	5	4	38	22	3	9	11	26	41	48
11	Chester	46	14	3	6	39	23	7	3	13	19	43	48
12	Scunthorpe United	46	11	6	6	34	23	7	4	12	33	42	46
13	York City	46	14	7	2	38	16	2	7	14	17	46	46
14	Northampton Town	46	11	7	5	41	19	5	5	13	23	36	44
15	Crewe Alexandra	46	12	6	5	37	18	4	6	13	14	33	44
16	Grimsby Town	46	9	9	5	33	24	5	6	12	21	34	43
17	Southend United	46	12	8	3	40	28	3	2	18	19	57	40
18	Exeter City	46	13	5	5	48	20	1	6	16	9	39	39
19	Oldham Athletic	46	11	4	8	45	28	2	9	12	15	37	39
20	Workington	46	9	9	5	31	21	3	5	15	15	43	38
21	Newport County	46	12	3	8	39	24	1	8	14	14	50	37
22	Darlington	46	8	7	8	31	27	5	3	15	22	46	36
23	HARTLEPOOL	46	7	7	9	31	30	3	3	17	11	52	30
24	Bradford Park Ave.	46	6	5	12	23	32	0	6	17	18	64	23

1970/71 23rd in Division 4

No	Month	Day	Opponent	Result	Scorers	Att	Ashurst L	Barlow P	Bircumshaw A	Bradbury A	Clarke MMG	Crook LR	Dawes M	Ellison WR	Forrest K	Gill JBA	Goad AM	Green W	Harvey D	Henderson G	Herd G	Hunter R	Kirk HJ	Lees N	McPartland D	Parry AJ	Sharkey D	Thompson KJ	Veart R	White D	Wright RL	Young R
1	Aug	15	Colchester United	0-1		4866					4	6					2				8		11		1	5	9			3	10	7
2		22	WORKINGTON	1-1	Wilson (og)	2945		7	12		6	10					2	5			8				1	4	11			3	9	
3		29	Grimsby Town	1-1	Sharkey	4456		9	2		7	6			12		3	5			8				1	4	10			11		
4		31	DARLINGTON	2-2	Wright, Crook	5032		12	2		8	6					3	5			7				1	4	9			11	10	
5	Sep	5	BARROW	2-1	Sharkey, Bircumshaw (p)	3667			2		10	6						5			8		12		1	4	11			3	9	7
6		11	Stockport County	1-2	Kirk	4146			2		11	6	3					5			8		12		1	4	9				10	7
7		19	ALDERSHOT	1-1	Bircumshaw (p)	3262			2		10	6	3					5			8		11		1	4	7				9	12
8		21	SOUTHEND UNITED	0-1		3755			2		10	6	3					5			8		11		1	4	7				9	12
9		26	Cambridge United	0-2		5225		9	2		6	12	3					5			8		11		1	4	10					7
10		30	NOTTS COUNTY	2-1	Young, Crook	2772			2		10	6	3			4		5			12		11		1	8	9					7
11	Oct	3	NEWPORT COUNTY	2-2	Crook, Bircumshaw (p)	3247			2		10	6	3			4		5			12		11		1	8	9					7
12		10	Exeter City	1-1	Bircumshaw	4857			2		10	6	3			4		5					11		1	8	9					7
13		17	COLCHESTER UNITED	1-2	Sharkey	2930			2		10	6	3			4		5			12		11		1	8	9					7
14		21	Crewe Alexandra	0-1		2031					10	6	3			4		5			12		11		1	8	9			2		7
15		24	SOUTHPORT	1-2	Sharkey	2174					4	6	3	10		5							11		1	8	9			2		7
16		31	Northampton Town	0-2		6049					10	6		11		4	3	5			12				1	8	9			2		7
17	Nov	7	PETERBOROUGH UTD.	1-2	Sharkey	2038			2		12		6	10		4	3	5			7				1	8	9					11
18		9	OLDHAM ATHLETIC	0-1		1762			2				10	8		4	6	5					11		1	12	9		7	3		
19		14	Bournemouth	0-3		5801			2		12	6	10	8		4	3	5					11		1	7	9					
20		28	Chester	1-0	Sharkey	4471			2			6	3			4	10	5							1	8	7				9	11
21	Dec	5	LINCOLN CITY	0-0		1965		12	2			6	3			4	10	5							1	8	7				9	11
22		19	Workington	1-0	Sharkey	2316			2			6	3			4	10	5							1	8	7				9	11
23		26	YORK CITY	2-1	Lees, Young	2368			2				3			4	10	5						6	1	8	7				9	11
24	Jan	9	Notts County	0-3		11540			2		7		3			4	6	5						8	1		9				10	11
25		16	CREWE ALEXANDRA	0-2		1989			2			6	3			4		5						10	1	8	7				9	11
26		23	Scunthorpe United	1-2	Sharkey	3867			2			12	3			4	6	5						9	1	8	7				10	11
27		30	CHESTER	0-2		1332			2	6	12		3			4	7	5						9	1	8	10					11
28	Feb	6	Lincoln City	0-2		3993			7			6	2			12	4	5						8	1		10	9		3		11
29		13	SCUNTHORPE UNITED	1-1	Bircumshaw	1267			7			6	2			9	4	5							1	8		10		3		11
30		24	Brentford	0-1		9246		12	2	10			3			9	4	5				8		7	1					6		11
31		27	NORTHAMPTON T	2-2	Thompson, Dawes	1288		10	2	6			3			12	4	5						8	1		7	9				11
32	Mar	5	Southport	0-5		1436			2	6			3			9	4	5						8	1		7	10				11
33		10	Southend United	0-2		3839	3		2	6			12			10	4	5						8	1		7				9	11
34		13	BOURNEMOUTH	2-1	Bircumshaw, Young	2111	3		2	6			8				4	5							1	10	7				9	11
35		15	BRENTFORD	0-0		2936	3		2	6			8				4	5							1	10	7		12		9	11
36		20	Peterborough United	0-5		3881	3		2				6				4	5						11	1	10	8		7		9	
37		27	Barrow	0-3		1776	3		2				6				4	5						11	1	10	8		7		9	
38		30	Oldham Athletic	0-2		9116			2		11		3				4	5		9				6	1	10	8		7			12
39	Apr	3	GRIMSBY TOWN	2-2	Young, Green	1734	3		2		11		10				4	5						6	1		8		7		9	12
40		9	STOCKPORT COUNTY	3-0	Veart 2, Young	2702	3		2		11						4	5						6	1	10	8		9		12	7
41		10	York City	0-4		7734	3		12		11						4	5						6	1	8		9	10	2		7
42		13	Newport County	0-2		3173	3	7	2			8				4		5	12					6	1	10			9			11
43		17	EXETER CITY	3-0	Wright 2, Veart	1525	3		12							4		5	7					6	1	10			9	2	8	11
44		24	Aldershot	0-1		3687	3	11								2		5	7					6	1	4			9		8	10
45		26	Darlington	0-2		2234	3	8					10					5	7					6	1	4			9	2		11
46	May	1	CAMBRIDGE UNITED	0-0		1767	3	8			11		6			4		5	12						1				9	2	7	10
						Apps	13	11	39	7	25	25	35	5	1	28	29	44	5	1	15	1	14	20	46	38	38	5	13	16	24	39
						Goals			6			3	1					1					1	1			8	1	3		3	5

One own goal

F.A. Cup

Round	Month	Day	Opponent	Result	Scorers	Att	Ashurst L	Barlow P	Bircumshaw A	Bradbury A	Clarke MMG	Crook LR	Dawes M	Ellison WR	Forrest K	Gill JBA	Goad AM	Green W	Harvey D	Henderson G	Herd G	Hunter R	Kirk HJ	Lees N	McPartland D	Parry AJ	Sharkey D	Thompson KJ	Veart R	White D	Wright RL	Young R
R1	Nov	21	Rhyl	0-1		3000			2		10	6	11			4	3	5							1	8	9			12		7

F.L. Cup

Round	Month	Day	Opponent	Result	Scorers	Att	Ashurst L	Barlow P	Bircumshaw A	Bradbury A	Clarke MMG	Crook LR	Dawes M	Ellison WR	Forrest K	Gill JBA	Goad AM	Green W	Harvey D	Henderson G	Herd G	Hunter R	Kirk HJ	Lees N	McPartland D	Parry AJ	Sharkey D	Thompson KJ	Veart R	White D	Wright RL	Young R
R1	Aug	19	YORK CITY	2-3	Young, Sharkey	3734					4	6	10				2				8				1	5	7			3	9	11

		P	W	D	L	F	A	W	D	L	F	A	Pts
1	Notts County	46	19	4	0	59	12	11	5	7	30	24	69
2	Bournemouth	46	16	5	2	51	15	8	7	8	30	31	60
3	Oldham Athletic	46	14	6	3	57	29	10	5	8	31	34	59
4	York City	46	16	6	1	45	14	7	4	12	33	40	56
5	Chester	46	17	2	4	42	18	7	5	11	27	37	55
6	Colchester United	46	14	6	3	44	19	7	6	10	26	35	54
7	Northampton Town	46	15	4	4	39	24	4	9	10	24	35	51
8	Southport	46	15	2	6	42	24	6	4	13	21	33	48
9	Exeter City	46	12	7	4	40	23	5	7	11	27	45	48
10	Workington	46	13	7	3	28	13	5	5	13	20	36	48
11	Stockport County	46	12	8	3	28	17	4	6	13	21	48	46
12	Darlington	46	15	3	5	42	22	2	8	13	16	35	45
13	Aldershot	46	8	10	5	32	23	6	7	10	34	48	45
14	Brentford	46	13	3	7	45	27	5	5	13	21	35	44
15	Crewe Alexandra	46	13	1	9	49	35	5	7	11	26	41	44
16	Peterborough Utd.	46	14	3	6	46	23	4	4	15	24	48	43
17	Scunthorpe United	46	9	7	7	36	23	6	6	11	20	38	43
18	Southend United	46	8	11	4	32	24	6	4	13	21	42	43
19	Grimsby Town	46	13	4	6	37	26	5	3	15	20	45	43
20	Cambridge United	46	9	9	5	31	27	6	4	13	20	39	43
21	Lincoln City	46	11	4	8	45	33	2	9	12	25	38	39
22	Newport County	46	8	3	12	32	36	2	5	16	23	49	28
23	HARTLEPOOL	46	6	10	7	28	27	2	2	19	6	47	28
24	Barrow	46	5	5	13	25	38	2	3	18	26	52	22

1971/72 18th in Division 4

						Ashurst L	Boylan A	Clarke MMG	Dawes M	Ellis K	Gadsby MD	Goad AM	Green W	Hillyard RW	Kelly JP	Naisbitt E	Noble B	Parkinson J	Parry AJ	Potter GR	Ross WE	Sharkey D	Smith RW	Spelman MT	Veart R	Waddell W	Ward W	Warnock N	Welsh E	White D	Young R
1	Aug	14 READING	3-1	Ellis 2 (2p), Young	2470	3		10		9	1	4	5							6								11	7	2	8
2		20 Colchester United	0-1		5672	3		10		9	1	4	5							6								11	7	2	8
3		28 SOUTHEND UNITED	2-2	Young 2	5479	3		10		9	1	4	5							6					12			11	7	2	8
4		30 DARLINGTON	2-3	Veart 2	7156	3		10		9	1	4	5							6					8			11	7	2	12
5	Sep	4 Brentford	0-6		8712	3				10	1	4	5							6					9			11	7	2	8
6		11 WORKINGTON	1-3	Wood (og)	3182	3				10	1	4	5						12	6					9			11	7	2	8
7		18 Gillingham	0-1		5477				12	10	1	3	5						4	6					9			11	7	2	8
8		25 BARROW	4-3	Ellis, Welsh, Green, Warnock	2641				10	9	1	3	5						4	6					12			11	7	2	8
9		27 PETERBOROUGH UTD.	1-0	Warnock	3487	3			10	9	1	4							5	6					12			11	7	2	8
10	Oct	1 Stockport County	1-2	Ashurst	2573	3		12	10	9	1	4							5	6								11	7	2	8
11		9 NEWPORT COUNTY	0-1		3010	3				8	1	4						6	5	10					9			11	7	2	12
12		16 Reading	0-3		3176	3		10		7	1	4							5	6		9						11	12	2	8
13		19 Bury	1-1	Warnock	2849	6		10		7	1	4			3				5	2		9						11			8
14		23 Chester	0-4		3466	6		10		7	1	4			3				5	2		9						11	12		8
15		30 ALDERSHOT	0-1		2197	4				7	1	2			3				5			9	8	6				11			10
16	Nov	6 Grimsby Town	2-3	Ellis, Sharkey	8709					7	1	4			3				5	2		9	8	6				11			10
17		13 DONCASTER ROVERS	0-0		2129	4	8			9	1	3							5	2			7	6	12			11			10
18		27 CREWE ALEXANDRA	1-0	Veart	2599	4				9	1	3							5	2	6		8		12			11	7		10
19	Dec	4 Northampton Town	1-2	Welsh	4507	4					1	3							5	2			8	6	9			11	7		10
20		18 BRENTFORD	1-2	Sharkey	2199	4			10			3					1		5	2	6	7	8		9			11			12
21		27 Scunthorpe United	2-2	Sharkey, Young	7270				4		1	3							5	2		7	8	6	9			11			10
22	Jan	1 GILLINGHAM	3-1	Young 2, Spelman	2932				4			3	9			1			5	2		7	8	6	12			11			10
23		7 Southend United	1-3	Young	6505				4			3	9	1					5	2		7	8	6	12			11			10
24		15 CAMBRIDGE UNITED	1-2	Green	2396				4	12		3	9	1					5	2		7	8	6				11			10
25		22 Peterborough United	2-2	Young, Ward	4525				4			3	5	1						2		12	8	6	9		7	11			10
26		29 BURY	3-1	Warnock, Veart 2	2128				4	12		3	5	1						2		8	6		9		7	11			10
27	Feb	5 Lincoln City	1-2	Young	7261				4		1	3	5							6		12	8		9		7	11		2	10
28		12 CHESTER	2-1	Young 2	2718	12			4	8		3	5	1						2			6		9		7	11			10
29		19 Aldershot	0-2		2760				4	8		3	5	1						2			6		9		7	11			10
30		26 GRIMSBY TOWN	0-1		3194	4				8		3	5	1						2		9	6				7	11			10
31	Mar	4 Doncaster Rovers	1-2	Young	2571				4			3	5	1						2		8	6		9		7	11			10
32		10 Newport County	2-0	Ashurst, Sharkey	3170	4			6			3	5	1						2		7	8		9			11			10
33		15 Cambridge United	1-2	Waddell	3619	4			6			3	5	1						2		7	8		9	12		11			10
34		18 COLCHESTER UNITED	3-2	Waddell, Smith (p), Young	2729	4			6			3	5	1						2			8		9	7		11			10
35		25 Workington	0-0		2147	4			6			3	5	1						2			8		9	7		11			10
36		27 EXETER CITY	1-0	Veart	3501				4	6		3	5	1						2			8		9	7		11			10
37		31 STOCKPORT COUNTY	5-0	Green, Young 2, Waddell, Smith	5537	12			4	6		3	5	1						2			8		9	7		11			10
38	Apr	1 SCUNTHORPE UNITED	1-0	Young	6197				4	6		3	5	1						2			8		9	7		11			10
39		3 Barrow	0-2		2717	4			6	9		3	5	1						2		12	8			7		11			10
40		8 LINCOLN CITY	2-1	Potter, Young	5975				4	6		3	5	1						2		12	8		9	7		11			10
41		10 SOUTHPORT	1-0	Young	6472				4	6		3	5	1						2			8		9	7		11			10
42		15 Crewe Alexandra	2-1	Waddell 2	1686				4	6		3	5	1						2			8		9	7		11			10
43		19 Exeter City	0-1		3791				4	6		3	5	1						2		12	8		9	7		11			10
44		22 NORTHAMPTON T	2-0	Waddell, Potter	6907				4	6		3	5	1						2			8		9	7		11			10
45		24 Darlington	2-1	Green, Waddell	8809	12			4	6		3	5	1						2		9	8			7		11			10
46		28 Southport	0-1		1550				4	6			5	1	3					2		9	8		11	7					10
					Apps	26	1	8	30	34	21	45	33	23	5	1	1	1	19	45	2	22	32	9	34	14	7	45	15	13	46
					Goals	2				4			4							2		4	2	1	6	7	1	4	2		18

One own goal

F.A. Cup

						Ashurst L	Boylan A	Clarke MMG	Dawes M	Ellis K	Gadsby MD	Goad AM	Green W	Hillyard RW	Kelly JP	Naisbitt E	Noble B	Parkinson J	Parry AJ	Potter GR	Ross WE	Sharkey D	Smith RW	Spelman MT	Veart R	Waddell W	Ward W	Warnock N	Welsh E	White D	Young R
R1	Nov	20 SCARBOROUGH	6-1	Ellis, Young 2, Warnock, Veart 2	3374	4				9	1	3							5	2			8	6	12			11	7		10
R2	Dec	11 Boston United	1-2	Veart	4400	4					1	3							5	2		12	8	6	9			11	7		10

F.L. Cup

						Ashurst L	Boylan A	Clarke MMG	Dawes M	Ellis K	Gadsby MD	Goad AM	Green W	Hillyard RW	Kelly JP	Naisbitt E	Noble B	Parkinson J	Parry AJ	Potter GR	Ross WE	Sharkey D	Smith RW	Spelman MT	Veart R	Waddell W	Ward W	Warnock N	Welsh E	White D	Young R
R1	Aug	18 Barnsley	0-0		5985	3		10		9	1	4	5						12	6								11	7	2	8
rep		23 BARNSLEY	0-1		9577	3		10		9	1	4	5							6					12			11	7	2	8

Replay a.e.t.

		P	W	D	L	F	A	W	D	L	F	A	Pts
1	Grimsby Town	46	18	3	2	61	26	10	4	9	27	30	63
2	Southend United	46	18	2	3	56	26	6	10	7	25	29	60
3	Brentford	46	16	2	5	52	21	8	9	6	24	23	59
4	Scunthorpe United	46	13	8	2	34	15	9	5	9	22	22	57
5	Lincoln City	46	17	5	1	46	15	4	9	10	31	44	56
6	Workington	46	12	9	2	34	7	4	10	9	16	27	51
7	Southport	46	15	5	3	48	21	3	9	11	18	25	50
8	Peterborough Utd.	46	14	6	3	51	24	3	10	10	31	40	50
9	Bury	46	16	4	3	55	22	3	8	12	18	37	50
10	Cambridge United	46	11	8	4	38	22	6	6	11	24	38	48
11	Colchester United	46	13	6	4	38	23	6	4	13	32	46	48
12	Doncaster Rovers	46	11	8	4	35	24	5	6	12	21	39	46
13	Gillingham	46	11	5	7	33	24	5	8	10	28	43	45
14	Newport County	46	13	5	5	34	20	5	3	15	26	52	44
15	Exeter City	46	11	5	7	40	30	5	6	12	21	38	43
16	Reading	46	14	3	6	37	26	3	5	15	19	50	42
17	Aldershot	46	5	13	5	27	20	4	9	10	21	34	40
18	HARTLEPOOL	46	14	2	7	39	25	3	4	16	19	44	40
19	Darlington	46	9	9	5	37	24	5	2	16	27	58	39
20	Chester	46	10	11	2	34	16	0	7	16	13	40	38
21	Northampton Town	46	8	9	6	43	27	4	4	15	23	52	37
22	Barrow	46	8	8	7	23	26	5	3	15	17	45	37
23	Stockport County	46	7	10	6	33	32	2	4	17	22	55	32
24	Crewe Alexandra	46	9	4	10	27	25	1	5	17	16	44	29

1972/73 20th in Division 4

							Ashurst L	Conlon B	Coyne JD	Dawes M	Gadston JE	Goad AM	Green W	Gibbin BT	Honour J	McGeough J	Potter GR	Pringle B	Smith RMS	Smith RW	Spelman MT	Veart R	Waddell W	Ward W	Warnock N	Watling BJ	White D	Young R
1	Aug	12	Lincoln City	2-1	Coyne, Green	5789			9	4		3	5				2		6	8	10		7		11	1		
2		19	COLCHESTER UNITED	2-1	Coyne, RW Smith (p)	5672			9	4		3	5				2		6	8	10	7		11		1		
3		26	Torquay United	0-1		4726			9	4		3	5				2		6	8	10		7		11	1		12
4		28	Exeter City	1-1	Warnock	4304			9	4		3	5				2		6	8	10		7		11	1		
5	Sep	2	READING	1-2	RW Smith (p)	5195			9	4		3	5				2		6	8	10		7		11	1		12
6		9	Cambridge United	1-1	Waddell	2627			9	4		3	5				2		6	8	10		7		11	1		
7		16	WORKINGTON	1-0	RW Smith (p)	4608		9	12	4		3	5				2		6	8	10		7		11	1		
8		18	DARLINGTON	0-0		7193		9	12	4		3	5				2		6	8	10		7		11	1		
9		23	Bradford City	2-0	Coyne, Conlon	3387		9	7	4		3	5				2		6		10				11	1		8
10		27	Aldershot	1-2	Young	3825		9	7	4		3	5				2		6	12	10				11	1		8
11		30	SOUTHPORT	0-2		4982		9	7	4		3	5				2		12	6	10				11	1		8
12	Oct	7	Hereford United	0-0		7521		9		4		3	5				2		6		10		7		11	1		8
13		11	Chester	0-2		3426		9	12	4		3	5				2		6		10		7		11	1		8
14		14	CREWE ALEXANDRA	1-1	R Smith	2528	5	9	8	4		3					2		6	12	10	7			11	1		
15		21	Newport County	1-5	Coyne	3392		9	7	4		3	5				2		6	8		11			12	1		10
16		23	GILLINGHAM	2-0	Veart, RW Smith (p)	3462		9	7	4		3	5		10		2		6	8		11				1		
17		28	BURY	1-1	Green	3942		9	7	4		3	5				2		6	8		11	12			1		10
18	Nov	4	ALDERSHOT	1-1	Waddell	3181	5	9		4		3					2		6	8		11	7		12	1		10
19		11	Darlington	2-1	Coyne 2	3724	5	9	12	4		3			10		2		6	8		11	7			1		
20		25	Peterborough United	0-3		4378			9	4		3	5		10		2		6		8	11	7			1		12
21	Dec	2	DONCASTER ROVERS	0-0		2964			9	4		3	5				2		6	8		11	7			1		10
22		8	Barnsley	1-2	Young	1897	4		9			3	5				2		6	8		11	7			1		10
23		16	STOCKPORT COUNTY	0-0		2448	4		9			3	5		12		2		6	8		11	7			1		10
24		23	Mansfield Town	0-2		4208			9	4		3	5		11		2		6	8		7	12			1		10
25		26	BRADFORD CITY	1-0	Veart	4139		12	9	4		3	5		10		2		6			11	7			1		8
26		29	Colchester United	1-1	Veart	3172			9	4		3	5		10		2		6			11	7			1		8
27	Jan	6	TORQUAY UNITED	1-0	Green	2951		12	9	4		3	5		10		2		6			11	7			1		8
28		13	Gillingham	0-2		2772		12	9	4		3	5		10		2		6			11	7			1		8
29		20	Reading	0-1		5360		9		4		3	5		7		2		6	8	12	11				1		10
30		27	CAMBRIDGE UNITED	0-0		3036		9		4		3	5		7		2		6	8		11	12			1		10
31	Feb	3	CHESTER	0-0		2845		11		4	9	3	5		12		2		6	8				7		1		10
32		10	Workington	0-0		1413		11	9	4		3	5				2		6	8	10			7		1		
33		17	LINCOLN CITY	1-0	Conlon	2892		11	9	4			5				2		3	8	6	12		7		1		10
34		23	Stockport County	1-0	Coyne	3324		11	9	4			5				2		3	8	6			7		1		10
35	Mar	3	HEREFORD UNITED	0-1		5253		11	9	4			5				2		3	8	6	12		7		1		10
36		5	NORTHAMPTON T	2-0	Coyne, Green	3822		11	9	4		3	5		10		2			8	6	12		7		1		
37		10	Crewe Alexandra	0-2		1760		11	9	4		3	5		10	12	2			8	6			7		1		
38		16	NEWPORT COUNTY	1-0	RW Smith (p)	3696		11	9	4		3	5			10	2			8	6		12	7		1		
39		24	Bury	1-1	Coyne	2358		11	9	4			5		10		2			8	6		7			1	3	
40		31	PETERBOROUGH UTD.	0-1		2888			9	4			5		10				3	8	6	11	7	12		1	2	
41	Apr	7	Doncaster Rovers	1-2	Conlon	1488		11	9	4			5		10				3	8	6	12	7			1	2	
42		14	BARNSLEY	1-4	Honour	2448			12	4		2	5	3	10				8		6	9	7	11		1		
43		20	MANSFIELD TOWN	1-1	Pate (og)	2855	12		9	4		3	5		10				2	8	6		7	11		1		
44		21	Northampton Town	1-3	Roberts (og)	1478	6		9	4		3	5		10				2	8	7		11	12		1		
45		23	Southport	1-1	Honour	6525			9	4		3	5		11		2		10	8	6			7		1		
46		28	EXETER CITY	0-0		1887			9	4		12	5		10		2	7	3	8	6			11		1		
						Apps	7	28	41	44	1	40	43	1	22	2	41	1	42	37	31	24	29	15	15	46	3	25
						Goals		3	9				4		2				1	5		3	2		1			2

Two own goals

F.A. Cup

							Ashurst L	Conlon B	Coyne JD	Dawes M	Gadston JE	Goad AM	Green W	Gibbin BT	Honour J	McGeough J	Potter GR	Pringle B	Smith RMS	Smith RW	Spelman MT	Veart R	Waddell W	Ward W	Warnock N	Watling BJ	White D	Young R
R1	Nov	18	SCUNTHORPE UNITED	0-0		4586	5		9	4		3			10		2		6	8		11	7			1		12
rep		21	Scunthorpe United	0-0		4478	5		9	4		3			10		2		6	8		11	7			1		
rep2		27	Scunthorpe United	1-2	Veart	7917	5		9	4		3			10		2		6	8		11	7			1		

Replay a.e.t. Replay 2 at Roker Park, Sunderland

F.L. Cup

							Ashurst L	Conlon B	Coyne JD	Dawes M	Gadston JE	Goad AM	Green W	Gibbin BT	Honour J	McGeough J	Potter GR	Pringle B	Smith RMS	Smith RW	Spelman MT	Veart R	Waddell W	Ward W	Warnock N	Watling BJ	White D	Young R
R1	Aug	16	DONCASTER ROVERS	1-0	RW Smith (p)	6752			9	4		3	5				2		6	8	10	12	7		11	1		
R2	Sep	5	Coventry City	0-1		8687			9	4		3	5				2		6	8	10		7		11	1		

		P	W	D	L	F	A	W	D	L	F	A	Pts
1	Southport	46	17	4	2	40	19	9	6	8	31	29	62
2	Hereford United	46	18	4	1	39	12	5	8	10	17	26	58
3	Cambridge United	46	15	6	2	40	23	5	11	7	27	34	57
4	Aldershot	46	14	6	3	33	14	8	6	9	27	24	56
5	Newport County	46	14	6	3	37	18	8	6	9	27	26	56
6	Mansfield Town	46	15	7	1	52	17	5	7	11	26	34	54
7	Reading	46	14	7	2	33	7	3	11	9	18	31	52
8	Exeter City	46	13	8	2	40	18	5	6	12	17	33	50
9	Gillingham	46	15	4	4	44	20	4	7	12	19	38	49
10	Lincoln City	46	12	7	4	38	27	4	9	10	26	30	48
11	Stockport County	46	14	7	2	38	18	4	5	14	15	35	48
12	Bury	46	11	7	5	37	19	3	11	9	21	32	46
13	Workington	46	15	7	1	44	20	2	5	16	15	41	46
14	Barnsley	46	9	8	6	32	24	5	8	10	26	36	44
15	Chester	46	11	6	6	40	19	3	9	11	21	33	43
16	Bradford City	46	12	6	5	42	25	4	5	14	19	40	43
17	Doncaster Rovers	46	10	8	5	28	19	5	4	14	21	39	42
18	Torquay United	46	8	10	5	23	17	4	7	12	21	30	41
19	Peterborough Utd.	46	10	8	5	42	29	4	5	14	29	47	41
20	HARTLEPOOL	46	8	10	5	17	15	4	7	12	17	34	41
21	Crewe Alexandra	46	7	8	8	18	23	2	10	11	20	38	36
22	Colchester United	46	8	8	7	36	28	2	3	18	12	48	31
23	Northampton Town	46	7	6	10	24	30	3	5	15	16	43	31
24	Darlington	46	5	9	9	28	41	2	6	15	14	44	29

1973/74 11th in Division 4

							Conlon B	Coyne JD	Dawes M	Embleton D	Gauden A	Goad AM	Heath D	Honour J	Maddison WH	McMahon FG	McMahon K	McNamee J	Moore M	Potter GR	Shoulder J	Smith RMS	Spelman MT	Waddell W	Ward W	Watling BJ
1	Aug	25	BRENTFORD	1-0	Gauden	3447	5			4	11	3	8				9		7	2		6	10		12	1
2		31	Chester	1-3	Smith	2369	5	12	4		11	3	8				9		7	2		6	10			1
3	Sep	8	READING	1-2	K McMahon	2736	5	7	4		11	3	8				9			2		6	10		12	1
4		11	Bury	0-1		4436		10	4	5	11	3		6			9		7	2		8				1
5		15	Rotherham United	2-2	Gauden (p), K McMahon	3764		10	4	5	11	3		6			9		7	2		8				1
6		17	EXETER CITY	1-3	Gauden (p)	2625		10	4	5	11	3	12	6			9		7			2	8			1
7		22	GILLINGHAM	2-1	Dawes, Moore	1399	5	9	4		11	3		6					7	2	10	8				1
8		29	Scunthorpe United	1-1	Gauden	2626	5		4		11	3		6			9		7	2	10	8				1
9	Oct	3	Exeter City	0-2		4461	5	12	4		11	3		6			9		7	2	10	8				1
10		6	COLCHESTER UNITED	0-0		1926	5	12	4		11	3		6			9		7	2	10	8				1
11		13	Mansfield Town	0-2		3086	5	10	4			3		7			9			12	8	2	6		11	1
12		20	Doncaster Rovers	2-2	Dawes, Coyne	1676	5	10	4		11	3				6	9				7	2	8		12	1
13		22	BURY	1-1	Gauden	1939	5	10	4		11	3				6	9				7	2	8		12	1
14		27	LINCOLN CITY	0-2		1898	5	9	4		11	3				6	12				10	2	8		7	1
15	Nov	3	Northampton Town	0-1		3715	5	9	4					7		6	12		10		3	2	8		11	1
16		10	CREWE ALEXANDRA	1-0	Ward	1221	5		4		11	3				6			7		12	2	8	10	9	1
17		12	NEWPORT COUNTY	0-1		1656		9	4		11	5				6					3	2	8	10	7	1
18		17	Swansea City	0-0		23[illegible]8					11	5		7		6				4	3	2	8	10	9	1
19	Dec	1	Peterborough United	0-2		7537					11	4		6				5	12	2	3	7	8	10	9	1
20		8	BARNSLEY	1-2	Gauden	1101			4		8	3		6				5	9	2		7	12	10	11	1
21		22	SCUNTHORPE UNITED	3-0	Goad, Moore 2	844			4		8	5	7	6			10		9	2	3				11	1
22		26	Workington	2-0	Moore, Gauden (p)	1312			4		8	5	7	6			10		9	2	3				11	1
23		29	Reading	1-1	Gauden	4663			4		8	5	7	6			10		9	2	3	12			11	1
24	Jan	1	CHESTER	0-0		3104			4		8	5	7	6			10		9	2	3				11	1
25		5	NORTHAMPTON T	1-0	Potter	2078			4		8	5	7	6			10		9	2	3	12			11	1
26		12	ROTHERHAM UNITED	2-0	K McMahon, Ward	2016			4		8	5	7	6			10		9	2	3	12			11	1
27		19	Brentford	2-1	Nelmes (og), K McMahon	4646			4		8		7	6			10		9	5	3	2			11	1
28		26	TORQUAY UNITED	0-0		2960			4		8	5	7	6			10		9	2	3				11	1
29	Feb	3	STOCKPORT COUNTY	3-0	K McMahon, Gauden (p), Dawes	5747			4		8	5	7	6			10		9	2	3	12			11	1
30		10	Gillingham	0-3		8724			4		8	5	7	6			10		9	2	3				11	1
31		17	MANSFIELD TOWN	4-0	K McMahon 2, Heath, Moore	4067			4		8	5	7	6			10		9	2	3				11	1
32		22	Colchester United	0-3		5608			4		8	5	7	6			10		9	2	3	12			11	1
33	Mar	3	WORKINGTON	3-0	Dawes 2, Heath	2827			4		8	5	7	6			10		9	2	3				11	1
34		6	Bradford City	0-2		2098			4		8	5	7	6			10		9	2	3		12		11	1
35		9	Lincoln City	1-0	Gauden	1800			4		8	5	7	6			10		9	2	3	12			11	1
36		17	DONCASTER ROVERS	3-0	Shoulder, Ward, Gauden	3502			4		8	5	7	6			10		9	2	3				11	1
37		23	Crewe Alexandra	3-1	Ward 2, K McMahon	1370			4		8	5	7	6			10		9	2	3				11	1
38		27	BRADFORD CITY	1-0	Dawes	3798			4		8	5	7	6			10		9	2	3				11	1
39	Apr	3	Torquay United	2-0	Moore 2	2014			4		8	5	7	6			10		9	2	3				11	1
40		6	Newport County	0-0		1685			4		8	5	7	6			10		9	2	3				11	1
41		12	DARLINGTON	1-2	Cattrell (og)	6739			4		8	5	7	6			10		9	2	3	12			11	1
42		13	SWANSEA CITY	0-1		2665			4		8	5	7				10		9	2	3		6		11	1
43		16	Darlington	1-1	Ward	6723			4		8	5	7	6			10		9	2	3	12			11	1
44		20	Barnsley	0-2		3555			4		8	5	7	6			10		9	2	3		12		11	1
45		22	Stockport County	1-1	Gauden	1311			4		10	5	7	6					9	2	3	8	12		11	1
46		27	PETERBOROUGH UTD.	0-1		2283			4		10	5	7	6	12				9	2	3	8			11	1
						Apps	13	14	43	4	44	44	30	37	1	7	38	2	39	39	39	31	18	5	38	46
						Goals		1	6		12	1	2				8		7	1	1	1			6	

Two own goals

F.A. Cup

R1	Nov	24	Altrincham	0-2		2923					11	5	7	6					12	4	3	2	8	10	9	1

F.L. Cup

R1	Aug	29	Rochdale	3-5	Gauden 2, K McMahon	1836	5			4	11	3	8				9		7	2		6	10		12	1

		P	W	D	L	F	A	W	D	L	F	A	Pts
1	Peterborough Utd.	46	19	4	0	49	10	8	7	8	26	28	65
2	Gillingham	46	16	5	2	51	16	9	7	7	39	33	62
3	Colchester United	46	16	5	2	46	14	8	7	8	27	22	60
4	Bury	46	18	3	2	51	14	6	8	9	30	35	59
5	Northampton Town	46	14	7	2	39	14	6	6	11	24	34	53
6	Reading	46	11	9	3	37	13	5	10	8	21	24	51
7	Chester	46	13	6	4	31	19	4	9	10	23	36	49
8	Bradford City	46	14	7	2	45	20	3	7	13	13	32	48
9	Newport County	46	13	6	4	39	23	3	8	12	17	42	45
10	Exeter City	45	12	5	6	37	20	6	3	13	21	35	44
11	HARTLEPOOL	46	11	4	8	29	16	5	8	10	19	31	44
12	Lincoln City	46	10	8	5	40	30	6	4	13	23	37	44
13	Barnsley	46	15	5	3	42	16	2	5	16	16	48	44
14	Swansea City	46	11	6	6	28	15	5	5	13	17	31	43
15	Rotherham United	46	10	9	4	33	22	5	4	14	23	36	43
16	Torquay United	46	11	7	5	37	23	2	10	11	15	34	43
17	Mansfield Town	46	13	8	2	47	24	0	9	14	15	45	43
18	Scunthorpe United	45	12	7	3	33	17	2	5	16	14	47	42
19	Brentford	46	9	7	7	31	20	3	9	11	17	30	40
20	Darlington	46	9	8	6	29	24	4	5	14	11	38	39
21	Crewe Alexandra	46	11	5	7	28	30	3	5	15	15	41	38
22	Doncaster Rovers	46	10	7	6	32	22	2	4	17	15	58	35
23	Workington	46	10	8	5	33	26	1	5	17	10	48	35
24	Stockport County	46	4	12	7	22	25	3	8	12	22	44	34

1974/75 13th in Division 4

	Date	Opponent	Score	Scorers	Att	Dawes M	Embleton D	Gauden A	Goad AM	Griffiths S	Guy EF	Heath D	Honour J	Johnson, David	Johnson KP	Maddison WH	McBurney ML	McMahon K	Moore M	Park RC	Potter GR	Shoulder J	Smith DB	Smith RMS	Spelman MT	Ward W	Watling BJ	Worthington PR
1	Aug 17	NEWPORT COUNTY	2-0	Moore, Gauden	2557	4		8	5				6					10	9	7	2	3				11	1	
2	24	Chester	0-3		2942	4		8	5				7					10	9	6	2	3		12		11	1	
3	31	SOUTHPORT	1-1	Dawes	1914	4		8	5				7					10	9	6	2	3		12		11	1	
4	Sep 7	Crewe Alexandra	0-2		2211	4		8	5			7						10	9		6	3		2	11		1	
5	14	ROTHERHAM UNITED	3-2	Moore, Goodfellow (og), Shoulder	2401	4		8	5			7						10	9		6	3		2	11		1	
6	21	Scunthorpe United	1-1	McMahon	2069	4		8	5			7						10	9		6	3		2	11		1	
7	28	SWANSEA CITY	0-2		2850	4		8	5			7	12					10	9		6	3		2		11	1	
8	Oct 1	Cambridge United	2-3	Shoulder, Smith	2774	4		8	5			7	11					10	9		6	3		2			1	
9	5	Shrewsbury Town	1-0	Moore	4222	4		8	5			7	11					10	9		6	3		2			1	
10	12	TORQUAY UNITED	0-0		2177	4		8	5			7	11					10	9		6	3		2			1	
11	19	Barnsley	1-2	McMahon	3135	4		8	5				7					10	9	11	6	3		2		12	1	
12	26	MANSFIELD TOWN	2-1	Dawes, Potter	2632	4		8	5				7					10	9		6	3		2		11	1	
13	28	Stockport County	1-1	Moore	2047	4		8	5				7					10	9		6	3		2		11	1	
14	Nov 2	WORKINGTON	3-0	Gauden 2, Dawes	2632	4		8	5				7					10	9		6	3		2		11	1	
15	6	READING	2-3	Dawes, Honour	3204	4		8	5				7					10	9		6	3		2	12	11	1	
16	9	Darlington	2-1	Spelman, McMahon	3974	4		8	5				7					10	9		6	3		2	11		1	
17	16	BRENTFORD	3-2	McMahon, Spelman, Honour	2864	4		8	5				7					10	9		6	3		2	11		1	
18	Dec 7	Doncaster Rovers	0-3		1357	4		8	5				7				12	10	9		6	3		2	11		1	
19	21	ROCHDALE	5-0	Honour, McMahon 2, Moore 2	1991	4		8	5				7					10	9		6	3		2		11	1	
20	26	Rotherham United	2-1	McBurney, McMahon	5784	4			5				12				8	10	9		6	3		2	11	7	1	
21	Jan 1	NORTHAMPTON T	2-0	McMahon, Moore	5178	4			5								8	10	9	6	2			3	11	7	1	
22	4	Exeter City	0-1		3424	4	5										8	10	9	6	2			3	11	7	1	
23	11	DONCASTER ROVERS	2-1	Moore, McMahon	2950	4			5								8	10	9		6	3		2	11	7	1	
24	17	Lincoln City	0-2		5459	4			5								8	10	9		6	3		2	11	7	1	
25	29	Bradford City	0-3		2225	4	12		5				8					10	9		6	3		2	11	7	1	
26	Feb 1	DARLINGTON	2-0	McMahon, Goad	4138	4	12		5				8					10	9	11	6	3		2		7	1	
27	12	LINCOLN CITY	2-0	Moore 2	2632	4	3		5				8					10	9	11	6			2		7	1	
28	15	BRADFORD CITY	1-2	Moore	3278	4	3		5				8		12			10	9	11	6			2		7	1	
29	22	Brentford	0-1		5516	4			5				6		11			10	9		3		8	2		7	1	
30	24	Reading	0-0		5980	4	3		5				10		11				9		6		8	2		7	1	
31	28	Southport	0-0		1451	4	3		5						11				9	10	6		8	2		7	1	
32	Mar 8	STOCKPORT COUNTY	1-1	Johnson	2593	4	3		5				10		11				9	6			8	2		7	1	
33	10	EXETER CITY	0-3		2178	4			5				6	10	11				9	3			8	2		7	1	
34	15	Swansea City	0-1		2303	4			5				10		11	7			9		6		8	2			1	3
35	17	Newport County	0-2		1535	4			5				10		11	7			9		6		8	2		12	1	3
36	22	CREWE ALEXANDRA	1-1	Johnson	1923	4			5				8		10	7			9	12	6			2		11	1	3
37	28	SCUNTHORPE UNITED	1-0	McMahon	2471		6		5				8		11			10	9		2			4		7	1	3
38	29	Rochdale	0-3		1297		6		5				8		11			10	9	12	2			4		7	1	3
39	Apr 1	Northampton Town	0-3		2758	4			5				7		11			10	9	8	6			2			1	3
40	5	Mansfield Town	0-2		8860	3	6		5						8			10	9		4			2	11	7	1	
41	7	CAMBRIDGE UNITED	1-1	Ward	1627	3	6		5						8			10	9		4			2	11	7	1	
42	12	SHREWSBURY TOWN	1-1	McMahon	2182	3	6		5				12		8			10	9		4			2	11	7	1	
43	15	Workington	1-1	Moore	1319		6		5				8		11			10	9	12	3			2	4	7	1	
44	19	Torquay United	1-2	McMahon	2444		6		5						11			10	9	8	3			2	4	7	1	
45	21	CHESTER	1-0	Moore	2047	4	6		5						11			10	9		3			2	8	7	1	
46	26	BARNSLEY	4-3	Ward 2, Moore, Dawes	2159	4	6		5	12	1				11			10	9		3			2	8	7		
					Apps	42	17	19	45	1	1	7	33	1	19	3	6	39	46	17	44	24	7	45	20	35	45	6
					Goals	5		3	1				3		2		1	13	14		1	2		1	2	3		

One own goal

F.A. Cup

	Date	Opponent	Score	Scorers	Att	Dawes M	Embleton D	Gauden A	Goad AM	Griffiths S	Guy EF	Heath D	Honour J	Johnson, David	Johnson KP	Maddison WH	McBurney ML	McMahon K	Moore M	Park RC	Potter GR	Shoulder J	Smith DB	Smith RMS	Spelman MT	Ward W	Watling BJ	Worthington PR
R1	Nov 23	BRADFORD CITY	1-0	Honour	3677	4		8	5				7					10	9		6	3		2	11		1	
R2	Dec 14	LINCOLN CITY	0-0		2838			8	5				7					10	9		6	3		2	11	4	1	
rep	17	Lincoln City	0-1		4985	12		8	5				7					10	9		6	3		2	11	4	1	

F.L. Cup

	Date	Opponent	Score	Scorers	Att	Dawes M	Embleton D	Gauden A	Goad AM	Griffiths S	Guy EF	Heath D	Honour J	Johnson, David	Johnson KP	Maddison WH	McBurney ML	McMahon K	Moore M	Park RC	Potter GR	Shoulder J	Smith DB	Smith RMS	Spelman MT	Ward W	Watling BJ	Worthington PR
R1	Aug 21	Workington	2-1	McMahon, Gauden	2011	4		8	5				7					10	9	6	2	3				11	1	
R2	Sep 11	Bournemouth	1-1	Gauden	4971	4		8	5			7						10	9		6	3		2	11		1	
rep	18	BOURNEMOUTH	2-2	Moore 2	5160	4		8	5			7						10	9		6	3		2	11		1	
rep2	23	Bournemouth	1-1	Moore	4498	4		8	5			7						10	9		6	3		2	11		1	
rep3	26	BOURNEMOUTH	1-0	Ward	6970	4		8	5			7						10	9		6	3		2	11	12	1	
R3	Oct 9	BLACKBURN ROVERS	1-1	Moore	5995	4		8	5			7	11					10	9		6	3		2			1	
rep	16	Blackburn Rovers	2-1	Potter, McMahon	11145	4		8	5				7					10	9	12	6	3		2	11		1	
R4	Nov 12	ASTON VILLA	1-1	Moore	12305	4		8	5				7					10	9		6	3		2	11		1	
rep	25	Aston Villa	1-6	Gauden	17686	4		8	5				7					10	9		6	3		2	11		1	

R2 replay and replay 2 a.e.t.

League table on a later page

1975/76 — 14th in Division 4

No	Date	Opponent	Score	Scorers	Att	Bielby PA	Charlton H	Crowther SJ	Dawes M	Elliott K	Embleton D	Endean B	Goad AM	Honour J	Hope JWM	Jacques J	Johnson KP	Luckett P	Maggiore A	McMahon K	Moore M	Potter GR	Richardson GC	Rowlands JH	Rylands DR	Scaife RH	Skillen K	Smith DB	Smith RMS	Spelman MT	Wann JD	Watling BJ
1	Aug 16	BOURNEMOUTH	1-1	D Smith	2228			3	6				5	7	1		11			10	9	4					12	8	2			
2	23	Brentford	1-1	Goad	4948			2			6		5	7			11			10	12	4	1				9	8	3			
3	30	LINCOLN CITY	2-2	D Smith 2	1908			3					5	4			11			10	9	6					7	8	2			1
4	Sep 6	Watford	1-2	Skillen	3598								5				11			10	9	6		12		4	7	8	2	3		1
5	13	SCUNTHORPE UNITED	1-2	Johnson	1972								5				11			10	9	6	1	12		4	7	8	2	3		
6	19	Southport	4-2	Johnson,McMahon,Moore,D Smith	1012						6						11			10	9	2	1	5		4		8	3	7		
7	22	READING	2-4	Rowlands, R Smith	2269						6						11			10	9	2	1	5		4		8	3	7		
8	27	TRANMERE ROVERS	1-2	Rowlands	1559								6		1		11			10	9	2		5		4	12	8	3	7		
9	Oct 4	Crewe Alexandra	0-0		2326						3		2	7	1		6				9	4		5		11		8		10		
10	11	TORQUAY UNITED	0-1		1695						3		2	7	1		6			12	9	4		5		11		8		10		
11	13	EXETER CITY	2-1	Moore, D Smith	1323								3	7	1		6			10	9	4		5				8	2	11		
12	18	Exeter City	1-3	Goad	2406								3	7	1		6			10	9	4		5				8	2	11		
13	22	STOCKPORT COUNTY	3-0	Moore, D Smith, McMahon	1683								3	7	1		6			10	9	4		5				8	2	11		
14	25	BARNSLEY	1-0	D Smith	2350								3	7	1		6			10	9	4		5				8	2	11		
15	Nov 1	Huddersfield Town	0-2		4183								3	7	1		6			10	9	4		5		12		8	2	11		
16	3	Darlington	2-1	McMahon, Scaife	4275								3	7	1		6			10	9	4		5		11		8	2			
17	8	DONCASTER ROVERS	2-1	Rowlands, McMahon	3592								3	7	1		6			10	9	4		5		11		8	2			
18	15	Bradford City	2-1	Johnson, Honour	2009	12							3	7	1		6			10	9	4		5		11		8	2			
19	29	NEWPORT COUNTY	4-1	Moore,Screen(og),Johnson,McMahon	2661	7							3		1		6		12	10	9	4		5		11		8	2			
20	Dec 6	Swansea City	1-3	McMahon	2354	7							3		1		6			10	9	4		5		11		8	2			
21	20	Rochdale	1-1	Scaife	1156	12							3		1		6			10	9	4		5		11		8	2	7		
22	26	NORTHAMPTON T	3-0	D Smith 2, McMahon	5077								3	7	1					10	9	4		5		11		8	2	6		
23	27	Workington	2-1	McMahon, Moore	2553	12							3	7	1					10	9	4		5		11		8	2	6		
24	Jan 10	Lincoln City	0-3		7581	6	7			9			3		1				4	10				5		11		8	2			
25	17	SOUTHPORT	0-0		2953	6	7						3		1				4	10				5		11		8	2		9	
26	30	Stockport County	0-2		1565									7	1	4	6		3	10	9			5		11		8	2			
27	Feb 7	DARLINGTON	2-3	Rowlands, D Smith	3689		12							7	1		6		3	10	9	4		5		11		8	2			
28	14	Doncaster Rovers	0-3		5035	12							3				6		2	10	9	4	1	5		11				7	8	
29	18	CAMBRIDGE UNITED	2-2	Goad, Moore	1434	12							3				6			10	9	4	1	5		11		8	2	7		
30	21	BRADFORD CITY	2-2	D Smith 2	1899								3	7		6					9	4	1	5		11		8	2	10		
31	25	Reading	0-1		6473								3	7		6					9	4	1	5		11		8	2	10		
32	28	Barnsley	1-3	Scaife	2772	12							3	7		6					9	4	1	5		11		8	2	10		
33	Mar 2	Scunthorpe United	1-5	D Smith	3098					7			3		1	5	6		2		9	4				11		8		10		
34	6	HUDDERSFIELD T	1-1	Rowlands	2058								3				6			10	9	4	1	5		11		8	2	7		
35	10	CREWE ALEXANDRA	1-3	Moore	1506	12							3				6			10	9	4	1	5		11		8	2	7		
36	13	Torquay United	1-1	Moore	2826							8					6	3	12		9	4	1	10	5	11			2	7		
37	20	Newport County	1-0	Moore	1230							8					6	3			9	4	1	10	5	11			2	7		
38	27	SWANSEA CITY	1-0	Rowlands	1708							8					6	3			9	4	1	10	5	11			2	7		
39	31	ROCHDALE	3-0	Spelman, Moore 2	1561							8	2				6	3			9	4	1	10	5	11				7		
40	Apr 3	Bournemouth	2-4	Endean, Johnson	3102							8	2				6	3			9	4	1		5	11		10		7		
41	6	Tranmere Rovers	2-1	Endean, Griffiths (og)	3450							8	2				10	3	6		9	4	1		5	11				7		
42	10	WATFORD	2-1	Endean, Moore	2028	12						8	2				10	3	6		9	4	1		5	11				7		
43	16	Cambridge United	0-4		2136	11						8	2				10	3	6		9	4	1		5	12				7		
44	17	Northampton Town	2-5	Moore, Johnson (p)	7555	11						8			1		10	3	6		9	4			5	7				2		
45	20	WORKINGTON	0-2		1765	11				7		8					6	3	12		9	4	1		5	10				2		
46	24	BRENTFORD	1-0	Scaife	1276	11				6		8	2					3	12		9	4	1		5	10				7		
					Apps	16	3	3	1	4	5	11	37	20	23	5	38	11	14	30	44	43	21	35	11	39	6	35	34	34	2	2
					Goals							3	3	1			6			8	13			6		4	1	13	1	1		

Two own goals

F.A. Cup

Rd	Date	Opponent	Score	Scorers	Att	Bielby PA	Charlton H	Crowther SJ	Dawes M	Elliott K	Embleton D	Endean B	Goad AM	Honour J	Hope JWM	Jacques J	Johnson KP	Luckett P	Maggiore A	McMahon K	Moore M	Potter GR	Richardson GC	Rowlands JH	Rylands DR	Scaife RH	Skillen K	Smith DB	Smith RMS	Spelman MT	Wann JD	Watling BJ
R1	Nov 22	STOCKPORT COUNTY	3-0	D Smith, McMahon, Potter	3348	7							3		1		6			10	9	4		5		11		8	2			
R2	Dec 13	Marine	1-1	Scaife	2300								3		1		6			10	9	4		5		11		8	2	7		
rep	15	MARINE	6-3	Moore 3,Johnson (p),Rowlands,Scaife	5673								3		1		6			10	9	4		5		11		8	2	7		
R3	Jan 3	Manchester City	0-6		26863	6							3	7	1					10	9	4		5		11		8	2			

F.L. Cup

Rd	Date	Opponent	Score	Scorers	Att	Bielby PA	Charlton H	Crowther SJ	Dawes M	Elliott K	Embleton D	Endean B	Goad AM	Honour J	Hope JWM	Jacques J	Johnson KP	Luckett P	Maggiore A	McMahon K	Moore M	Potter GR	Richardson GC	Rowlands JH	Rylands DR	Scaife RH	Skillen K	Smith DB	Smith RMS	Spelman MT	Wann JD	Watling BJ
R1/1	Aug 19	Halifax Town	1-4	Johnson	1476			2					5	7	1		11			10	9	4						8	3			
R1/2	25	HALIFAX TOWN	2-1	McMahon, Skillen	1725			3					5	4			11			10	9	6	1				7	8	2			

Played in R1/1: B Albeson (at 6)

		P	W	D	L	F	A	W	D	L	F	A	Pts
1	Lincoln City	46	21	2	0	71	15	11	8	4	40	24	74
2	Northampton Town	46	18	5	0	62	20	11	5	7	25	20	68
3	Reading	46	19	3	1	42	9	5	9	9	28	42	60
4	Tranmere Rovers	46	18	3	2	61	16	6	7	10	28	39	58
5	Huddersfield Town	46	11	6	6	28	17	10	8	5	28	24	56
6	Bournemouth	46	15	5	3	39	16	5	7	11	18	32	52
7	Exeter City	46	13	7	3	37	17	5	7	11	19	30	50
8	Watford	46	16	4	3	38	18	6	2	15	24	44	50
9	Torquay United	46	12	6	5	31	24	6	8	9	24	39	50
10	Doncaster Rovers	46	10	6	7	42	31	9	5	9	33	38	49
11	Swansea City	46	14	8	1	51	21	2	7	14	15	36	47
12	Barnsley	46	12	8	3	34	16	2	8	13	18	32	44
13	Cambridge United	46	7	10	6	36	28	7	5	11	22	34	43
14	HARTLEPOOL	46	10	6	7	37	29	6	4	13	25	49	42
15	Rochdale	46	7	11	5	27	23	5	7	11	13	31	42
16	Crewe Alexandra	46	10	7	6	36	21	3	8	12	22	36	41
17	Bradford City	46	9	7	7	35	26	3	10	10	28	39	41
18	Brentford	46	12	7	4	37	18	2	6	15	19	42	41
19	Scunthorpe United	46	11	3	9	31	24	3	7	13	19	35	38
20	Darlington	46	11	7	5	30	14	3	3	17	18	43	38
21	Stockport County	46	8	7	8	23	23	5	5	13	20	53	38
22	Newport County	46	8	7	8	35	33	5	2	16	22	57	35
23	Southport	46	6	6	11	27	31	2	4	17	14	46	26
24	Workington	46	5	4	14	19	43	2	3	18	11	44	21

1976/77

22nd in Division 4

	Date		Opponent	Score	Scorers	Att	Bielby PA	Creamer PA	Cunningham D	Davies GP	Edgar E	Elliott K	Endean B	Goad AM	Goldthorpe W	Harley JR	Johnson KP	Luckett P	Maggiore A	McMaster C	McMordie AA	O'Donnell JD	Poskett M	Prudham CE	Reed HD	Richardson GC	Rowlands JH	Scaife RH	Scott RW	Simpkin CJ	Smith TM	Spelman MT	Turnbull TM	Veitch T	Wiggett DJ
1	Aug	21	EXETER CITY	2-2	Endean, Elliott	1599	11					8	9	3					6			2				1		10	5			7		4	
2		24	Watford	0-4		4667	11					8	9	3					6			2				1		10	5			7		4	
3		28	Crewe Alexandra	1-3	Lugg (og)	2012	12				1	8		9			11	3	6			2						7	5			10		4	
4	Sep	4	BOURNEMOUTH	0-1		1548	11				1	12	8	2		10	9	3									6		5			7		4	
5		11	Workington	1-1	Harley	1505					1	7		2		9	11	3						10			6	12	5			8		4	
6		18	SOUTHEND UNITED	1-1	Rowlands	1612					1	12		2		9	11	3						10			6	7	5			8		4	
7		24	Halifax Town	0-1		1393					1	8	9	2				3	11					10			6	7	5					4	
8	Oct	2	Scunthorpe United	0-2		3514					1	12	8	2		9		3	4								6	11	5			7		10	
9		9	CAMBRIDGE UNITED	2-2	Scaife, Rowlands	1452	12				1	4	8	2				3							9		6	11	5			7		10	
10		16	Colchester United	2-6	Bielby 2	3180	11				1			2				3							9		8	10	5			7		4	6
11		23	ROCHDALE	2-0	Scaife, Reed (p)	1492	11	2			1	10		6					4						9		8	7	5						3
12		26	Newport County	1-1	Scaife	2334	11	2			1	10	12	6					4						9		8	7	5						3
13		30	HUDDERSFIELD T	0-1		2628	11	2			1	10		6					4	12					9		8	7	5						3
14	Nov	1	STOCKPORT COUNTY	1-1	Rowlands	1685	11	2			1	10		6						9					4		8	7	5						3
15		5	Doncaster Rovers	1-2	Scaife	2631	11	2		9	1	10		8								4					6	7	5						3
16		13	BRENTFORD	2-0	Davies (p), Rowlands	1888	11	2		9	1	10		8								4	12				6	7	5						3
17		27	Aldershot	0-3		3494	11	2			1	10		8								4	9				6	7							3
18	Dec	18	Barnsley	0-3		3667	11	2		9	1			12							8	4	10					7	5	6					3
19		22	Bradford City	2-2	Poskett, Bielby	3552	11	2		9	1			12							8	4	10					7	5	6					3
20		27	DARLINGTON	1-1	O'Donnell	4885	11	2		9	1			12							8	4	10					7	5	6					3
21	Jan	1	DONCASTER ROVERS	0-0		2206	11	2					9		12						8	4	10			1		7	5	6					3
22		8	TORQUAY UNITED	4-0	Poskett 3, Bielby	2128	11	2							9						8	4	10			1		7	5	6					3
23		15	WATFORD	1-0	Wiggett (p)	2411	11	2						12	9						8	4	10			1		7	5	6					3
24		22	Exeter City	1-3	Goldthorpe	3285	12	2						11	9						8	4	10			1		7	5	6					3
25		29	Swansea City	2-4	Bartley (og), Creamer	5034	11	2							9						8	4	10			1		7	5	6					3
26	Feb	5	CREWE ALEXANDRA	3-0	Poskett 2, Scaife	1972	11	2							9						8	4	10			1		7	5	6					3
27		12	Bournemouth	0-2		4409	11	2						12	9						8	4	10			1		7	5	6					3
28		15	Huddersfield Town	1-4	Creamer	5493	11	2				4	9	12							8		10			1		7	5	6					3
29		19	WORKINGTON	2-0	Endean, Johnston (og)	1774	11	2			1	4	9								8		10					7	5	6					3
30		25	Southend United	0-1		6619		2			1	4	9								8	11	10					7	5	6					3
31	Mar	5	HALIFAX TOWN	1-0	Bielby	1673	12	2			1	4	9	5							8	11	10					7		6					3
32		7	Stockport County	0-1		2649	12	2			1	4	9	5							8	11	10					7		6					3
33		12	SCUNTHORPE UNITED	3-0	Poskett, Creamer, Scaife	1698	11	2	12		1			5							8	4	10					7		6			9		3
34		19	Cambridge United	0-2		3853	11	2	12		1			5							8	4	10					7		6			9		3
35		26	COLCHESTER UNITED	2-2	Poskett 2 (1p)	1831		2	11		1			4							8		10					7	5	6			9		3
36		28	SOUTHPORT	1-1	Turnbull	1539	4	5	11		1			6					2		8	12	10					7					9		3
37	Apr	2	Rochdale	1-0	Cunningham	858			11		1			8					2			4	10					7	5	6			9		3
38		8	Darlington	1-3	Poskett	4419	12		11		1	8		7					2			4	10						5	6			9		3
39		9	BRADFORD CITY	0-1		2765	12	7	11		1								2		8	4	10						5	6			9		3
40		16	NEWPORT COUNTY	0-1		1522	12	7	11		1		9						2		8	4	10						5	6					3
41		18	SWANSEA CITY	2-2	Goad, McMordie	1169	11	2	7		1			10					3		8	4							5	6			9		
42		23	Brentford	1-3	Turnbull	5978	11	2			1			7							8	4	10						5	6			9		3
43		30	ALDERSHOT	0-2		1202	11	2			1	8		12								4	10					7	5	6			9		3
44	May	4	Torquay United	0-1		1831	11	2	8		1			5								4	10					7		6			9		3
45		7	Southport	2-1	Turnbull, Bielby	880	11	2	8		1											4	10					7		6	5		9		3
46		14	BARNSLEY	0-2		1274	11	2	8		1			4						7			10							6	5		9		3
						Apps	39	34	12	5	36	23	14	37	7	4	4	8	14	3	23	31	30	3	6	10	14	39	37	28	2	9	13	10	36
						Goals	6	3	1	1		1	2	1	1	1					1	1	10		1		4	6					3		1

Played in one game: GR Potter (game 2, at 12); F Spraggon (17, at 5)

Three own goals

F.A. Cup

	Date		Opponent	Score	Scorers	Att	Bielby PA	Creamer PA	Cunningham D	Davies GP	Edgar E	Elliott K	Endean B	Goad AM	Goldthorpe W	Harley JR	Johnson KP	Luckett P	Maggiore A	McMaster C	McMordie AA	O'Donnell JD	Poskett M	Prudham CE	Reed HD	Richardson GC	Rowlands JH	Scaife RH	Scott RW	Simpkin CJ	Smith TM	Spelman MT	Turnbull TM	Veitch T	Wiggett DJ
R1	Nov	20	Chester	0-1		3724	11	2			1	10		8					9			4					6	7	5						3

F.L. Cup

	Date		Opponent	Score	Scorers	Att	Bielby PA	Creamer PA	Cunningham D	Davies GP	Edgar E	Elliott K	Endean B	Goad AM	Goldthorpe W	Harley JR	Johnson KP	Luckett P	Maggiore A	McMaster C	McMordie AA	O'Donnell JD	Poskett M	Prudham CE	Reed HD	Richardson GC	Rowlands JH	Scaife RH	Scott RW	Simpkin CJ	Smith TM	Spelman MT	Turnbull TM	Veitch T	Wiggett DJ
R1/1	Aug	14	Huddersfield Town	0-2		3603	11					7	10	3			9		6			2				1		8	5			4			
R1/2		18	HUDDERSFIELD TOWN	1-2	Turnbull	2000	11					12	8	3			9		6			2				1		7	5			4	10		

		P	W	D	L	F	A	W	D	L	F	A	Pts
1	Cambridge United	46	16	5	2	57	18	10	8	5	30	22	65
2	Exeter City	46	17	5	1	40	13	8	7	8	30	33	62
3	Colchester United	46	19	2	2	51	14	6	7	10	26	29	59
4	Bradford City	46	16	7	0	51	18	7	6	10	27	33	59
5	Swansea City	46	18	3	2	60	30	7	5	11	32	38	58
6	Barnsley	46	16	5	2	45	18	7	4	12	17	21	55
7	Watford	46	15	7	1	46	13	3	8	12	21	37	51
8	Doncaster Rovers	46	16	2	5	47	25	5	7	11	24	40	51
9	Huddersfield Town	46	15	5	3	36	15	4	7	12	24	34	50
10	Southend United	46	11	9	3	35	19	4	10	9	17	26	49
11	Darlington	46	13	5	5	37	25	5	8	10	22	39	49
12	Crewe Alexandra	46	16	6	1	36	15	3	5	15	11	45	49
13	Bournemouth	46	13	8	2	39	13	2	10	11	15	31	48
14	Stockport County	46	10	10	3	29	19	3	9	11	24	38	45
15	Brentford	46	14	3	6	48	27	4	4	15	29	49	43
16	Torquay United	46	12	5	6	33	22	5	4	14	26	45	43
17	Aldershot	46	10	8	5	29	19	6	3	14	20	40	43
18	Rochdale	46	8	7	8	32	25	5	5	13	18	34	38
19	Newport County	46	11	6	6	33	21	3	4	16	9	37	38
20	Scunthorpe United	46	11	6	6	32	24	2	5	16	17	49	37
21	Halifax Town	46	11	6	6	36	18	0	8	15	11	40	36
22	HARTLEPOOL	46	8	9	6	30	20	2	3	18	17	53	32
23	Southport	46	3	12	8	17	28	0	7	16	16	49	25
24	Workington	46	3	7	13	23	42	1	4	18	18	60	19

1977/78 21st in Division 4

	Date	Opponent	Score	Scorers	Att	Ayre W	Bielby PA	Creamer PA	Darling M	Downing DG	Edgar E	Foggon A	Gaffney T	Gibb T	Goad AM	Harris M	Hogan RD	Houchen KM	Larkin GT	Lawrence M	Linacre J	Livsey GW	Malone RP	McMaster C	McMordie AA	Newton R	Poskett M	Richardson GC	Scaife RH	Simpkin CJ	Smith G	Smith TM	Wiggett DJ
1	Aug 20	TORQUAY UNITED	1-2	Malone	2351	5	11	6		8	1		12	4									2		7	9	10						3
2	23	Halifax Town	0-3		1714	5				8	1			4	9								2		7		10		11	6			3
3	27	Southport	1-1	Goad	1628	5	11			8	1			4	9								2		7		10			6			3
4	Sep 3	SCUNTHORPE UNITED	1-0	Malone	1960	5	11			8	1			4	9								2		7		10			6			3
5	10	WIMBLEDON	2-0	McMordie, Poskett	2731	5	11			8	1			4									2		7	9	10			6			3
6	13	Grimsby Town	1-2	Downing	4021	5	11			8	1			4							12		2		7	9	10			6			3
7	17	Northampton Town	3-5	Poskett 2, Newton	3499	5	11	2		8	1										4				7	9	10			6			3
8	24	READING	2-1	Ayre, Downing	2402	5	11	2	12	8	1										4					9	10		7	6			3
9	27	ROCHDALE	1-0	Ayre	3389	5	11	2		8	1			4							7					9	10			6			3
10	Oct 1	Crewe Alexandra	0-1		2051	5	11	2	12	8	1			4							7					9	10			6			3
11	4	Huddersfield Town	1-3	Ayre	3966	5	12	2	11	8				4							7					9	10	1		6			3
12	8	BOURNEMOUTH	0-1		2601	5	11	2		8	1			4											7	9	10			6			3
13	14	Southend United	1-1	Poskett	5686	5			11	3	1			4							8		2		7	9	10			6		
14	22	BRENTFORD	3-1	Poskett 2, Ayre	2470	5	11			3	1			4							8		2		7	9	10			6		
15	29	Barnsley	2-3	Poskett 2	4287	5	11			3	1			4							12		2		7	9	10			6	8	
16	Nov 5	WATFORD	1-2	Poskett	3143	5	11			3	1		7	4							8					9	10			6	2	
17	11	Stockport County	0-6		4179	5				3	1		7	4	11						8					9				6	2	10	
18	19	DONCASTER ROVERS	0-2		2309	5	11			2	1		10	4	12						7					9					8	6	3
19	Dec 3	Newport County	2-4	Ayre, Newton	3323	5	11			8	1		10	4							7					9					2	6	3
20	10	ALDERSHOT	2-2	Gaffney, Ayre	2082	5	11	2		8			12	4	10						7					9		1				6	3
21	26	York City	0-1		3603	5	11			8				4								1	2			9	10			6	7		3
22	27	DARLINGTON	2-1	Downing, Poskett	5299	5	12			8				4							7	1	2			9	10			6		11	3
23	31	SWANSEA CITY	0-4		3211	5	11			3				4		12					7	1	2			9	10			6		8	
24	Jan 2	Watford	0-1		16866	5		11		3				4							7	1	2			9	10				6	8	
25	14	Torquay United	0-0		2421	5	11	7		3	1			4									2		8	9	10				6	12	
26	Feb 7	HALIFAX TOWN	1-1	Downing	3537	5	11	7		3	1	10		4									2		8	9					6		
27	18	Reading	3-2	Gibb, Ayre, White (og)	4322	5	11	7		3	1	10		4									2		8	9					6		
28	20	Wimbledon	0-3		1440	5	11	7		3	1	10		4									2		8	9					6	12	
29	25	CREWE ALEXANDRA	1-1	Roberts (og)	2506	5	11			3	1	10		4				9			7		2		8						6		
30	28	SOUTHPORT	2-1	Gibb, Ayre	2432	5	11			3	1	10		4				9			7		2		8						6		
31	Mar 4	Bournemouth	0-1		2992	5		11		3	1	10		4							7		2		8	9					6		
32	7	GRIMSBY TOWN	3-1	Bielby (p), Foggon, G Smith	2595	5	11	7		3	1	10		4							12		2		8	9					6		
33	11	SOUTHEND UNITED	1-0	Bielby (p)	3115	5	11	7		3	1	10		4									2		8	9					6		
34	14	YORK CITY	4-2	G Smith, Newton, Ayre, Gibb	3496	5	11	7		3	1	10		4									2		8	9					6		
35	18	Brentford	0-2		7499	5	11	7			1			4							10		2		8	9					6	12	3
36	24	BARNSLEY	1-2	Houchen	4315	5	11	7			1	10		4				9			12		2		8						6	3	
37	25	Darlington	2-1	Foggon, Houchen	3372	5	11	7		3		10	8	2				9			4							1			6		
38	Apr 1	Swansea City	0-8		7149	5	3	7				10	11	4				9			8		2					1			6	12	
39	4	Rochdale	1-0	Houchen	972	5	11	2		3	1	10	12	4				9			8										6	7	
40	8	STOCKPORT COUNTY	2-0	Gibb, Ayre	2416	5	11	7		3	1	10		4				9			8		2								6		
41	11	NORTHAMPTON T	0-2		2844	5	11	7		3	1	10		4				9			8		2		12						6		
42	15	Doncaster Rovers	0-2		2040	5	11	6		3	1		7		10		4	9			8		2										
43	18	Scunthorpe United	0-2		2317	5	12	7		3	1	10	11	4				9			8		2								6		
44	22	NEWPORT COUNTY	1-1	Houchen	2027	5	12	3			1	10	7					9	11	4	8		2									6	
45	25	HUDDERSFIELD T	3-2	Ayre 2, Larkin	1926	5		3				10	7				4	9	11	12	8	1	2								6		
46	29	Aldershot	0-3		3624	5	12	3									4	9	11	8	7	1	2	10							6		
					Apps	46	40	29	4	40	36	18	13	40	7	1	3	13	3	3	33	6	33	1	24	30	21	4	2	19	27	14	18
					Goals	12	2			4		2	1	4	1			4	1				2		1	3	10					2		

Two own goals

F.A. Cup

	Date	Opponent	Score	Scorers	Att	Ayre W	Bielby PA	Creamer PA	Darling M	Downing DG	Edgar E	Foggon A	Gaffney T	Gibb T	Goad AM	Harris M	Hogan RD	Houchen KM	Larkin GT	Lawrence M	Linacre J	Livsey GW	Malone RP	McMaster C	McMordie AA	Newton R	Poskett M	Richardson GC	Scaife RH	Simpkin CJ	Smith G	Smith TM	Wiggett DJ
R1	Nov 26	Tranmere Rovers	1-1	T Smith	3564	5	11			8	1			4	10						7					9					2	6	3
rep	29	TRANMERE ROVERS	3-1	Newton, Ayre, Bielby	4827	5	11			8	1			4	2						7					9					10	6	3
R2	Dec 17	RUNCORN	4-2	Bielby, Newton 2, Poskett (p)	6112	5	11			8	1			4							7					9	10				2	6	3
R3	Jan 7	CRYSTAL PALACE	2-1	Newton 2	4502	5	11	7		3	1			4									2		8	9	10				6		
R4	Feb 28	Ipswich Town	1-4	Downing	24207	5	11	7		3	1			4							12		2		8	9	10				6		

F.L. Cup

	Date	Opponent	Score	Scorers	Att	Ayre W	Bielby PA	Creamer PA	Darling M	Downing DG	Edgar E	Foggon A	Gaffney T	Gibb T	Goad AM	Harris M	Hogan RD	Houchen KM	Larkin GT	Lawrence M	Linacre J	Livsey GW	Malone RP	McMaster C	McMordie AA	Newton R	Poskett M	Richardson GC	Scaife RH	Simpkin CJ	Smith G	Smith TM	Wiggett DJ
R1/1	Aug 13	Grimsby Town	0-3		2318	5	11			8	1		12	4									2		7	9	10			6			3
R1/2	16	GRIMSBY TOWN	1-2	Bielby	2733	5	11			8	1		12	4									2		7	9	10			6			3

		P	W	D	L	F	A	W	D	L	F	A	Pts
1	Watford	46	18	4	1	44	14	12	7	4	41	24	71
2	Southend United	46	15	5	3	46	18	10	5	8	20	21	60
3	Swansea City	46	16	5	2	54	17	7	5	11	33	30	56
4	Brentford	46	15	6	2	50	17	6	8	9	36	37	56
5	Aldershot	46	15	8	0	45	16	4	8	11	22	31	54
6	Grimsby Town	46	14	6	3	30	15	7	5	11	27	36	53
7	Barnsley	46	15	4	4	44	20	3	10	10	17	29	50
8	Reading	46	12	7	4	33	23	6	7	10	22	29	50
9	Torquay United	46	12	6	5	43	25	4	9	10	14	31	47
10	Northampton Town	46	9	8	6	32	30	8	5	10	31	38	47
11	Huddersfield Town	46	13	5	5	41	21	2	10	11	22	34	45
12	Doncaster Rovers	46	11	8	4	37	26	3	9	11	15	39	45
13	Wimbledon	46	8	11	4	39	26	6	5	12	27	41	44
14	Scunthorpe United	46	12	6	5	31	14	2	10	11	19	41	44
15	Crewe Alexandra	46	11	8	4	34	25	4	6	13	16	44	44
16	Newport County	46	14	6	3	43	22	2	5	16	22	51	43
17	Bournemouth	46	12	6	5	28	20	2	9	12	13	31	43
18	Stockport County	46	14	4	5	41	19	2	6	15	15	37	42
19	Darlington	46	10	8	5	31	22	4	5	14	21	37	41
20	Halifax Town	46	7	10	6	28	23	3	11	9	24	39	41
21	HARTLEPOOL UNITED	46	12	4	7	34	29	3	3	17	17	55	37
22	York City	46	8	7	8	27	31	4	5	14	23	38	36
23	Southport	46	5	13	5	30	32	1	6	16	22	44	31
24	Rochdale	46	8	6	9	29	28	0	2	21	14	57	24

1978/79 13th in Division 4

						Ayre W	Brooks SM	Crumplin I	Edgar E	Evans DT	Goldthorpe W	Gorry MC	Guy K	Harding A	Hogan RD	Houchen KM	Larkin GT	Lawrence M	Linacre J	Loadwick D	Malone RP	Newton R	Norton DJ	Platt JA	Richardson GC	Smith G	Smith TM	Watson J
1	Aug 19	DONCASTER ROVERS	3-4	Linacre, Newton, Crumplin	2634	6	5	10				3	11			8	12		7		2	9			1	4		
2	23	Northampton Town	1-1	Newton	4288	6	5	10			12	3	11					8	7			9		1		4	2	
3	25	PORTSMOUTH	1-1	Crumplin	3136	6	5	10			12	3	11			8			7			9		1		4	2	
4	Sep 2	Bournemouth	1-0	Newton (p)	2658	6	5	10			12	3	11		4			8	7			9		1		2		
5	9	HEREFORD UNITED	2-1	Linacre, Hogan	2995	6	5	10			8		11		4				7		2	9		1		3		
6	11	Stockport County	0-4		4259	6	5	10			12	3	11		8				7		2	9		1		4		
7	16	Grimsby Town	1-0	Goldthorpe	4958	6	5				8	3	12		4	10		11	7			9		1		2		
8	23	HALIFAX TOWN	3-1	Houchen, Newton (p), Goldthorpe	3760	6	5	12			8	3			4	10		11	7			9		1		2		
9	25	NEWPORT COUNTY	0-0		5495	6	5	12			8	3			4	10		11	7			9		1		2		
10	30	Torquay United	1-4	Houchen	3033	6	5				8	3	12		4	10		11	7			9		1		2		
11	Oct 7	DARLINGTON	0-2		4854	6	5	10			8	3	11			9		4	7					1		2		
12	14	Aldershot	1-1	Brooks	2968	6	5	10			8	3				9		4	7	11				1		2		
13	17	SCUNTHORPE UNITED	1-1	Lawrence	2981	6	5	10			8		12			11		4	7			9		1		2	3	
14	21	Crewe Alexandra	1-0	T Smith	2023	6	5	12			8					10		4	7	11		9		1		2	3	
15	28	ROCHDALE	5-1	Ayre,Goldthorpe 2,Lawrence,Houchen	3084	6	5		1		8				11	10		4	7			9				2	3	
16	Nov 4	Port Vale	0-2		3195	6	5		1		8					10		4	7	11		9				2	3	
17	11	BOURNEMOUTH	0-0		3239	6	5				8	3				10		4	7	11		9			1	2		
18	18	Portsmouth	0-3		10957	6	5				8	3				10		4	7	11		9			1	2		
19	Dec 9	WIMBLEDON	1-1	Ayre	3098	6	5	9			8	3				10		4	7	11			12		1	2		
20	23	BARNSLEY	1-1	Goldthorpe	5956	6	5	9			8	3						4	7	11		10			1	2		
21	26	York City	1-1	Crumplin	3825	6	5	9			8	3						4	7	11		10			1	2		
22	Jan 20	GRIMSBY TOWN	1-0	Newton (p)	2222			9			8	3			4	12			7	11		10	6		1	2	5	
23	Feb 2	Newport County	2-3	Newton (p), Linacre	3659		5	9			8	3			4				7	11		10	12		1	2	6	
24	10	TORQUAY UNITED	3-2	Newton 2, Houchen	2419		5	9				3			4	8			7	11		10			1	2	6	
25	24	ALDERSHOT	2-2	Ayre, Houchen	2908	6	5	9				3			4	8			7	11		10			1	2		
26	26	Reading	1-3	Houchen	7052	6	5	9				3			4	8		12	7	11		10			1	2		
27	Mar 3	CREWE ALEXANDRA	2-2	Houchen, Crumplin	2470	6	5	9	1		10	3				8		4	7	11							2	
28	7	Hereford United	0-1		2439	6	5	9			8	3				10		4	7	11					1	2		
29	10	Rochdale	1-1	Crumplin	1931	6	5	9			8	3				10		4	7	11					1	2	12	
30	13	STOCKPORT COUNTY	1-3	Linacre	2449	6		9			8	3			12	10		4	7	11					1	2	5	
31	23	Doncaster Rovers	0-0		2552	6		9				3		10		8		4	7	11					1	2	5	
32	31	Huddersfield Town	0-2		2420			9			5	3		10	11	8		4	7				6		1	2		
33	Apr 3	WIGAN ATHLETIC	1-1	Houchen	2128	6		9			5	3		4		8	10	12	7	11					1	2		
34	7	BRADFORD CITY	2-2	Lawrence, Houchen	2183	6		9			5	3		4		8		10	7	11					1	2	12	
35	12	Barnsley	0-1		11398	6					5	3		10	4	8		9	7	12			11			2		1
36	14	YORK CITY	1-1	Houchen	2357	6		12			5	3		10		8		9	7	11			4				2	1
37	16	Wigan Athletic	2-2	Goldthorpe (p), Linacre	8217	6				12	5	3		10	11	8		9	7				4			2		1
38	21	READING	0-0		2526	6				12	5	3		10	11	8		9	7				4			2		1
39	24	Scunthorpe United	1-3	Houchen	1339	6				9	5	3		10	11	8	12	7					4			2		1
40	28	Wimbledon	1-3	Houchen	3546	6					5	3		10	11	8		12	7	9						4	2	1
41	May 2	Bradford City	2-1	Ayre, Harding	1950	6	5				4	3		10		9		12	7	11						8	2	1
42	5	HUDDERSFIELD T	2-0	Norton 2	2251	6	5				2	3			12	9		8	7	11			10			4		1
43	7	Darlington	1-0	Lawrence	3513	6	5				2	3		10		9		8	7	11						4		1
44	10	PORT VALE	1-2	Houchen	2007	6	5				2	3		10	12	9		8	7	11						4		1
45	14	Halifax Town	4-2	Lawrence 4	1012	6	5				2	3		10		9		8	7	11						4		1
46	17	NORTHAMPTON T	2-0	Lawrence, Ayre	1769	6	5				2	3		10	4	9		8	7	11			12					1
					Apps	42	34	29	3	3	41	41	10	15	23	39	3	38	45	29	3	23	11	13	18	43	17	12
					Goals	5	1	5			6			1	1	13		9	5			8	2				1	

F.A. Cup

						Ayre W	Brooks SM	Crumplin I	Edgar E	Evans DT	Goldthorpe W	Gorry MC	Guy K	Harding A	Hogan RD	Houchen KM	Larkin GT	Lawrence M	Linacre J	Loadwick D	Malone RP	Newton R	Norton DJ	Platt JA	Richardson GC	Smith G	Smith TM	Watson J
R1	Nov 25	GRIMSBY TOWN	1-0	Goldthorpe	3584	6	5	9			8	3			12	10		4	7	11					1	2		
R2	Dec 16	Crewe Alexandra	1-0	Crumplin	2626	6	5	9			8	3						4	7	11		10			1		2	
R3	Jan 18	LEEDS UNITED	2-6	Newton 2 (2p)	16000			9			8	3						4	7	11		10	6		1	2	5	

F.L. Cup

						Ayre W	Brooks SM	Crumplin I	Edgar E	Evans DT	Goldthorpe W	Gorry MC	Guy K	Harding A	Hogan RD	Houchen KM	Larkin GT	Lawrence M	Linacre J	Loadwick D	Malone RP	Newton R	Norton DJ	Platt JA	Richardson GC	Smith G	Smith TM	Watson J
R1/1	Aug 12	Rotherham United	0-5		2431	6	5	10				3	11			8	12		7		2	9			1	4		
R1/2	15	ROTHERHAM UNITED	1-1	Newton	1746	6	5	10				3	11			8			7		2	9			1	4		

		P	W	D	L	F	A	W	D	L	F	A	Pts
1	Reading	46	19	3	1	49	8	7	10	6	27	27	65
2	Grimsby Town	46	15	5	3	51	23	11	4	8	31	26	61
3	Wimbledon	46	18	3	2	50	20	7	8	8	28	26	61
4	Barnsley	46	15	5	3	47	23	9	8	6	26	19	61
5	Aldershot	46	16	5	2	38	14	4	12	7	25	33	57
6	Wigan Athletic	46	14	5	4	40	24	7	8	8	23	24	55
7	Portsmouth	46	13	7	3	35	12	7	5	11	27	36	52
8	Newport County	46	12	5	6	39	28	9	5	9	27	27	52
9	Huddersfield Town	46	13	8	2	32	15	5	3	15	25	38	47
10	York City	46	11	6	6	33	24	7	5	11	18	31	47
11	Torquay United	46	14	4	5	38	24	5	4	14	20	41	46
12	Scunthorpe United	46	12	3	8	33	30	5	8	10	21	30	45
13	HARTLEPOOL UNITED	46	7	12	4	35	28	6	6	11	22	38	44
14	Hereford United	46	12	8	3	35	18	3	5	15	18	35	43
15	Bradford City	46	11	5	7	38	26	6	4	13	24	42	43
16	Port Vale	46	8	10	5	29	28	6	4	13	28	42	42
17	Stockport County	46	11	5	7	33	21	3	7	13	25	39	40
18	Bournemouth	46	11	6	6	34	19	3	5	15	13	29	39
19	Northampton Town	46	12	4	7	40	30	3	5	15	24	46	39
20	Rochdale	46	11	4	8	25	26	4	5	14	22	38	39
21	Darlington	46	8	8	7	25	21	3	7	13	24	45	37
22	Doncaster Rovers	46	8	8	7	25	22	5	3	15	25	51	37
23	Halifax Town	46	7	5	11	24	32	2	3	18	15	40	26
24	Crewe Alexandra	46	3	7	13	24	41	3	7	13	19	49	26

1979/80 19th in Division 4

	Date		Opponent	Score	Scorers	Att	Ayre W	Brooks SM	Brown P	Burleigh MS	Carr P	Fagan MJ	Fowler M	Goldthorpe W	Gorry MC	Hampton D	Harding A	Higgins RJ	Hogan RD	Houchen KM	Larkin GT	Lawrence M	Linacre J	Loadwick D	McNamee G	Newton R	Normanton GS	Norton DJ	Pimblett FR	Richardson GC	Smith G	Staff P	Sweeney A	Vass S	Watson J
1	Aug	18	PORTSMOUTH	0-3		3110	6	5						4	3		10			9		11	7					2			8				1
2		21	Scunthorpe United	3-1	Brooks, Lawrence, Linacre	1822	6	5						4	3		10			9		11	7					2			8				1
3		24	Rochdale	0-1		2180	6	5						4	3		10			9		11	7	12				2			8				1
4	Sep	1	ALDERSHOT	1-0	Houchen	3084	6	5						4	3		10			8		11	7			9					2	12			1
5		8	DARLINGTON	3-1	Goldthorpe 2 (1p), Ayre	3697	6	5						4	3		10			8		2	7	11		9						12			1
6		15	Walsall	1-3	Ayre	4205	6	5						4	3		10			8		2	7	11		9					12				1
7		19	Wigan Athletic	1-2	Houchen	4877	6	5									10			8	12	3	7	11		9	2				4				1
8		22	TORQUAY UNITED	2-2	Houchen, Ayre	2520	6	5									10			8		2	7	11		9	3			1	4				
9		29	Halifax Town	1-2	Newton	2293	6	5									10			8	12	7		11		9	3				4		2		1
10	Oct	6	Bournemouth	1-2	Harding	3180	6				5						10			8	12	4		11		9	3			1	7		2		
11		9	SCUNTHORPE UNITED	3-2	Lawrence, Newton 2	2803	6			1	5						10		12	8		4	7	11		9	3						2		
12		13	PORT VALE	2-1	Newton, Ayre	2441	6	5		1	4						10			8		7		11		9	3				12		2		
13		20	Peterborough United	0-2		3412	6			1	5						10		7	8	12	4		11		9	3						2		
14		22	Stockport County	0-0		1983	6			1	5						10			8		4	7	11		9	3						2		
15		27	CREWE ALEXANDRA	3-1	Harding, Lawrence, Newton	2619	6			1	5						10			8		4	7	11		9	3						2		
16	Nov	3	Portsmouth	1-2	Newton	14295	6			1	5						10			8		4	7	11		9	3						2		
17		6	STOCKPORT COUNTY	1-2	Ayre	2639	6	12		1	5						10			8		4	7	11		9	3						2		
18		10	HEREFORD UNITED	3-0	Loadwick, Newton 2	2282	6			1	5				7		10			8		4		11		9	3						2		
19		17	Northampton Town	1-2	Newton	2251	6			1	3				7		10	5		8		4		11		9							2		
20		30	Lincoln City	3-3	Lawrence 2, Hampton	3526	6			1	3				7	11	10	5		12		4		8		9							2		
21	Dec	8	NEWPORT COUNTY	0-0		2565	6	5		1	3					11				8	12	4		7		9						10	2		
22		21	Bradford City	0-2		3789	6	5		1	3					11	10			12		4	7	8		9							2		
23		26	YORK CITY	3-1	Ayre, Houchen, Hampton	2947	6	5		1	3					11	10			12		4	7	8		9							2		
24		29	ROCHDALE	1-1	Houchen	3151	6	5		1	3					11	10			12		4	7	8		9							2		
25	Jan	5	TRANMERE ROVERS	2-1	Houchen 2	2517	6	5		1					3	11				10		4	7	8		9							2		
26		12	Aldershot	2-0	Houchen, Newton	3516	6	5		1	3					11				8		4	7			9	10						2		
27		19	Darlington	1-0	Lawrence	4045	6	5		1	3				10	11	9			8		4	7									12	2		
28		26	HUDDERSFIELD T	1-1	Ayre (p)	5959	6	5		1	3				10	11	9			8		4			7								2		
29	Feb	2	WALSALL	2-2	Newton, Houchen	4598	6			1	3	5			10	11	8			12		4	7			9							2		
30		16	HALIFAX TOWN	1-2	Newton	3410	6			1	3	5			10	11	8			12		4	7			9							2		
31		23	Port Vale	1-1	Houchen	3702				1	3	5			10	11				8		4	7			9	6						2		
32	Mar	1	PETERBOROUGH UTD.	1-2	Hampton	2887			6	1	3	5				11				8		4	7			9							2	10	
33		8	Crewe Alexandra	1-2	Houchen	2425			6	1		5				11	10			8		4	7			9							2	3	
34		11	Doncaster Rovers	2-0	Houchen, Hampton	2453	6			1		5				11	10		12	8		4	7			9							2	3	
35		15	BOURNEMOUTH	3-1	Cunningham(og),Ayre(p),Hampton	2201	6			1			5			11	10			8		4	7			9		3					2		
36		22	Hereford United	1-2	Hampton	2782	6		5	1			4			11	10		12	8		9	7					3					2		
37		29	NORTHAMPTON T	2-1	Hampton, Houchen	1995	6	5		1			4			11	10			8		3	7			9							2		
38	Apr	4	BRADFORD CITY	0-1		3860	6	5		1			4			11	10			8		3	7			9							2		
39		5	York City	1-2	McNamee	2711	6	5		1			4			11	10			8		3	7		12	9							2		
40		8	DONCASTER ROVERS	1-2	Houchen	2228	6	5	3	1			10			11				8		4	7								12	9	2		
41		11	Tranmere Rovers	0-1		1590	6	5	3	1							10				12	4	7					2	11		8				
42		15	WIGAN ATHLETIC	1-1	Ayre (p)	1836	6	5	3	1						9	10				12	4	7						11		2	8			
43		19	LINCOLN CITY	0-0		1706	6	5	2						3	9	10		4		8		7						11	1					
44		23	Torquay United	1-3	Harding	1581	6	5	2						3	11	10		4				7		8		9			1	12				
45		26	Newport County	0-1		8383	6	5	2						3	9	10		4			11	7				12			1	8				
46	May	3	Huddersfield Town	1-2	Linacre	16807	6	5	4			3				11	10		8	9			7							1				2	
						Apps	43	29	10	32	22	7	6	6	18	26	40	2	8	41	8	43	37	22	3	33	16	6	3	6	15	6	32	4	8
						Goals	9	1						2		7	3			14		6	2	1	1	12									

Played in one game: DT Evans (41, at 9)

One own goal

F.A. Cup

	Date		Opponent	Score	Scorers	Att	Ayre W	Brooks SM	Brown P	Burleigh MS	Carr P	Fagan MJ	Fowler M	Goldthorpe W	Gorry MC	Hampton D	Harding A	Higgins RJ	Hogan RD	Houchen KM	Larkin GT	Lawrence M	Linacre J	Loadwick D	McNamee G	Newton R	Normanton GS	Norton DJ	Pimblett FR	Richardson GC	Smith G	Staff P	Sweeney A	Vass S	Watson J
R1	Nov	24	Barnsley	2-5	Linacre, Newton	12548	6			1	3				2		10	5		8		4	7	11		9									

F.L. Cup

	Date		Opponent	Score	Scorers	Att	Ayre W	Brooks SM	Brown P	Burleigh MS	Carr P	Fagan MJ	Fowler M	Goldthorpe W	Gorry MC	Hampton D	Harding A	Higgins RJ	Hogan RD	Houchen KM	Larkin GT	Lawrence M	Linacre J	Loadwick D	McNamee G	Newton R	Normanton GS	Norton DJ	Pimblett FR	Richardson GC	Smith G	Staff P	Sweeney A	Vass S	Watson J
R1/1	Aug	11	Chesterfield	1-5	Harding	3493	6	5							3		10		12	9		4	7	11							2				1
R1/2		14	CHESTERFIELD	2-1	Goldthorpe (p), Lawrence	1763	6	5						4	3		10			9		12	7	11				2			8				1

Played in R1/1: I Crumplin (at 8)

		P	W	D	L	F	A	W	D	L	F	A	Pts
1	Huddersfield Town	46	16	5	2	61	18	11	7	5	40	30	66
2	Walsall	46	12	9	2	43	23	11	9	3	32	24	64
3	Newport County	46	16	5	2	47	22	11	2	10	36	28	61
4	Portsmouth	46	15	5	3	62	23	9	7	7	29	26	60
5	Bradford City	46	14	6	3	44	14	10	6	7	33	36	60
6	Wigan Athletic	46	13	5	5	42	26	8	8	7	34	35	55
7	Lincoln City	46	14	8	1	43	12	4	9	10	21	30	53
8	Peterborough Utd.	46	14	3	6	39	22	7	7	9	19	25	52
9	Torquay United	46	13	7	3	47	25	2	10	11	23	44	47
10	Aldershot	46	10	7	6	35	23	6	6	11	27	30	45
11	Bournemouth	46	8	9	6	32	25	5	9	9	20	26	44
12	Doncaster Rovers	46	11	6	6	37	27	4	8	11	25	36	44
13	Northampton Town	46	14	5	4	33	16	2	7	14	18	50	44
14	Scunthorpe United	46	11	9	3	37	23	3	6	14	21	52	43
15	Tranmere Rovers	46	10	4	9	32	24	4	9	10	18	32	41
16	Stockport County	46	9	7	7	30	31	5	5	13	18	41	40
17	York City	46	9	6	8	35	34	5	5	13	30	48	39
18	Halifax Town	46	11	9	3	29	20	2	4	17	17	52	39
19	HARTLEPOOL UNITED	46	10	7	6	36	28	4	3	16	23	36	38
20	Port Vale	46	8	6	9	34	24	4	6	13	22	46	36
21	Hereford United	46	8	7	8	22	21	3	7	13	16	31	36
22	Darlington	46	7	11	5	33	26	2	6	15	17	48	35
23	Crewe Alexandra	46	10	6	7	25	27	1	7	15	10	41	35
24	Rochdale	46	6	7	10	20	28	1	6	16	13	51	27

1980/81 9th in Division 4

						Ayre W	Bird JC	Brown P	Burleigh MS	Fagan MJ	Forster GP	Granycome N	Hampton D	Harding A	Hogan RD	Houchen KM	Howard DF	Johnson KP	Kerr R	Lawrence M	Linacre J	Linacre P	Linighan A	Newton R	Normanton GS	Richardson GC	Staff P	Stimpson BG	Sweeney A
1	Aug 16	Wigan Athletic	3-0	Forster 2, Houchen	5233		5	2	1	6	10		11		4	9			8		7								3
2	19	BURY	1-2	Forster	3656	6	5	2	1		10		11		4	9			8	12	7								3
3	23	Rochdale	1-1	Brown	5230	6	5	3		2	10		11	9	4				8	12	7					1			
4	30	DONCASTER ROVERS	1-0	Bird	2112	6	5	3		2	10			11	4	12			8	9	7					1			
5	Sep 6	NORTHAMPTON T	2-3	Hogan, Forster	2435	6	5	3		2	10			11	4	12			8	9	7					1			
6	13	York City	1-0	Houchen	2504		5	3		6	10		12	11	4	9			8	7						1			2
7	16	Bournemouth	0-1		2413	6	5	3			12			11	4	10			8	7				9		1			2
8	20	HEREFORD UNITED	2-0	Houchen, Ayre	2345	6	5	3			12			11	4	10			8	7				9		1			2
9	26	Southend United	0-4		4971	6	5	3			12			11	4	10			7	8				9		1			2
10	30	BOURNEMOUTH	1-0	Lawrence	2419	6	5	3			11				4	10			7	8				9		1			2
11	Oct 4	ALDERSHOT	1-0	Linacre	2872		5	3			11				4	10			7	8	6			9		1			2
12	7	Scunthorpe United	3-3	Newton 2, Houchen	2900		5	3			11		12		4	10			7	8	6			9		1			2
13	11	Wimbledon	0-5		1971		5	3			11				4	10			7	8	6			9		1			2
14	18	LINCOLN CITY	2-0	Bird, Newton	2712		5	3	1				11		4	10			7	8	6			9					2
15	21	MANSFIELD TOWN	0-1		3419		5	3	1		12		11		4	10			7	8	6			9					2
16	25	Port Vale	1-1	Kerr	3072		5	3	1				11		4	10			7	8	6			9					2
17	27	Stockport County	2-0	Newton, Houchen	2066		5	3	1				11		4	10			7	8	6			9					2
18	Nov 1	CREWE ALEXANDRA	6-2	Kerr,Houchen 2,Newton 2,Hampton	3098		5	3	1				11		4	10			7	8	6			9					2
19	4	SCUNTHORPE UNITED	2-0	Sweeney, Hampton	4400		5	3	1				11		4	10			7	8	6			9					2
20	8	Halifax Town	2-1	Hampton, Hogan	1692		5	3	1				11		4	10			7	8	6			9					2
21	11	Bury	0-0		2301		5	3	1				11		4	10			7	8	6			9					2
22	15	WIGAN ATHLETIC	3-1	Hogan, Houchen 2	5035		5	3	1				11		4	10			7	8	6			9					2
23	29	TORQUAY UNITED	0-2		3419		5	3	1				11	12	4	10			7	8	6			9					2
24	Dec 5	Tranmere Rovers	2-2	Houchen, Hamilton (og)	1523		5	3	1				11		4	10			7	8	6			9					2
25	20	PETERBOROUGH UTD.	1-1	Hampton	3121			3	1	5			11		4	10			7	8	6	9							2
26	26	Darlington	0-3		7155	2	5	3	1				11	9	4	10			7	8	6								
27	27	BRADFORD CITY	2-2	Hampton, Hogan	3695	2	5	3	1	12			11		4	10			7	8	6			9					
28	Jan 10	PORT VALE	3-0	Newton 2 (1p), Hogan	3116		5	3		2			11		4	10		12	7	8	6			9		1			
29	17	Torquay United	1-2	Newton	1647		5	3		2			11		4	10		12	7	8	6			9		1			
30	24	Doncaster Rovers	2-1	Hogan, Hampton	6814		5	3		6			11		4	12		10	7		2			9		1			8
31	31	ROCHDALE	2-2	Houchen 2 (1p)	3867		5	3		6			11		4	9		10	7	12	2					1			8
32	Feb 7	YORK CITY	1-0	Bird	3119		5	3		6			11		4	9		10	7	12	2					1			8
33	14	Northampton Town	1-3	Hampton	2032		5	3		6			11		4	9		12	7	10	2					1			8
34	21	SOUTHEND UNITED	1-3	Bird	3748		5	3				10	11		4	9		12	7	8					6	1			2
35	28	Hereford United	0-3		2313		5	2					12		4	10		11	7	8				9	6	1			3
36	Mar 7	Aldershot	1-2	Houchen	2252		5	6		8				4		10		11	7		2			9		1			3
37	14	WIMBLEDON	2-3	Houchen, Newton	2138		5	6		8				4	12	10		11	7		2			9		1			3
38	16	Mansfield Town	1-0	Harding	3737		5	6		8				4	11	10		12	7	3	2			9		1			
39	21	Lincoln City	0-2		3969		5	6		8				4	11	10			7	3	2			9		1			
40	28	STOCKPORT COUNTY	1-0	Harding	1928		5	6					12	11		10		9	7	4	2		8			1		3	
41	Apr 3	Crewe Alexandra	0-2		2419		5	6					12	11		10		9	7	4	2		8			1		3	
42	11	HALIFAX TOWN	3-0	Hogan, Houchen, Lawrence	1579		5	6							11	10	9		7	4	2		8			1	12	3	
43	17	DARLINGTON	2-0	Howard, Linacre	5578		5	6							11	10	9		7	4	2		8			1		3	
44	19	Bradford City	0-2		1614		5	6		8			9		11	10		12	7	4	2					1			3
45	25	Peterborough United	1-1	Lawrence	3560		5	6					12		11	10			7	4	2		8			1	9		3
46	May 2	TRANMERE ROVERS	3-0	Houchen 2 (1p), Sweeney	1826		5	6							11	10	12		7	4	2		8			1	9		3
					Apps	10	45	46	16	18	14	1	31	15	43	45	3	14	46	42	39	1	6	27	2	30	3	4	33
					Goals	1	4	1			4		7	2	7	17	1		2	3	2			10					2

One own goal

F.A. Cup

						Ayre W	Bird JC	Brown P	Burleigh MS	Fagan MJ	Forster GP	Granycome N	Hampton D	Harding A	Hogan RD	Houchen KM	Howard DF	Johnson KP	Kerr R	Lawrence M	Linacre J	Linacre P	Linighan A	Newton R	Normanton GS	Richardson GC	Staff P	Stimpson BG	Sweeney A
R1	Nov 22	Scunthorpe United	1-3	Hampton	5162		5	3	1				11		4	10			7	8	6			9					2

F.L. Cup

						Ayre W	Bird JC	Brown P	Burleigh MS	Fagan MJ	Forster GP	Granycome N	Hampton D	Harding A	Hogan RD	Houchen KM	Howard DF	Johnson KP	Kerr R	Lawrence M	Linacre J	Linacre P	Linighan A	Newton R	Normanton GS	Richardson GC	Staff P	Stimpson BG	Sweeney A
R1/1	Aug 9	York City	1-2	Forster	2444		5	2	1	6	10		11			9			8	4	7								
R1/2	12	YORK CITY	0-0		3496		5	2	1	6	10		11			9			8	4	7								3

Played at 3 in R1/1: S Vass

		P	W	D	L	F	A	W	D	L	F	A	Pts
1	Southend United	46	19	4	0	47	6	11	3	9	32	25	67
2	Lincoln City	46	15	7	1	44	11	10	8	5	22	14	65
3	Doncaster Rovers	46	15	4	4	36	20	7	8	8	23	29	56
4	Wimbledon	46	15	4	4	42	17	8	5	10	22	29	55
5	Peterborough Utd.	46	11	8	4	37	21	6	10	7	31	33	52
6	Aldershot	46	12	9	2	28	11	6	5	12	15	30	50
7	Mansfield Town	46	13	5	5	36	15	7	4	12	22	29	49
8	Darlington	46	13	6	4	43	23	6	5	12	22	36	49
9	HARTLEPOOL UNITED	46	14	3	6	42	22	6	6	11	22	39	49
10	Northampton Town	46	11	7	5	42	26	7	6	10	23	41	49
11	Wigan Athletic	46	13	4	6	29	16	5	7	11	22	39	47
12	Bury	46	10	8	5	38	21	7	3	13	32	41	45
13	Bournemouth	46	9	8	6	30	21	7	5	11	17	27	45
14	Bradford City	46	9	9	5	30	24	5	7	11	23	36	44
15	Rochdale	46	11	6	6	33	25	3	9	11	27	45	43
16	Scunthorpe United	46	8	12	3	40	31	3	8	12	20	38	42
17	Torquay United	46	13	2	8	38	26	5	3	15	17	37	41
18	Crewe Alexandra	46	10	7	6	28	20	3	7	13	20	41	40
19	Port Vale	46	10	8	5	40	23	2	7	14	17	47	39
20	Stockport County	46	10	5	8	29	25	6	2	15	15	32	39
21	Tranmere Rovers	46	12	5	6	41	24	1	5	17	18	49	36
22	Hereford United	46	8	8	7	29	20	3	5	15	9	42	35
23	Halifax Town	46	9	3	11	28	32	2	9	12	16	39	34
24	York City	46	10	2	11	31	23	2	7	14	16	43	33

1981/82 14th in Division 4

							Bainbridge T	Bird JC	Brown P	Burleigh MS	Clarke H	Dobson P	Fagan MJ	Hampton D	Harding A	Hogan RD	Houchen KM	Howard DF	Johnson KP	Kerr R	Lawrence M	Linacre J	Linacre P	Linighan A	Linighan D	Lowe K	Newton R	Staff P	Stimpson BG	Sweeney A	Watson J
1	Aug	29	COLCHESTER UNITED	1-3	Harding	2006		5	2	1				12	11	4	10			7				6				9	3	8	
2	Sep	5	Rochdale	1-2	Houchen	1481			2	1			5		11	4	10		12	7				6				9	3	8	
3		12	WIGAN ATHLETIC	2-1	J Linacre, Hampton	1712		5	7	1			6	9		4	10		11			8							3	2	
4		18	York City	2-1	Houchen, Newton	2241			6	1				9		4	10		11			7		5			8		3	2	
5		22	Scunthorpe United	1-2	Newton	2060			6	1				9		4	10		11			7		5			8		3	2	
6		26	HALIFAX TOWN	3-2	Hampton 2, Houchen	1800		5	12	1				9		4	10		11			7		6			8		3	2	
7		30	HULL CITY	3-2	Houchen (p), Hampton, Newton	2654		5	12	1				9		4	10		11			7		6			8		3	2	
8	Oct	3	Hereford United	1-1	Bird	2247		5	3	1				9		4	10		11			7		6			8			2	
9		10	PETERBOROUGH UTD.	0-1		2450		5	3	1				9		4	10		11			7		6			8	12		2	
10		17	Sheffield United	1-1	Bird	12752		5		1				9	12	4	10		11			7		6			8		3	2	
11		20	Tranmere Rovers	0-1		1456		5		1				9	12	4	10		11			7		6			8		3	2	
12		24	TORQUAY UNITED	0-0		2099		5	2	1				9	4	12	10					7	11	6			8		3		
13		31	Aldershot	2-1	Newton, J Linacre	2658		5	2	1				9	4		10					7	11	6			8		3		
14	Nov	4	CREWE ALEXANDRA	1-2	Houchen	2328		5	2	1				9	4	12	10					7	11	6			8		3		
15		8	Bradford City	0-1		5753		5	2	1					4	12						7	11	6			8	10	3	9	
16		14	NORTHAMPTON T	3-1	Newton 2, Hogan	1641		5	2	1						4			11			7	9	6			8		3	10	
17		28	Port Vale	2-5	Howard, Hogan	2477		5	2	1						4	10	7	11	12			9	6			8		3		
18	Dec	5	BOURNEMOUTH	1-1	Newton	1763		5	2	1						4	10		11			7	3	6			8			9	
19	Jan	16	Mansfield Town	2-3	Brown, Houchen	2011		5	4	1			6				10	12	11			7	8					9	3	2	
20		19	Bury	1-1	Houchen (p)	2997		5	4	1			6				10	12	11			7	3				9	8		2	
21		23	Colchester United	3-3	Houchen 2 (1p), Bird	2862		5	4	1			6			8	10					7	3				9	11		2	
22		25	Stockport County	2-0	Bird, Brown	1924		5	4	1			6			8	10					7	3				9	11		2	
23		30	YORK CITY	3-2	Houchen, Fagan, Newton	2291		5	4	1			6			8	10					7	3				9	11		2	
24	Feb	3	DARLINGTON	1-2	Bird	4548		5	4	1			6			8	10		12			7	3				9	11		2	
25		6	Wigan Athletic	1-1	Newton	6315		5	4	1			6			8	10		12			7	3				9	11		2	
26		10	SCUNTHORPE UNITED	3-3	Houchen (p), Johnson 2	2001		5	4	1		12	6			8	10		11			7	3				9			2	
27		13	HEREFORD UNITED	2-1	Howard 2	1811	6	5	2	1						4	10	9	11			7	3					8			
28		20	Hull City	2-5	Houchen 2 (1p)	3040	6	5	2	1				12		4	10	9	11			7	3			8					
29		27	Peterborough United	4-4	Houchen 3 (1p), Staff	4610		5	2	1			6			4	10					7	11				9	8	3		
30	Mar	6	SHEFFIELD UNITED	2-3	P Linacre, Staff	4145	6	5	2	1							10		4			7	11				9	8	3		
31		10	TRANMERE ROVERS	0-0		1633		5	6	1							10		4			7	11				9	8	3	2	
32		13	Torquay United	1-1	Staff	1532		5	6	1					7	4	10		11			2	12				9	8	3		
33		16	Crewe Alexandra	2-1	Houchen, Hogan	1116	5		6	1					7	4	10		11			2	3				9	8	12		
34		20	ALDERSHOT	2-2	Newton, Bainbridge	1702	7	5	6	1						4	10		11			2	3				9	8			
35		27	BRADFORD CITY	0-2		2512	7	5	6			12				4		9	11			2	3		10			8			1
36		31	ROCHDALE	1-1	Brown	1259	6	5	10			9				4			11			2	3		7	12		8			1
37	Apr	3	Northampton Town	1-2	Bird	1890	6	5	10			9			12	4			11			2	3		7			8			1
38		10	STOCKPORT COUNTY	2-2	Stimpson, Brown	1506	6	5	9					10		4			11			2			7			12	3	8	1
39		12	Darlington	2-5	Harding, Clarke	4575		5	9	1	8				7	4			11			2			6			12	3	10	
40		17	Bournemouth	1-5	Hogan	6567	12	5	9	1	8				7	4			10						6			11	3	2	
41		24	PORT VALE	3-1	P Linacre, Newton (p), Staff	1439		5	6							4			11		12	7	10				9	8	3	2	1
42		28	BLACKPOOL	2-2	Newton 2	1387		5	6		8			11							12	7	10			4	9		3	2	1
43	May	1	Halifax Town	0-2		1305		5	6		12			11							4	7	10			8	9		3	2	1
44		5	MANSFIELD TOWN	3-0	Newton, Staff, J Linacre	1202		5	6		12					4					11	7	10				9	8	3	2	1
45		8	BURY	1-0	P Linacre	1370		5	6		8	12				4					11	7	10				9		3	2	1
46		15	Blackpool	2-2	P Linacre, Newton	1824		5	6		8					4					12	7	10				9	11	3	2	1
						Apps	10	42	44	36	7	5	11	17	13	39	32	6	32	3	6	42	32	17	6	4	34	27	30	32	10
						Goals	1	6	4		1		1	4	2	4	17	3	2			3	4				15	5	1		

F.A. Cup

							Bainbridge T	Bird JC	Brown P	Burleigh MS	Clarke H	Dobson P	Fagan MJ	Hampton D	Harding A	Hogan RD	Houchen KM	Howard DF	Johnson KP	Kerr R	Lawrence M	Linacre J	Linacre P	Linighan A	Linighan D	Lowe K	Newton R	Staff P	Stimpson BG	Sweeney A	Watson J
R1	Nov	21	Wigan Athletic	2-2	P Linacre, Newton	5303		5	2	1	12					4			11			7	9	6			8		3	10	
rep		25	WIGAN ATHLETIC	1-0	Newton	3739		5	2	1						4	12		11			7	9	6			8		3	10	
R2	Jan	4	Hull City	0-2		4975	5		4	1				9			10		11	8		7	3	6						2	

F.L. Cup (Milk Cup)

							Bainbridge T	Bird JC	Brown P	Burleigh MS	Clarke H	Dobson P	Fagan MJ	Hampton D	Harding A	Hogan RD	Houchen KM	Howard DF	Johnson KP	Kerr R	Lawrence M	Linacre J	Linacre P	Linighan A	Linighan D	Lowe K	Newton R	Staff P	Stimpson BG	Sweeney A	Watson J
R1/1	Sep	1	Northampton Town	0-2		1480			2	1			5		11	4	10		12	7				6				9	3	8	
R1/2		16	NORTHAMPTON TOWN	2-1	Newton, Houchen	1975			6	1			5	9		4	10		11			7		12			8		3	2	

F.L. Group Cup

							Bainbridge T	Bird JC	Brown P	Burleigh MS	Clarke H	Dobson P	Fagan MJ	Hampton D	Harding A	Hogan RD	Houchen KM	Howard DF	Johnson KP	Kerr R	Lawrence M	Linacre J	Linacre P	Linighan A	Linighan D	Lowe K	Newton R	Staff P	Stimpson BG	Sweeney A	Watson J
R1	Aug	15	ROTHERHAM UNITED	0-1		2031		5	2	1				10	11	4	9	12		8		7		6					3		
R1		19	BRADFORD CITY	0-1		1221		5	2	1				11		4	10	9	12	7				6				13	3	8	
R1		22	Hull City	0-1		1621		5	2	1				12	11	4	10	13		7				6				9	3	8	

1982/83 22nd in Divison 4

							Bainbridge T	Barker AM	Bird JC	Blackburn EH	Borthwick JR	Brown P	Dobson P	Fagan MJ	Hamilton J(2)	Higgins AM	Hogan RD	Johnson KP	Langridge J	Lawrence M	Linacre P	Linighan A	Linighan D	Lowe K	Newton R	Robinson MW	Smith TM	Smithies MH	Staff P	Stalker JAH	Stewart DC	Stimpson BG	Taylor M	Watson J	Wright GJ
1	Aug	28	SCUNTHORPE UNITED	0-0		1009	7		5			2	12				4	11		8		6					9		10			3		1	
2	Sep	4	Peterborough United	1-2	Stimpson	3499	7		5			2					4	11		10		6			9		8					3		1	
3		7	Rochdale	0-2		987	7		5			2					4	11		10		6			9		8					3		1	
4		11	NORTHAMPTON T	2-1	Bird, Hogan	947	7	12	5			2					4	11		10		6			9		8					3		1	
5		18	Hull City	1-1	Smith	3913	7	5	12			2					4	11		10	9	6					8					3		1	
6		25	TRANMERE ROVERS	4-0	Linacre, A Linighan 2, Lawrence(p)	1233	7	5				2					4	11		10	9	6					8					3		1	
7		29	CREWE ALEXANDRA	1-0	Higgins	1654	7		5			2				9	4	11		10		6					8					3		1	
8	Oct	2	Torquay United	2-3	Brown, Hogan	2164	7		5			2				9	4	11		10		6					8					3		1	
9		8	Stockport County	1-1	Johnson	1915	7		5			2	12				4	11		10	9	6							8			3		1	
10		16	BRISTOL CITY	3-1	Bird, Lawrence (p), Dobson	1449	7	11	5			2	8							10	9	6		4								3		1	
11		18	Port Vale	0-3		3664	6	11	5			2	8			12	4			10	9			7								3		1	
12		23	ALDERSHOT	1-1	Bird	1412	12	7	5							9	4	11				6					8		10			3	2	1	
13		30	York City	1-5	Smith	1971		11	5			2					4	10		9		6		12			8		7			3		1	
14	Nov	3	MANSFIELD TOWN	0-4		1325		11	5			2			12		4	10		9		6					8		7			3		1	
15		6	WIMBLEDON	1-0	Linacre	1081		11	5			2	12				4			9	10	6		8					7			3			1
16		13	Hereford United	0-1		2298		11	5			2			7		4			9	10	6		8					12			3			1
17		27	HALIFAX TOWN	1-2	A Linighan	1367		5				2	8		11		4	12		10	9	6							7			3			1
18	Dec	4	Chester	1-2	Lane (og)	1243	11	5				10	8				4			12	9	6					2		7			3			1
19		18	Swindon Town	0-3		4291		7	5			2	8				4	3		11	9	6					10		12						1
20		27	DARLINGTON	2-0	Lawrence 2 (1p)	3337	11	5				2					4	3		10	9	6					8		7						1
21		28	Bury	0-4		3275	11	5				2					4	3		10	9	6					8	12	7						1
22	Jan	1	BLACKPOOL	2-1	Linacre, Smith	1569		5				4						11		10	9	6					8	2	7			3			1
23		3	Colchester United	1-4	Brown	2239		5			12	4						11		10	9	6					8	2	7			3			1
24		12	PETERBOROUGH UTD.	0-0		1161		3	5	1		10					4	11		8		6						2	7	9					
25		16	Scunthorpe United	0-3		4261		3	5	1		10	12				4	11		8		6						2	7	9					
26		22	HULL CITY	0-0		2295		3	5	1		10					4	11		8		6		7				2		9					
27		29	Northampton Town	1-3	Lowe	2181		3	5	1		2	10					11		8	9	6		7		4				12					
28	Feb	5	Tranmere Rovers	1-1	Dobson	1545		3	5	1	10	2	9								11	6		7		4			8						
29		12	TORQUAY UNITED	0-2		1159		3	5	1		2	9							10	11	6		7		4	12		8						
30		19	STOCKPORT COUNTY	3-2	Lawrence 2 (1p), Dobson	1029		5		1		2	9							10	11	6		7		4	12		8			3			
31		26	Bristol City	0-2		4207		5		1		2	9						12	10	11	6		7		4	8					3			
32	Mar	2	PORT VALE	2-2	Staff, Linacre	1398		3	5	1		2	9						10		12	6		7		4	8		11						
33		5	Aldershot	2-0	Staff, Robinson	1439			5	1		2	9								10	6		7		4	8		11			3			
34		12	YORK CITY	2-0	Staff, Linacre	1606			5	1		2	10								9	6		7		4	8		11			3			
35		14	Mansfield Town	0-3		1991			5			2	12						10		9	6		7		4	8		11			3			1
36		19	Wimbledon	0-2		2324		3		1		2	10								9	6	5	7		4	8		11						
37		26	HEREFORD UNITED	0-1		1151		3	5	1		2						11	10		9	6		7		4					12				
38	Apr	2	BURY	0-1		1288			5	1								12	10		9	6		7		4	8	2			11	3			
39		4	Darlington	1-2	Robinson	3131		11	5	1		12									9	6	3	7		4	8	2							
40		9	CHESTER	1-0	Dobson	1039		11	5	1		7	10								9	6	3			12	4	2			8				
41		15	Crewe Alexandra	0-3		2042		11	5	1		7	10						9			6	3	12			4	2			8				
42		23	SWINDON TOWN	1-2	Dobson	1126			5	1		7	10								12	6				11	4	2	9		8	3			
43		29	Halifax Town	1-1	Dobson	1245			5	1		7	10				4					6				11		2	9		8	3			
44	May	2	COLCHESTER UNITED	1-4	Linacre	804			5	1		7	10				4				12	6				11		2	9		8	3			
45		7	ROCHDALE	3-0	Hogan (p), Staff, Dobson	1015		11				12	10	5			4					7	6	8			2		9			3			1
46		14	Blackpool	2-1	D Linighan, Dobson	2184		11				5	10				4					7	6	8			2		9		12	3			1
						Apps	15	33	34	20	2	44	26	1	3	4	27	24	6	29	30	45	6	22	3	17	32	13	29	4	8	31	1	14	12
						Goals			3			2	8			1	3	1		6	6	3	1	1		2	3		4			1			

Played in one game: SW Boam (37, at 8), A Harding (28, at 12), G McNamee (36, at 12), S Winn (39, at 10).

One own goal

F.A. Cup

							Bainbridge T	Barker AM	Bird JC	Blackburn EH	Borthwick JR	Brown P	Dobson P	Fagan MJ	Hamilton J(2)	Higgins AM	Hogan RD	Johnson KP	Langridge J	Lawrence M	Linacre P	Linighan A	Linighan D	Lowe K	Newton R	Robinson MW	Smith TM	Smithies MH	Staff P	Stalker JAH	Stewart DC	Stimpson BG	Taylor M	Watson J	Wright GJ
R1	Nov	20	LINCOLN CITY	3-0	Linacre 2, Hogan	2204		11				2	9		8		4			10	5	6							7			3		1	
R2	Dec	11	YORK CITY	1-1	Dobson	3344		5				10	8				4			11	9	6					2		7			3		1	
rep		14	York City	0-4		4206		7	5			10	8				4	12		11	9	6					2					3		1	

F.L. Cup (Milk Cup)

							Bainbridge T	Barker AM	Bird JC	Blackburn EH	Borthwick JR	Brown P	Dobson P	Fagan MJ	Hamilton J(2)	Higgins AM	Hogan RD	Johnson KP	Langridge J	Lawrence M	Linacre P	Linighan A	Linighan D	Lowe K	Newton R	Robinson MW	Smith TM	Smithies MH	Staff P	Stalker JAH	Stewart DC	Stimpson BG	Taylor M	Watson J	Wright GJ
R1/1	Aug	31	Chesterfield	1-2	A Linighan	1690	7		5			2					4	11		8		6			9		10					3		1	
R1/2	Sep	15	CHESTERFIELD	2-0	Barker, Bainbridge	1122	7	5				2					4	11		8	9	6					10					3		1	
R2/1	Oct	6	Derby County	0-2		7656	7		5			2				9	4	11		10	12	6					8					3		1	
R2/2		25	DERBY COUNTY	4-2	Barker, Smith, Staff. Johnson	3596		11	5			2					4	10		9		6					8		7			3		1	

R1/2 and R2/2 a.e.t. Derby County won on the away goals rule.

F.L. Trophy

							Bainbridge T	Barker AM	Bird JC	Blackburn EH	Borthwick JR	Brown P	Dobson P	Fagan MJ	Hamilton J(2)	Higgins AM	Hogan RD	Johnson KP	Langridge J	Lawrence M	Linacre P	Linighan A	Linighan D	Lowe K	Newton R	Robinson MW	Smith TM	Smithies MH	Staff P	Stalker JAH	Stewart DC	Stimpson BG	Taylor M	Watson J	Wright GJ
R1	Aug	14	HULL CITY	1-2	Lawrence	962	13					6		5			4	11		8	10		7	2	9				12			3		1	
R1		18	BRADFORD CITY	0-4		655						6		7			4	11		8	10	5			9				12			3	2	1	
R1		21	Halifax Town	0-3		938	7		5			6					4	11		8				12	9		10					3	2		1

Played against Halifax Town: J Gollogly (at 13)

1983/84 23rd in Division 4

						Bainbridge T	Barker AM	Bassett GR	Bird JC	Blackburn EH	Borthwick JR	Brown P	Buckley MJ	Campbell PJ	Dixon KL	Dobson P	Hogan RD	Johnson KP	Kennedy R	Lawrence M	Linacre J	Linacre P	Linighan A	Linighan D	Lowe K	Ray P	Robinson DA	Robinson MW	Smithies MH	Staff P	Taylor PMR	Waddle AR	Weir A	Whitfield M	Wilson H
1	Aug 27	Peterborough United	1-3	M Robinson	3213	6				1		2	4					10					5					11		7		9		8	3
2	Sep 3	ALDERSHOT	0-1		1831	6				1		2	4					10					5					11		7		9		8	3
3	7	CHESTERFIELD	2-2	Waddle, A Linighan	1661	6				1		2	4					10					5		7			11				9	12	8	3
4	10	Bristol City	0-2		5310					1		2	4					10					5		7			11		12		9	6	8	3
5	17	DONCASTER ROVERS	1-0	Staff	1611					1		2	4										5		10			11		7		9	6	8	3
6	23	Halifax Town	2-3	Waddle, Lowe	1416					1		2	4										5	12	7			11		10		9	6	8	3
7	27	Rochdale	0-2		1380					1		2								4			5	11	7					10		9	6	8	3
8	Oct 1	TRANMERE ROVERS	0-1		1226					1		2								4			5	12	10			11		7		9	6	8	3
9	8	Torquay United	0-0		1850				5	1		2						11		8			10	6	7							9	4		3
10	15	WREXHAM	1-1	Bird	982			12	4	1		2						11		8			5	10	7							9	6		3
11	19	CHESTER CITY	1-1	Bird	1150			12	4	1		2						6		11			5					7		10		9		8	
12	22	Mansfield Town	0-5		1906			12	4	1		2								11			5	6				7		10		9		8	
13	29	BURY	1-3	Dixon	1125			10	4	1		2		12	9					11			5					8		7				6	3
14	Nov 1	Crewe Alexandra	0-2		2117	12		11	4	1				10	9								5			2		7					6	8	3
15	5	HEREFORD UNITED	0-0		1021			10	4			12			9								5		11	7		8					2	6	3
16	12	Swindon Town	2-3	Gibson (og), Ray	3257							7			9								5	4	11	2		8		10				6	3
17	26	YORK CITY	2-3	Dixon 2	2012		6				10	7			9			11					5	4		2		8						12	3
18	Dec 3	Colchester United	0-6		1935		6			1		7			9			11					5	4		2		8		10					3
19	17	Reading	1-5	Kennedy	2955	5	8	9		1		4		12					7					3	11					10				2	
20	26	DARLINGTON	2-1	Dobson 2	2968		3			1	9	2				10	4	12	7		8		5	6						11					
21	27	Blackpool	0-1		4562	6	3			1	9	2				10	4		7		8		5							11					
22	31	NORTHAMPTON T	2-0	Burrows (og), Hogan (p)	1706	6	3			1	10	2				9	4		7		8		5							11					
23	Jan 2	Stockport County	0-1		1799	6	3			1	10	2				9	4	7			8		5		12					11					
24	7	Aldershot	1-2	Staff	1637	6	3			1	10	2				9	4		7		8		5						12	11					
25	28	BRISTOL CITY	2-2	Dobson, Staff	1881		3			1						10	4		7		8	9	5	6					2	11					
26	Feb 3	Tranmere Rovers	1-0	P Linacre	1770		3			1						10	4		7		8	9	5	6					2	11					
27	11	HALIFAX TOWN	3-0	P Linacre, Kennedy, Hogan	1658		3			1						10	4		7			9	5	6	8				2	11					
28	15	CREWE ALEXANDRA	2-1	Lowe, Dobson	2059	6	3			1						10	4		7			9	5		8				2	11					
29	18	Bury	0-3		1565	6	3			1		12				10	4		7		11	9	5		8				2						
30	25	MANSFIELD TOWN	4-1	Kennedy, P Linacre(p), Dobson 2	1730		3			1		6				10	4		7			9	5		8				2	11					
31	Mar 3	Chester City	1-4	Staff (p)	1402		3			1	9	6				10	4	12	7				5		8				2	11					
32	7	Hereford United	0-5		2071		3			1						10	4	8	7			9	5	6					2	11					
33	10	SWINDON TOWN	0-1		1274		3		6	1		2				10	4		12		8	9	5		7					11					
34	17	TORQUAY UNITED	2-1	Bird, Dobson	969				6	1						10	4		12		2	9	5	3	7			8		11					
35	24	Wrexham	4-1	Dobson 3, Barker	1181		3		6	1						10	4	8	12		2	9	5		7					11					
36	27	PETERBOROUGH UTD.	1-1	Robinson	1689		3			1						10	4	8	12		2	9	5	6				7		11					
37	31	ROCHDALE	1-2	P Linacre (p)	1245		3			1						10	4	8	12		2	9	5	6	11			7							
38	Apr 7	Chesterfield	1-4	P Linacre	2263		3									10	4	8	7		2	9	5	12					6	11					
39	10	Northampton Town	1-1	Staff	1109		3			1						10	4		7			9	5		8		2		6	11					
40	14	COLCHESTER UNITED	0-0		1001		3			1						10	4		7			9	5		8		2		6		11				
41	20	BLACKPOOL	0-1		1817				6	1	12					10	4		7			9	5		8		2		3		11				
42	21	Darlington	0-2		2574				6	1	9					10	4		7				5	12	8		2		3		11				
43	28	York City	0-2		6063		3		6	1	12	7				10	4					9	5		8				2		11				
44	May 5	STOCKPORT COUNTY	1-2	P Linacre	790		3		6	1		7				10	4				11	9		5	8		12		2						
45	12	READING	3-3	D Linighan, P Linacre, Dobson	1214		3		5	1		8				10	4					9		6			2			7	11				
46	15	Doncaster Rovers	1-0	Dobson	3770	5	3					8				10	4							6	9		2			7	11				
					Apps	12	27	7	15	41	10	31	6	3	6	27	27	17	23	7	15	19	42	23	28	5	7	18	16	33	6	12	10	16	16
					Goals		1		3						3	12	2		3			7	1	1	2	1		2		5		2			

Played in one game: Colin Dixon (19, at 6), M Finch (46, 1), P Malley (18, at 12), J Roberts (38, at 1). Played in games 45,46 at 12: P Harrington

Played in games 15,16,17 at 1: M Prudhoe

Played in games 1 (at 12), 11,12 (at 3): BG Stimpson

Two own goals

F.A. Cup

						Bainbridge T	Barker AM	Bassett GR	Bird JC	Blackburn EH	Borthwick JR	Brown P	Buckley MJ	Campbell PJ	Dixon KL	Dobson P	Hogan RD	Johnson KP	Kennedy R	Lawrence M	Linacre J	Linacre P	Linighan A	Linighan D	Lowe K	Ray P	Robinson DA	Robinson MW	Smithies MH	Staff P	Taylor PMR	Waddle AR	Weir A	Whitfield M	Wilson H
R1	Nov 19	Rotherham United	0-0		3325			9				7											5	4	11	2		8		10				6	3
rep	23	ROTHERHAM UNITED	0-1	a.e.t.	2635			9				7											5	4	11	2		8		10				6	3

Played at 12 in both games: W Woof. Played at 1 in both games: J Roberts.

F.L. Cup (Milk Cup)

						Bainbridge T	Barker AM	Bassett GR	Bird JC	Blackburn EH	Borthwick JR	Brown P	Buckley MJ	Campbell PJ	Dixon KL	Dobson P	Hogan RD	Johnson KP	Kennedy R	Lawrence M	Linacre J	Linacre P	Linighan A	Linighan D	Lowe K	Ray P	Robinson DA	Robinson MW	Smithies MH	Staff P	Taylor PMR	Waddle AR	Weir A	Whitfield M	Wilson H
R1/1	Aug 30	Rotherham United	0-0		4384	6				1		2	4					10					5		12			11		7		9		8	3
R1/2	Sep 14	ROTHERHAM UNITED	0-1		2321					1		2	4					10					5	12	7			11		9			6	8	3

Associate Members Cup

						Bainbridge T	Barker AM	Bassett GR	Bird JC	Blackburn EH	Borthwick JR	Brown P	Buckley MJ	Campbell PJ	Dixon KL	Dobson P	Hogan RD	Johnson KP	Kennedy R	Lawrence M	Linacre J	Linacre P	Linighan A	Linighan D	Lowe K	Ray P	Robinson DA	Robinson MW	Smithies MH	Staff P	Taylor PMR	Waddle AR	Weir A	Whitfield M	Wilson H
R1	Feb 22	Bradford City	2-3	Dobson, A Linighan	1179		3			1		6				10	4	11	7			9	5		8				2						

1984/85

19th in Division 4

	Date	Opponent	Score	Scorers	Att	Bird JC	Blackburn EH	Borthwick JR	Brown P	Brownlie JJ	Dixon KL	Dobson P	Farnaby C	Finch M	Gavin MW	Gollogly J	Hedley G	Hogan RD	Honour B	Liddle B	Linighan D	Mutrie LA	Pollard BE	Proudlock P	Robinson DA	Smith A	Stevenson A	Stimpson BG	Taylor PMR	Venus M	Waddle AR	Wardrobe B
1	Aug 25	Stockport County	1-4	Dixon	1619	6			7	2	10	11		1			4			3	12					5			8			9
2	Sep 1	SWINDON TOWN	2-2	Hogan, Brownlie	1703	6			8	2	10	11		1			4	7		12		9			3	5						
3	8	Port Vale	1-1	Linighan	3232	2			7		9	10					4	11		3	6	8				5	1		12			
4	15	ROCHDALE	0-2		1574				7	2	9	10					4	11		3	6	8				5	1					12
5	19	CHESTERFIELD	1-0	Hedley	1686				6		11	12					4	8		3		10			2	5	1		7			9
6	22	Peterborough United	1-3	Hogan	3491				6			7					4	10		3		8			2	5	1		11			9
7	29	CREWE ALEXANDRA	3-0	Hogan, Mutrie, Wardrobe	1502				6		7						4	10		3		8			2	5	1		11			9
8	Oct 2	Darlington	1-0	Mutrie	5221				6		7						4	10		3		8			2	5	1		11			9
9	6	Tranmere Rovers	2-1	Mutrie, Wardrobe	1619	12			6		7		4					10		3		8			2	5	1		11			9
10	13	HEREFORD UNITED	2-2	Smith, Dixon	3138				6		7	12					4	10		3		8			2	5	1		11			9
11	20	Torquay United	1-0	Mooney (og)	1285				6		7	12					4	10		3	5	8			2		1		11			9
12	24	SOUTHEND UNITED	2-1	Hedley (p), Dobson	4297				6		7	12					4	10		3	5	8			2		1		11			9
13	27	MANSFIELD TOWN	0-0		4349				6		7	12					4	10		3		8			2	5	1		11			9
14	Nov 3	Wrexham	1-1	Taylor	1368				6	3	7	12					4	10				8			2	5	1		11			9
15	5	EXETER CITY	1-1	Hedley	3657				6	3	7	12					4	10				8			2	5	1		11			9
16	9	Colchester United	0-1		2136				6	3	7	8					4	10						12	2	5	1		11			9
17	24	SCUNTHORPE UNITED	3-2	Mutrie (p), Dobson, Taylor	3292				6	3	7	9					4	10				8			2	5	1		11			
18	Dec 1	Aldershot	0-1		2069				6	3	7	9					4	10				8			2	5	1		11			
19	15	NORTHAMPTON T	0-0		2207					3	7	9					4	10			6	8			2	5	1		11			12
20	22	CHESTER CITY	2-1	Dixon, Dobson	1949					3	8	12					4	10			6				2	5	1	7	11			9
21	26	Halifax Town	3-2	Dixon 2, Linighan	1409				7	2	8						4	10			6					5	1	3	11			9
22	29	Blackpool	1-2	Smith	4778				7	2	8	12					4	10			6					5	1	3	11			9
23	Jan 2	BURY	0-1		3199				7	2	8	9						10			6	11		12		5	1	3				4
24	19	PORT VALE	2-2	Dixon 2	2285				12	2	8						4	10			6		7	11		5	1	3				9
25	Feb 1	Crewe Alexandra	0-2		1547				6		9						4	10					7		2	5	1	3	11		8	
26	9	PETERBOROUGH UTD.	0-3		1353		1		6		7	9	10						4		3			12	2	5			11		8	
27	12	Chesterfield	0-0		2617				6		7	9							4		10			12	2	5	1	3	11		8	
28	17	DARLINGTON	1-2	Taylor	5947				6		7	9							4		10				2	5	1	3	11		8	12
29	23	WREXHAM	2-0	Hedley (p), Dobson	1432				6		7	9					11		4		10			8	2	5	1	3				
30	Mar 2	Mansfield Town	0-2		1940			12				9	11				8		4		6			10	2	5	1	3	7			
31	4	Southend United	1-1	Hedley (p)	1644	6						9					11	8	4					10	2	5	1	3				7
32	9	TORQUAY UNITED	3-1	Dixon, Hedley 2 (1p)	1364				6		10						8	7	4					11	2	5	1	3				9
33	16	Hereford United	1-2	Hedley (p)	3279				6		10	9					8	7	4					11	2	5	1	3				
34	23	TRANMERE ROVERS	2-4	Hedley (p), Dixon	1326				6		10	9					8	7	4		12				2	5	1	3	11			
35	30	Exeter City	2-3	Gollogly, Dobson	1578				6		10	9				4	8	7						12	2	5	1	3	11			
36	31	Swindon Town	1-2	Dixon	2414				6		10	9				4	8	7						12	2	5	1	3	11			
37	Apr 3	STOCKPORT COUNTY	5-1	Borthwick, Dixon(p), Dobson 2, Brown	1148			12	6		10	9				4	8	7							2	5	1	3	11			
38	6	HALIFAX TOWN	0-1		1577			8	6			9	10		11	4								12	2	5	1	3	7			
39	8	Bury	0-1		3726		1	12	6		8	9			11	10			4						2	5			7	3		
40	13	COLCHESTER UNITED	2-1	Dobson 2	1329		1		6		8	9			11	10		4	7						2	5			12	3		
41	15	Northampton Town	0-2		1181		1	12	6		10	9			11			4	7					8	2	5				3		
42	19	Scunthorpe United	0-2		2037		1		6	3	10	9			11			4	7						2	5						8
43	27	ALDERSHOT	1-0	Taylor	1201		1		6	3	10				11			4	8						2	5			7			9
44	30	Rochdale	3-4	Dixon (p), Dobson, Gavin	910		1		6	3	10	12			11			4	8						2	5			7			9
45	May 6	BLACKPOOL	0-2		2496		1	12	6	3	10	9				8		4	7						2	5			11			
46	11	Chester City	0-1		1626		1		6	2	9	10	8					4	7							5			11	3		12
					Apps	5	9	6	42	19	42	38	5	2	7	7	32	38	17	13	17	18	2	14	38	44	35	18	36	4	4	27
					Goals			1	1	1	12	10			1	1	9	3			2	4				2			4			2

One own goal

F.A. Cup

	Date	Opponent	Score	Scorers	Att	Bird JC	Blackburn EH	Borthwick JR	Brown P	Brownlie JJ	Dixon KL	Dobson P	Farnaby C	Finch M	Gavin MW	Gollogly J	Hedley G	Hogan RD	Honour B	Liddle B	Linighan D	Mutrie LA	Pollard BE	Proudlock P	Robinson DA	Smith A	Stevenson A	Stimpson BG	Taylor PMR	Venus M	Waddle AR	Wardrobe B
R1	Nov 17	DERBY COUNTY	2-1	Taylor, Dixon	7431				6	3	7	9					4	10				8			2	5	1		11			
R2	Dec 8	YORK CITY	0-2		8554				6	3	7	9					4	10				8			2	5	1		11			

F.L. Cup (Milk Cup)

	Date	Opponent	Score	Scorers	Att	Bird JC	Blackburn EH	Borthwick JR	Brown P	Brownlie JJ	Dixon KL	Dobson P	Farnaby C	Finch M	Gavin MW	Gollogly J	Hedley G	Hogan RD	Honour B	Liddle B	Linighan D	Mutrie LA	Pollard BE	Proudlock P	Robinson DA	Smith A	Stevenson A	Stimpson BG	Taylor PMR	Venus M	Waddle AR	Wardrobe B
R1/1	Aug 29	Derby County	1-5	Hedley	9281	6			8	3	10	11		1			4	7				9			2	5						
R1/2	Sep 5	DERBY COUNTY	0-1		1862				7	2	9	10					4	11			6	8			3	5	1		12			

A.M. Cup (Freight Rover Trophy)

	Date	Opponent	Score	Scorers	Att	Bird JC	Blackburn EH	Borthwick JR	Brown P	Brownlie JJ	Dixon KL	Dobson P	Farnaby C	Finch M	Gavin MW	Gollogly J	Hedley G	Hogan RD	Honour B	Liddle B	Linighan D	Mutrie LA	Pollard BE	Proudlock P	Robinson DA	Smith A	Stevenson A	Stimpson BG	Taylor PMR	Venus M	Waddle AR	Wardrobe B
R1/1	Jan 23	LINCOLN CITY	2-1	Waddle, Brown	1202				6		9						4	10					7		2	5	1	3	11		8	
R1/2	Feb 6	Lincoln City	0-4		1316		1		6	3	9						4	10			7		12		2	5			11	13	8	

1985/86 7th in Division 4

	Date	Opponent	Score	Scorers	Att	Blackburn EH	Borthwick JR	Carney S	Chambers PM	Chilton AJT	Dixon KL	Dobson P	Gollogly J	Hewitt MD	Hogan RD	Honour B	Kelly TJ	Lester MJ	Linighan D	Little A	Newton R	Nobbs AK	Poskett M	Proudlock P	Robinson DA	Shoulder A	Smith A	Taylor PMR	Walker NS
1	Aug 17	Cambridge United	2-4	Shoulder, Newton (p)	1821	1					11		12			8	3		6	4	9	2				7	5		10
2	24	CREWE ALEXANDRA	4-1	Davis(og),Dixon,Newton,Shoulder	2160	1					11					8	3		6	4	9	2				7	5		10
3	26	Chester City	1-1	Smith	1473	1					11				12	8	3		6	4	9	2				7	5		10
4	31	ORIENT	1-2	Shoulder	2206	1	12				11					8	3		6	4	9	2				7	5		10
5	Sep 7	Burnley	0-2		3175	1					11	7	12		4	8	3		6		9	2					5		10
6	13	ROCHDALE	2-0	Dixon, Borthwick	2148	1	9				11		8		4	7	3		6			2					5		10
7	18	NORTHAMPTON T	2-1	Honour, Walker	2200	1	9				11	12	8		4	7	3		6						2		5		10
8	21	Torquay United	3-1	Borthwick, Honour 2	946	1	9				11		8		4	7	3		6			2					5		10
9	28	SWINDON TOWN	1-0	Dobson	2411	1	9				11	12	8		4	7	3		6			2					5		10
10	30	Port Vale	0-4		3015	1					11	9	8		4	7	3		6			2					5	12	10
11	Oct 5	PETERBOROUGH UTD.	2-1	Borthwick, Hogan (p)	2138	1	9					12	8		4	7	3		6			2				11	5		10
12	11	Stockport County	3-1	Gollogly, Honour, Shoulder	1827	1	9						8		4	7	3		6			2				11	5		10
13	19	HEREFORD UNITED	2-1	Smith, Shoulder	2974	1	9				8				4	7	3		6			2				11	5	12	10
14	22	Preston North End	1-2	Hogan (p)	3608	1	9			3	8				4	7			6			2				11	5	12	10
15	26	Exeter City	2-1	Hogan, Shoulder	1934	1	9			3	12				4	7			6			11			2	8	5		10
16	Nov 2	MANSFIELD TOWN	1-1	Hogan (p)	4195	1	9			3		12			4	7			6			11			2	8	5		10
17	6	ALDERSHOT	2-1	Nobbs, Dobson	3324	1	9		3			12			4	7			6			11			2	8	5		10
18	9	Southend United	2-3	Walker, Borthwick	2748	1	9		3		11	12			4	7			6			2				8	5		10
19	23	TRANMERE ROVERS	1-0	Walker	2707	1	9		3			12	11			7			6			2			4	8	5		10
20	Dec 14	COLCHESTER UNITED	4-1	Shoulder 2 (1p), Dixon, Robinson	2161	1			3		9		11			7			6			2			4	8	5		10
21	20	Crewe Alexandra	0-0		1070	1			3		9		11		12	7			6			2			4	8	5		10
22	26	Scunthorpe United	0-1		2495	1			3		9				4	7			6			2			11	8	5		10
23	Jan 1	HALIFAX TOWN	3-0	Shoulder 2, Dixon	3391	1			3		9				4	7			6			2			11	8	5		10
24	8	CHESTER CITY	1-1	Holden (og)	3675	1			3		9				4	7			6		12	2			11	8	5		10
25	11	Orient	1-1	Honour	3667	1			3		9	8	6		4	7					12	2			11		5		10
26	18	CAMBRIDGE UNITED	2-1	Honour 2	3045	1			3						4	7		11			9	2			6	8	5		10
27	25	Rochdale	2-0	Borthwick, Shoulder (p)	2301	1	9		3						4	7		11	6			2				8	5		10
28	Feb 1	BURNLEY	3-1	Shoulder 2 (2p), Linighan	3359	1	9		3						4	7		11	6			2				8	5		10
29	5	PRESTON NORTH END	1-0	Shoulder	2986	1	9		3						4	7		11	6			2				8	5		10
30	25	Wrexham	0-1		957	1	9		3						4	7		11	6			2				8	5		10
31	Mar 5	PORT VALE	1-1	Sproson (og)	2550	1	9		3			12			4	7		11	6			2				8	5		10
32	8	Peterborough United	1-3	Borthwick	2324	1	9		3						4	7		11	6			2			12	8	5		10
33	11	Northampton Town	0-3		1815	1	9		3			12				7		11	6			2			4	8	5	10	
34	14	STOCKPORT COUNTY	1-1	Lester	2675	1	9		3							7		11	6	4	12	2				8	5		10
35	22	EXETER CITY	0-0		2204	1	12		3							7		11	6	4	9	2				8	5		10
36	25	Swindon Town	1-3	Smith	6172	1			3			10			4	7		11	6		9				2	8	5		12
37	28	Halifax Town	2-3	Shoulder 2 (1p)	2064	1	9	11	3						4	7			6			2				8	5		10
38	Apr 1	SCUNTHORPE UNITED	0-1		2575	1	9		3			12			4	7			6			2	8			11	5		10
39	5	Aldershot	1-0	Walker	1277	1		6	3						4	7			12	9			8		2	11	5		10
40	9	Hereford United	2-2	Hogan (p), Honour	2023	1	12	6	3						4	7				11			9		2	8	5		10
41	12	SOUTHEND UNITED	3-2	Little, Honour, Walker	1927	1	12	6	3						4	7				11			9		2	8	5		10
42	15	TORQUAY UNITED	1-0	Compton (og)	1348	1	9	6	3						4	7				11					2	8	5		10
43	18	Tranmere Rovers	2-4	Shoulder (p), Hogan	1161	1	9	6	3						4	7				11		2	12			8	5		10
44	22	Mansfield Town	0-4		5545	1	9	2				8			4	7	3		6			12		11			5		10
45	26	WREXHAM	3-3	Borthwick, Dixon, Hogan (p)	1282	1	9		3		8			12	4	7			6			2			11		5		10
46	May 2	Colchester United	1-3	Hogan (p)	2410	1	9		3		8				4	7	12			11					6		5	2	10
					Apps	46	32	7	29	3	22	15	13	1	38	46	15	11	39	12	11	39	5	1	21	36	46	5	45
					Goals		7				5	2	1		8	9		1	1	1	2	1			1	17	3		5

Four own goals

F.A. Cup

	Date	Opponent	Score	Scorers	Att	Blackburn EH	Borthwick JR	Carney S	Chambers PM	Chilton AJT	Dixon KL	Dobson P	Gollogly J	Hewitt MD	Hogan RD	Honour B	Kelly TJ	Lester MJ	Linighan D	Little A	Newton R	Nobbs AK	Poskett M	Proudlock P	Robinson DA	Shoulder A	Smith A	Taylor PMR	Walker NS
R1	Nov 16	Macclesfield Town	2-1	Shoulder 2	3217	1	9		3						4	7			6			2		8		11	5		10
R2	Dec 7	FRICKLEY ATHLETIC	0-1		4100	1	9		3			12	11			7			6			2			4	8	5		10

F.L. Cup (Milk Cup)

	Date	Opponent	Score	Scorers	Att	Blackburn EH	Borthwick JR	Carney S	Chambers PM	Chilton AJT	Dixon KL	Dobson P	Gollogly J	Hewitt MD	Hogan RD	Honour B	Kelly TJ	Lester MJ	Linighan D	Little A	Newton R	Nobbs AK	Poskett M	Proudlock P	Robinson DA	Shoulder A	Smith A	Taylor PMR	Walker NS
R1/1	Aug 21	Derby County	0-3		8419	1					11					8	3		6	4	9	2				7	5		10
R1/2	Sep 4	DERBY COUNTY	2-0	Linighan, Hogan	1611	1					11	7			4	8	3		5		9	2					6		10

A.M. Cup (Freight Rover Trophy)

	Date	Opponent	Score	Scorers	Att	Blackburn EH	Borthwick JR	Carney S	Chambers PM	Chilton AJT	Dixon KL	Dobson P	Gollogly J	Hewitt MD	Hogan RD	Honour B	Kelly TJ	Lester MJ	Linighan D	Little A	Newton R	Nobbs AK	Poskett M	Proudlock P	Robinson DA	Shoulder A	Smith A	Taylor PMR	Walker NS
R1	Jan 21	Rotherham United	0-3		1309	1	12		3			8			4	7		11			9	2			6		5		10
R1	28	YORK CITY	3-2	Honour 2, Lester	1080		9							12	4	7	3	11	6			2		13		8	5	10	

Played against York City: S Wilson (at 1)

1986/87 18th in Division 4

						Barratt A	Blackburn EH	Borthwick JR	Cochrane GT	Dixon KL	Edwards R	Gibb DA	Gollogly J	Hewitt MD	Hogan RD	Honour B	Lockhart KS	Lowe SJ	McCaffery A	McGinley J	McKinnon R	McLean DJ	Nobbs AK	Robinson A	Robson DM	Shoulder A	Smith A	Smithies MH	Stokle D	Sword TW	Tinkler J	Toman JA	Turner RP	Walker NS
1	Aug	23 CARDIFF CITY	1-1	Smith	2804		1	9		12			2		4	7		11			3					8	5			6				10
2		29 Southend United	1-1	Shoulder	2216		1	9				11	2		4	7		12			3					8	5			6				10
3	Sep	6 CAMBRIDGE UNITED	2-2	Gibb, Dixon	1956		1			11		10	2		4	7		9			3					8	5			6				
4		13 Burnley	1-1	Lowe	2465		1			11		7	2		4			9			3		12			8	5			6				10
5		16 Colchester United	1-2	Hogan (p)	2326		1			11		7	2		4			9			3					8	5			6				10
6		21 WREXHAM	0-1		2437		1			11		10	2		4	7		9			3					8	5			6				12
7		27 Orient	0-2		2610		1			11		10			4	7		9			3		2			8	5			6				12
8	Oct	1 CREWE ALEXANDRA	0-5		1512		1			9		10			4	7					3		2	11		8	5							12
9		5 Lincoln City	4-1	Stodder (og), Gollogly 2, Walker	2101		1			9			4		8	7		11			3		2				5			6				10
10		10 HEREFORD UNITED	0-0		1939		1			9		12	4		8	7		11			3		2				5			6				10
11		18 PETERBOROUGH UTD.	1-2	Gollogly	1482		1			9		2	4		8	7		11			3		6	12									5	10
12		22 Exeter City	0-2		2660		1			9		12	4		8	7		11			3		2				5						6	10
13		25 Aldershot	1-1	Turner	1902		1			11		8			4	7		12			3		2				5			6			9	10
14	Nov	1 NORTHAMPTON T	3-3	Hogan (p), Dixon, Wilcox (og)	1657		1			11					4	7		8			3		2				5			6			9	10
15		4 TORQUAY UNITED	2-1	Dixon, Honour	1623		1			9			8	12	4	7		11			3		2				5			6				10
16		8 Rochdale	2-0	Honour, Dixon	1467		1			8				12	4	7					3		2		11		5			6			9	10
17		22 Swansea City	0-1		4420					8	1				4	7					3		2			11	5	12		6			9	10
18		28 STOCKPORT COUNTY	1-0	Hogan (p)	1586		1			8					4	7					3		2			11	5			6			9	10
19	Dec	13 WOLVERHAMPTON W.	0-1		1785		1	9		7		12			4		11				3		2			8	5			6				10
20		26 HALIFAX TOWN	0-0		1676		1	9		7		2			4	12	11				3		6			8	5							10
21		27 Preston North End	0-0		7782		1			11		9		8	4	7					3		6				5	2						10
22	Jan	1 Scunthorpe United	2-1	Hewitt, Dixon	2726	10	1			11		9		8	6	7					3		4				5	2						
23		3 SWANSEA CITY	1-1	Dixon	1784	7	1			10		9		8	6	12				11	3		4				5	2						
24		10 Tranmere Rovers	1-1	Walker	2395		1	9		10				8	6					11	3		4				5	2						7
25		24 Cambridge United	0-3		1749		1	9		10				8		11					3		4				5	2			12	6		7
26		31 BURNLEY	2-2	Hewitt, Dixon	1506	2	1		11	9				8		12					3		4				5			6		10		7
27	Feb	6 COLCHESTER UNITED	1-0	Walker	1245	7	1			9				8	4	12					3		2				5			6		10		11
28		14 Wrexham	1-1	Toman	1824	2	1			9		12		8	4	10			6				3				5					7		11
29		21 ORIENT	1-3	Dixon	1439	2	1			9				8	4	12			6		11		3				5					7		10
30		28 Crewe Alexandra	0-1		1314	2	1	8	7	9					4	12			6		11		3				5							10
31	Mar	4 Northampton Town	1-1	Hogan	5470	2	1	8		9					4						11		3				5		6			7		10
32		7 ALDERSHOT	1-1	Toman	1018	2	1	8		9		12			4						11		3				5		6			7		10
33		14 Peterborough United	1-3	McCaffery	4116	2	1	9						8	4				6		11		3				5					7		10
34		18 EXETER CITY	1-0	Shoulder	1092	2	1			9					4	11					3		6			8	5					7		10
35		21 Hereford United	0-4		1832	2	1			9		11		7							3		6			8	5				12	4		10
36		29 LINCOLN CITY	2-1	Shoulder 2 (1p)	1483	2	1			9		12							4		3	11				8	5		6			7		10
37	Apr	4 ROCHDALE	1-1	Shoulder (p)	1168	11	1			9		12									3	4	2			8	5		6			7		10
38		11 Torquay United	1-0	Shoulder (p)	1773	11	1			9		10									3	4	2			8	5		6			7		
39		14 SOUTHEND UNITED	1-0	Shoulder (p)	1323	2	1			10		9			12						3	4	6			8	5					7		11
40		17 SCUNTHORPE UNITED	0-2		1805	2	1			10		9			4	12					3		6			8	5					7		11
41		20 Halifax Town	0-1		1115	11	1			10		9			4				6		3		2			8	5					7		12
42		24 TRANMERE ROVERS	1-1	Toman	1195	2	1	9		10		11			4						3		6			8	5					7		
43	May	1 Stockport County	2-0	Gibb, Toman	2228	2	1	9				11			4	10					3		6			8	5					7		
44		4 PRESTON NORTH END	2-2	Gibb, Toman	2449	2	1	9		12		11			4	10					3		6			8	5					7		
45		7 Cardiff City	0-4		1334	2	1	9		12		11				10					3	4	6			8	5					7		
46		9 Wolverhampton Wan.	1-4	Dixon	8610	2	1			9		11				10					3	4	6			8	5					7		
					Apps	23	45	14	2	43	1	30	11	13	38	32	2	14	6	2	45	6	40	2	1	25	45	6	5	18	2	21	7	37
					Goals					9		3	3	2	4	2		1		1						7	1					5	1	3

Played in one game: PB Byron (game 8, at 6), AP Dixon (46, at 12)

Two own goals

F.A. Cup

						Barratt A	Blackburn EH	Borthwick JR	Cochrane GT	Dixon KL	Edwards R	Gibb DA	Gollogly J	Hewitt MD	Hogan RD	Honour B	Lockhart KS	Lowe SJ	McCaffery A	McGinley J	McKinnon R	McLean DJ	Nobbs AK	Robinson A	Robson DM	Shoulder A	Smith A	Smithies MH	Stokle D	Sword TW	Tinkler J	Toman JA	Turner RP	Walker NS
R1	Nov	15 Wrexham	1-2	Hogan	4420		1			9				11	4	7							2			8	5	3		6				10

F.L. Cup (Littlewoods Challenge Cup)

						Barratt A	Blackburn EH	Borthwick JR	Cochrane GT	Dixon KL	Edwards R	Gibb DA	Gollogly J	Hewitt MD	Hogan RD	Honour B	Lockhart KS	Lowe SJ	McCaffery A	McGinley J	McKinnon R	McLean DJ	Nobbs AK	Robinson A	Robson DM	Shoulder A	Smith A	Smithies MH	Stokle D	Sword TW	Tinkler J	Toman JA	Turner RP	Walker NS
R1/1	Aug	26 MIDDLESBROUGH	1-1	Hogan	2356		1	9		12		10	2		4	7		13			3					8	5			6				11
R1/2	Sep	2 Middlesbrough	0-2		7735		1			12		11	2		4	7		9			3					8	5			6				10

A.M. Cup (Freight Rover Trophy)

						Barratt A	Blackburn EH	Borthwick JR	Cochrane GT	Dixon KL	Edwards R	Gibb DA	Gollogly J	Hewitt MD	Hogan RD	Honour B	Lockhart KS	Lowe SJ	McCaffery A	McGinley J	McKinnon R	McLean DJ	Nobbs AK	Robinson A	Robson DM	Shoulder A	Smith A	Smithies MH	Stokle D	Sword TW	Tinkler J	Toman JA	Turner RP	Walker NS
PR	Dec	2 Scunthorpe United	0-1		952		1	9		8					4	7		12			3		2			11	5			6				10
PR		6 LINCOLN CITY	0-0		938		1	9		11		4				7		12			3		2			8	5			6				10

Also played v. Lincoln City: A Little (at 14)

1987/88 16th in Division 4

							Baker DP	Barratt A	Borthwick JR	Butler PJ	Carr K	Danskin J	Dixon AP	Doig R	Gibb DA	Grayson SD	Haigh P	Hall AD	Honour B	Kennedy AP	McCarthy JD	McKinnon R	Nobbs AK	Owers P	Prudhoe M	Shoulder A	Smith A	Stokes WD	Stokle D	Thomson R	Tinkler J	Toman JA	Whellans R
1	Aug	15	NEWPORT COUNTY	0-0		1846	9	2		11					12		4		7				3	1		10	5	6				8	
2		22	Wrexham	1-2	McKinnon	1816	9	2	12	11							4		7			3		1		10	5	6				8	
3		29	DARLINGTON	2-5	Dixon, Baker	1808	9	11		12			14				4		7			3	2		1		5	6		10		8	
4		31	Swansea City	1-2	Toman	3569	9	12		11			10						7			3	2		1		5	6		4		8	
5	Sep	5	LEYTON ORIENT	2-2	Toman, Baker	1110	9	14		12			10				4		7			3	2		1	11	5	6				8	
6		12	Carlisle United	3-1	Baker 2, Toman	2463	9	12					10				4		7			3	2		1	11	5	6		14		8	
7		16	CAMBRIDGE UNITED	2-1	Baker 2	1454	9		10	12							4		7			3	2		1	11	5	6				8	
8		19	COLCHESTER UNITED	3-1	Baker 3 (2p)	1619	9	11	10								4		7			3	2		1		5	6				8	
9		26	Bolton Wanderers	2-1	McKinnon, Baker (p)	4398	9	11	10								4		7			3	2		1		5	6				8	
10		30	EXETER CITY	3-1	Baker 3	2971	9	11	10								4		7			3	2		1		5	6				8	
11	Oct	3	Crewe Alexandra	1-1	Baker (p)	2128	9	11	10								4		7			3	2		1		5	6				8	
12		10	Burnley	0-1		5216	9	11	10						12		4		7	14		3	2		1		5	6				8	
13		17	TORQUAY UNITED	0-0		2462	9	2	10										7	3		11	4		1		5	6				8	
14		21	HALIFAX TOWN	2-1	Toman, Barratt	2472	9	2					10						7	3		11	4		1		5	6				8	
15		24	Scarborough	1-1	Toman (p)	3909	9	2	12						10		11		7			3	4		1		5	6				8	
16		31	SCUNTHORPE UNITED	1-0	Toman	2532	9			11	1				10		2		7	3			4				5	6				8	
17	Nov	3	Stockport County	0-1		1408	9	11			1				10		2		7	3		12	4				5	6				8	
18		7	Peterborough United	1-0	Toman	3232	9			11	1				10		2		7			3	4				5	6				8	
19		21	TRANMERE ROVERS	1-2	Toman	2443	9	14	12	11	1				10		2		7			3	4				5	6				8	
20		28	Cardiff City	1-1	Barratt	3232	9	11	10		1				12		2		7			3	4				5	6				8	
21	Dec	12	WOLVERHAMPTON W.	0-0		2631	9	11	10		1						2		7			3					5	6			4	8	
22		19	Hereford United	2-4	Toman 2 (1p)	1676		11	10		1		9		12		2	14	7			3					5	6			4	8	
23		26	BOLTON WANDERERS	0-0		4304		11	10		1				9		2		7			3	4				5	6				8	
24		28	Rochdale	2-0	Baker, Whellans	1851	9	11			1						2		7			3	4				5	6				8	10
25	Jan	1	Darlington	1-1	Baker	4735	9	11			1				12		2		7			3	4				5				6	8	10
26		2	CARLISLE UNITED	0-0		3139	9	11			1				12		2		7			3	4				5				6	8	10
27		15	Colchester United	0-0		1768	9	2	11		1	7					6					3	4				5				12	8	10
28		26	WREXHAM	1-0	Borthwick	1524	9	2	11		1	7					6					3	4				5				12	8	10
29		30	SWANSEA CITY	0-2		2050	9	2	11		1	7			10		6		14			3	4				5				12	8	
30	Feb	6	Leyton Orient	2-0	Baker, Toman	4188	9	2	11		1						6		7			3	4				5				10	8	
31		13	ROCHDALE	1-1	Toman	2120	9	2	11		1						6		7			3	4				5				10	8	
32		19	Newport County	3-2	Toman (p), Borthwick 2	1880		2	11		1		12		9		6		7			3	4				5				10	8	
33		27	CREWE ALEXANDRA	2-1	Toman (p), Baker	1624	9	2	11		1						6		7			3	4				5				10	8	12
34	Mar	2	Exeter City	0-1		1573	9	2	11		1				12				7			3	4				5				6	8	10
35		5	Torquay United	1-1	Barratt	2857	9	2	11		1								7			3	4				5		6		10	8	
36		12	BURNLEY	2-1	Baker, Borthwick	2893	9	2	11		1								7			3	4				5		6		10	8	
37		19	Scunthorpe United	0-3		3783		2	11		1		14		12				7			3	4				5		6		10	8	9
38		26	SCARBOROUGH	1-0	Borthwick	2453		2	11		1			10	9		6		7			3	4				5					8	12
39	Apr	2	PETERBOROUGH UTD.	0-1		2315	9	2	11		1			10			6		7			3	4				5				14	8	12
40		4	Tranmere Rovers	1-3	Toman	3921	9	2	11		1			10			6		12			3	4				5				7	8	
41		9	STOCKPORT COUNTY	1-3	Toman	1269	9	2	11		1		12	10			6		7			3	4				5					8	
42		19	Cambridge United	1-1	Crowe (og)	1492	12	2	11		1			10			6		7			3	4				5					8	9
43		23	Halifax Town	1-3	Baker	876	9	2	11		1		12	10			6		7			3	14				5				4	8	
44		30	CARDIFF CITY	0-1		1101	9	2	12		1		10	11			6		7			3	4				5					8	
45	May	2	Wolverhampton Wan.	0-2		17895		2	9		1		10	11	12		3		7				4				5				6	8	
46		7	HEREFORD UNITED	1-2	Toman	823		2	10		1		12	11		9	3		7		14		4				5				6	8	
						Apps	39	43	34	9	31	3	13	9	18	1	39	1	44	5	1	42	43	2	13	5	46	24	3	3	20	46	11
						Goals	20	3	5				1									2										17	1

One own goal

F.A. Cup

							Baker DP	Barratt A	Borthwick JR	Butler PJ	Carr K	Danskin J	Dixon AP	Doig R	Gibb DA	Grayson SD	Haigh P	Hall AD	Honour B	Kennedy AP	McCarthy JD	McKinnon R	Nobbs AK	Owers P	Prudhoe M	Shoulder A	Smith A	Stokes WD	Stokle D	Thomson R	Tinkler J	Toman JA	Whellans R
R1	Nov	14	Chorley	2-0	Gibb, Baker	2462	9			11	1				10		2		7			3	4				5	6				8	
R2	Dec	5	York City	1-1	Baker	3394	9	11	10		1						2	12	7			3	4				5	6				8	
rep		9	YORK CITY	3-1	Baker, Toman 2	4057	9	11	10		1						2		7			3					5	6			4	8	
R3	Jan	9	LUTON TOWN	1-2	Toman	6056	9	2			1				11		6		7			3	4				5				12	8	10

F.L. Cup (Littlewoods Challenge Cup)

							Baker DP	Barratt A	Borthwick JR	Butler PJ	Carr K	Danskin J	Dixon AP	Doig R	Gibb DA	Grayson SD	Haigh P	Hall AD	Honour B	Kennedy AP	McCarthy JD	McKinnon R	Nobbs AK	Owers P	Prudhoe M	Shoulder A	Smith A	Stokes WD	Stokle D	Thomson R	Tinkler J	Toman JA	Whellans R
R1/1	Aug	18	Scunthorpe United	1-3	Baker	1613	9	2		11			12				4		7				3	1		10	5	6				8	
R1/2		26	SCUNTHORPE UNITED	0-1		972	9	2		11			12				4		7			3		1			5	6		10		8	

A.M. Cup (Sherpa Van Trophy)

							Baker DP	Barratt A	Borthwick JR	Butler PJ	Carr K	Danskin J	Dixon AP	Doig R	Gibb DA	Grayson SD	Haigh P	Hall AD	Honour B	Kennedy AP	McCarthy JD	McKinnon R	Nobbs AK	Owers P	Prudhoe M	Shoulder A	Smith A	Stokes WD	Stokle D	Thomson R	Tinkler J	Toman JA	Whellans R
PR	Oct	27	Mansfield Town	2-3	Smith, Kennedy	2710	9	2	14		1				10		11	7		12		3	4				5	6				8	
PR	Nov	24	DONCASTER ROVERS	1-0	Stokes	782	9	11	10		1				12		2		7			3	4				5	6				8	
R1	Feb	3	Carlisle United	2-0	Baker, Borthwick	1433	9	2	11		1						6		7			3	4				5				10	8	
QF	Feb	9	Sunderland	1-0	Honour	8976	9	2	11		1						6		7			3	4				5				10	8	
SFN	Mar	9	PRESTON NORTH END	0-2		4989	9	2	11		1				12				7			3	4				5		6		10	8	14

1988/89 19th in Division 4

							Allon JB	Atkinson PD	Baker DP	Barras A	Barratt A	Borthwick JR	Dalton P	Dixon KL	Doig R	Grayson SD	Haigh P	Hepple JA	Honour B	Locker S	McAndrew A	McKellar DN	McKinnon R	Moverley R	Muggleton CD	Nobbs AK	Norton P	Ogden P	Plaskett SC	Smith A	Stokes WD	Tinkler J	Toman JA	Tunks RW
1	Aug	27	Lincoln City	1-0	Toman	3547					11	9		10		12	2		7			1	3							5	6	4	8	
2	Sep	3	DARLINGTON	2-1	Toman, Smith	2477					11	10		9		12	2		7			1	3							5	6	4	8	
3		10	Torquay United	0-2		2027					11	10		9	14	12	2		7			1	3							5	6	4	8	
4		17	LEYTON ORIENT	1-0	Tinkler	1873					2			9	11	10			7			1	3							5	6	4	8	
5		20	York City	3-2	Honour, Doig, Dixon	2611		14			2	12		9	11	10			7			1	3							5	6	4	8	
6		24	CAMBRIDGE UNITED	3-2	Dixon 2 (2p), Toman	2357					2			9	11	10			7				3							5	6	4	8	1
7		30	Tranmere Rovers	1-2	Dixon	3624			12		2			9	11	10			7				3							5	6	4	8	1
8	Oct	4	ROCHDALE	0-1		2363			5		2			9	11	10			7				3								6	4	8	1
9		8	Doncaster Rovers	0-1		2091			5		2			9	11	10	12		7				3					14			6	4	8	1
10		15	WREXHAM	1-3	Baker	2194			10		2			9	11	12	5		7				3								6	4	8	1
11		22	CREWE ALEXANDRA	0-3		1794			10		12			9	11		2		7				3				1			5	6	4	8	
12		24	Stockport County	0-3		2098			10		2			9			11		7				3				1			5	6	4	8	
13		29	HEREFORD UNITED	1-1	Barratt	1585	9		10		2						11		7				3		1					5	6	4	8	
14	Nov	4	Halifax Town	0-1		2182	9		10		2				14	12	11		7				3		1					5	6	4	8	
15		9	Peterborough United	1-0	Grayson	3148	9		6		11			4	12	10	2		7				3		1					5			8	
16		12	GRIMSBY TOWN	2-1	Grayson, Toman	1787	9		6		11			4		10	2		7				3		1					5			8	
17		26	EXETER CITY	2-2	Grayson, Smith	2107		12	6		11	9			4	10			7				3		1	2				5			8	
18	Dec	3	Burnley	0-0		6289	9		6						4	10			7				3		1	2		11		5			8	
19		17	CARLISLE UNITED	0-2		1863	9	14	6		4	12				10			7				3		1	2		11			5		8	
20		26	Scunthorpe United	1-1	Allon	4595	9		6		11	12				10			7				3		1	2					5	4	8	
21		30	Colchester United	2-1	Borthwick, Stokes	2359			6		11	9				10			7				3	1		2					5	4	8	
22	Jan	2	ROTHERHAM UNITED	1-1	Grayson	3471			6		11	9				10			7				3	1		2					5	4	8	
23		14	Darlington	0-0		3521	9		6		11					10			7				3	1		2					5	4	8	
24		21	LINCOLN CITY	3-2	Atkinson 2, Grayson	2808	9	11	6		2					10			7				3	1				8			5	4		
25	Feb	4	YORK CITY	0-1		2794	9	11	6		2					10			7				3	1							5	4	8	
26		11	Cambridge United	0-6		2273	9		6		11				12	10			7				3	1		2					5	4	8	
27		18	DONCASTER ROVERS	2-1	Tinkler, Grayson	1919	9		6		11	12			14	10			7				3	1		2					5	4	8	
28		28	STOCKPORT COUNTY	2-2	Toman, Grayson	1598		11	6		2	9			12	10			7				3	1							5	4	8	
29	Mar	4	Crewe Alexandra	0-3		3981		11	6		2	9			12	10			7				3	1		14					5	4	8	
30		7	Wrexham	3-4	Grayson 2, Baker	2438			6		2	9	11			10			7				3	1							5	4	8	
31		11	HALIFAX TOWN	2-0	Grayson, Toman	1706			6	12	2	9	11			10			7				3	1		5						4	8	
32		15	Hereford United	0-2		2157			6		2	9	11		12	10			7				3	1							5	4	8	
33		18	TORQUAY UNITED	0-1		1351			6	12	2	9	11		10				7				3	1							5	4	8	
34		21	Leyton Orient	3-4	Baker 2 (1p), Atkinson	3408		12	6	10		9	11						7				3	1					2		5	4	8	
35		25	Rotherham United	0-4		4889		7	9				11			10		12			6		3	1				14	2		5	4	8	
36		27	SCUNTHORPE UNITED	0-2		1895			9				11			10					6		3				1	7	2		5	4	8	
37	Apr	1	Carlisle United	1-2	Grayson	3158	7		9				11			10					6		3				1		2		5	4	8	
38		5	Scarborough	0-2		2155	7		9				11			10					6		3				1		2		5	4	8	
39		8	COLCHESTER UNITED	2-1	Tinkler, Baker	1371	7	12	9				11			10							3	1		6			2		5	4	8	
40		11	SCARBOROUGH	3-1	Allon, Baker (p), Dalton	1845	7		9				11			10							3	1		6			2		5	4	8	
41		15	TRANMERE ROVERS	2-2	Baker (p), McKinnon	2355	7		9				11			10							3	1		6			2		5	4	8	
42		22	Rochdale	0-0		1406	7	12	9				11			10							3	1		6			2		5	4	8	
43		29	Exeter City	1-2	Allon	2380	7		9				11			10							3	1		6		12	2	5		4	8	
44	May	1	PETERBOROUGH UTD.	2-1	Grayson, Dalton	1553	7		9				11			10							3	1		6		4	2	5			8	
45		6	BURNLEY	2-2	Grayson, McKinnon	2038	7	14	9			12	11			10							3	1		6		4	2	5			8	
46		13	Grimsby Town	0-3		3801		7	9			6	11			10		2		12			3	1				4		5			8	
						Apps	21	13	40	3	32	19	17	14	19	41	11	2	34	1	4	5	46	23	8	18	5	10	12	19	37	38	45	5
						Goals	3	3	7		1	1	2	4	1	13			1				2							2	1	3	6	

F.A. Cup

							Allon JB	Atkinson PD	Baker DP	Barras A	Barratt A	Borthwick JR	Dalton P	Dixon KL	Doig R	Grayson SD	Haigh P	Hepple JA	Honour B	Locker S	McAndrew A	McKellar DN	McKinnon R	Moverley R	Muggleton CD	Nobbs AK	Norton P	Ogden P	Plaskett SC	Smith A	Stokes WD	Tinkler J	Toman JA	Tunks RW
R1	Nov	19	WIGAN ATHLETIC	2-0	Smith, Borthwick	2476			6		11	9		4		10	2		7				3				1			5			8	
R2	Dec	10	NOTTS COUNTY	1-0	Allon	3182	9		6		4					10			7				3	1		2		11		5			8	
R3	Jan	7	BRISTOL CITY	1-0	Baker (p)	4033	12		6		11	9				10			7				3	1		2					5	4	8	
R4		28	BOURNEMOUTH	1-1	Honour	6240	9	11	6		2				12	10			7				3	1							5	4	8	
rep		31	Bournemouth	2-5	Allon, Toman	10142	9	11	6		2					10			7				3	1							5	4	8	

F.L. Cup (Littlewoods Challenge Cup)

							Allon JB	Atkinson PD	Baker DP	Barras A	Barratt A	Borthwick JR	Dalton P	Dixon KL	Doig R	Grayson SD	Haigh P	Hepple JA	Honour B	Locker S	McAndrew A	McKellar DN	McKinnon R	Moverley R	Muggleton CD	Nobbs AK	Norton P	Ogden P	Plaskett SC	Smith A	Stokes WD	Tinkler J	Toman JA	Tunks RW
R1/1	Aug	30	SHEFFIELD UNITED	2-2	Powell (og), Dixon (p)	2480					11	10		9		12	2		7			1	3			14				5	6	4	8	
R1/2	Sep	6	Sheffield United	0-2	a.e.t.	6577		12			11	10		4		9	2		7			1	3					14		5	6		8	

A.M. Cup (Sherpa Van Trophy)

							Allon JB	Atkinson PD	Baker DP	Barras A	Barratt A	Borthwick JR	Dalton P	Dixon KL	Doig R	Grayson SD	Haigh P	Hepple JA	Honour B	Locker S	McAndrew A	McKellar DN	McKinnon R	Moverley R	Muggleton CD	Nobbs AK	Norton P	Ogden P	Plaskett SC	Smith A	Stokes WD	Tinkler J	Toman JA	Tunks RW
PR	Nov	29	Burnley	0-3		3748	9	11	6						4	10			7				3		1	2		12		5			8	
PR	Dec	13	YORK CITY	0-2		1396	9	14	6		2	12			4	10			7				3		1			11			5		8	

1989/90 19th in Division 4

#	Date	Opponent	Score	Scorers	Att	Allon JB	Atkinson PD	Atkinson P	Baker DP	Barras A	Bennyworth IR	Dalton P	Davies KF	Dearden KC	Doig R	Grayson SD	Honour B	Hutchison D	Lamb A	Macdonald G	McEwan S	McKinnon R	Moverley R	Nobbs AK	Ogden P	Olsson P	Plaskett SC	Priestley JA	Siddall B	Sinclair J	Smith M	Tinkler J	Trewick J	Tupling S	Williams PA
1	Aug 19	Halifax Town	0-4		1686		7		9	2		11				10						3			8							4			
2	26	EXETER CITY	0-3		1618	9	13		5	6		11	8		7	10						3		2								4			
3	Sep 1	Southend United	0-3		3236	7			9	6		11	8	1							5	3		2								4			
4	9	GILLINGHAM	1-2	Dalton	1379	7	12		9	6		11		1							5	3		8			2					4			
5	15	Stockport County	0-6		3884	7			9	6		11		1							5	3			8		2					4			
6	23	PETERBOROUGH UTD.	2-2	Allon, Baker	1760	7	12		9	6		11		1					10		8	3		5			2					4			
7	26	Rochdale	0-0		1511	7			9	6		11		1					10		8	3		5			2					4			
8	30	DONCASTER ROVERS	0-6		1757	7			9	6		11		1					10		8	3		5			2					4			
9	Oct 7	SCUNTHORPE UNITED	3-2	Baker, McEwan(p), Tinkler	1815	7			9			11		1				10			6	3		2							5	4	8		
10	14	Burnley	0-0		7450	7	12		9			11		1				10			2	3									5	4	8		6
11	17	Torquay United	3-4	Allon 2, Hutchison	2108	7	12		9			11		1				10			2	3									5	4	8		6
12	21	YORK CITY	1-2	Dalton	2252	7	9					11		1				10			2	3									5	4	8		6
13	28	Carlisle United	0-1		3699	7						11						10	12		2	3	1				9				5	4	8		6
14	31	CAMBRIDGE UNITED	1-2	Hutchison	1695	7	9					11						10	12		5	3	1				2					4	8		6
15	Nov 4	WREXHAM	3-0	McEwan(p), Allon, Dalton	1724	7			2			11						10	12		6	3	1								5	4	8		9
16	11	Aldershot	1-6	Smith	2137	7			2	13		11						10	9		6	3	1				12			4	5		8		
17	25	Chesterfield	1-3	Baker	3488	7			9			11						10				3	1							8	5	4			6
18	Dec 2	HEREFORD UNITED	1-2	Dalton	1491	7			9			11						10				3	1	6						8	5	4			12
19	16	Maidstone United	2-4	Baker, Doig	1501	7			9			11			8				12			3		6				1		10	5	4			
20	26	SCARBOROUGH	4-1	*See below	3698	7			9		6	11			12			13				3		10		2		1			5	4		8	
21	30	GRIMSBY TOWN	4-2	Dalton 2, Bennyworth, Allon	3418	7			9		6	11								12		3		10		2		1			5	4		8	
22	Jan 1	Colchester United	1-3	Dalton	3826	7			9		6	11								12		3		10		2		1			5	4		8	
23	6	LINCOLN CITY	1-1	McKinnon	2499	7			9		6	11								12		3		10		2		1			5	4		8	
24	13	Exeter City	1-3	Allon	4959	7			9		6	11					12		13			3		10		2		1			5	4		8	
25	20	HALIFAX TOWN	2-0	Allon, Smith	2409	7			9		6	11					12			2		3		10				1			5	4		8	
26	27	Gillingham	0-0		3690	7			9		6	12					13			2		3		10		11		1			5	4		8	
27	Feb 7	Peterborough United	2-0	Allon, Tinkler	2813	7			9		6	13					11			2		3		10		12		1			5	4		8	
28	10	STOCKPORT COUNTY	5-0	Baker 4, Macdonald	2938	7			9		6	11					13			2		3		10		12		1			5	4		8	
29	13	SOUTHEND UNITED	1-1	Allon	3578	7			9		6	11					12			2		'3		10		8		1			5	4			
30	17	Hereford United	1-4	Baker	2049	7			9		6	12					11			2		3		10		13		1			5	4		8	
31	24	CHESTERFIELD	3-1	Baker, Dalton, Allon	2907	7			9		6	10					11					3		2				1			5	4		8	
32	Mar 3	Lincoln City	1-4	Allon	3503	7			9		6	10			12		11					3				2		1			5	4		8	
33	6	Doncaster Rovers	2-2	Smith, Allon	2518	7			9		6	10										3		2		11		1			5	4		8	
34	10	ROCHDALE	2-1	Brown (og), Tupling	2771	7			9		6	10			12					11		3		2				1			5	4		8	
35	17	Scunthorpe United	1-0	Dalton	3868	7			9		6	10										3		2		11			1		5	4		8	
36	20	BURNLEY	3-0	Baker, Olsson, Dalton	3187	7		12	9		6	10							13			3		2		11			1		5	4		8	
37	24	TORQUAY UNITED	1-1	Allon	2723	7		12	9		6	10										3		2		11			1		5	4		8	
38	31	York City	1-1	P Atkinson	2891	7		12	9		6	10										3		2		11			1		5	4		8	
39	Apr 7	CARLISLE UNITED	1-0	Allon	3724	7		11	9		6	10										3		2					1		5	4		8	
40	10	Cambridge United	1-2	Smith	3254	7		13	9		6	12						10		2		3				11					5	4		8	
41	14	COLCHESTER UNITED	0-2		3407	7		11	9		6	10								5		3				2			1			4		8	
42	16	Scarborough	1-4	Baker	2762	7		13	9		6	10	5					11		12		3				2			1			4		8	
43	21	MAIDSTONE UNITED	4-2	Berry(og), Allon 2, Baker	2177	7		11	9		6	12								13		3		2		10			1		5	4		8	
44	24	Grimsby Town	0-0		8687	7		11	9		6											3		2		10			1		5	4		8	
45	28	ALDERSHOT	2-0	Dalton, Baker	2638	7		12	9		6	11								13		3		2		10			1		5	4		8	
46	May 5	Wrexham	2-1	Allon, Olsson	2759	7		10	9		6	11								13		3		2		12			1		5	4		8	
		Apps				45	8	11	43	9	27	45	3	10	5	2	9	13	10	16	14	46	6	32	2	23	8	16	11	4	35	45	8	26	8
		Goals				17		1	15		2	11			1			2		1	2	1				2					5	2		1	

Played in one game: SC Berryman (40, at 1), I Bowling (1, at 1), SP Curry (1, 12), I Dunbar (3, at 10), WD Stokes (1, at 5), PM Wilson (41, at 12)
GGJ Carr (2, at 1), G Speirs (2, at 10), D Stokle (1, at 6).
Played in games 4,5 at 10: WP Entwistle. In games 17,18,19 at 2: WJ McStay.
Scorers in game 20: Smith, Baker, Bennyworth, Kamara (og).

Three own goals

F.A. Cup

Rd	Date	Opponent	Score	Scorers	Att	Allon JB	Atkinson PD	Atkinson P	Baker DP	Barras A	Bennyworth IR	Dalton P	Davies KF	Dearden KC	Doig R	Grayson SD	Honour B	Hutchison D	Lamb A	Macdonald G	McEwan S	McKinnon R	Moverley R	Nobbs AK	Ogden P	Olsson P	Plaskett SC	Priestley JA	Siddall B	Sinclair J	Smith M	Tinkler J	Trewick J	Tupling S	Williams PA
R1	Nov 18	HUDDERSFIELD TOWN	0-2		3160	7	13		9	6		11						10	12		2	3	1							8		4			5

F.L. Cup (Littlewoods Challenge Cup)

Rd	Date	Opponent	Score	Scorers	Att	Allon JB	Atkinson PD	Atkinson P	Baker DP	Barras A	Bennyworth IR	Dalton P	Davies KF	Dearden KC	Doig R	Grayson SD	Honour B	Hutchison D	Lamb A	Macdonald G	McEwan S	McKinnon R	Moverley R	Nobbs AK	Ogden P	Olsson P	Plaskett SC	Priestley JA	Siddall B	Sinclair J	Smith M	Tinkler J	Trewick J	Tupling S	Williams PA
R1/1	Aug 23	YORK CITY	3-3	Grayson 2, Baker	1507				9	5		11	8		7	10						3		2								4			
R1/2	29	York City	1-4	Dalton	2236	7			9	6		11	8		12						5	3		2								4			

Played in both games: GGJ Carr (at 1). Played at 6 in R1/1: D Stokle. Played at 10 in R1/2: G Speirs.

A.M. Cup (Leyland DAF Cup)

Rd	Date	Opponent	Score	Scorers	Att	Allon JB	Atkinson PD	Atkinson P	Baker DP	Barras A	Bennyworth IR	Dalton P	Davies KF	Dearden KC	Doig R	Grayson SD	Honour B	Hutchison D	Lamb A	Macdonald G	McEwan S	McKinnon R	Moverley R	Nobbs AK	Ogden P	Olsson P	Plaskett SC	Priestley JA	Siddall B	Sinclair J	Smith M	Tinkler J	Trewick J	Tupling S	Williams PA
PR	Nov 7	York City	1-7	McEwan(p)	1444	7	12		6			11						10	9		5	3	1				2					4	8		
PR	28	ROTHERHAM UNITED	1-4	Baker	818	7	12		9			11	8						10			3	1				2				5	4			6

1990/91 3rd in Division 4: Promoted

							Allon JB	Baker DP	Bennyworth IR	Cox BR	Dalton P	Davies AJ	Davies KF	Duggan AJ	Dunbar I	Fletcher SM	Gabbiadini R	Heaney NA	Honour B	Hutchison D	Lamb A	Macdonald G	MacPhail J	McKinnon R	Nesbitt MT	Nobbs AK	Olsson P	Poole K	Shotton JM	Smith M	Tinkler J	Tupling S
1	Aug	25	Chesterfield	3-2	Tupling, Baker, Fletcher	3821	7	9	6	1	11					10			12					3			2			5	4	8
2	Sep	1	CARDIFF CITY	0-2		2897	7	9	6	1	11			10		12			13					3		5	2				4	8
3		8	Gillingham	0-3		3180	7	12	6	1	11			5		9			10	13				3			2				4	8
4		18	ROCHDALE	2-2	Dalton, O' Shaughnessy(og)	5725	7	9	6	1	11								10				5	3		12	2				4	8
5		22	Carlisle United	0-1		3303	7	9	6	1	11												5	3		10	2		12		4	8
6		29	Blackpool	0-2		4092	7	9	6	1	11								12	13			5	3		10	2				4	8
7	Oct	2	ALDERSHOT	1-0	Allon	1916	7	9	6	1	11								2	4			5	3		10						8
8		6	MAIDSTONE UNITED	1-0	Dalton	2069	7	12	6	1	11								2	4			5	3		10				9		8
9		13	Doncaster Rovers	2-2	Place(og), Allon	2801	7	9	6	1	11									4		12	2	3		10	13			5		8
10		16	YORK CITY	0-1		2746	7	9	6	1	12									13		11	2	3		10	4			5		8
11		20	Wrexham	2-2	Smith, Hutchison	1733	7	9		1	11					13			10	12			6	3		2	4			5		8
12		23	PETERBOROUGH UTD.	2-0	Allon, Baker	2190	7	9	6	1	11					12			10	8			5	3		2	4					13
13		27	HEREFORD UNITED	2-1	Allon(p), Olsson	2139	7	9	6	1	11				12				10	8			5	3		2	4					
14	Nov	3	Northampton Town	2-3	Fletcher, Baker	3342	7	9	6	1	12					11			10	8			5	3		2	4					
15		10	Darlington	1-0	Allon	5113	7	9	6	1	12					11			10				5	3		2	4				13	8
16		24	SCARBOROUGH	2-0	Baker, Tinkler	2122	7	9		1	11		6		12	13			10	8			5	3			2				4	
17	Dec	1	Torquay United	1-0	Allon	2835	7	9	6	1	11	8							10				5	3			2				4	
18		15	LINCOLN CITY	2-0	Allon 2	2055	7	9	6	1	11					12			10				5	3		4	2					8
19		22	Burnley	0-4		8514	7	9	12	1	11	6							10		13		5	3		2	4					8
20	Jan	1	Halifax Town	2-1	Allon 2	1707	7	9	6	1	11								10		12		5	3		2	4					8
21		12	Cardiff City	0-1		2619	7	9	6	1	11								10		13		5	3		2	4				12	8
22		19	CHESTERFIELD	2-0	Allon, Tupling	2134	7	9	6	1	11							13	10				5	3		2	4				12	8
23		26	York City	0-0		3089	7	9	6	1	12							11	10				5	3		2	4					8
24		29	STOCKPORT COUNTY	3-1	Baker, Allon 2	2384	7	9	6	1	12	13						11	10				5	3		2	4					8
25	Feb	5	CARLISLE UNITED	4-1	Allon 2(1p), Honour, Dalton	2670	7	9	6	1	11	12							10		13		5	3		2	4					8
26		16	Scarborough	0-2		1804	7	9	6	1	11								10				5	3		2	4			12		8
27		23	DARLINGTON	0-0		6100	7	9	6	1	11								10				5	3		2					4	8
28		26	Scunthorpe United	1-2	Allon(p)	2220	7	9	6	1	12		13						10				5	3		2				11	4	8
29	Mar	2	TORQUAY UNITED	0-0		2209	7	12	6	1	11					9			10				5	3		2					4	8
30		9	Lincoln City	1-3	Allon	2575	7	9	6	1	11					12			10					3		2				5	4	8
31		12	Aldershot	5-1	Dalton 3, Allon, Tinkler	1579	7	9	6	1	11		13			12			10				3			2				5	4	8
32		16	BLACKPOOL	1-2	McKinnon	2840	7	9	6	1	11					12			10				2	3						5	4	8
33		23	Maidstone United	4-1	Honour 2, Dalton, Baker	1704	7	9	6	1	11								10				2	3						5	4	8
34		26	WALSALL	2-1	Allon 2	2556	7	9	6	1	11								10				2	3		12				5	4	8
35		29	Stockport County	3-1	Baker, Allon 2	5217	7	9	6		11					12			10				5	3		2		1			4	8
36	Apr	1	BURNLEY	0-0		4967	7	9	6		11								10				5	3		2		1			4	8
37		6	Walsall	1-0	Allon	2758	7	9	6		11						12		10				5	3		2		1			4	8
38		9	SCUNTHORPE UNITED	2-0	Dalton, Baker	3040	7	9	6		11								10				5	3		2		1			4	8
39		13	HALIFAX TOWN	2-1	Baker, Allon	3195	7	9	6		11						12		10				5	3		2	13	1			4	8
40		16	DONCASTER ROVERS	1-1	MacPhail	3363	7	9	6		11						12		10				5	3		2		1			4	8
41		20	WREXHAM	2-1	Allon, Baker	3077	7	9	6		11						13		10				5	3		2	8	1			4	12
42		23	Rochdale	0-0		1686	7	9			11						10						5	3	2	6	4	1				8
43		27	Peterborough United	1-1	Allon	7636	7	9	6		11								10				5	3		2	8	1				4
44		30	GILLINGHAM	1-0	Allon	3782	7	9	6		11								10				5	3		2	8	1				4
45	May	4	Hereford United	3-1	Baker, Dalton 2	2387	7	9	6		11								10				5	3		2	8	1				4
46		11	NORTHAMPTON T	3-1	Dalton, Allon, Baker	6957	7	9	6		11								10				5	3		2	8	1				4
						Apps	46	46	43	34	46	4	3	2	2	14	5	3	42	11	4	2	42	45	1	40	31	12	1	12	26	42
						Goals	28	12			11					2			3	1			1	1			1			1	2	2

Two own goals

F.A. Cup

							Allon JB	Baker DP	Bennyworth IR	Cox BR	Dalton P	Davies AJ	Davies KF	Duggan AJ	Dunbar I	Fletcher SM	Gabbiadini R	Heaney NA	Honour B	Hutchison D	Lamb A	Macdonald G	MacPhail J	McKinnon R	Nesbitt MT	Nobbs AK	Olsson P	Poole K	Shotton JM	Smith M	Tinkler J	Tupling S
R1	Nov	17	Runcorn	3-0	Allon 3	1695	7	9	6	1	11					12			10	8			5	3			4				2	
R2	Dec	8	Wigan Athletic	0-2		2492	7	9	6	1	11	8							10				5	3		12	2				4	

F.L. Cup (Rumbelows Cup)

							Allon JB	Baker DP	Bennyworth IR	Cox BR	Dalton P	Davies AJ	Davies KF	Duggan AJ	Dunbar I	Fletcher SM	Gabbiadini R	Heaney NA	Honour B	Hutchison D	Lamb A	Macdonald G	MacPhail J	McKinnon R	Nesbitt MT	Nobbs AK	Olsson P	Poole K	Shotton JM	Smith M	Tinkler J	Tupling S
R1/1	Aug	28	Chesterfield	2-1	Allon, Honour	2934	7	9	6	1	11		10						12					3		5	2				4	8
R1/2	Sep	11	CHESTERFIELD	2-2	Allon, Baker	2911	7	9	6	1	11			12					13					3		10	2				4	8
R2/1	Sep	26	Tottenham Hotspur	0-5		19760	7	9	6	1	11								13	12				3		10	2			5	4	8
R2/2	Oct	9	TOTTENHAM HOTSPUR	1-2	Dalton	9631	7	9	6	1	11								2	4		13		3		10	12			5		8

Played at 5 in R1/2: A Harbron

A.M. Cup (Leyland DAF Cup)

							Allon JB	Baker DP	Bennyworth IR	Cox BR	Dalton P	Davies AJ	Davies KF	Duggan AJ	Dunbar I	Fletcher SM	Gabbiadini R	Heaney NA	Honour B	Hutchison D	Lamb A	Macdonald G	MacPhail J	McKinnon R	Nesbitt MT	Nobbs AK	Olsson P	Poole K	Shotton JM	Smith M	Tinkler J	Tupling S
PR	Nov	28	Huddersfield Town	4-1	Dalton 2, Allon, Olsson	1405	7	9	8	1	11	6				13			10				5	3			2				4	12
PR	Dec	18	BRADFORD CITY	0-4		1147	7	9	6	1	11								10				5	3		2	12				4	8
R1	Jan	22	Bradford City	2-3	Baker, Allon	2308	7	9	6	1	11	10											5	3		2					4	8

1991/92 11th in Division 3

No	Date	Opponent	Score	Scorers	Att	Baker DP	Bennyworth IR	Cross P	Dalton P	Davies AJ	Fletcher SM	Gabbiadini R	Hodge MJ	Honour B	Johnrose L	Johnson DA	Jones S	McCreery D	McGuckin TI	McKinnon R	MacPhail J	Nesbitt MT	Nobbs AK	Olsson P	Peake JW	Rush D	Saville AV	Smith A (3)	Smith M	Southall LN	Thomas JW	Tinkler J	Tupling S
1	Aug 17	Torquay United	1-3	Baker	4163	9	6		11				1	10				4		3	12	2	5	8		7							
2	24	READING	2-0	Baker, Olsson	2858	9	6		11				1	10				4		3	5		2	8		7						12	
3	31	Bradford City	1-1	Rush	5872	9	6		11				1	10				4		3	5		2	8		7						12	
4	Sep 3	BRENTFORD	1-0	Gabbiadini	3660		6		11		9	12	1	10						3	5		2	8		7						4	
5	7	LEYTON ORIENT	2-3	Dalton, Rush	3581		6		11		9	12	1	10						3	5		2	8		7						4	
6	14	Exeter City	1-1	Baker(p)	2906	9	6		11				1	10						3	5		2	8		7						4	
7	17	Stoke City	2-3	Baker, Olsson	9419	9	6		11				1	10				12		3	5		2	8		7						4	13
8	21	BIRMINGHAM CITY	1-0	Baker	4643	9	6		11				1	10						3	5		2	8		7						4	
9	28	Bury	1-1	Gabbiadini	2600	9	6		11			12	1	10				7		3	5		2	8								4	
10	Oct 5	WIGAN ATHLETIC	4-3	Honour, Dalton 2, McKinnon	3047	9	6		11		12	7	1	10						3	5		2	8								4	13
11	12	Bournemouth	0-2		4817	9			11			12	1	10						3	5		2	8					6	7		4	
12	19	HULL CITY	2-3	Southall 2	2868	9			11				1	10						3	5		2	8					6	7		4	
13	26	Peterborough United	2-3	Bennyworth, Honour	3385	9	6		11			12	1	10				4		3	5		2	8						7			
14	Nov 2	Darlington	0-4		5041		6		11			12	1	10		9		13		3	5		2	8						7		4	
15	5	WEST BROMWICH ALB.	0-0		2970				11		9		1	10				4		3	5		2	8						12		7	6
16	9	FULHAM	2-0	Honour, Morgan(og)	2999				11		9		1	10				4		3	5		2	8						12		7	6
17	23	Shrewsbury Town	4-1	Olsson 2, Dalton, Baker	2368	9			11				1	10		7				3	5		2	8						12		4	6
18	30	HUDDERSFIELD T	0-0		4017	9			11				1	10		7				3	5		2	8					13	12		4	6
19	Dec 14	Preston North End	4-1	Baker 2, Dalton, Johnson	5034	9			11				1	10		7		4		3	5			8					2				6
20	20	Reading	1-0	Baker	2535	9			11				1	10		7		4		3	5		2	8								12	6
21	26	BRADFORD CITY	1-0	Baker	5413	9							1	10		7		4		3	5		2	8					11				6
22	28	TORQUAY UNITED	1-1	Johnson	3812	9			11				1	10		7		4		3	5		2	8								12	6
23	Jan 1	Brentford	0-1		7102	9			11				1	10				4		3	5		2	8						7		12	6
24	11	CHESTER CITY	1-0	Honour	3088	9			11		7		1	10				4			5		2	8				3				12	6
25	18	Bolton Wanderers	2-2	Olsson, Kelly(og)	6129	9			11		7		1	10							5		2	8				3		12		4	6
26	Feb 1	Hull City	2-0	Dalton, Baker	3483	9		3	11				1	10							5		2	8				7		12		4	6
27	8	PETERBOROUGH UTD.	0-1		2479	9		3	11			13	1	10				4			5		2	8						7		12	6
28	11	Huddersfield Town	0-1		5559	9		3	11			12	1	10							5		2	8						7		4	6
29	15	PRESTON NORTH END	2-0	Peake, Baker	2140	9		3	11				1	10							5		2	8	7							4	6
30	18	STOCKPORT COUNTY	0-1		2473	9		3	11				1	10							5		2	8	7			12				4	6
31	22	Chester City	0-2		1072	9		3	11				1	10							5		2	8	7			6		12		4	13
32	29	SWANSEA CITY	0-1		2669	9		3			12		1	10	7						5		2	8	11				6			4	
33	Mar 3	BOLTON WANDERERS	0-4		2254	9		3					1	10	7			12			5			8	11				6			4	2
34	6	Stockport County	1-0	Baker	4473	9		3	11				1	10	7			2			5			8	13				6	12		4	
35	11	West Bromwich Albion	2-1	Dalton 2(1p)	10307			3	11	6	9		1	10	7			2			5			8								4	
36	14	DARLINGTON	2-0	Saville, Dalton	4442			3	11	6			1	10	9			2	5					8			7					4	
37	20	Fulham	0-1		4359			3	11	12	7		1	10	9			2	5				6	8								4	
38	28	SHREWSBURY TOWN	4-2	Thomas,Dalton,Fletcher,Johnrose(p)	2515			3	11		12		1	10	9			2	5				6	8							7	4	
39	31	EXETER CITY	3-1	Dalton 2, Southall	2222			3	11				1	10	9			2	5				6	8						12	7	4	
40	Apr 4	Leyton Orient	0-4		4245			3	11		12		1	10	9			2	5				6	8							7	4	
41	11	STOKE CITY	1-1	Olsson	4362			3	11		10				9		1	2	5		4		6	8						7	12		
42	18	Birmingham City	1-2	Fletcher	13698			3	11		10				9		1	2	5		4		6	8						7	12		
43	20	BURY	0-0		2503			3	11		10				9		1	2			5		6	8						4	7		
44	24	Wigan Athletic	1-1	MacPhail	2002			3	11		10				9		1	2			5		6	8						4	7	12	
45	28	Swansea City	1-1	Dalton	2167			3	11		10				9		1	2			5		6	8						7		4	
46	May 2	BOURNEMOUTH	1-0	Johnrose	2612			3	11		10				9		1	2			5		6	8						7		4	12
					Apps	29	12	21	43	3	18	9	40	40	15	7	6	30	7	23	41	1	41	46	6	8	1	5	8	22	7	39	21
					Goals	13	1		13		2	2		4	2	2				1	1			6	1	2	1			3	1		

Two own goals

F.A. Cup

Rd	Date	Opponent	Score	Scorers	Att	Baker DP	Bennyworth IR	Cross P	Dalton P	Davies AJ	Fletcher SM	Gabbiadini R	Hodge MJ	Honour B	Johnrose L	Johnson DA	Jones S	McCreery D	McGuckin TI	McKinnon R	MacPhail J	Nesbitt MT	Nobbs AK	Olsson P	Peake JW	Rush D	Saville AV	Smith A (3)	Smith M	Southall LN	Thomas JW	Tinkler J	Tupling S
R1	Nov 16	SHREWSBURY TOWN	3-2	Tinkler, Johnson, Baker(p)	2864	9			11				1	10		7				3	5		2	8						12		4	6
R2	Dec 17	Darlington	2-1	Dalton, Honour	5509	9			11				1	10		7		4		3	5		2	8									6
R3	Jan 4	Ipswich Town	1-1	Baker	12507	9			11		12		1					4		3	5		2	8						7		10	6
rep	15	IPSWICH TOWN	0-2		6700	9			11		7		1	10				4			5		2	8						12		3	6

F.L. Cup (Rumbelows Cup)

Rd	Date	Opponent	Score	Scorers	Att	Baker DP	Bennyworth IR	Cross P	Dalton P	Davies AJ	Fletcher SM	Gabbiadini R	Hodge MJ	Honour B	Johnrose L	Johnson DA	Jones S	McCreery D	McGuckin TI	McKinnon R	MacPhail J	Nesbitt MT	Nobbs AK	Olsson P	Peake JW	Rush D	Saville AV	Smith A (3)	Smith M	Southall LN	Thomas JW	Tinkler J	Tupling S
R1/1	Aug 20	BURY	1-0	Baker	2833	9	6		11			7	1	10				4		3	5		2	8								12	
R1/2	27	Bury	2-2	Gabbiadini, Fletcher	1917	9	6		11		12	7	1	10				4		3			2	8								13	5
R2/1	Sep 25	CRYSTAL PALACE	1-1	Honour	6697	9	6		11			7	1	10				12		3	5		2	8								4	
R2/2	Oct 8	Crystal Palace	1-6	Tinkler	9153	9	6		11		12	7	1	10						3	5		2	8								4	13

A.M. Cup (Autoglass Trophy)

Rd	Date	Opponent	Score	Scorers	Att	Baker DP	Bennyworth IR	Cross P	Dalton P	Davies AJ	Fletcher SM	Gabbiadini R	Hodge MJ	Honour B	Johnrose L	Johnson DA	Jones S	McCreery D	McGuckin TI	McKinnon R	MacPhail J	Nesbitt MT	Nobbs AK	Olsson P	Peake JW	Rush D	Saville AV	Smith A (3)	Smith M	Southall LN	Thomas JW	Tinkler J	Tupling S
PR	Nov 19	Bradford City	3-3	Tinkler, Baker, Fletcher	1562	9			11		12		1	10						3			2	8					5	7		4	6
PR	Jan 7	HULL CITY	2-0	Dalton, Baker	1550	9			11		10		1								5		2	8				3		7		4	6
R1	21	SCUNTHORPE UNITED	2-1	Honour, Tinkler	1351	9			11		7		1	10							5		2	8				3		12		4	6
R2	Feb 4	Stockport County	0-3		2255	9			11			12	1	10							5		2	8						3		4	6

Played at 7 in R2: PDZ Thompson

1992/93

16th in the new Football League Division 3

							Cross P	Cross R	Ellison AL	Emerson D	Gallacher J	Gilchrist PA	Hodge MJ	Honour B	Johnrose L	Johnson DA	Jones S	Lynch CJ	McGuckin TI	MacPhail J	Nobbs AK	Olsson P	Peverell NJ	Proudlock P	Saville AV	Skedd AS	Southall LN	Tait MP	Talia F	Thompson PDZ	Wratten P
1	Aug	15	READING	1-1	Saville(p)	4129	3	2		6	11		1	10	7					5		8			9			4			
2		22	Rotherham United	0-0		4427	3	2		6	11		1	10	7					5		8			9		12	4			
3		29	HUDDERSFIELD T	1-0	Olsson	4120	3	2		6			1	10	7					5		8			9		11	4			
4	Sep	1	CHESTER CITY	2-0	R.Cross, Emerson	2983	3	2		6			1		7					5	10	8			9		11	4			
5		5	Bournemouth	2-0	R.Cross, Saville	4446	3	2		6			1		7					5	10	8			9		11	4			
6		11	Wigan Athletic	2-2	Saville 2	2073	3	2		6			1		7					5	10	8		12	9		11	4			
7		15	LEYTON ORIENT	0-2		3286	3	2		6	12		1		7					5	10	8		13	9		11	4			
8		19	PORT VALE	1-1	Olsson	2815	3	13		6	11		1		7					5	10	8		2	9		12	4			
9		26	Preston North End	2-0	Gallacher, Johnrose	4347	3	2		6	11		1		7					5	10	8			9			4			
10	Oct	2	BLACKPOOL	1-0	Saville(p)	2675	3	2		6	11		1	12	7					5	10	8		13	9			4			
11		10	Bolton Wanderers	2-1	Johnrose, Saville	5097	3	2		6			1	11	7						10	8		5	9		12	4			
12		17	SWANSEA CITY	0-1		4396	3	2					1	11	7						10	8		5	9		12	4			6
13		24	Brighton & Hove Albion	1-1	Honour	5918	3	2		6			1	11	7					5	10	8			9		12	4			
14		31	BRADFORD CITY	2-0	Southall, Wratten	4349	3	2		6			1	10						5		8			9		7	4			11
15	Nov	3	West Bromwich Albion	1-3	Southall	13046	3	2		6	12		1	10	13					5		8			9		7	4			11
16		7	EXETER CITY	1-3	P.Cross	2893	3	2		6				10	12		1		5			8			9		7	4			11
17		28	STOCKPORT COUNTY	3-2	Johnrose, McGuckin, Saville	2949	3	2		6			1	10	7	11			4	5		8			9						
18	Dec	12	Plymouth Argyle	2-2	Johnrose, Saville	5996	3	2		6			1	10	7	11			4	5		8			9						
19		19	STOKE CITY	1-2	Honour	4136	3	2		6		4	1	10	7	11				5		8	13		9		12				
20		26	HULL CITY	1-0	Johnrose	4232	3	2		6		4		10	7		1			5		8			9		11				
21		28	Fulham	3-1	Saville 2(1p), Southall	4403	3	2		6	12	4		10	7		1			5		8			9		11				
22	Jan	9	Leyton Orient	0-0		5531	3	2		6		4		10	7					5		8			9		11		1		
23		16	PRESTON NORTH END	0-0		2748	3	2		6		4		10	7					5		8	11		9		13		1		12
24		27	Huddersfield Town	0-3		4153	3	2			11	4		10	7					5			13		9		8	6	1		12
25		30	ROTHERHAM UNITED	0-2		3869	3				11			10	7				2	5			8		9			6	1	12	4
26	Feb	6	Reading	0-2		3431	3				11	6		10	7				2	5	8				9		12		1		4
27		9	Port Vale	0-2		6629	3	2			11	4		10	7				12	5					9		6		1		8
28		13	BOURNEMOUTH	0-1		2197	3	2			11	4		10	7					5			13		9		12	6	1		8
29		16	Mansfield Town	0-2		2655	3	2			11	4		10	7					5					9		8	6	1		
30		20	Chester City	0-1		1912	3				11	4		10	7				13	5			12		9		2	6	1		8
31		27	BOLTON WANDERERS	0-2		2717					11	4		10	7					5	2	8			9		3	6	1		
32	Mar	2	WIGAN ATHLETIC	0-0		1791						4		10	7				3	5	2	8			9		11	6	1		
33		6	Blackpool	1-1	Saville	4926						4		10	7				3	5	2	8	12		9		11	6	1		
34		9	BURNLEY	0-0		3021						4		10	7				3	5	2	8	12		9		11	6	1		
35		13	Exeter City	1-3	Tait	2636						4		10					3	5	2	8	7		9		11	6	1		12
36		20	WEST BROMWICH ALB.	2-2	Saville 2(1p)	3697				6		4	1	10					3	5	2	8	7		9			11			12
37		23	Stockport County	1-4	Southall	4154				6		4	1	10					3	5	2	8	7				9	11			12
38		27	MANSFIELD TOWN	0-1		2316		2	9	6	12	4	1	10						5	3	8	13				7	11			
39	Apr	3	Burnley	0-3		8226	13	2	9	6	12	4	1							5	3	8					7	11			10
40		5	PLYMOUTH ARGYLE	1-0	Honour	1822		2		6	9	4	1	10						5	3	8	12				7	11			
41		10	Hull City	2-3	Ellison, Southall	3562	3	2	9	6	10	4	1		12						5	8	13				7	11			
42		12	FULHAM	0-3		2361	3			6	9	4	1	10						5	2	8	12				7	11			
43		17	Stoke City	1-0	Johnrose	17331	3	2				4	1	10	9					5	6	8	12				7	11			
44		24	Swansea City	0-3		5301	3		12	6			1	10	9				4	5	11	8	7				2				
45	May	1	BRIGHTON & HOVE ALB	2-0	Southall, Peverell	2693	3			6			1	10	9					5	2	8	7				11	4			
46		8	Bradford City	2-0	MacPhail, Thompson	5612	3	2		6			1		9			12		5	4	8	10			11	7			13	
						Apps	37	33	4	32	21	24	29	37	38	3	3	1	14	42	27	39	19	6	36	1	39	35	14	2	15
						Goals	1	2	1	1	1			3	6				1	1		2	1		13		6	1		1	1

F.A. Cup

							Cross P	Cross R	Ellison AL	Emerson D	Gallacher J	Gilchrist PA	Hodge MJ	Honour B	Johnrose L	Johnson DA	Jones S	Lynch CJ	McGuckin TI	MacPhail J	Nobbs AK	Olsson P	Peverell NJ	Proudlock P	Saville AV	Skedd AS	Southall LN	Tait MP	Talia F	Thompson PDZ	Wratten P
R1	Nov	14	Doncaster Rovers	2-1	Johnrose, Saville(p)	4513	3	2		6			1	10	7					5		8			9			4			11
R2	Dec	6	SOUTHPORT	4-0	Peverell, Saville 3	4171	3	2		6			1	10	7				4	5		8	11		9		12				13
R3	Jan	2	CRYSTAL PALACE	1-0	Saville(p)	6721	3	2		6		4		10	7		1			5		8			9		11				
R4		23	Sheffield United	0-1		20074	3	2		6		4		10	7		1			5		8			9		11				

F.L. Cup (Coca Cola Cup)

							Cross P	Cross R	Ellison AL	Emerson D	Gallacher J	Gilchrist PA	Hodge MJ	Honour B	Johnrose L	Johnson DA	Jones S	Lynch CJ	McGuckin TI	MacPhail J	Nobbs AK	Olsson P	Peverell NJ	Proudlock P	Saville AV	Skedd AS	Southall LN	Tait MP	Talia F	Thompson PDZ	Wratten P
R1/1	Aug	18	Halifax Town	2-1	MacPhail, Johnrose	1370	3	2		6	11		1	10	7					5		8			9		12	4			
R1/2		25	HALIFAX TOWN	3-2	Johnrose 2, Southall	2191	3	2		6			1	10	7					5		8			9		11	4			
R2/1	Sep	23	Sheffield Wednesday	0-3		10112	3	2		6	11		1		7					5	10	8			9			4			12
R2/2	Oct	6	SHEFFIELD WEDNESDAY	2-2	Saville(p), Johnrose	4667	3	2		6			1	11	7					5	10	8			9			4			

A.M. Cup (Autoglass Trophy)

							Cross P	Cross R	Ellison AL	Emerson D	Gallacher J	Gilchrist PA	Hodge MJ	Honour B	Johnrose L	Johnson DA	Jones S	Lynch CJ	McGuckin TI	MacPhail J	Nobbs AK	Olsson P	Peverell NJ	Proudlock P	Saville AV	Skedd AS	Southall LN	Tait MP	Talia F	Thompson PDZ	Wratten P
PR	Dec	8	SCARBOROUGH	4-1	Olsson, Johnson, Honour, Saville	1193	3	2			11		1	10	7				4	5					9		8	6			
PR		15	Carlisle United	0-2		859	3	2		6		4	1	10	7	11				5		8	12		9						
R1	Jan	12	Stockport County	0-1		2383	3	2		6	12	4		10	7					5		8			9		11		1		

1993/94

23rd in Division 2: Relegated

	Date	Opponent	Score	Scorers	Att	Carter TD	Cross P	Cross R	Emerson D	Gallacher J	Garrett S	Gilchrist PA	Halliday SW	Honour B	Houchen KM	Ingram SD	Johnrose L	Jones S	Lynch CJ	MacPhail J	McGuckin TI	Oliver K	Olsson P	Peverell NJ	Skedd AS	Southall LN	Tait MP	Thompson PDZ	West CW	Wratten P
1	Aug 14	FULHAM	0-1		2542	1	3	2	6	7		13		10						5	4			11		12			9	8
2	21	Brighton & Hove Albion	1-1	Gallacher	5230	1	3	2	12	7				10						5	4					11	6		9	8
3	28	BOURNEMOUTH	1-1	Honour	2482	1	3	2	6			4		10						5				13		11	7	12	9	8
4	31	Leyton Orient	2-1	West, Southall	3399	1	3	2	6					10						5	4			12		11		7	9	8
5	Sep 4	Exeter City	1-2	Southall	2644	1	3	2	6					10						5	4			12		11		7	9	8
6	11	STOCKPORT COUNTY	1-0	Thompson	2473	1	3	2	6					10			12			5	4					11		7	9	8
7	14	BLACKPOOL	2-0	West, Honour	2214	1	3	2	6					10			12			5	4					11		7	9	8
8	18	Port Vale	0-1		7279	1	3	2	6					10			12			5	4					11		7	9	8
9	25	YORK CITY	0-2		3050	1	3	2	6					10			12			5	4					11		7	9	8
10	Oct 2	Burnley	0-2		9528	1	3	2	6			12		10	9		11			5	4								7	8
11	9	BRENTFORD	0-1		1802	1	3	2	6			13		10	9		11			5	4		12						7	8
12	16	Cambridge United	0-1		3318	1	3	2	6			4			9		10			5			11	13		12	7			8
13	23	BRADFORD CITY	1-2	Johnrose	2536	1	3	2	6						9		10			5	4		11	12			7			8
14	30	Cardiff City	2-2	Johnrose, West	3710	1	3	2							9		10			5	4		6	12			7		11	8
15	Nov 2	BARNET	2-1	Houchen, Johnrose	1960	1	3	2				12			9		10			5	4		6				7		11	8
16	6	Bristol Rovers	1-1	West	5205	1	3	2				7			9		10			5	4		6						11	8
17	20	WREXHAM	1-2	Southall	1530	1						3	10		9	2	8			5	4		12		11	7	6			
18	27	Plymouth Argyle	0-2		5881	1		2				6		10	9		8			5					3	7	4		12	11
19	Dec 4	Blackpool	1-2	Stoneman(og)	3121							6		10	9	2		1		5	12		13		3	7	4		11	8
20	11	BRIGHTON & HOVE ALB	2-2	Southall, Honour(p)	1558							6		10	9	2		1			5				3	7	4		11	8
21	17	Fulham	0-2		2998							6		10	9	2		1	12	5					3	7	4	13	11	8
22	27	HUDDERSFIELD T	1-4	Southall(p)	3286									10	9	2		1	3	5			6		12	7	4	13	11	8
23	28	Hull City	0-1		4607							6			9			1	3	5			4		10	7	2		11	8
24	Jan 1	ROTHERHAM UNITED	2-0	Houchen 2	2101							6			9			1	3	5			4		10	7	2		11	8
25	8	Reading	0-4		6217							6			9			1	3	5			4		10	7	2		11	8
26	15	CAMBRIDGE UNITED	0-2		1690							6	12					1	3	5			4	13	10	7	2	9	11	8
27	22	Brentford	0-1		6334							6	13			2		1	3	12	5		4		10	7	11	9		8
28	28	Swansea City	1-1	Thompson	2573								11		9	2		1	3	12	5		4		10	7	6	13		8
29	Feb 5	Bradford City	1-2	Thompson	7907							11	13		9	2		1	3		5		4		10	7	6	12		8
30	12	READING	1-4	McGuckin	2218							11	13		9	2		1	3		5		4		10	7	6	12		8
31	19	Bournemouth	0-0		3201							11			9			1	3		5		4		10	2	6	7		8
32	26	EXETER CITY	1-2	McGuckin	1695							6	11	10	9			1	3	12	5		4			2		7	13	8
33	Mar 5	Stockport County	0-5		4076						2	3			9			1		6	5	13	4	12		11		7	10	8
34	8	LEYTON ORIENT	1-1	Southall	1251						2	3			9			1		4	5				6	11		7	10	8
35	12	PORT VALE	1-4	MacPhail	1798						2	3			9			1		4	5		8	12	6	11		7	10	
36	19	York City	0-3		3191						2	3			9			1		4	5		8		6	11		7	10	
37	22	CARDIFF CITY	3-0	Olsson, Southall(p), Houchen	1077						2	4			9			1	3		5		8		6	11		7		10
38	26	BURNLEY	4-1	Houchen 2, Southall, Thompson	2879						2	4			9			1	3		5		8		6	11		7	12	10
39	29	SWANSEA CITY	1-0	Houchen	1354						2	4			9			1	3		5		8	13	6	11		7	12	10
40	Apr 2	Huddersfield Town	1-1	West	5717						2	4			9			1	3		5		8			11		7	6	10
41	4	HULL CITY	0-1		2448						2	4			9			1	3		5		8			11		7	6	10
42	9	Rotherham United	0-7		2792						2	4						1	3		5		8	9		11	12	7	6	10
43	23	BRISTOL ROVERS	2-1	Houchen, Peverell	1409						2	4	10		9	3		1					7	8		11	5			6
44	26	Barnet	2-3	Southall, Olsson	1352						2	4	10		9	3		1			13		7	8		11	5		12	6
45	30	Wrexham	0-2		2090						2	12	10		9	3		1			5		7	8		11	4		13	6
46	May 7	PLYMOUTH ARGYLE	1-8	Peverell	2389						2	5	10		9	3		1	13				7	8	6	11	4		12	
					Apps	18	16	17	13	2	14	35	11	17	34	13	13	28	19	32	35	1	32	16	22	40	26	26	36	42
					Goals					1				3	8		3			1	2		2	2		9		4	5	

One own goal

F.A. Cup

	Date	Opponent	Score	Scorers	Att	Carter TD	Cross P	Cross R	Emerson D	Gallacher J	Garrett S	Gilchrist PA	Halliday SW	Honour B	Houchen KM	Ingram SD	Johnrose L	Jones S	Lynch CJ	MacPhail J	McGuckin TI	Oliver K	Olsson P	Peverell NJ	Skedd AS	Southall LN	Tait MP	Thompson PDZ	West CW	Wratten P
R1	Nov 13	Macclesfield Town	0-2		2747	1		2				7		12	9		10			5	4		6		3	13			11	8

F.L. Cup (Coca Cola Cup)

	Date	Opponent	Score	Scorers	Att	Carter TD	Cross P	Cross R	Emerson D	Gallacher J	Garrett S	Gilchrist PA	Halliday SW	Honour B	Houchen KM	Ingram SD	Johnrose L	Jones S	Lynch CJ	MacPhail J	McGuckin TI	Oliver K	Olsson P	Peverell NJ	Skedd AS	Southall LN	Tait MP	Thompson PDZ	West CW	Wratten P
R1/1	Aug 17	Stockport County	1-1	West	2915	1	3	2		7				10						5	4					11			9	8
R1/2	24	STOCKPORT COUNTY	2-1	Tait, Honour	2273	1	3	2	6			13		10						5	4			12		11	7		9	8
R2/1	Sep 21	Grimsby Town	0-3		2353	1	3	2	6					10			12			5	4					11		7	9	8
R2/2	Oct 5	GRIMSBY TOWN	0-2		1385	1	3	2	6					10	9		11			5	4		12						7	8

Played at 6 in R1/1: AK Nobbs

A.M. Cup (Autoglass Trophy)

	Date	Opponent	Score	Scorers	Att	Carter TD	Cross P	Cross R	Emerson D	Gallacher J	Garrett S	Gilchrist PA	Halliday SW	Honour B	Houchen KM	Ingram SD	Johnrose L	Jones S	Lynch CJ	MacPhail J	McGuckin TI	Oliver K	Olsson P	Peverell NJ	Skedd AS	Southall LN	Tait MP	Thompson PDZ	West CW	Wratten P
PR	Sep 28	DARLINGTON	1-1	Honour	1454	1	3	2	6					10			9			5	4		11	7					12	8
PR	Nov 9	York City	0-2		1630	1	3	2	14			7	12		9		10			5	4		6						11	8

1994/95 18th in Division 3

						Ainsley J	Burgess DJ	Cook MC	Daughtry PW	Foster WP	Gilchrist PA	Halliday SW	Henderson DM	Holmes SP	Honour B	Horne BS	Houchen KM	Hyson MA	Ingram SD	Jones S	Lynch CJ	MacPhail J	McCreery D	McGuckin TI	Oliver K	Reddish S	Skedd AS	Sloan SM	Southall LN	Sunley M	Sweeney PMF	Tait MP	Thompson PDZ	Walsh A
1	Aug 13	Gillingham	0-0		2959	7					4				10	1	9		2					5	6			8	11		3			
2	20	DARLINGTON	1-0	Lynch	3053						4	12				1	9		2		10			5	6		3	8	11				7	
3	27	Bury	0-2		2145	6					4	8				1	9	12	2		10			5			3		11				7	
4	30	BARNET	0-1		2098						4	8				1	9	12	2		10			5	6		3		11				7	
5	Sep 3	CHESTERFIELD	0-2		2173	8					4	12				1	9	13	2		10			5	6		3		11				7	
6	10	Colchester United	0-1		2428	8					4					1	9	12	2		10				6		3	11				5	7	
7	13	Northampton Town	1-1	Halliday	2466	8					4	10				1	9		2		3				6			11				5	7	
8	17	GILLINGHAM	2-0	Houchen, Walsh(p)	1756		2				4	10				1	9				12			5	6			11				8	7	3
9	24	LINCOLN CITY	0-3		1537		2				4	10				1	9	11			13			5	6		12					8	7	3
10	Oct 1	Exeter City	1-2	Halliday	2390	11	2				4	10				1	9		8					5	6			12					7	3
11	8	Mansfield Town	0-2		2545	11	2				4	10				1	9		8					5	6			12	7				13	3
12	15	PRESTON NORTH END	3-1	Houchen, Ainsley, Foster	2003	6	2			10	4					1	9		3				8	5				7	11					
13	22	WALSALL	1-1	Houchen	1862	6	2			10	4					1	9		3				8	5				7	11				12	
14	29	Scunthorpe United	0-0		2624	6	2			10	4					1	9		3				8	5				7	11					
15	Nov 5	WIGAN ATHLETIC	0-1		1683	6	2			10	4					1	9		3				8	5			13	7	11				12	
16	19	Doncaster Rovers	0-3		2507	6	2	3			4	12				1			10				13	5		8		9	11				7	
17	26	ROCHDALE	1-0	Sloan	1387		2	3	7		4	12				1						5				8	6	10	11				9	
18	Dec 10	Darlington	2-1	Southall, Houchen	3193		2	3	7		4					1	9							5			6	10	11			8		
19	17	BURY	3-1	Houchen 3	1746			3	7		4					1	9		2					5			6	10	11			8		
20	26	CARLISLE UNITED	1-5	Skedd	3854			3	7		4	12				1			2							8	6	10	11			5	9	
21	27	Torquay United	2-2	Southall(p), Thompson	3172	8		3	7		4					1			2			5						10	11			6	9	
22	31	FULHAM	1-2	Southall(p)	1698	8			7		4					1			2					5			3	10	11			6	9	
23	Jan 14	SCARBOROUGH	3-3	Thompson 2, Sloan	1784			3	7			12				1			2	13		4		5		8		10	11			6	9	
24	28	SCUNTHORPE UNITED	1-4	Thompson	1660			3	7			12							2	1		4		5		8		10	11			6	9	
25	Feb 4	Rochdale	0-1		1848	13		3	7		4	12				1			2					5		8		10	11			6	9	
26	18	Scarborough	2-2	McGuckin, Houchen	1517			3	7							1	9		2				13	5		8	12	10	11			6	4	
27	21	Hereford United	0-1		1741			3	7							1	9		2					5		8		10	11			6	4	
28	25	EXETER CITY	2-2	Houchen, McGuckin	1452			3	7			12				1	9		2					5		8	13	10	11			6	4	
29	28	Wigan Athletic	0-2		1452			3				7				1	9		2			4		5		8	12	10	11	13		6		
30	Mar 4	Lincoln City	0-3		6477			3				7				1	9					5			4	8		10	11	2		6		
31	7	Walsall	1-4	McGuckin	3314			3				7	9			1							8	5	4	2	12	10	11			6		
32	11	COLCHESTER UNITED	3-1	Southall 3(2p)	1371			3				7	10	4		1	9							5	8	2			11			6		
33	18	Barnet	0-4		1557			3	8			7	10	4		1	9		2					5		6			11					
34	21	DONCASTER ROVERS	2-1	Houchen 2	1354				13			7	10	4		1	9		8					5		2	3	12	11			6		
35	25	Chesterfield	0-2		4125				8			7	10			1	9		6					5		2	3		11				4	
36	Apr 1	NORTHAMPTON T	1-1	Houchen	2113			12				7	10			1	9		6				8	5		2	3		11				4	
37	8	Fulham	0-1		3465			3				7	5			1			9		12		8			2	10		11				4	
38	15	TORQUAY UNITED	1-1	Henderson	1596			12				7	5			1	9		6						4	2	3	10	11				8	
39	17	Carlisle United	1-0	Houchen	10242			7					10	6		1	9		2					5	4	8	3		11					
40	22	HEREFORD UNITED	4-0	Holmes 2, Henderson 2	1784			7					10	6		1	9		2		3			5	4	8			11					
41	29	Preston North End	0-3		9129			7				10	6			1	9		2					5	4	8	3		11				12	
42	May 6	MANSFIELD TOWN	3-2	Halliday 3	3049			7				8	10			1	9		6		3			5	4	2			11					
					Apps	15	11	24	15	4	23	28	12	5	1	41	32	5	35	2	11	6	9	34	18	23	23	29	37	2	1	20	28	4
					Goals	1				1		5	3	2			13				1			3			1	2	6				4	1

Played in one game: S Garrett (6, at 13), AM Gourlay (7, at 13), C Homer (37, at 6), NJ Peverell (22, at 12)

F.A. Cup

						Ainsley J	Burgess DJ	Cook MC	Daughtry PW	Foster WP	Gilchrist PA	Halliday SW	Henderson DM	Holmes SP	Honour B	Horne BS	Houchen KM	Hyson MA	Ingram SD	Jones S	Lynch CJ	MacPhail J	McCreery D	McGuckin TI	Oliver K	Reddish S	Skedd AS	Sloan SM	Southall LN	Sunley M	Sweeney PMF	Tait MP	Thompson PDZ	Walsh A
R1	Nov 12	Port Vale	0-6		6199	6					4	10				1	9		2				8	5			13	12	11				7	3

F.L. Cup (Coca Cola Cup)

						Ainsley J	Burgess DJ	Cook MC	Daughtry PW	Foster WP	Gilchrist PA	Halliday SW	Henderson DM	Holmes SP	Honour B	Horne BS	Houchen KM	Hyson MA	Ingram SD	Jones S	Lynch CJ	MacPhail J	McCreery D	McGuckin TI	Oliver K	Reddish S	Skedd AS	Sloan SM	Southall LN	Sunley M	Sweeney PMF	Tait MP	Thompson PDZ	Walsh A
R1/1	Aug 16	Bury	0-2		1515	7					4				10		9		2	1	12			5	6			8	11		3		13	
R1/2	23	BURY	5-1	*see below	1505						4	12					9		2	1	10			5	6		3	8	11				7	
R2/1	Sep 21	ARSENAL	0-5		4421		2				4	10				1	9	12	13		11			5	6							8	7	3
R2/2	Oct 5	Arsenal	0-2		20250	11	2				4	10				1	9		8					5	6		12	13					7	3

R1/2 a.e.t.. Scorers Houchen, Southall 2, Jackson (og), Thompson

A.M. Cup (Auto Windscreens Shield)

						Ainsley J	Burgess DJ	Cook MC	Daughtry PW	Foster WP	Gilchrist PA	Halliday SW	Henderson DM	Holmes SP	Honour B	Horne BS	Houchen KM	Hyson MA	Ingram SD	Jones S	Lynch CJ	MacPhail J	McCreery D	McGuckin TI	Oliver K	Reddish S	Skedd AS	Sloan SM	Southall LN	Sunley M	Sweeney PMF	Tait MP	Thompson PDZ	Walsh A
PR	Oct 18	Carlisle United	0-2		2563	6				10	4					1	9		2					5	8			7	11				12	3
PR	Nov 8	DARLINGTON	0-2		1211	6				10	4	8				1	9		2					5	7				11					3

1995/96 20th in Division 3

No	Date	Opponent	Score	Scorers	Att	Allinson J	Allon JB	Billing PG	Canham A	Conlon PR	Dixon AP	Ford G	Halliday SW	Henderson DM	Homer C	Horne BS	Houchen KM	Howard SJ	Hutt S	Ingram SD	Jones S	Key LW	Lee GB	Lowe K	Lynch CJ	McAuley S	McGuckin TI	Oliver K	Reddish S	Roberts BJ	Sloan SM	Stokoe G	Tait MP	Walton PA
1	Aug 12	Chester City	0-2		2286			4	11				7	10			9	6		2	1					3	5						8	
2	19	EXETER CITY	0-0		2346			4	11				10	9		1	12	6		2					7	3	5						8	
3	26	Rochdale	0-4		1794			4	2				10	5		1	9	7							11	3		6			12		8	
4	29	NORTHAMPTON T	2-1	Hughes(og), Henderson	2390			4	11				10	9	13	1		6							7	3	5	12	2				8	
5	Sep 2	Doncaster Rovers	0-1		2304			4	11				7	10		1	9							6	12	3	5		2				8	
6	9	DARLINGTON	1-1	Houchen	2706			4	11			12	7	10		1	9							6		3	5		2				8	
7	12	TORQUAY UNITED	2-2	Houchen, Lowe	1945			4	11			7	10			1	9							6	12	3	5	13	2				8	
8	16	Leyton Orient	1-4	Houchen	4520			4	11			7	10	12		1	9							6		3	5		2				8	
9	23	CARDIFF CITY	2-1	Lowe 2	2172			4	7				10	13		1	9							6	3	11	5	12	2				8	
10	30	Cambridge United	1-0	Howard	2849				2				10	4		1	9	11		13	12			6		3	5	7					8	
11	Oct 7	Colchester United	1-4	Howard	2618			4					10	9	12			11		2	1			6		3	5	7					8	
12	14	SCUNTHORPE UNITED	2-0	Howard, Henderson	2603		7	4					10	9	12			11		2				6		3	5						8	
13	21	Wigan Athletic	0-1		2104		7	4						12	10		9	11		2				6		3	5			1			8	
14	28	GILLINGHAM	1-1	Halliday	2355		7	4					12	10			9	11		2				6		3	5		13	1			8	
15	31	BARNET	0-0		1713		7	4					11	6			9	12		2				10	13	3	5		8	1				
16	Nov 4	Lincoln City	1-1	Allon	2939		7	4					13	6			9	12		2				10		3	5		11	1			8	
17	18	PLYMOUTH ARGYLE	2-2	Ingram, Howard	1830			4	11		9		10	6		1	13	12		2				8		3	5				7		14	
18	25	Preston North End	0-3		9466			4	12		7		10	6		1	9	11		2						3	5		13		14		8	
19	Dec 9	Cardiff City	0-2		2934			4			7		10	5		1	9	11		2					3	6					12		8	
20	16	CAMBRIDGE UNITED	1-2	Allon	1612		7	4					10				9	11		2		1			12	3	5		6				8	
21	23	Mansfield Town	3-0	Houchen 2, Halliday	1982			4					10	6		1	9			2					11	3	5	12	7				8	
22	Jan 1	Bury	3-0	Houchen, Halliday, McGuckin	2927			4					10		13	1	9	7					6		11	3	5	8	2		12			
23	6	SCARBOROUGH	1-1	Allon	2252		7	4					10			1		9					6		11	3	5	8	2		12			
24	20	CHESTER CITY	2-1	Halliday, Tait	1864		7	4					10			1	9	12		2					3	11	5		6				8	
25	30	Exeter City	0-1		2468		7	4					10			1	9	12		2					3	11	5		6				8	
26	Feb 3	ROCHDALE	1-1	Tait	1929		7	4					10			1	9	11		2						3	5	12	6				8	
27	10	Fulham	2-2	Allon 2	3700		7	4					10			1	9	11		2						3	5	12	6				8	
28	17	Torquay United	0-0		2580		7		11	13				4		1	9	6					12		10	3	5	8	2					
29	20	DONCASTER ROVERS	0-1		1367		7		12	13				5		1	9	6		4					11	3		10	2				8	
30	24	LEYTON ORIENT	4-1	Conlon, Allon, McGuckin, Lynch	1915		7		11	10				4		1	9	12		2					13	3	5					6	8	
31	27	Darlington	0-1		4332		7		11	10				4		1	9	12		2					13	3	5					6	8	
32	Mar 2	Scarborough	2-1	Conlon 2	2420			4	11	10				7		1	9			2						3	5					6	8	
33	5	HEREFORD UNITED	0-1		1473		7	4	11	10						1		9		2						3	5					6	8	
34	9	MANSFIELD TOWN	1-1	Howard	1758		7	4		10			12			1		9		2					11	3	5					6	8	
35	12	FULHAM	1-0	Conlon	1198					7			10	4		1	9	11		2						3	5					6	8	
36	19	Northampton Town	0-0		3537				12	7			10	4		1	9	11		2						3	5					6	8	
37	23	BURY	1-2	Ingram	1802				12	7			10	4		1	9	11		2						3	5					6	8	
38	30	COLCHESTER UNITED	2-1	Halliday, Howard	1364	14		12	11	7			10	4		1	9	6		2						3	5						8	13
39	Apr 2	Scunthorpe United	1-2	Halliday	2100	5		2	11	7			10	4		1	9	6					13			3							8	12
40	6	Gillingham	0-2		6263	5		7	11				10	4		1	9	6		2	12					3							8	13
41	8	WIGAN ATHLETIC	1-2	Canham	1877	5		2	11	7			10	4			9	6			1					3							8	12
42	13	Barnet	1-5	Halliday	2530		7	2	11				10	4			9	6			1					3	5						8	
43	20	LINCOLN CITY	3-0	Henderson, Allon 2	2112		7	8	11	13			10	4			9	6		2			12			3	5							
44	27	PRESTON NORTH END	0-2		5076		7		11				10	4			9	6		2	1					3	5						8	
45	30	Hereford United	1-4	Howard	4045		7	2	11	12			10	4				6		8	1					3	5							9
46	May 4	Plymouth Argyle	0-3		11526		7		11				10	4				9	13	2	1		6			3	5							12
					Apps	4	22	36	29	15	3	3	39	36	5	32	38	39	1	33	9	1	6	13	19	46	40	13	20	4	6	8	39	6
					Goals		8		1	4			7	3			6	7		2				3	1		2						2	

Played in one game: AC Debont (12, at 1), L Foster (3, at 13), I Gallagher (46, at 8) PD O'Connor (43, at 1), D Slater (41, at 13).

One own goal

F.A. Cup

Rd	Date	Opponent	Score	Scorers	Att	Allinson J	Allon JB	Billing PG	Canham A	Conlon PR	Dixon AP	Ford G	Halliday SW	Henderson DM	Homer C	Horne BS	Houchen KM	Howard SJ	Hutt S	Ingram SD	Jones S	Key LW	Lee GB	Lowe K	Lynch CJ	McAuley S	McGuckin TI	Oliver K	Reddish S	Roberts BJ	Sloan SM	Stokoe G	Tait MP	Walton PA
R1	Nov 11	DARLINGTON	2-4	Sloan, Halliday	3834	3		4					10	6		1		9		2					13	11	5	12			7		8	

F.L. Cup (Coca Cola Cup)

Rd	Date	Opponent	Score	Scorers	Att	Allinson J	Allon JB	Billing PG	Canham A	Conlon PR	Dixon AP	Ford G	Halliday SW	Henderson DM	Homer C	Horne BS	Houchen KM	Howard SJ	Hutt S	Ingram SD	Jones S	Key LW	Lee GB	Lowe K	Lynch CJ	McAuley S	McGuckin TI	Oliver K	Reddish S	Roberts BJ	Sloan SM	Stokoe G	Tait MP	Walton PA
R1/1	Aug 15	Scarborough	0-1		1555			4	11				7	10			9	6		2	1				12	3	5	13					8	
R1/2	22	SCARBOROUGH	1-0	McGuckin	2134			4	11				7	10		1	9	6		2					12	3	5	13					8	
R2/1	Sep 19	ARSENAL	0-3		4945			4	7			14	10	13		1	9							6	3	11	5	12	2				8	
R2/2	Oct 3	Arsenal	0-5		27194			4					10	9	12			11		2	1		14	6	13	3	5	7					8	

R1/2 after extra time. Hartlepool won 7-6 on penalties.

A.M. Cup (Auto Windscreens Shield)

Rd	Date	Opponent	Score	Scorers	Att	Allinson J	Allon JB	Billing PG	Canham A	Conlon PR	Dixon AP	Ford G	Halliday SW	Henderson DM	Homer C	Horne BS	Houchen KM	Howard SJ	Hutt S	Ingram SD	Jones S	Key LW	Lee GB	Lowe K	Lynch CJ	McAuley S	McGuckin TI	Oliver K	Reddish S	Roberts BJ	Sloan SM	Stokoe G	Tait MP	Walton PA
PR	Oct 17	Crewe Alexandra	0-8		2344		7	4	6				10	9	12			11		2	1					3	5						8	
PR	Nov 7	BLACKPOOL	3-2	Howard 2, Allon	888	3	7	4					10	5		12		9		2			13		6	11		8		1	14			

1996/97 20th in Division 3

No	Date		Opponent	Score	Scorers	Att	Allon JB	Baker DP	Barron MJ	Beech CS	Bradley R	Brown MR	Clegg DL	Cooper MN	Cullen DJ	Davies G	Elliott A	Halliday SW	Hislop TK	Houchen KM	Howard SJ	Ingram SD	Irvine SC	Knowles DT	Lee GB	Lucas R	McAuley S	McDonald C	McGuckin TI	Mike AR	O'Connor PD	Pears S	Proctor MG	Sunderland JP	Tait MP	Walton PA
1	Aug	17	Colchester United	2-0	Allon, McAuley	2942	7			4			11	8		5		10			9	2					3	6				1			12	
2		24	FULHAM	2-1	Cooper, Davies	2457				7			12	8		4		10		9		2					3	6	5			1			11	
3		27	MANSFIELD TOWN	2-2	Cooper, Ingram	2750	7			6			9	8		4		10		12		2					3		5			1			11	
4		31	Leyton Orient	0-2		4344	7			9			13	8		4		10		12		2					3	6	5			1			11	
5	Sep	7	Hereford United	1-0	Halliday	2729	7		5	11			9	8		4		10				2					3	6	12			1				
6		10	CARLISLE UNITED	1-2	Cooper	3077	7		5	11			9	8		4		10		13	12	2					3	6				1				
7		14	WIGAN ATHLETIC	1-1	Cooper	2433			5	11			7	8		4		10		9	12	2					3	6				1				
8		21	Hull City	0-1		3886	7		5	11			12	8		4		10	13		9	2					3	6				1				
9		28	CHESTER CITY	2-0	Allon, Cooper(p)	2042	7		5	6			11	8		4		10	12		9						3					1			2	
10	Oct	1	Doncaster Rovers	1-2	Beech	1471	7		5	6			11	8		4		10	12		9	13					3					1			2	
11		5	Cambridge United	0-1		3406			5	7				8				10	11			2			4		3	6		9		1				
12		12	DARLINGTON	1-2	Halliday	3799			5	7			12	8				10	11		13	2			4		3		6	9		1				
13		15	SWANSEA CITY	1-1	Halliday	1810	13		5	7			4	8				10	11		12	2					3		6	9		1				
14		19	Barnet	0-1		2265			5	4			7	8		2		10	11			12					3	6		9		1				
15		26	Exeter City	0-2		3043			5					8		4		10	11		7	2					3			9		1			6	
16		29	NORTHAMPTON T	0-2		1254			5	4			7	8				10	11		13	2					3		6	9		1			12	
17	Nov	2	BRIGHTON & HOVE ALB	2-3	Mike, Cooper	1683	7		5	4			12	8		6		13	11		10						3			9	1				2	
18		9	Scarborough	4-2	Howard, Clegg, Halliday 2	3157			5	4			7	8				10	11		9				2		3		6		1					
19		23	Torquay United	1-0	Allon	1856	7			4			9	8				10	11			2	12		5		3		6		1					
20		30	EXETER CITY	1-1	Irvine	1419	7		8	4			9						11			2	10		5		3		6		1					
21	Dec	3	Scunthorpe United	1-2	Clegg	1778			8	4			7			5			11		9	2	10		6		3				1					
22		14	Rochdale	3-1	Beech, Howard, Allon	1618	7			4			10	8		6			11		9	2			5		3				1					
23		21	LINCOLN CITY	2-1	Cooper(p), Sunderland	1344	7			4				8		10			11		9	2			5		3		6		1			12		
24		26	Carlisle United	0-1		6947	7			4				8		6			11		9	2			5		3				1			10		12
25		28	HEREFORD UNITED	2-1	Allon, Howard	1923	7			4			10	8		3			11		9	2			5				6		1			13	12	
26	Jan	1	HULL CITY	1-1	Beech	1944	7			4			10	8					11		9	2			5		3		6		1					
27	Jan	11	Chester City	0-0		1885	7			4			10	8		6			11		9	2			5		3				1			12		
28		18	DONCASTER ROVERS	2-4	Howard, Cooper(p)	1708	7			4			10	8		6					9	2			5		3				1			11		
29		25	Northampton Town	0-3		5039	7			4			10	8		12					9	2			5		3		6		1			11		
30	Feb	1	SCARBOROUGH	1-0	Cooper	1843	7			4				8							9	2			5		3		6		1			11	10	
31		8	Brighton & Hove Albion	0-5		8412	7			4			12	8							9	2			5		3		6		1			11	10	
32	Feb	11	CARDIFF CITY	2-3	Beech 2	1120				4			8			5	7				9	2					3		6		1			11	10	
33		15	TORQUAY UNITED	1-1	Beech	1548	12			4	6		8				7		11		9	2			5		3				1			13	10	
34		22	Cardiff City	0-2		2971					4		7	8			12	10	11			2			5		3		6		1			13	9	
35	Mar	1	SCUNTHORPE UNITED	0-1		1300	7			9	4			8			12	10	11			2			5		3		6		1					
36		4	Wigan Athletic	2-2	Halliday, Howard	3229				7	4					6		10			9	2			5		3				1				8	11
37		8	Lincoln City	1-2	Allon	2915	7			10	4		12			6					9	2			5		3				1			13	8	11
38		15	ROCHDALE	1-2	Beech	1448	7			8	4		11			6		10	12		9	2					3				1			13	5	
39		22	Fulham	0-1		7222				8	4		12			6		10	11		9	2	13				3				1		7		5	14
40		29	COLCHESTER UNITED	1-0	Beech	2725		9		4	5	10			7	6		12	11					2	13	3					1		8			
41		31	Mansfield Town	0-1		2229		9		4	5	10			7	6		12	11		13			2		3					1		8			
42	Apr	5	LEYTON ORIENT	3-1	Bradley, Baker, Halliday	2576	7	9			5	11	12	8	4			10						2	6	3					1					
43		12	CAMBRIDGE UNITED	0-2		3186	7	9			5	11	13	8	4	12		10						2	6	3					1					
44		19	Darlington	2-1	Brown, Allon	4662	14			7	5	11			13	4		10			9	12		2		3			6		1		8			
45		26	BARNET	4-0	Allon 2, Baker, Halliday	3070	7	9		4		11				5		10						2		3			6		1		8			
46	May	3	Swansea City	2-2	Howard 2	5423		9		4			12		7	5		10			11			2		3			6		1		8			
						Apps	30	6	16	42	12	6	35	33	6	32	4	31	27	5	32	37	4	7	24	7	38	9	22	7	30	16	6	13	19	4
						Goals	9	2		8	1	1	2	9		1		8			7	1	1				1			1				1		

Played in one game: C Homer (20, at 12), A Horace (16, at 14), CJ Winstanley (29, at 13).

F.A. Cup

Rd	Date		Opponent	Score	Scorers	Att	Allon JB	Baker DP	Barron MJ	Beech CS	Bradley R	Brown MR	Clegg DL	Cooper MN	Cullen DJ	Davies G	Elliott A	Halliday SW	Hislop TK	Houchen KM	Howard SJ	Ingram SD	Irvine SC	Knowles DT	Lee GB	Lucas R	McAuley S	McDonald C	McGuckin TI	Mike AR	O'Connor PD	Pears S	Proctor MG	Sunderland JP	Tait MP	Walton PA
R1	Nov	16	YORK CITY	0-0		3011				4			7	8				10	11		9	2			5		3		6		1					
rep		26	York City	0-3		3257	7			4			9					10	11			2	12		5		3		6			1			8	

F.L. Cup (Coca Cola Cup)

Rd	Date		Opponent	Score	Scorers	Att	Allon JB	Baker DP	Barron MJ	Beech CS	Bradley R	Brown MR	Clegg DL	Cooper MN	Cullen DJ	Davies G	Elliott A	Halliday SW	Hislop TK	Houchen KM	Howard SJ	Ingram SD	Irvine SC	Knowles DT	Lee GB	Lucas R	McAuley S	McDonald C	McGuckin TI	Mike AR	O'Connor PD	Pears S	Proctor MG	Sunderland JP	Tait MP	Walton PA
R1/1	Aug	20	LINCOLN CITY	2-2	Bos(og), Allon	2073	7			4				8		5		10		13	9	2			14		3	6	12			1			11	
R1/2	Sep	3	Lincoln City	2-3	Allon, Beech	2389	7			10			11	8		4		12		9		2					3	6	5			1				

A.M. Cup (Auto Windscreens Shield)

Rd	Date		Opponent	Score	Scorers	Att	Allon JB	Baker DP	Barron MJ	Beech CS	Bradley R	Brown MR	Clegg DL	Cooper MN	Cullen DJ	Davies G	Elliott A	Halliday SW	Hislop TK	Houchen KM	Howard SJ	Ingram SD	Irvine SC	Knowles DT	Lee GB	Lucas R	McAuley S	McDonald C	McGuckin TI	Mike AR	O'Connor PD	Pears S	Proctor MG	Sunderland JP	Tait MP	Walton PA
R1	Dec	10	BURNLEY	0-2		921	7			4			10	8		6			11		9	2	12		5		3				1					

Also played: S Hutt (at 13), I Gallagher (at 14)

1997/98 17th in Division 3

	Date	Opponent	Res	Scorers	Att	Allon JB	Baker DP	Barron MJ	Beech CS	Bradley R	Clark ID	Connor P	Cullen DJ	Davies G	Davis KG	Di Lella GM	Dobson WE	Elliott A	Gavin MW	Halliday SW	Harper SA	Hollund M	Howard SJ	Hutt S	Ingram SD	Irvine SC	Knowles DT	Larsen SO	Lee GB	Lucas R	McDonald C	Midgley CS	Miller TW	Nash M	Pedersen JO	Stephenson P
1	Aug 9	Exeter City	1-1	Cullen	3409	7	9		10	6			8	5	1					12			11		4		2			3						
2	16	COLCHESTER UNITED	3-2	Baker, Allon 2	2174	7	9	10		6			8	5	1					12			11		4		2			3						
3	23	Rotherham United	1-2	Cullen	3086	7	9	10	11	6			8	5			1			13			14		4		2		12	3						
4	30	MACCLESFIELD TOWN	0-0		2283	12	9	7		6			8							10	1		11		4		2		5	3						
5	Sep 2	NOTTS COUNTY	1-1	Howard	2010		9	7	11	6			8							10	1		12		4		2		5	3						
6	7	Scarborough	1-1	Cullen	3027		9	7	11	6			8					13		10	1		12		4		2		5	3						
7	13	TORQUAY UNITED	3-0	Baker, Cullen, Lee	1927		9	7	11	6			8					13		10	1		12		4		2		5	3						
8	20	Darlington	1-1	Cullen	3169		9	7	11	6			8					14		10	1		13		4		2		5	3	12					
9	27	SHREWSBURY TOWN	2-1	Ingram(p), Cullen	2253		9			6			8							10	1		11		4		2		5	3	7					
10	Oct 4	Chester City	1-3	Baker	2163		9			6			8						12	10	1		11		4		2		5	3	7		13			
11	11	Doncaster Rovers	2-2	Cullen, Lucas	1526		9			6			8	12					14	13	1		11		4	10	2		5	3			7			
12	18	LEYTON ORIENT	2-2	Howard, Ingram	2108		9		10	6			8	7							1		11		4	12	2		5	3						
13	21	PETERBOROUGH UTD.	2-1	Howard 2	1990				11	6			8	7					12	10	1		9		4		2		5	3						
14	25	Cardiff City	1-1	Baker	3383		9		11	6			8	7							1		10		4		2		5	3						
15	Nov 1	BRIGHTON & HOVE ALB	0-0		2561		9		11	6	13		8	7						12	1		10		4		2		5	3						
16	4	Swansea City	2-0	Cullen, Baker	2949		9			6			8	7							1		10		4		2		5	3					11	
17	8	Scunthorpe United	1-1	Knowles	3272		9	12		6			8	7						13	1		10		4		2		5	3					11	
18	18	ROCHDALE	2-0	Beech, Halliday	1666			7	11	6			8							10	1				4		2		5	3					9	
19	22	BARNET	2-0	Cullen 2	2225			11	7	6			8							10		1			4		2		5	3					9	
20	29	Cambridge United	0-2		2513			11	7	6	13		8	4						10		1	12				2		5	3					9	
21	Dec 2	HULL CITY	2-2	Beech, Lucas	1933			11	7	6	4		8							10		1	12				2		5	3					9	
22	13	Lincoln City	1-1	Cullen	2849			4	7	6			8							10		1	11				2		5	3					9	
23	20	MANSFIELD TOWN	2-2	Halliday, Howard	2309			4	7	6			8							10		1	11		12		2	13	5	3					9	
24	26	SCARBOROUGH	3-0	Halliday 2, Clark	3905			4	7		12		8							10		1	11		6		2			3	5				9	
25	28	Notts County	0-2		6073			4	7		13		8							10		1	11		6		2	14	12	3	5				9	
26	Jan 3	Colchester United	2-1	Clark, Howard	2885			4	7	6	10		8									1	11				2	12	5	3					9	
27	10	EXETER CITY	1-1	Clark	2507				7	6	10		8							12		1	11		4		2		5	3					9	
28	17	Macclesfield Town	1-2	Cullen	2334				7	6	11		8							10		1	12		4		2	13	5	3					9	
29	24	ROTHERHAM UNITED	0-0		2375			4	7	6	10											1	11		8		2		5	3					9	
30	31	Torquay United	0-1		2238			4		6	7									10		1	11		8	12	2		5	3					9	
31	Feb 7	DARLINGTON	2-2	Pedersen, Clark	3212			4		6	7	10		5						12		1	11		8		2			3					9	
32	14	CHESTER CITY	0-0		2186			4	8	6	7	10		5								1	11			12	2			3					9	
33	21	Shrewsbury Town	0-1		2160			11		6	7	10		4								1	9	8		13	2		5	3			12	14		
34	24	Leyton Orient	1-2	Clark	3713			4		6	7	10								12		1	9	11	8		2		5	3						
35	28	DONCASTER ROVERS	3-1	Clark, Bradley, Howard	1920			4	10	6	7											1	9	11	8		2		5	3						
36	Mar 3	SCUNTHORPE UNITED	0-1		1588			4	10	6	7	14		12						13		1	9	11	8		2		5	3						
37	7	Brighton & Hove Albion	0-0		2811			4	11	6	7			5						10		1	9				2			3			8			
38	14	SWANSEA CITY	4-2	Halliday, Lee 2, Beech	1727			4	11	6				5				12		10		1					2		7	3		9	8			
39	21	Rochdale	1-2	Clark	1395			4	11	6	14			5		12				10		1	13				2		7	3		9	8			
40	28	Barnet	1-1	Midgley	2344			4	11	6	7											1	10				2		5	3		9	8			
41	Apr 4	CAMBRIDGE UNITED	3-3	Miller, Di Lella 2	1867			4	11		7					13						1	10		6	14	2		5	3	12	9	8			
42	11	Hull City	1-2	Midgley	3343			4	12	6						11						1	10		7		2		5	3		9	8			
43	13	LINCOLN CITY	1-1	Beech	1997			4	11	6	3					12						1	10		7		2		5			9	8			
44	18	Mansfield Town	2-2	Beech 2	2047				7	6	3			5								1	10		4	12	2					9	8			11
45	25	CARDIFF CITY	2-0	Midgley, Ingram(p)	2817				7	6	3			5		12						1	10		4	13	2					9	8			11
46	May 2	Peterborough United	0-0		4727			5	7	6	3											1	10		4	12	2					9	8			11
					Apps	4	16	33	35	43	24	5	28	20	2	5	1	4	3	31	15	28	43	4	36	9	46	4	37	42	6	9	13	1	17	3
					Goals	2	5		6	1	7		12			2				5			7		3		1		3	2		3	1		1	

F.A. Cup

	Date	Opponent	Res	Scorers	Att	Allon JB	Baker DP	Barron MJ	Beech CS	Bradley R	Clark ID	Connor P	Cullen DJ	Davies G	Davis KG	Di Lella GM	Dobson WE	Elliott A	Gavin MW	Halliday SW	Harper SA	Hollund M	Howard SJ	Hutt S	Ingram SD	Irvine SC	Knowles DT	Larsen SO	Lee GB	Lucas R	McDonald C	Midgley CS	Miller TW	Nash M	Pedersen JO	Stephenson P
R1	Nov 15	MACCLESFIELD T	2-4	Beech, Pedersen	3165			6	10		13		8	7			1	14		12			9		4		2		5	3					11	

F.L. Cup (Coca Cola Cup)

	Date	Opponent	Res	Scorers	Att	Allon JB	Baker DP	Barron MJ	Beech CS	Bradley R	Clark ID	Connor P	Cullen DJ	Davies G	Davis KG	Di Lella GM	Dobson WE	Elliott A	Gavin MW	Halliday SW	Harper SA	Hollund M	Howard SJ	Hutt S	Ingram SD	Irvine SC	Knowles DT	Larsen SO	Lee GB	Lucas R	McDonald C	Midgley CS	Miller TW	Nash M	Pedersen JO	Stephenson P
R1/1	Aug 12	Tranmere Rovers	1-3	Howard	3878	7	9		10	6			8	5	1					12			11		4		2			3						
R1/2	26	TRANMERE ROVERS	2-1	Baker, Lee	1626		9	7		6			8				1			10			11		4		2		5	3						

A.M. Cup (Auto Windscreens Shield)

	Date	Opponent	Res	Scorers	Att	Allon JB	Baker DP	Barron MJ	Beech CS	Bradley R	Clark ID	Connor P	Cullen DJ	Davies G	Davis KG	Di Lella GM	Dobson WE	Elliott A	Gavin MW	Halliday SW	Harper SA	Hollund M	Howard SJ	Hutt S	Ingram SD	Irvine SC	Knowles DT	Larsen SO	Lee GB	Lucas R	McDonald C	Midgley CS	Miller TW	Nash M	Pedersen JO	Stephenson P
R1	Dec 6	Shrewsbury Town	2-1	Beech, Pedersen	1130			4	7	6			8							10		1	11				2		5	3					9	
R2	Jan 6	SCUNTHORPE UTD.	1-2	Lee	1491			4	7	6	3		8							10		1	11				2	12	5						9	

1974/75 Division 4

1	Mansfield Town	46	17	6	0	55	15	11	6	6	35	25	68
2	Shrewsbury Town	46	16	3	4	46	18	10	7	6	34	25	62
3	Rotherham United	46	13	7	3	40	19	9	8	6	31	22	59
4	Chester	46	17	5	1	48	9	6	6	11	16	29	57
5	Lincoln City	46	14	8	1	47	14	7	7	9	32	34	57
6	Cambridge United	46	15	5	3	43	16	5	9	9	19	28	54
7	Reading	46	13	6	4	38	20	8	4	11	25	27	52
8	Brentford	46	15	6	2	38	14	3	7	13	15	31	49
9	Exeter City	46	14	3	6	33	24	5	8	10	27	39	49
10	Bradford City	46	10	5	8	32	21	7	8	8	24	30	47
11	Southport	46	13	7	3	36	19	2	10	11	20	37	47
12	Newport County	46	13	5	5	43	30	6	4	13	25	45	47
13	HARTLEPOOL	46	13	6	4	40	24	3	5	15	12	38	43
14	Torquay United	46	10	7	6	30	25	4	7	12	16	36	42
15	Barnsley	46	10	7	6	34	24	5	4	14	28	41	41
16	Northampton Town	46	12	6	5	43	22	3	5	15	24	51	41
17	Doncaster Rovers	46	10	9	4	41	29	4	3	16	24	50	40
18	Crewe Alexandra	46	9	9	5	22	16	2	9	12	12	31	40
19	Rochdale	46	9	9	5	35	22	4	4	15	24	53	39
20	Stockport County	46	10	8	5	26	27	2	6	15	17	43	38
21	Darlington	46	11	4	8	38	27	2	6	15	16	40	36
22	Swansea City	46	9	4	10	25	31	6	2	15	21	42	36
23	Workington	46	7	5	11	23	29	3	6	14	13	37	31
24	Scunthorpe United	46	7	8	8	27	29	0	7	16	14	49	29

1981/82 Division 4

1	Sheffield United	46	15	8	0	53	15	12	7	4	41	26	96
2	Bradford City	46	14	7	2	52	23	12	6	5	36	22	91
3	Wigan Athletic	46	17	5	1	47	18	9	8	6	33	28	91
4	Bournemouth	46	12	10	1	37	15	11	9	3	25	15	88
5	Peterborough Utd.	46	16	3	4	46	22	8	7	8	25	35	82
6	Colchester United	46	12	6	5	47	23	8	6	9	35	34	72
7	Port Vale	46	9	12	2	26	17	9	4	10	30	32	70
8	Hull City	46	14	3	6	36	23	5	9	9	34	38	69
9	Bury	46	13	7	3	53	26	4	10	9	27	33	68
10	Hereford United	46	10	9	4	36	25	6	10	7	28	33	67
11	Tranmere Rovers	46	7	9	7	27	25	7	9	7	24	31	60
12	Blackpool	46	11	5	7	40	26	4	8	11	26	34	58
13	Darlington	46	10	5	8	36	28	5	8	10	25	34	58
14	HARTLEPOOL UNITED	46	9	8	6	39	34	4	8	11	34	50	55
15	Torquay United	46	9	8	6	30	25	5	5	13	17	34	55
16	Aldershot	46	8	7	8	34	29	5	8	10	23	39	54
17	York City	46	9	5	9	45	37	5	3	15	24	54	50
18	Stockport County	46	10	5	8	34	28	2	8	13	14	39	49
19	Halifax Town	46	6	11	6	28	30	3	11	9	23	42	49
20	Mansfield Town	46	8	6	9	39	39	5	4	14	24	42	47
21	Rochdale	46	7	9	7	26	22	3	7	13	24	40	46
22	Northampton Town	46	9	5	9	32	27	2	4	17	25	57	42
23	Scunthorpe United	46	7	9	7	26	35	2	6	15	17	44	42
24	Crewe Alexandra	46	3	6	14	19	32	3	3	17	10	52	27

1982/83 Division 4

1	Wimbledon	46	17	4	2	57	23	12	7	4	39	22	98
2	Hull City	46	14	8	1	48	14	11	7	5	27	20	90
3	Port Vale	46	15	4	4	37	16	11	6	6	30	18	88
4	Scunthorpe United	46	13	7	3	41	17	10	7	6	30	25	83
5	Bury	46	15	4	4	43	20	8	8	7	31	26	81
6	Colchester United	46	17	5	1	51	19	7	4	12	24	36	81
7	York City	46	18	4	1	59	19	4	9	10	29	39	79
8	Swindon Town	46	14	3	6	45	27	5	8	10	16	27	68
9	Peterborough Utd.	46	13	6	4	38	23	4	7	12	20	29	64
10	Mansfield Town	46	11	6	6	32	26	5	7	11	29	44	61
11	Halifax Town	46	9	8	6	31	23	7	4	12	28	43	60
12	Torquay United	46	12	3	8	38	30	5	4	14	18	35	58
13	Chester	46	8	6	9	28	24	7	5	11	27	36	56
14	Bristol City	46	10	8	5	32	25	3	9	11	27	45	56
15	Northampton Town	46	10	8	5	43	29	4	4	15	22	46	54
16	Stockport County	46	11	8	4	41	31	3	4	16	19	48	54
17	Darlington	46	8	5	10	27	30	5	8	10	34	41	52
18	Aldershot	46	11	5	7	40	35	1	10	12	21	47	51
19	Tranmere Rovers	46	8	8	7	30	29	5	3	15	19	42	50
20	Rochdale	46	11	8	4	38	25	0	8	15	17	48	49
21	Blackpool	46	10	8	5	32	23	3	4	16	23	51	49
22	HARTLEPOOL UNITED	46	11	5	7	30	24	2	4	17	16	52	48
23	Crewe Alexandra	46	9	5	9	35	32	2	3	18	18	39	41
24	Hereford United	46	8	6	9	19	23	3	2	18	23	56	41

1983/84 Division 4

1	York City	46	18	4	1	58	16	13	4	6	38	23	101
2	Doncaster Rovers	46	15	6	2	46	22	9	7	7	36	32	85
3	Reading	46	17	6	0	51	14	5	10	8	33	42	82
4	Bristol City	46	18	3	2	51	17	6	7	10	19	27	82
5	Aldershot	46	14	6	3	49	29	8	3	12	27	40	75
6	Blackpool	46	15	4	4	47	19	6	5	12	23	33	72
7	Peterborough Utd.	46	15	5	3	52	16	3	9	11	20	32	68
8	Colchester United	46	14	7	2	45	14	3	9	11	24	39	67
9	Torquay United	46	13	7	3	32	18	5	6	12	27	46	67
10	Tranmere Rovers	46	11	5	7	33	26	6	10	7	20	27	66
11	Hereford United	46	11	6	6	31	21	5	9	9	23	32	63
12	Stockport County	46	12	5	6	34	25	5	6	12	26	39	62
13	Chesterfield	46	10	11	2	34	24	5	4	14	25	37	60
14	Darlington	46	13	4	6	31	19	4	4	15	18	31	59
15	Bury	46	9	7	7	34	32	6	7	10	27	32	59
16	Crewe Alexandra	46	10	8	5	35	27	6	3	14	21	40	59
17	Swindon Town	46	11	7	5	34	23	4	6	13	24	33	58
18	Northampton Town	46	10	8	5	32	32	3	6	14	21	46	53
19	Mansfield Town	46	9	7	7	44	27	4	6	13	22	43	52
20	Wrexham	46	7	6	10	34	33	4	9	10	25	41	48
21	Halifax Town	46	11	6	6	36	25	1	6	16	19	64	48
22	Rochdale	46	8	9	6	35	31	3	4	16	17	49	46
23	HARTLEPOOL UNITED	46	7	8	8	31	28	3	2	18	16	57	40
24	Chester City	46	7	5	11	23	35	0	8	15	22	47	34

1984/85 Division 4

1	Chesterfield	46	16	6	1	40	13	10	7	6	24	22	91
2	Blackpool	46	15	7	1	42	15	9	7	7	31	24	86
3	Darlington	46	16	4	3	41	22	8	9	6	25	27	85
4	Bury	46	15	6	2	46	20	9	6	8	30	30	84
5	Hereford United	46	16	2	5	38	21	6	9	8	27	26	77
6	Tranmere Rovers	46	17	1	5	50	21	7	2	14	33	45	75
7	Colchester United	46	13	7	3	49	29	7	7	9	38	36	74
8	Swindon Town	46	16	4	3	42	21	5	5	13	20	37	72
9	Scunthorpe United	46	14	6	3	61	33	5	8	10	22	29	71
10	Crewe Alexandra	46	10	7	6	32	28	8	5	10	33	41	66
11	Peterborough Utd.	46	11	7	5	29	21	5	7	11	25	32	62
12	Port Vale	46	11	8	4	39	24	3	10	10	22	35	60
13	Aldershot	46	11	6	6	33	20	6	2	15	23	43	59
14	Mansfield Town	46	10	8	5	25	15	3	10	10	16	23	57
15	Wrexham	46	10	6	7	39	27	5	3	15	28	43	54
16	Chester City	46	11	3	9	35	30	4	6	13	25	42	54
17	Rochdale	46	8	7	8	33	30	5	7	11	22	39	53
18	Exeter City	46	9	7	7	30	27	4	7	12	27	52	53
19	HARTLEPOOL UNITED	46	10	6	7	34	29	4	4	15	20	38	52
20	Southend United	46	8	8	7	30	34	5	3	15	28	49	50
21	Halifax Town	46	9	3	11	26	32	6	2	15	16	37	50
22	Stockport County	46	11	5	7	40	26	2	3	18	18	53	47
23	Northampton Town	46	10	1	12	32	32	4	4	15	21	42	47
24	Torquay United	46	5	11	7	18	24	4	3	16	20	39	41

1985/86 Division 4

1	Swindon Town	46	20	2	1	52	19	12	4	7	30	24	102
2	Chester City	46	15	5	3	44	16	8	10	5	39	34	84
3	Mansfield Town	46	13	8	2	43	17	10	4	9	31	30	81
4	Port Vale	46	13	9	1	42	11	8	7	8	25	26	79
5	Orient	46	11	6	6	39	21	9	6	8	40	43	72
6	Colchester United	46	12	6	5	51	22	7	7	9	37	41	70
7	HARTLEPOOL UNITED	46	15	6	2	41	20	5	4	14	27	47	70
8	Northampton Town	46	9	7	7	44	29	9	3	11	35	29	64
9	Southend United	46	13	4	6	43	27	5	6	12	26	40	64
10	Hereford United	46	15	6	2	55	30	3	4	16	19	43	64
11	Stockport County	46	9	9	5	35	28	8	4	11	28	43	64
12	Crewe Alexandra	46	10	6	7	35	26	8	3	12	19	35	63
13	Wrexham	46	11	5	7	34	24	6	4	13	34	56	60
14	Burnley	46	11	3	9	35	30	5	8	10	25	35	59
15	Scunthorpe United	46	11	7	5	33	23	4	7	12	17	32	59
16	Aldershot	46	12	5	6	45	25	5	2	16	21	49	58
17	Peterborough Utd.	46	9	11	3	31	19	4	6	13	21	45	56
18	Rochdale	46	12	7	4	41	29	2	6	15	16	48	55
19	Tranmere Rovers	46	9	1	13	46	41	6	8	9	28	32	54
20	Halifax Town	46	10	8	5	35	27	4	4	15	25	44	54
21	Exeter City	46	10	4	9	26	25	3	11	9	21	34	54
22	Cambridge United	46	12	2	9	45	38	3	7	13	20	42	54
23	Preston North End	46	7	4	12	32	41	4	6	13	22	48	43
24	Torquay United	46	8	5	10	29	32	1	5	17	14	56	37

1986/87 Division 4

1	Northampton Town	46	20	2	1	56	20	10	7	6	47	33	99
2	Preston North End	46	16	4	3	36	18	10	8	5	36	29	90
3	Southend United	46	14	4	5	43	27	11	1	11	25	28	80
4	Wolverhampton Wan.	46	12	3	8	36	24	12	4	7	33	26	79
5	Colchester United	46	15	3	5	41	20	6	4	13	23	36	70
6	Aldershot	46	13	5	5	40	22	7	5	11	24	35	70
7	Orient	46	15	2	6	40	25	5	7	11	24	36	69
8	Scunthorpe United	46	15	3	5	52	27	3	9	11	21	30	66
9	Wrexham	46	8	13	2	38	24	7	7	9	32	27	65
10	Peterborough Utd.	46	10	7	6	29	21	7	7	9	28	29	65
11	Cambridge United	46	12	6	5	37	23	5	5	13	23	39	62
12	Swansea City	46	13	3	7	31	21	4	8	11	25	40	62
13	Cardiff City	46	6	12	5	24	18	9	4	10	24	32	61
14	Exeter City	46	11	10	2	37	17	0	13	10	16	32	56
15	Halifax Town	46	10	5	8	32	32	5	5	13	27	42	55
16	Hereford United	46	10	6	7	33	23	4	5	14	27	38	53
17	Crewe Alexandra	46	8	9	6	38	35	5	5	13	32	37	53
18	HARTLEPOOL UNITED	46	6	11	6	24	30	5	7	11	20	35	51
19	Stockport County	46	9	6	8	25	27	4	6	13	15	42	51
20	Tranmere Rovers	46	6	10	7	32	37	5	7	11	22	35	50
21	Rochdale	46	8	8	7	31	30	3	9	11	23	43	50
22	Burnley	46	9	7	7	31	35	3	6	14	22	39	49
23	Torquay United	46	8	8	7	28	29	2	10	11	28	43	48
24	Lincoln City	46	8	7	8	30	27	4	5	14	15	38	48

1987/88 Division 4

1	Wolverhampton Wan.	46	15	3	5	47	19	12	6	5	35	24	90
2	Cardiff City	46	15	6	2	39	14	9	7	7	27	27	85
3	Bolton Wanderers	46	15	6	2	42	12	7	6	10	24	30	78
4	Scunthorpe United	46	14	5	4	42	20	6	12	5	34	31	77
5	Torquay United	46	10	7	6	34	16	11	7	5	32	25	77
6	Swansea City	46	9	7	7	35	28	11	3	9	27	28	70
7	Peterborough Utd.	46	10	5	8	28	26	10	5	8	24	27	70
8	Leyton Orient	46	13	4	6	55	27	6	8	9	30	36	69
9	Colchester United	46	10	5	8	23	22	9	5	9	24	29	67
10	Burnley	46	12	5	6	31	22	8	2	13	26	40	67
11	Wrexham	46	13	3	7	46	26	7	3	13	23	32	66
12	Scarborough	46	12	8	3	38	19	5	6	12	18	29	65
13	Darlington	46	13	6	4	39	25	5	5	13	32	44	65
14	Tranmere Rovers	46	14	2	7	43	20	5	7	11	18	33	64
15	Cambridge United	46	10	6	7	32	24	6	7	10	18	28	61
16	HARTLEPOOL UNITED	46	9	7	7	25	25	6	7	10	25	32	59
17	Crewe Alexandra	46	7	11	5	25	19	6	8	9	32	34	58
18	Halifax Town	46	11	7	5	37	25	3	7	13	17	34	55
19	Hereford United	46	8	7	8	25	27	6	5	12	16	32	54
20	Stockport County	46	7	7	9	26	26	5	8	10	18	32	51
21	Rochdale	46	5	9	9	28	34	6	6	11	19	42	48
22	Exeter City	46	8	6	9	33	29	3	7	13	20	39	46
23	Carlisle United	46	9	5	9	38	33	3	3	17	19	53	44
24	Newport County	46	4	5	14	19	36	2	2	19	16	69	25

1988/89 Division 4

1	Rotherham United	46	13	6	4	44	18	9	10	4	32	17	82
2	Tranmere Rovers	46	15	6	2	34	13	6	11	6	28	30	80
3	Crewe Alexandra	46	13	7	3	42	24	8	8	7	25	24	78
4	Scunthorpe United	46	11	9	3	40	22	10	5	8	37	35	77
5	Scarborough	46	12	7	4	33	23	9	7	7	34	29	77
6	Leyton Orient	46	16	2	5	61	19	5	10	8	25	31	75
7	Wrexham	46	12	7	4	44	28	7	7	9	33	35	71
8	Cambridge United	46	13	7	3	45	25	5	7	11	26	37	68
9	Grimsby Town	46	11	9	3	33	18	6	6	11	32	41	66
10	Lincoln City	46	12	6	5	39	26	6	4	13	25	34	64
11	York City	46	10	8	5	43	27	7	5	11	19	36	64
12	Carlisle United	46	9	6	8	26	25	6	9	8	27	27	60
13	Exeter City	46	14	4	5	46	23	4	2	17	19	45	60
14	Torquay United	46	15	2	6	32	23	2	6	15	13	37	59
15	Hereford United	46	11	8	4	40	27	3	8	12	26	45	58
16	Burnley	46	12	6	5	35	20	2	7	14	17	41	55
17	Peterborough Utd.	46	10	3	10	29	32	4	9	10	23	42	54
18	Rochdale	46	10	10	3	32	26	3	4	16	24	56	53
19	HARTLEPOOL UNITED	46	10	6	7	33	33	4	4	15	17	45	52
20	Stockport County	46	8	10	5	31	20	2	11	10	23	32	51
21	Halifax Town	46	10	7	6	42	27	3	4	16	27	48	50
22	Colchester United	46	8	7	8	35	30	4	7	12	25	48	50
23	Doncaster Rovers	46	9	6	8	32	32	4	4	15	17	46	49
24	Darlington	46	3	12	8	28	38	5	6	12	25	38	42

1989/90 Division 4

1	Exeter City	46	20	3	0	50	14	8	2	13	33	34	89
2	Grimsby Town	46	14	4	5	41	20	8	9	6	29	27	79
3	Southend United	46	15	3	5	35	14	7	6	10	26	34	75
4	Stockport County	46	13	6	4	45	27	8	5	10	23	35	74
5	Maidstone United	46	14	4	5	49	21	8	3	12	28	40	73
6	Cambridge United	46	14	3	6	45	30	7	7	9	31	36	73
7	Chesterfield	46	12	9	2	41	19	7	5	11	22	31	71
8	Carlisle United	46	15	4	4	38	20	6	4	13	23	40	71
9	Peterborough Utd.	46	10	8	5	35	23	7	9	7	24	23	68
10	Lincoln City	46	11	6	6	30	27	7	8	8	18	21	68
11	Scunthorpe United	46	9	9	5	42	25	8	6	9	27	29	66
12	Rochdale	46	11	4	8	28	23	9	2	12	24	32	66
13	York City	46	10	5	8	29	24	6	11	6	26	29	64
14	Gillingham	46	9	8	6	28	21	8	3	12	18	27	62
15	Torquay United	46	12	2	9	33	29	3	10	10	20	37	57
16	Burnley	46	6	10	7	19	18	8	4	11	26	37	56
17	Hereford United	46	7	4	12	31	32	8	6	9	25	30	55
18	Scarborough	46	10	5	8	35	28	5	5	13	25	45	55
19	HARTLEPOOL UNITED	46	12	4	7	45	33	3	6	14	21	55	55
20	Doncaster Rovers	46	7	7	9	29	29	7	2	14	24	31	51
21	Wrexham	46	8	8	7	28	28	5	4	14	23	39	51
22	Aldershot	46	8	7	8	28	26	4	7	12	21	43	50
23	Halifax Town	46	5	9	9	31	29	7	4	12	26	36	49
24	Colchester United	46	9	3	11	26	25	2	7	14	22	50	43

1990/91 Division 4

1	Darlington	46	13	8	2	36	14	9	9	5	32	24	83
2	Stockport County	46	16	6	1	54	19	7	7	9	30	28	82
3	HARTLEPOOL UNITED	46	15	5	3	35	15	9	5	9	32	33	82
4	Peterborough Utd.	46	13	9	1	38	15	8	8	7	29	30	80
5	Blackpool	46	17	3	3	55	17	6	7	10	23	30	79
6	Burnley	46	17	5	1	46	16	6	5	12	24	35	79
7	Torquay United	46	14	7	2	37	13	4	11	8	27	34	72
8	Scunthorpe United	46	17	4	2	51	20	3	7	13	20	42	71
9	Scarborough	46	13	5	5	36	21	6	7	10	23	35	69
10	Northampton Town	46	14	5	4	34	21	4	8	11	23	37	67
11	Doncaster Rovers	46	12	5	6	36	22	5	9	9	20	24	65
12	Rochdale	46	10	9	4	29	22	5	8	10	21	31	62
13	Cardiff City	46	10	6	7	26	23	5	9	9	17	31	60
14	Lincoln City	46	10	7	6	32	27	4	10	9	18	34	59
15	Gillingham	46	9	9	5	35	27	3	9	11	22	33	54
16	Walsall	46	7	12	4	25	17	5	5	13	23	34	53
17	Hereford United	46	9	10	4	32	19	4	4	15	21	39	53
18	Chesterfield	46	8	12	3	33	26	5	2	16	14	36	53
19	Maidstone United	46	9	5	9	42	34	4	7	12	24	37	51
20	Carlisle United	46	12	3	8	30	30	1	6	16	17	59	48
21	York City	46	8	6	9	21	23	3	7	13	24	34	46
22	Halifax Town	46	9	6	8	34	29	3	4	16	25	50	46
23	Aldershot	46	8	7	8	38	43	2	4	17	23	58	41
24	Wrexham	46	8	7	8	33	34	2	3	18	15	40	40

1991/92 Division 3

1	Brentford	46	17	2	4	55	29	8	5	10	26	26	82
2	Birmingham City	46	15	6	2	42	22	8	6	9	27	30	81
3	Huddersfield Town	46	15	4	4	36	15	7	8	8	23	23	78
4	Stoke City	46	14	5	4	45	24	7	9	7	24	25	77
5	Stockport County	46	15	5	3	47	19	7	5	11	28	32	76
6	Peterborough Utd.	46	13	7	3	38	20	7	7	9	27	38	74
7	West Bromwich Alb.	46	12	6	5	45	25	7	8	8	19	24	71
8	Bournemouth	46	13	4	6	33	18	7	7	9	19	30	71
9	Fulham	46	11	7	5	29	16	8	6	9	28	37	70
10	Leyton Orient	46	12	7	4	36	18	6	4	13	26	34	65
11	HARTLEPOOL UNITED	46	12	5	6	30	21	6	6	11	27	36	65
12	Reading	46	9	8	6	33	27	7	5	11	26	35	61
13	Bolton Wanderers	46	10	9	4	26	19	4	8	11	31	37	59
14	Hull City	46	9	4	10	28	23	7	7	9	26	31	59
15	Wigan Athletic	46	11	6	6	33	21	4	8	11	25	43	59
16	Bradford City	46	8	10	5	36	30	5	9	9	26	31	58
17	Preston North End	46	12	7	4	42	32	3	5	15	19	40	57
18	Chester City	46	10	6	7	34	29	4	8	11	22	30	56
19	Swansea City	46	10	9	4	35	24	4	5	14	20	41	56
20	Exeter City	46	11	7	5	34	25	3	4	16	23	55	53
21	Bury	46	8	7	8	31	31	5	5	13	24	43	51
22	Shrewsbury Town	46	7	7	9	30	31	5	4	14	23	37	47
23	Torquay United	46	13	3	7	29	19	0	5	18	13	49	47
24	Darlington	46	5	5	13	31	39	5	2	16	25	51	37

1992/93 The new Football League Division 2

1	Stoke City	46	17	4	2	41	13	10	8	5	32	21	93
2	Bolton Wanderers	46	18	2	3	48	14	9	7	7	32	27	90
3	Port Vale	46	14	7	2	44	17	12	4	7	35	27	89
4	West Bromwich Alb.	46	17	3	3	56	22	8	7	8	32	32	85
5	Swansea City	46	12	7	4	38	17	8	6	9	27	30	73
6	Stockport County	46	11	11	1	47	18	8	4	11	34	39	72
7	Leyton Orient	46	16	4	3	49	20	5	5	13	20	33	72
8	Reading	46	14	4	5	44	20	4	11	8	22	31	69
9	Brighton & Hove A.	46	13	4	6	36	24	7	5	11	27	35	69
10	Bradford City	46	12	5	6	36	24	6	9	8	33	43	68
11	Rotherham United	46	9	7	7	30	27	8	7	8	30	33	65
12	Fulham	46	9	9	5	28	22	7	8	8	29	33	65
13	Burnley	46	11	8	4	38	21	4	8	11	19	38	61
14	Plymouth Argyle	46	11	6	6	38	28	5	6	12	21	36	60
15	Huddersfield Town	46	10	6	7	30	22	7	3	13	24	39	60
16	Hartlepool United	46	8	6	9	19	23	6	6	11	23	37	54
17	Bournemouth	46	7	10	6	28	24	5	7	11	17	28	53
18	Blackpool	46	9	9	5	40	30	3	6	14	23	45	51
19	Exeter City	46	5	8	10	26	30	6	9	8	28	39	50
20	Hull City	46	9	5	9	28	26	4	6	13	18	43	50
21	Preston North End	46	8	5	10	41	47	5	3	15	24	47	47
22	Mansfield Town	46	7	8	8	34	34	4	3	16	18	46	44
23	Wigan Athletic	46	6	6	11	26	34	4	5	14	17	38	41
24	Chester City	46	6	2	15	30	47	2	3	18	19	55	29

1993/94 Division 2

1	Reading	46	15	6	2	40	16	11	5	7	41	28	89
2	Port Vale	46	16	6	1	46	18	10	4	9	33	28	88
3	Plymouth Argyle	46	16	4	3	46	26	9	6	8	42	30	85
4	Stockport County	46	15	3	5	50	22	9	10	4	24	22	85
5	York City	46	12	7	4	33	13	9	5	9	31	27	75
6	Burnley	46	17	4	2	55	18	4	6	13	24	40	73
7	Bradford City	46	13	5	5	34	20	6	8	9	27	33	70
8	Bristol Rovers	46	10	8	5	33	26	10	2	11	27	33	70
9	Hull City	46	9	9	5	33	20	9	5	9	29	34	68
10	Cambridge United	46	11	5	7	38	29	8	4	11	41	44	66
11	Huddersfield Town	46	9	8	6	27	26	8	6	9	31	35	65
12	Wrexham	46	13	4	6	45	33	4	7	12	21	44	62
13	Swansea City	46	12	7	4	37	20	4	5	14	19	38	60
14	Brighton & Hove A.	46	10	7	6	38	29	5	7	11	22	38	59
15	Rotherham United	46	11	4	8	42	30	4	9	10	21	30	58
16	Brentford	46	7	10	6	30	28	6	9	8	27	27	58
17	Bournemouth	46	8	7	8	26	27	6	8	9	25	32	57
18	Leyton Orient	46	11	9	3	38	26	3	5	15	19	45	56
19	Cardiff City	46	10	7	6	39	33	3	8	12	27	46	54
20	Blackpool	46	12	2	9	41	37	4	3	16	22	38	53
21	Fulham	46	7	6	10	20	23	7	4	12	30	40	52
22	Exeter City	46	8	7	8	38	37	3	5	15	14	46	45
23	HARTLEPOOL UNITED	46	8	3	12	28	40	1	6	16	13	47	36
24	Barnet	46	4	6	13	22	32	1	7	15	19	54	28

1994/95 Division 3

1	Carlisle United	42	14	5	2	34	14	13	5	3	33	17	91
2	Walsall	42	15	3	3	42	18	9	8	4	33	22	83
3	Chesterfield	42	11	7	3	26	10	12	5	4	36	27	81
4	Bury	42	13	7	1	39	13	10	4	7	34	23	80
5	Preston North End	42	13	3	5	37	17	6	7	8	21	24	67
6	Mansfield Town	42	10	5	6	45	27	8	6	7	39	32	65
7	Scunthorpe United	42	12	2	7	40	30	6	6	9	28	33	62
8	Fulham	42	11	5	5	39	22	5	9	7	21	32	62
9	Doncaster Rovers	42	9	5	7	28	20	8	5	8	30	23	61
10	Colchester United	42	8	5	8	29	30	8	5	8	27	34	58
11	Barnet	42	8	7	6	37	27	7	4	10	19	36	56
12	Lincoln City	42	10	7	4	34	22	5	4	12	20	33	56
13	Torquay United	42	10	8	3	35	25	4	5	12	19	32	55
14	Wigan Athletic	42	7	6	8	28	30	7	4	10	25	30	52
15	Rochdale	42	8	6	7	25	23	4	8	9	19	44	50
16	Hereford United	42	9	6	6	22	19	3	7	11	23	43	49
17	Northampton Town	42	8	5	8	25	29	2	9	10	20	38	44
18	Hartlepool United	42	9	5	7	33	32	2	5	14	10	37	43
19	Gillingham	42	8	7	6	31	25	2	4	15	15	39	41
20	Darlington	42	7	5	9	25	24	4	3	14	18	33	41
21	Scarborough	42	4	7	10	26	31	4	3	14	23	39	34
22	Exeter City	42	5	5	11	25	36	3	5	13	11	34	34

1995/96 Division 3

1	Preston North End	46	11	8	4	44	22	12	9	2	34	16	86
2	Gillingham	46	16	6	1	33	6	6	11	6	16	14	83
3	Bury	46	11	6	6	33	21	11	7	5	33	27	79
4	Plymouth Argyle	46	14	5	4	41	20	8	7	8	27	29	78
5	Darlington	46	10	6	7	30	21	10	12	1	30	21	78
6	Hereford United	46	13	5	5	40	22	7	9	7	25	25	74
7	Colchester United	46	13	7	3	37	22	5	11	7	24	29	72
8	Chester City	46	11	9	3	45	22	7	7	9	27	31	70
9	Barnet	46	13	6	4	40	19	5	10	8	25	26	70
10	Wigan Athletic	46	15	3	5	36	21	5	7	11	26	35	70
11	Northampton Town	46	9	10	4	32	22	9	3	11	19	22	67
12	Scunthorpe United	46	8	8	7	36	30	7	7	9	31	31	60
13	Doncaster Rovers	46	11	6	6	25	19	5	5	13	24	41	59
14	Exeter City	46	9	9	5	25	22	4	9	10	21	31	57
15	Rochdale	46	7	8	8	32	33	7	5	11	25	28	55
16	Cambridge United	46	8	8	7	34	30	6	4	13	27	41	54
17	Fulham	46	10	9	4	39	26	2	8	13	18	37	53
18	Lincoln City	46	8	7	8	32	26	5	7	11	25	47	53
19	Mansfield Town	46	6	10	7	25	29	5	10	8	29	35	53
20	HARTLEPOOL UNITED	46	8	9	6	30	24	4	4	15	17	43	49
21	Leyton Orient	46	11	4	8	29	22	1	7	15	15	41	47
22	Cardiff City	46	8	6	9	24	22	3	6	14	17	42	45
23	Scarborough	46	5	11	7	22	28	3	5	15	17	41	40
24	Torquay United	46	4	9	10	17	36	1	5	17	13	48	29

1996/97 Division 3

1	Wigan Athletic	46	17	3	3	53	21	9	6	8	31	30	87
2	Fulham	46	13	5	5	41	20	12	7	4	31	18	87
3	Carlisle United	46	16	3	4	41	21	8	9	6	26	23	84
4	Northampton Town	46	14	4	5	43	17	6	8	9	24	27	72
5	Swansea City	46	13	5	5	37	20	8	3	12	25	38	71
6	Chester City	46	11	8	4	30	16	7	8	8	25	27	70
7	Cardiff City	46	11	4	8	30	23	9	5	9	26	31	69
8	Colchester United	46	11	9	3	36	23	6	8	9	26	28	68
9	Lincoln City	46	10	8	5	35	25	8	4	11	35	44	66
10	Cambridge United	46	11	5	7	30	27	7	6	10	23	32	65
11	Mansfield Town	46	9	8	6	21	17	7	8	8	26	28	64
12	Scarborough	46	9	9	5	36	31	7	6	10	29	37	63
13	Scunthorpe United	46	11	3	9	36	33	7	6	10	23	29	63
14	Rochdale	46	10	6	7	34	24	4	10	9	24	34	58
15	Barnet	46	9	9	5	32	23	5	7	11	14	28	58
16	Leyton Orient	46	11	6	6	28	20	4	6	13	22	38	57
17	Hull City	46	9	8	6	29	26	4	10	9	15	24	57
18	Darlington	46	11	5	7	37	28	3	5	15	27	50	52
19	Doncaster Rovers	46	9	7	7	29	23	5	3	15	23	43	52
20	HARTLEPOOL UNITED	46	8	6	9	33	32	6	3	14	20	34	51
21	Torquay United	46	9	4	10	24	24	4	7	12	22	38	50
22	Exeter City	46	6	9	8	25	30	6	3	14	23	43	48
23	Brighton & Hove A.	46	12	6	5	41	27	1	4	18	12	43	47
24	Hereford United	46	6	8	9	26	25	5	6	12	24	40	47

1997/98 Division 3

1	Notts County	46	14	7	2	41	20	15	5	3	41	23	99
2	Macclesfield Town	46	19	4	0	40	11	4	9	10	23	33	82
3	Lincoln City	46	11	7	5	32	24	9	8	6	28	27	75
4	Colchester United	46	14	5	4	41	24	7	6	10	31	36	74
5	Torquay United	46	14	4	5	39	22	7	7	9	29	37	74
6	Scarborough	46	14	6	3	44	23	5	9	9	23	35	72
7	Barnet	46	10	8	5	35	22	9	5	9	26	29	70
8	Scunthorpe United	46	11	7	5	30	24	8	5	10	26	28	69
9	Rotherham United	46	10	9	4	41	30	6	10	7	26	31	67
10	Peterborough Utd.	46	13	6	4	37	16	5	7	11	26	35	67
11	Leyton Orient	46	14	5	4	40	20	5	7	11	22	27	66
12	Mansfield Town	46	11	9	3	42	26	5	8	10	22	29	65
13	Shrewsbury Town	46	12	3	8	35	28	4	10	9	26	34	61
14	Chester City	46	12	7	4	34	15	5	3	15	26	46	61
15	Exeter City	46	10	8	5	39	25	5	7	11	29	38	60
16	Cambridge United	46	11	8	4	39	27	3	10	10	24	30	60
17	HARTLEPOOL UNITED	46	10	12	1	40	22	2	11	10	21	31	59
18	Rochdale	46	15	3	5	43	15	2	4	17	13	40	58
19	Darlington	46	13	6	4	43	28	1	6	16	13	44	54
20	Swansea City	46	8	8	7	24	16	5	3	15	25	46	50
21	Cardiff City	46	5	13	5	27	22	4	10	9	21	30	50
22	Hull City	46	10	6	7	36	32	1	2	20	20	51	41
23	Brighton & Hove A.	46	3	10	10	21	34	3	7	13	17	32	35
24	Doncaster Rovers	46	3	3	17	14	48	1	5	17	16	65	20

1990/91: Back: Fletcher, Baker, Errington, McKinnon, Bennyworth
Centre: Craggs (youth team coach), Macdonald, Smith, Nobbs, Lamb, Henderson (phsio), Andy Davies, Tupling, Kenny Davies, Pop Robson (assistant manager)
Front: Olsson, Tinkler, Allon, Knowles (manager), Dalton, Honour, Hutchison

George Smith in action

Brian Honour

HARTLEPOOL AGAINST OTHER LEAGUE CLUBS

Present day names used throughout. League games to end 1997/98 season.

	p	*hw*	*hd*	*hl*	*hf*	*ha*	*aw*	*ad*	*al*	*af*	*aa*	*tf*	*ta*	*% won*
Accrington Stanley	62	20	6	5	62	30	8	6	17	41	69	103	99	45.16
Aldershot	54	11	8	8	35	33	6	4	17	28	58	63	91	31.48
Ashington	16	4	0	4	12	10	1	1	6	8	17	20	27	31.25
Barnet	10	3	1	1	8	2	0	1	4	4	14	12	16	30.00
Barnsley	32	5	2	9	21	30	1	2	13	18	38	39	68	18.75
Barrow	84	25	8	9	91	44	9	11	22	46	80	137	124	40.48
Birmingham City	2	1	0	0	1	0	0	0	1	1	2	2	2	50.00
Blackpool	14	3	1	3	8	8	1	2	4	7	11	15	19	28.57
Bolton Wan.	6	0	1	2	0	6	2	1	0	6	4	6	10	33.33
Bournemouth	24	4	5	3	11	9	2	1	9	7	24	18	33	25.00
Bradford City	70	13	12	10	40	37	11	8	16	36	57	76	94	34.29
Bradford Park Avenue	46	11	4	8	40	30	7	3	13	25	57	65	87	39.13
Brentford	26	8	3	2	18	9	3	1	9	7	25	25	34	42.31
Brighton & Hove Alb.	14	1	4	2	11	13	0	4	3	4	17	15	30	7.14
Bristol City	4	1	1	0	5	3	0	0	2	0	4	5	7	25.00
Bristol Rovers	4	2	0	0	3	1	0	1	1	2	3	5	4	50.00
Burnley	16	4	4	0	16	7	0	3	5	1	13	17	20	25.00
Bury	24	4	3	5	14	14	1	6	5	10	18	24	32	20.83
Cambridge U	30	3	7	5	20	24	1	2	12	9	34	29	58	13.33
Cardiff City	14	3	1	3	10	8	0	3	4	4	13	14	21	21.43
Carlisle United	68	17	6	11	55	52	5	6	23	34	76	89	128	32.35
Chester City	90	22	11	12	71	56	7	10	28	40	96	111	152	32.22
Chesterfield	66	17	6	10	57	35	5	4	24	32	81	89	116	33.33
Colchester U	42	11	5	5	32	26	3	4	14	19	50	51	76	33.33
Coventry City	4	2	0	0	5	3	0	0	2	3	9	8	12	50.00
Crewe Alexandra	120	33	14	13	115	79	10	7	43	50	124	165	203	35.83
Crystal Palace	6	1	0	2	6	6	1	1	1	6	8	12	14	33.33
Darlington	122	32	11	18	106	70	20	10	31	64	119	170	189	42.62
Derby County	4	2	0	0	4	1	0	0	2	2	5	6	6	50.00
Doncaster Rovers	86	20	13	10	67	53	7	13	23	45	86	112	139	31.40
Durham City	14	4	2	1	10	4	2	1	4	5	9	15	13	42.86
Exeter City	58	10	13	6	41	37	1	6	22	19	59	60	96	18.97
Fulham	12	3	0	3	6	7	1	1	4	5	8	11	15	33.33
Gateshead	50	11	6	8	48	40	4	6	15	27	53	75	93	30.00
Gillingham	28	8	4	2	22	12	0	3	11	6	36	28	48	28.57
Grimsby Town	34	10	4	3	29	16	2	2	13	7	32	36	48	35.29
Halifax Town	100	28	11	11	98	50	8	4	38	39	101	137	151	36.00
Hereford United	34	8	4	5	24	15	2	3	12	13	37	37	52	29.41
Huddersfield Town	16	3	3	2	9	9	0	1	7	4	18	13	27	18.75
Hull City	36	4	8	6	30	30	1	3	14	12	44	42	74	13.89
Leyton Orient	22	3	4	4	17	17	3	2	6	11	20	28	37	27.27
Lincoln City	88	23	13	8	78	51	7	7	30	49	108	127	159	34.09
Luton Town	8	4	0	0	7	2	1	0	3	3	6	10	8	62.50
Macclesfield Town	2	0	1	0	0	0	0	0	1	1	2	1	2	0.00
Maidstone U	4	2	0	0	5	2	1	0	1	6	5	11	7	75.00
Mansfield Town	68	17	10	7	67	42	4	2	28	25	91	92	133	30.88
Millwall	10	3	1	1	8	5	0	1	4	6	15	14	20	30.00
Nelson	18	5	1	3	29	17	1	1	7	14	26	43	43	33.33
New Brighton	42	15	3	3	53	21	3	5	13	22	41	75	62	42.86
Newport County	36	5	6	7	22	19	4	3	11	17	32	39	51	25.00

Northampton Town	50	16	5	4	48	26	1	7	17	22	54	70	80	34.00
Notts County	16	5	2	1	18	10	1	1	6	3	12	21	22	37.50
Oldham Ath.	46	10	6	7	37	21	4	3	16	25	59	62	80	30.43
Oxford United	6	1	1	1	4	4	0	0	3	3	14	7	18	16.67
Peterborough United	40	6	4	10	20	25	3	5	12	21	44	41	69	22.50
Plymouth Aryle	8	1	2	1	5	11	0	1	3	2	10	7	21	12.50
Port Vale	38	10	5	4	33	26	1	6	12	12	40	45	66	28.95
Portsmouth	4	0	1	1	1	4	0	0	2	1	5	2	9	0.00
Preston North End	12	3	2	1	8	5	2	1	3	7	9	15	14	41.67
Reading	24	4	3	5	20	21	2	2	8	7	29	27	50	25.00
Rochdale	120	30	17	13	116	68	15	11	34	62	120	178	188	37.50
Rotherham U	56	14	6	8	55	41	6	5	17	35	73	90	114	35.71
Scarborough	16	6	2	0	18	6	2	3	3	11	15	29	21	50.00
Scunthorpe U	64	16	6	10	49	38	4	10	18	27	60	76	98	31.25
Sheffield United	2	0	0	1	2	3	0	1	0	1	1	3	4	0.00
Shrewsbury T	12	3	2	1	8	6	2	1	3	6	7	14	13	41.67
Southend Utd.	24	5	3	4	15	15	1	3	8	9	23	24	38	25.00
Southport	94	28	10	9	91	55	8	16	23	47	80	138	135	38.30
Stalybridge Celtic	4	1	0	1	4	1	1	1	0	4	2	8	3	50.00
Stockport County	116	29	16	13	105	58	13	10	35	56	121	161	179	36.21
Stoke City	6	0	1	2	3	6	1	0	2	4	6	7	12	16.67
Swansea City	28	5	3	6	15	17	2	4	8	12	29	27	46	25.00
Swindon Town	10	1	2	2	4	5	0	1	4	5	12	9	17	10.00
Torquay United	62	10	12	9	38	36	7	7	17	30	49	68	85	27.42
Tranmere Rovers	94	23	11	13	85	55	9	6	32	55	115	140	170	34.04
Walsall	34	8	6	3	38	22	5	5	7	21	39	59	61	38.24
Watford	12	4	1	1	10	7	0	1	5	4	18	14	25	33.33
West Bromwich Alb.	4	0	2	0	2	2	1	0	1	3	4	5	6	25.00
Wigan Athletic	18	3	4	2	13	11	1	5	3	12	13	25	24	22.22
Wigan Borough	20	4	5	1	15	6	2	1	7	8	17	23	23	30.00
Wimbledon	8	2	1	1	6	4	0	0	4	1	13	7	17	25.00
Wolves	6	0	1	2	0	2	0	0	3	2	8	2	10	0.00
Workington	44	11	4	7	33	28	5	10	7	17	26	50	54	36.36
Wrexham	92	25	9	12	90	53	8	7	31	55	112	145	165	35.87
York City	86	23	9	11	85	59	8	11	24	39	87	124	146	36.05

Complete Playing Record:

	p	*hw*	*hd*	*hl*	*hf*	*ha*	*aw*	*ad*	*al*	*af*	*aa*	*tf*	*ta*	*pts.*
	3116	756	395	407	2641	1852	271	311	976	1479	3281	4120	5133	2999
comprising:														
New Div.2/old Div. 3	184	34	26	32	102	113	17	25	50	78	161	180	274	194
New Div. 3/old Div. 4	1650	362	231	232	1263	997	145	169	511	730	1650	1993	2647	1612
Div. 3 (North)	1282	360	138	143	1276	742	109	117	415	671	1470	1947	2212	1193

HARTLEPOOLS UNITED IN THE WAR SEASONS

1918/19 Northern Victory League

1	Jan	11	Newcastle United	0-0		18000
2		18	SOUTH SHIELDS	2-1	R Thompson 2	6000
3		25	Darlington Forge Albion	7-1	R Thompson 6, Connor	2000
4	Feb	1	MIDDLESBROUGH	1-2	J Hibbert(p)	7000
5		8	SCOTSWOOD	0-2		4000
6		15	Sunderland	2-6	Butler, J Hibbert(p)	12000
7		22	DURHAM CITY	6-1	Butler 3, R Thompson, Winship 2	4000
8	Mar	1	Middlesbrough	2-8	W Hibbert 2	12000
9		15	South Shields	1-2	Metcalf	8000
10		22	DARLINGTON FORGE ALBION	1-4	W Hibbert(p)	3000
11		29	Durham City	5-0	W Hibbert 2, Butler 3	3000
12	Apr	5	Scotswood	1-4	W Thompson	
13		12	SUNDERLAND	0-2		6000
14		21	NEWCASTLE UNITED	6-1	Hewitt 2, Butler 2, Cook, Toward	5000

		p	w	d	l	f	a	pts
1	Middlesbrough	14	10	1	3	29	12	21
2	Sunderland	14	8	2	4	32	20	18
3	South Shields	14	5	5	4	27	25	15
4	Scotswood	14	5	4	5	29	24	14
5	Newcastle United	14	5	4	5	21	23	14
6	Darlington FA	14	5	2	7	15	27	12
7	HARTLEPOOLS U	14	5	1	8	34	34	11
8	Durham City	14	2	3	9	8	30	7

1939/40 Regional League North East Division

1	Oct	21	NEWCASTLE UNITED	1-2	Wilson	4000
2		28	Hull City	3-2	Maguire 2, Stephens	2500
3	Nov	11	HALIFAX TOWN	3-2	Stephens, Norton, West	2000
4		18	Leeds United	1-2	Stephens	4000
5		25	BRADFORD CITY	4-1	Stephens 3, West	1100
6	Dec	2	Darlington	0-4		2536
7		25	YORK CITY	1-2	Scrimshaw	2000
8	Feb	10	Newcastle United	0-3		4333
9		24	HULL CITY	3-2	Stephens 3	1500
10	Mar	2	Middlesbrough	0-2		1480
11		9	Halifax Town	1-3	Marshall	2000
12		16	LEEDS UNITED	2-1	Howe(p), West	1500
13		22	BRADFORD PARK AVENUE	0-4		2500
14		23	Bradford City	0-4		2500
15		25	Huddersfield Town	1-4	West	4326
16		30	DARLINGTON	3-1	Armes, Middleton, Glassey	1300
17	May	18	York City	1-2	West	
18		20	Bradford Park Avenue	0-2		469
19		25	MIDDLESBROUGH	1-2	Middleton	1000
20	Jun	1	HUDDERSFIELD TOWN	2-2	Carr 2	

		p	w	d	l	f	a	pts
1	Huddersfield T	20	15	4	1	54	22	34
2	Newcastle United	20	12	0	8	58	39	24
3	Bradford Park Ave.	19	10	2	7	44	38	22
4	Middlesbrough	20	9	4	7	49	42	22
5	Leeds United	18	9	3	6	36	27	21
6	Bradford City	19	9	3	7	41	36	21
7	Hull City	20	8	1	11	35	41	17
8	York City	20	8	1	11	36	51	17
9	Darlington	19	6	3	10	44	57	15
10	HARTLEPOOLS U	20	6	1	13	27	47	13
11	Halifax T	19	3	2	14	29	53	8

Some fixtures not played

1943/44 Football League North First and Second Championships

1	Aug	28	MIDDLESBROUGH	1-0	Scrimshaw	2584
2	Sep	4	Middlesbrough	2-3	Bamford(p), Mullen	4000
3		11	SUNDERLAND	0-3		6208
4		18	Sunderland	0-3		9840
5		25	Gateshead	3-3	Barrett(p), Adams, Short	3000
6	Oct	2	GATESHEAD	5-0	Johnson 2, Adams 2, Robinson	4649
7		9	York City	0-2		5868
8		16	YORK CITY	4-1	Robinson, Phillips, Corbett, Johnson	5241
9		23	Newcastle United	1-0	Barrett(p)	10056
10		30	NEWCASTLE UNITED	5-4	Short 2, Scott, Mullen, Newman	7472
11	Nov	6	DARLINGTON	2-1	Short, Bamford(p)	7200
12		13	Darlington	2-2	Robinson, Short	7009
13		20	Middlesbrough	3-1	Newman, Robinson, Short	4000
14		27	MIDDLESBROUGH	3-4	Newman, Short, Mullen	7000
15	Dec	4	Sunderland	2-1	Short, Johnson	6000
16		11	SUNDERLAND	1-1	Skinner	6585
17		18	DARLINGTON	5-1	Short 3, Robinson, Newman	4492
18		25	Darlington	5-1	Corbett, Robinson 2, Drake, Skinner	8890
19		27	Middlesbrough	1-1	Robinson	8500
20	Jan	1	MIDDLESBROUGH	1-1	Skinner	9100
21		8	NEWCASTLE UNITED	1-2	Short	6326
22		15	Newcastle United	1-5	Robinson	13835
23		22	Sunderland	4-3	Bamford 2, Newman, Ward	7500
24		29	SUNDERLAND	4-2	Farrington 2, Wardle, Hamilton	7000
25	Feb	5	DARLINGTON	2-1	Short, Skinner	8000
26		12	Darlington	4-2	Tooze 2(og), Robinson, Farrington	10000
27		19	GATESHEAD	5-6	Short 2(1p), Scott, Smallwood 2	7000
28		26	Gateshead	2-2	Short 2(1p)	2000
29	Mar	4	NEWCASTLE UNITED	3-1	Scott, Short, Bamford	8432
30		11	Newcastle United	0-3		26110
31		18	Sunderland	0-3		3000
32		25	SUNDERLAND	2-1	Short, Scott	4835
33	Apr	1	Gateshead	2-3	Short, Farrington	2000
34		8	GATESHEAD	3-3	Baines 2, Drake	5419
35		15	MIDDLESBROUGH	2-6	Bamford, Short	3670
36		22	Middlesbrough	5-0	One og, Scott, Nettleton 2, Baines	2000
37		29	Gateshead	1-3	Baines	500
38	May	6	GATESHEAD	6-2	Baines 3, Farrington, Scott, Short	2000

First Championship (top 12 clubs only)

		p	w	d	l	f	a	pts
1	Blackpool	18	12	4	2	46	20	28
2	Manchester United	18	13	2	3	56	30	28
3	Liverpool	18	13	1	4	72	26	27
4	Doncaster	18	11	5	2	45	25	27
5	Bradford Park Ave.	18	11	4	3	65	28	26
6	Huddersfield T	18	12	2	4	48	35	26
7	Northampton T	18	10	5	3	43	25	25
8	Aston Villa	18	11	3	4	43	27	25
9	Sunderland	18	10	3	5	46	30	23
10	HARTLEPOOLS U	18	10	3	5	44	31	23
11	Everton	18	9	4	5	60	34	22
12	Blackburn Rovers	18	10	2	6	47	32	22

Second Championship

Finished mid-table with the following record:

HARTLEPOOLS U 20 8 4 8 49 50 20

League North Cup

Hartlepool's record in the Second Championship meant they qualified for the knock out stages of the League Cup (see games 37 and 38).

Games 1- 18 in the First Championship, 19-38 in the Second Championship. League Cup results were included in the Second Championship

1944/45: Football League North First and Second Championships

1	Aug	26	York City	1-3	Nettleton	4000
2	Sep	2	YORK CITY	5-0	Horton 3, Copeland, Short	2500
3		9	DARLINGTON	4-2	Horton 2, Copeland, Smallwood	6240
4		16	Darlington	1-2	Horton	6736
5		23	Gateshead	3-1	Horton, Nettleton, Smallwood	2000
6		30	GATESHEAD	2-5	Barrett(p), Short	6000
7	Oct	7	BRADFORD PARK AVENUE	0-0		8057
8		14	Bradford Park Avenue	1-4	Nettleton	7184
9		21	SUNDERLAND	2-6	Catterick, Short	8484
10		28	Sunderland	2-4	Scott, West	10000
11	Nov	4	MIDDLESBROUGH	2-3	Harrison 2	4784
12		11	Middlesbrough	3-0	West, Short, Turney	6000
13		18	Leeds United	2-6	Cochrane, Copeland	8000
14		25	LEEDS UNITED	3-0	Nettleton, Scott, Cochrane	4940
15	Dec	2	NEWCASTLE UNITED	2-3	Nettleton, Cochrane	7204
16		9	Newcastle United	0-3		12000
17		16	Bradford City	4-2	Horton, Cochrane(p), Harrison 2	2000
18		23	BRADFORD CITY	4-3	Brown 3, Wardle	5500
19		26	Middlesbrough	0-0		10000
20		30	MIDDLESBROUGH	6-4	Short, Cochrane 2, Brown 2, Harrison	8000
21	Jan	6	Gateshead	2-1	Harrison, Brown	3000
22		13	GATESHEAD	1-1	Brown	6756
23		20	Darlington	2-3	Brown, Cochrane	4199
24	Feb	10	Newcastle United	1-4	Short	15467
25		17	Sunderland	2-6	Short, Robinson	12200
26		24	SUNDERLAND	3-1	Adams, Brown 2	9817
27	Mar	3	NEWCASTLE UNITED	2-1	Douglas, Brown	9523
28		10	YORK CITY	1-1	Brown	5590
29		17	DARLINGTON	0-3		11869
30		24	MIDDLESBROUGH	3-0	Short, Brown 2	4132
31		31	Middlesbrough	3-1	Lyons 2, Skinner	3000
32	Apr	7	HUDDERSFIELD TOWN	1-6	Lyons	6046
33		14	Huddersfield Town	3-6	Williams 2, Howe(og)	2210
34		21	Sunderland	0-5		10000
35		28	SUNDERLAND	0-2		3275
36	May	5	DARLINGTON	2-0	Bainbridge, Skinner	2000
37		12	Darlington	0-3		3173
38		19	Middlesbrough	2-1	Short, Robertson	2500
39		21	DARLINGTON	0-5		2500

First Championship

Finished mid-table with the following record:

HARTLEPOOLS U	18	7	1	10	41	47	15

Second Championship

Finished mid-table with the following record:

HARTLEPOOLS U	21	8	3	10	34	54	19

and failed to qualify for knock-out stages of the League Cup North

Games 1- 18 in the First Championship, 19-39 in the Second championship

1945/46: Football League Division 3 (North East)

1	Aug	25	DONCASTER ROVERS	1-1	Short	5997
2	Sep	1	Doncaster Rovers	0-2		7000
3		8	Rotherham United	0-3		7000
4		15	ROTHERHAM UNITED	2-4	Dryden, Robertson	5000
5		22	BRADFORD CITY	3-2	Baines, Robertson, Short	3754
6		29	Bradford City	0-2		7647
7	Oct	6	Carlisle United	3-1	Short 2, Robertson	6000
8		13	CARLISLE UNITED	3-2	Short 2(1p), Robertson	5813
9		20	GATESHEAD	0-2		6000
10		27	Gateshead	1-3	Harrison	5613
11	Nov	3	YORK CITY	0-2		4000
12		10	York City	2-5	Morris 2	4000
13	Dec	1	Halifax Town	2-3	Robinson, McMahon	4000
14		8	HALIFAX TOWN	0-0		3000
15		22	Lincoln City	2-4	McMahon, Johnson	5000
16		25	DARLINGTON	0-0		5961
17		26	Darlington	2-5	Johnson, McMahon	8518
18	Jan	1	LINCOLN CITY	1-4	Price	4689
19	Jan	5	Halifax Town	5-2	Copeland 2, Johnson, McMahon, Woollett	3000
20		12	Rotherham United	1-1	McMahon	8436
21		19	ROTHERHAM UNITED	2-3	Short, Johnson	5000
22		26	Darlington	1-3	Johnson	5161
23	Feb	2	DARLINGTON	5-1	McMahon 2(1p), Copeland, Short, Johnson	4596
24		9	CARLISLE UNITED	5-3	Johnson 4, Short	5238
25		16	Carlisle United	3-1	Johnson 3	7000
26		23	BRADFORD CITY	0-0		5144
27	Mar	2	Bradford City	2-6	Short 2	5000
28		9	HALIFAX TOWN	1-1	Moses	5874
29	Mar	23	Crewe Alexandra	2-1	Price, Oakes	5000
30		30	CREWE ALEXANDRA	3-3	Tabram, McMahon, Price	6000
31	Apr	6	SOUTHPORT	1-2	Copeland	7122
32		13	Southport	1-1	Price	5000
33		19	BARROW	3-1	Harden, McMahon, Copeland	5837
34		20	Darlington	1-4	Tabram	3372
35		22	Barrow	1-2	Spelman(p)	3600
36		27	York City	3-2	Price 2, Harden	2000
37	May	4	YORK CITY	6-2	Price 2, McMahon 2, Scott, Spelman(p)	4150

		p	w	d	l	f	a	pts
1	Rotherham U	18	12	2	4	56	28	26
2	Darlington	18	12	2	4	61	36	26
3	Gateshead	18	11	2	5	51	34	24
4	Doncaster Rovers	18	8	4	6	34	35	20
5	York City	18	6	6	6	34	34	18
6	Halifax Town	18	7	4	7	39	46	18
7	Bradford City	18	6	4	8	45	40	16
8	Carlisle United	18	5	3	10	34	58	13
9	Lincoln City	18	4	2	12	34	54	10
10	HARTLEPOOLS U	18	3	3	12	22	45	9

Games 1 - 18 Div. 3 (NE), 19-28 Div.3 (NE) Cup Qualifying games, 29-37 Div. 3 (NE) Cup. Games 33-37: Division 3 (North) Second Championship.

Division 3 (North East) Cup Qualifying

		p	w	d	l	f	a	pts
1	Doncaster Rovers	10	6	3	1	24	15	15
2	Carlisle United	10	7	0	3	30	17	14
3	Bradford City	10	4	3	3	27	22	11
4	HARTLEPOOLS U	10	4	3	3	25	21	11
5	Gateshead	10	4	2	4	21	23	10
6	Darlington	10	5	0	5	26	31	10
7	Rotherham U	10	3	2	5	24	26	8
8	York City	10	2	4	4	14	18	8
9	Halifax Town	10	2	4	4	15	18	8
10	Lincoln City	10	2	1	7	21	38	5

Qualified for Competitiion Proper (games 29-32)
March 30th: extra time played

See later page for two FA Cup games on Nov. 17 and 24.

F.A. CUP IN NON-LEAGUE SEASONS

Player's appearances and goals are included in the A-Z section only if they also made a League appearance

1908/09

Q1	Oct	3 West Hartlepool	2-1	Brown, Smith	7,000	Mearns	Priest	Smith	S Tweddle	Hand	Ledger	Fletcher	F Tweddle	Edgley	Brown	Roberts
Q2		17 South Bank	2-2	Edgley 2		Mearns	Priest	Harvey	S Tweddle	Hand	Ledger	Fletcher	F Tweddle	Edgley	Brown	Roberts
rep		21 SOUTH BANK	0-2		3,000	Mearns	Priest	Harvey	S Tweddle	Hand	Ledger	F Tweddle	Fletcher	Edgley	Brown	Seal

1909/10

Q1	Oct	2 WINGATE ALBION	6-3	Edgley, Brown 2, Fletcher 2, Thompson	6,000	Kelley	T Hegarty	Billam	Hand	Smith	Ledger	F Tweddle	Fletcher	Edgley	Brown	Thompson
Q2		16 DARLINGTON	0-1		8,000	McIver	T Hegarty	R Hegarty	S Tweddle	Hand	Smith	F Tweddle	Fletcher	Edgley	Brown	Thompson

1910/11

PR	Sep	17 HORDEN ATHLETIC	5-0	Featherstone, Stokoe, Fletcher 3(1p)		McIver	Hogg	Hedley	S Tweddle	Hand	Ledger	Bainbridge	Fletcher	Featherstone	Stokoe	Griffin
Q1	Oct	1 Darlington	1-1	Fletcher		McIver	Hogg	Hedley	S Tweddle	Larkin	Ledger	Bainbridge	Fletcher	Morgan	Stokoe	Griffin
rep		6 DARLINGTON	0-1			McIver	Hogg	Hedley	S Tweddle	Larkin	Ledger	Bainbridge	Fletcher	Morgan	Stokoe	Griffin

1911/12

Q4	Nov	18 North Shields Ath.	1-2	Stokoe		Carmichael	McDonald	Hedley	Gorman	Penman	Prosser	F Tweddle	Fletcher	Stokoe	Grierson	Griffin

1912/13

Q1	Oct	12 HOUGHTON ROVERS	3-1	Humphreys(p), Fletcher 2	4,000	Pearson	Ellis	Gatenby	Baker	Hibbert	Little	Mayo	Fletcher	Humphreys	Stokoe	Marsh
Q2	Nov	2 WINGATE ALBION	4-1	Stokoe, Humphreys 3	3,800	Pearson	Ellis	Gatenby	Baker	Hibbert	Little	Mayo	Fletcher	Humphreys	Stokoe	Marsh
Q3		16 SUNDERLAND ROVERS	2-1	Fletcher, Henderson		Pearson	Ellis	Gatenby	Baker	Hibbert	Pickering	Mayo	Fletcher	Henderson	Stokoe	Marsh
Q4		30 CASTLEFORD TOWN	1-0	Mayo	4,700	Pearson	Ellis	Gatenby	Baker	Hibbert	Pickering	Mayo	Fletcher	Humphreys	Stokoe	Outhwaite
Q5	Dec	14 Gainsborough Trinity	0-4			Pearson	Ellis	Gatenby	Baker	Butler	Pickering	Mayo	Fletcher	Humphreys	Mason	Bennett

Q2 and Q3 played at Hartlepools by arrangement.

1913/14

PR	Sep	27 SUNDERLAND ROVERS	0-0		4,000	Gill	Ellis	Graham	Baker	Hibbert	Manners	Bennett	Walker	Smith	Lowe	Young
rep	Oct	1 Sunderland Rovers	3-1	Smith, Hibbert 2(1p)	3,000	Gill	Ellis	Graham	Baker	Hibbert	Manners	Jobling	Walker	Smith	Lowe	Young
Q1		11 ANNFIELD PLAIN	6-1	Lowe 2, Walker 2, Smith 2	4,327	Gill	Ellis	Graham	Varty	Hibbert	Manners	Bennett	Walker	Smith	Lowe	Young
Q2	Nov	1 BIRTLEY	4-0	Lowe, Smith 2, Bryden	5,143	Gill	Ellis	Gatenby	Baker	Hibbert	Manners	Bennett	Young	Smith	Lowe	Bryden
Q3		15 HORDEN ATHLETIC	4-0	Smith 3, Manners	5,300	Gill	Ellis	Graham	Baker	Hibbert	Manners	Bennett	Young	Smith	Lowe	Bryden
Q4		29 SOUTH SHIELDS	0-1			Gill	Ellis	Graham	Baker	Hibbert	Manners	Bennett	Young	Smith	Lowe	Bryden

Q1 played at home by arrangement.

1914/15

Q4	Nov	21 BISHOP AUCKLAND	6-2	Strugnell, Butler 3, Hibbert, Luke		Gill	Taylor	Graham	McDougall	Hibbert	Manners	Luke	McGill	Butler	Stugnell	Bell
Q5	Dec	5 Rochdale	0-2		2,000	Gill	Taylor	Graham	McDougall	Hibbert	Manners	Luke	McGill	Butler	Stugnell	Bell

1919/20

Q4	Nov	22	Bishop Auckland	0-1			Gill	Franks	Mordue	Gray	Scott	Topping	Toward	Hafekost	Reed	Hewitt	Bryden

1920/21

PR	Sep	25	SOUTH BANK EAST END	7-0	Kessler, Short 3, Hewitt, Ramsey 2	5,000	Gill	Franks	Crilly	Potter	Thoms	Topping	Yews	Hewitt	Ramsey	Short	Kessler
Q1	Oct	9	HAVERTON HILL	3-3	Short, Sotheran, Topping	4,000	Gill	Stephenson	Crilly	Potter	Thoms	Topping	Yews	Hewitt	Sotheran	Short	Kessler
rep		13	HAVERTON HILL	0-0			Summerfield	Franks	Crilly	Ashton	Thoms	Topping	Yews	Hewitt	Potter	Short	Kessler
rep2		18	Haverton Hill	1-0	Potter	3,000	Summerfield	Franks	Crilly	Ashton	Thoms	Stephenson	Yews	Hewitt	Potter	Short	Kessler
Q2		23	Scarborough	4-1	Mulholland 2, Hewitt 2(1p)		Gill	Stephenson	Crilly	Potter	Thoms	Ashton	Yews	Mulholland	Lister	Hewitt	Kessler
Q3	Nov	6	LOFTUS ALBION	2-1	Kessler, Lister	5,815	Gill	Stephenson	Crilly	Potter	Thoms	Ashton	Yews	Mulholland	Lister	Hewitt	Kessler
Q4		20	HOUGHTON ROVERS	3-0	Lister 2, Thoms	7,743	Summerfield	Stephenson	Crilly	Potter	Thoms	Ashton	Yews	Mulholland	Lister	Hewitt	Kessler
Q5	Dec	11	BISHOP AUCKLAND	1-1	Thoms	8,000	Gill	Stephenson	Crilly	Potter	Thoms	Ashton	Yews	Mulholland	Lister	Hewitt	Kessler
rep		15	Bishop Auckland	5-0	Lister 3, Hardy, Kessler		Gill	Summerfield	Crilly	Potter	Thoms	Short	Hewitt	Mulholland	Lister	Hardy	Kessler
Q6		18	Swansea Town	0-3			Gill	Lawson	Crilly	Potter	Thoms	Short	Hewitt	Mulholland	Lister	Hardy	Kessler

Q1 played at home by arrangement. Q1 replay a.e.t.
Q1 second replay at Ayresome Park, Middlesbrough.

THE F.A. CUP IN 1945/46

R1/1	Nov	17	GATESHEAD	1-2	McMahon(p)	5,148	Jarrie	Gorman	Porter	Cliff	Keeys	Troman	Morris	Robertson	Lewis	West	McMahon
R1/2		24	Gateshead	2-6	Holland, McMahon	6,152	Jarrie	Gorman	Porter	Brown	Troman	Woods	Morris	Holland	West	Robertson	McMahon

The League Season of 1939/40 (Abandoned on the outbreak of war)

Aug	26	BARROW	1-1	Mantle	6380	Robinson	Wright	Brown	Price	Turner	Deacon	Foreman	Earl	Mantle	West	Dodds
	30	Gateshead	0-3		2702	Robinson	Wright	Wilson	Daniels	Turner	Deacon	Foreman	Earl	Mantle	West	Dodds
Sep	2	Crewe Alexandra	0-0		3849	Wallace	Wright	Brown	Thomas	Turner	Deacon	Foreman	Earl	Love	West	Dodds

F.A. Cup action from 1908.
Hartlepools' second goal against West Hartlepool.

HARTLEPOOL'S MANAGERS

Fred Priest	1908-12
Percy Humphreys	1912-13
Jack Manners	1913-20
Cecil Potter	1920-22
David Gordon	1922-24
Jack Manners	1924-27
Bill Norman	1927-31
Jackie Carr	1931-35
Jimmy Hamilton	1935-40
Fred Westgarth	1943-57
Ray Middleton	1957-59
Bill Robinson	1959-62
Allenby Chilton	1962-63
Bob Gurney	1963-64
Alvan Williams	1964-65
Geoff Twentyman	1965
Brian Clough	1965-67
Angus McLean	1967-70
John Simpson	1970-71
Len Ashurst	1971-74
Ken Hale	1974-76
Billy Horner	1976-83
John Duncan	1983
Mick Docherty	1983
Billy Horner	1983-86
John Bird	1986-88
Bobby Moncur	1988-89
Cyril Knowles	1989-91
Alan Murray	1991-93
Viv Busby	1993
John MacPhail	1993-94
David McCreery	1994-95
Keith Houchen	1995-96
Mick Tait	1996-

CHAIRMEN

Bill Paterson	1908-14
Bill Coates	1914-23
Bob Stonehouse	1923-24
Bill Yeats	1924-52
Harold Sargeant	1952-60
Norman Hope	1960-63
Ernest Ord	1963-66
John Curry	1966-73
Tom Aird	1973-75
Ernest Ord	1975
Vince Barker	1975-84
John Smart	1984-89
Garry Gibson	1989-94
Harold Hornsey	1994-97
Ken Hodcroft	1997-

SECRETARIES

Robert Martin	1908-10
Bob Stonehouse	1910-13
Tom Robertson	1913-16
George Morris	1916-20
Cecil Potter	1920-22
Bob Nicholson	1922-30
Frank Perryman	1930-61
Bill Hillan	1961-83
Linda Holmes	1983-85
Malcolm Kirby	1985-90
Alan Murray *	1990-91
Ken Green *	1991-92
Stuart Bagnall *	1992-97
Maureen Smith	1997-

* *Chief Executive*

Name		Date of Birth	Place of Birth	Died	First Season	Last Season	Previous Club	Next Club	Appearances				Goals			
									League	FAC	FLC	Oth.	Leag	FAC	FLC	Oth.
Abdallah T	Tewfik	23 Jun 1897	Cairo, Egypt		1923		Bridgend Town	Providence Clamdiggers	11	0	0	0	1	0	0	0
Adamson T	Terry	15 Oct 1948	Shiney Row		1967		Luton Town	Scarborough	1	0	0	0	0	0	0	0
Ainsley J	Jason	30 Jul 1970	Stockton-on-Tees		1994		Spennymoor United	Inglewood Kiev	15	1	2	2	1	0	0	0
Aitken AL	Andy		Newcastle upon Tyne		1935		Mickley		1	0	0	0	0	0	0	0
Allan W	William		Strathaven		1931		Greenock Morton	Scottish football	1	0	0	0	0	0	0	0
Allen JT	Jack	1899	Sneinton		1924		Crystal Palace	Jarrow	29	5	0	0	3	0	0	0
Allen KR	Ken	12 Jan 1949	Thornaby-on-Tees		1968		Tow Law Town	Fulham	7	0	0	0	0	0	0	0
Allinson J	Jamie	15 Jun 1978	Stockton-on-Tees		1995		Trainee	Guiseley	4	1	0	1	0	0	0	0
Allison JJ	John	17 Nov 1913	Consett	1971	1946		Barnsley		13	0	0	0	0	0	0	0
Allison WML	Billy	13 Jan 1908	Shildon	1981	1935	1937	Eden Colliery	Spennymoor United	107	12	0	3	0	0	0	0
Allon JB	Joe	12 Nov 1966	Gateshead		1988	1990	Swansea City	Chelsea	168	8	8	10	67	5	4	3
					1995	1997	Lincoln City	retired								
Anderson C	Chris	30 Aug 1925	Aberdeen	1986	1946		Aberdeen	Army football	2	0	0	0	0	0	0	0
Anderson JB	Jimmy				1922		Musselburgh Bruntonians		13	0	0	0	0	0	0	0
Anderson WB	Billy	28 Mar 1935	Sunderland		1955	1960	Barnsley		179	8	0	0	11	0	0	0
Arch WH	Harry	29 Nov 1894	Tipton	1978	1926		Grimsby Town	Bilston United	23	1	0	0	0	0	0	0
Ashurst L	Len	10 Mar 1939	Liverpool		1970	1972	Sunderland	retired	46	5	2	0	2	0	0	0
Ashworth B	Barry	18 Aug 1942	Stockport		1964	1965	Southend United	Tranmere Rovers	45	2	2	0	4	0	0	0
Aston S	Stan	10 May 1940	Nuneaton		1966	1967	Burton Albion	Nuneaton Borough	21	0	0	0	0	0	0	0
Atkinson CBC	Charlie	05 May 1938	Haswell		1959	1963	Eppleton CW	Boston United	47	1	1	0	0	0	0	0
Atkinson DJ	David	03 Apr 1951	Hull		1968		Hull City	Charlton Athletic	8	0	0	0	1	0	0	0
Atkinson P	Paul	19 Jan 1966	Chester-le-Street		1989		Port Vale (loan)		11	0	0	0	1	0	0	0
Atkinson PD	Paddy	22 May 1970	Singapore		1988	1989	Sheffield United	Gateshead	21	3	1	4	3	0	0	0
Ayre W	Billy	07 May 1952	Crookhill		1977	1980	Scarborough	Halifax Town	141	8	6	0	27	1	0	0
Bain WC	Billy	16 Nov 1924	Alloa		1950		Dunfermline Athletic	Dunfermline Athletic	2	0	0	0	0	0	0	0
Bainbridge T	Terry	23 Dec 1962	Hartlepool		1981	1983	Henry Smith BC	Peterlee Newtown	37	1	4	2	1	0	1	0
Baines PC	Peter		Australia		1947		Crewe Alexandra	New Brighton	9	0	0	0	1	0	0	0
Baker DP	Paul	05 Jan 1963	Newcastle upon Tyne		1987	1991	Carlisle United	Motherwell	219	16	14	16	74	6	5	5
					1996	1997	Scunthorpe United									
Ballantyne JD	Dick	16 Sep 1927	Newburn		1950	1951	West Ham United	Millwall	13	0	0	0	0	0	0	0
Bannister N	Neville	21 Jul 1937	Brierfield		1964		Lincoln City	Rochdale	41	2	0	0	8	0	0	0
Barker AM	Allan	23 Feb 1956	Newcastle upon Tyne		1982	1983	Bishop Auckland	Bishop Auckland	60	3	2	1	1	0	2	0
Barlow P	Peter	09 Jan 1950	Portsmouth		1970		Workington	Stafford Rangers	11	0	0	0	0	0	0	0
Barras A	Tony	29 Mar 1971	Billingham		1988	1989	Trainee	Stockport County	12	1	2	0	0	0	0	0
Barratt A	Tony	18 Oct 1965	Salford		1986	1988	Billingham Town	York City	98	8	4	6	4	0	0	0
Barron MJ	Michael	22 Dec 1974	Chester-le-Street		1996		Middlesbrough (loan)		49	1	1	2	0	0	0	0
					1997		Middlesbrough									
Barson F	Frank	10 Apr 1891	Grimethorpe	1968	1929		Watford	Wigan Borough	9	0	0	0	2	0	0	0
Bassett GR	Graham	06 Oct 1964	Sunderland		1983		Ipswich Town	Burnley	7	2	0	0	0	0	0	0
Bates JW	John	28 Apr 1942	Newcastle upon Tyne		1965		Consett	Horden CW	11	0	0	0	0	0	0	0
Beech CS	Chris	16 Sep 1974	Blackpool		1996	1997	Blackpool		77	3	3	3	14	1	1	1
Bell ED	Dorman	22 Mar 1905	Hartlepool		1929		Belle Vue Temperance	Sheffield Wednesday	4	1	0	0	0	0	0	0
Bell JJ	Jack	02 Mar 1891	South Shields		1923		Newport County	Watford	12	0	0	0	4	0	0	0
Bell TJ	Terry	01 Aug 1944	Sherwood		1966	1969	Nuneaton Borough	Reading	117	4	2	0	34	3	1	0
Bennyworth IR	Ian	15 Jan 1962	Hull		1989	1991	Scarborough	Scarborough	82	2	8	3	3	0	0	0
Beresford JT	John	02 Jan 1943	Sunderland		1966		Local amateur	Ryhope CW	3	0	0	0	0	0	0	0
Berryman SC	Steve	26 Dec 1966	Blackburn		1989		Leyland Motors	Leyland Motors	1	0	0	0	0	0	0	0
Best R	Bobbie	12 Sep 1891	Mickley		1924	1926	Durham City		72	4	0	0	8	1	0	0
Bielby PA	Paul	24 Nov 1956	Darlington		1975	1977	Manchester United	Huddersfield Town	95	8	4	0	8	2	1	0
Bilcliff R	Ray	24 May 1931	Blaydon		1960	1963	Middlesbrough	retired	117	5	3	0	0	0	0	0
Billing PG	Peter	24 Oct 1964	Liverpool		1995		Port Vale	Crewe Alexandra	36	1	4	2	0	0	0	0
Bircham WC	Clive	07 Sep 1939	Philadelphia		1959	1962	Sunderland	Boston United	105	3	4	0	15	0	1	0
Bircumshaw A	Tony	08 Feb 1945	Mansfield		1966	1970	Notts County	Nuneaton Borough	185	7	2	0	11	0	0	0
Bird JC	John	09 Jun 1948	Doncaster		1980	1984	Newcastle United	retired	141	4	6	4	16	0	0	0
Birnie J	Jack				1923		Fraserburgh		5	0	0	0	0	0	0	0
Birtles F	Fred	05 Apr 1903	Stockport		1925		Crewe Alexandra	Crewe Alexandra	15	0	0	0	6	0	0	0
Blackburn EH	Eddie	18 Apr 1957	Easington Lane		1982	1986	York City		161	3	6	5	0	0	0	0
Blowman P	Peter	12 Dec 1949	Thornaby-on-Tees		1967	1969	Billingham Synthonia	Stockton	66	3	1	0	15	0	0	0
Blythe JD	David	21 Jul 1947	Huddersfield		1969		Crook Town		2	0	0	0	0	0	0	0
Boam SW	Stuart	28 Jan 1948	Kirkby-in-Ashfield		1982		Mansfield Town	Guisborough Town	1	0	0	0	0	0	0	0
Boland GA	Dicky	06 Oct 1902	Marley Hill	1977	1925	1927	White-le-Head Rangers	Reading	64	1	0	0	9	0	0	0
Bonass AE	Albert	01 Jan 1912	York	1945	1934	1935	York City	Chesterfield	77	9	0	3	31	4	0	1
Borthwick JR	John	24 Mar 1964	Hartlepool		1982	1988	Owton Manor SC	Darlington	117	6	3	10	14	1	0	1
Borthwick JW	Walter	1897	Poplar		1922		Cowdenbeath	Nithsdale Wanderers	2	0	0	0	0	0	0	0
Boulton JWC	John	1899	Southwick		1923		Southwick		4	0	0	0	0	0	0	0
Bowling I	Ian	27 Jul 1965	Sheffield		1989		Lincoln City (loan)		1	0	0	0	0	0	0	0
Bowron S	Steve	1903	Chilton		1929	1933	Ferryhill Athletic	Aldershot	194	8	0	1	0	0	0	0
Boylan A	Tony	19 Feb 1950	Hartlepool		1969	1971	Bishop Auckland	Bishop Auckland	11	0	0	0	0	0	0	0
Bradbury A	Allen	23 Jan 1947	Barnsley		1970		Kettering Town		7	0	0	0	0	0	0	0
Bradford JR	Jimmy	1914	Walker	1990	1935	1936	Huddersfield Town	Frickley Colliery	9	0	0	0	0	0	0	0
Bradley R	Russell	28 Mar 1966	Birmingham		1996	1997	Scunthorpe United	Hednesford Town	55	0	2	2	2	0	0	0
Bradley W	Willie	26 Jun 1937	Glasgow		1963	1965	Ayr United		98	5	2	0	15	0	0	0
Braidford L	Lowe	1898			1922		Southern League football	USA football	29	0	0	0	9	0	0	0
Brass RA	Bobby	09 Nov 1943	Middlesbrough		1964	1965	Middlesbrough	Stockton	28	2	0	0	0	1	0	0
Bratt W	Bill	1896	Hartlepool		1921	1922	West Hartlepool Expansion	Wingate Albion	15	3	0	0	2	0	0	0
Briggs H	Harold	1904			1928		Newark	Barrow	18	1	0	0	3	0	0	0
Briggs W	Wally	29 Nov 1922	Middlesbrough	1990	1949	1951	Southport	Blyth Spartans	44	0	0	0	0	0	0	0
Broadbent AH	Albert	20 Aug 1934	Dudley		1966	1967	Bradford Park Avenue	Rotherham United	25	0	2	0	3	0	1	0
Brooks SM	Steve	18 Jun 1955	Liverpool		1978	1979	Southport	Barrow	63	2	4	0	2	0	0	0

Name		Date of Birth	Place of Birth	Died	First Season	Last Season	Previous Club	Next Club	Appearances League	FAC	FLC	Oth.	Goals Leag	FAC	FLC	Oth.
Brown CM	Charlie	1915	Tinsley		1938		Bolton Wanderers		5	0	0	0	0	0	0	0
Brown GA	George	1913	Whitton Park		1933	1935	Cockfield	Halifax Town	51	9	0	2	0	0	0	0
Brown J	Jimmy				1923		Lambton Star		1	0	0	0	0	0	0	0
Brown, John	Jack				1927		Marley Hill	West Stanley	5	0	0	0	0	0	0	0
Brown JH	Jack	19 Mar 1899	Worksop	1962	1937		Sheffield Wednesday	retired	1	0	0	0	0	0	0	0
Brown JT	John	02 Apr 1935	Edinburgh		1962	1963	Tranmere Rovers	Scarborough	68	2	3	0	10	0	0	0
Brown MR	Michael	25 Jan 1977	Hartlepool		1996		Manchester City (loan)		6	0	0	0	1	0	0	0
Brown P	Phil	30 May 1959	South Shields		1979	1984	St Hilda's Juniors	Halifax Town	217	11	12	9	8	0	0	1
Brown RB	Berry	06 Sep 1927	Hartlepool		1951	1955	Stockton		126	13	0	0	0	0	0	0
Brown W	Billy	22 Aug 1900	Fence Houses	1985	1931		Stockport County	Blackhall CW	13	0	0	0	3	0	0	0
Brown WH	Billy	11 Mar 1909	Choppington		1946	1947	Middlesbrough	Stockton	80	5	0	0	0	0	0	0
Brownlie JJ	John	11 Mar 1952	Caldercruix		1984		Middlesbrough	Berwick Rangers	19	2	2	1	1	0	0	0
Brownlow JM	Jackie	18 Jun 1916	Belfast		1948		Ipswich Town		3	0	0	0	0	0	0	0
Buckley MJ	Mick	04 Nov 1953	Manchester		1983		Sunderland	Carlisle United	6	0	2	0	0	0	0	0
Buller J	Joe	1909	Chilton		1929	1931	Chilton Colliery	Stoke City	86	0	0	0	2	0	0	0
Burgess DJ	Dave	20 Jan 1960	Liverpool		1994		Carlisle United (loan)		11	0	2	0	0	0	0	0
Burleigh MS	Martin	02 Feb 1951	Durham		1979	1981	Darlington	Bishop Auckland	84	5	4	3	0	0	0	0
Burlison TH	Tommy	23 May 1936	Edmondsley		1957	1963	Lincoln City	Darlington	148	6	3	0	5	1	0	0
Burluraux F	Fred	1907	Skelton		1932		South Bank	Scarborough	1	0	0	0	0	0	0	0
Burn F	Fred		Annfield Plain		1921		Annfield Plain		9	0	0	0	1	0	0	0
Burnett WJ	Billy	01 Mar 1926	Pelaw		1948	1953	Grimsby Town		194	10	0	0	17	2	0	0
Butler A	Arthur	1892	Norton		1921		Stockton		2	0	0	0	0	0	0	0
Butler E	Ernie	17 Jun 1896	Stillington		1924	1925	Queens Park Rangers	Durham City	58	5	0	0	4	1	0	0
Butler K	Ken	23 Aug 1936	Whitburn		1959	1960	Whitburn	South Shields	20	0	1	0	2	0	0	0
Butler PJ	Paul	09 Jun 1964	Stockton-on-Tees		1987		Hereford United	Brandon United	9	1	2	0	0	0	0	0
Byron PB	Paul	09 May 1965	Preston		1986		Blackburn Rovers	Southport	1	0	0	0	0	0	0	0
Cain JP	Jimmy	29 Dec 1933	Fishburn		1960	1961	South Shields	Blyth Spartans	30	2	2	0	0	0	0	0
Cairns JG	Jackie	13 Apr 1922	Newcastle upon Tyne		1947	1949	Local amateur		16	0	0	0	2	0	0	0
Calder JH	John	13 Oct 1911	Lochgelly		1938		Torquay United		4	0	0	0	0	0	0	0
Cameron J	Jack	07 Mar 1931	Dumbarton		1953	1959	Dumbarton	retired	175	18	0	0	0	0	0	0
Campbell PJ	Paul	07 Oct 1964	Newcastle upon Tyne		1983		Gateshead	Burnley	3	0	0	0	0	0	0	0
Canham A	Tony	08 Jun 1960	Leeds		1995		York City	Harrogate RA	29	0	3	1	1	0	0	0
Carney S	Steve	22 Sep 1957	Wallsend		1985		Darlington	Tow Law Town	7	0	0	0	0	0	0	0
Carr GGJ	Graham	08 Dec 1970	Darlington		1989		Trainee	Gateshead	1	0	2	0	0	0	0	0
Carr J	Jack	26 Nov 1891	South Bank	1942	1931		Blackpool	retired	10	0	0	0	1	0	0	0
Carr K	Kevin	06 Nov 1958	Morpeth		1987		Middlesbrough	Blyth Spartans	31	4	0	5	0	0	0	0
Carr P	Peter	25 Aug 1951	Darlington		1979		New England Teamen	New England Teamen	22	1	0	0	0	0	0	0
Carr T	Tommy	1903	Annfield Plain		1924	1928	Burnhope	West Stanley	131	4	0	0	13	0	0	0
Carswell R	Robert		Port Glasgow		1923		Greenock Morton		2	0	0	0	0	0	0	0
Carter TD	Tim	05 Oct 1967	Bristol		1993		Sunderland	Millwall	18	1	4	2	0	0	0	0
Catton E	Edwin		Langley Park		1933		Eden Colliery	Blackhall CW	8	0	0	1	3	0	0	0
Chambers PM	Phil	10 Nov 1953	Barnsley		1985		Rochdale	Rotherham United	29	2	0	1	0	0	0	0
Chape GE	George	1902	Longhoughton		1924		South Shields	Robert Thompsons	4	0	0	0	0	0	0	0
Chapman J	John	1917	Lumley		1938		Bury	Consett	9	2	0	0	0	0	0	0
Charlton H	Harry	22 Jun 1951	Gateshead		1975		Middlesbrough (loan)		3	0	0	0	0	0	0	0
Chatterton W	Walter	1911	Ferryhill		1935		Trimdon Grange	Blackhall CW	2	0	0	0	1	0	0	0
Chesser JM	Jimmy	27 Dec 1899	Stockton-on-Tees	1970	1922	1923	Stockton		41	0	0	0	0	0	0	0
Chilton AJT	Tony	07 Sep 1965	Maryport		1985		Burnley	Whitley Bay	3	0	0	0	0	0	0	0
Christon L	Len	1906	Skelton		1928		Carlin How		2	0	0	0	0	0	0	0
Clark HM	Harry	29 Dec 1932	Newcastle upon Tyne		1958	1960	Sheffield Wednesday		118	5	1	0	43	0	0	0
Clark ID	Ian	23 Oct 1974	Stockton-on-Tees		1997		Doncaster Rovers		24	1	0	1	7	0	0	0
Clarke H	Harry	26 Nov 1960	Sunderland		1981		Middlesbrough	Belgian football	7	1	0	0	1	0	0	0
Clarke JH	Harry	27 Mar 1921	Broomhill		1949		Darlington	Stockton	7	2	0	0	1	1	0	0
Clarke MMG	Malcolm	29 Jun 1944	Clydebank		1970	1971	Bristol City	Apia Leichardt	33	1	3	0	0	0	0	0
Clarke N	Neville	09 Oct 1930	Gateshead		1953		Sunderland	Horden CW	2	0	0	0	0	0	0	0
Clegg DL	David	23 Oct 1976	Liverpool		1996		Liverpool	Winsford United	35	2	1	1	2	0	0	0
Cleugh W	Billy	1914	Gateshead		1934		Local amateur	Horden CW	1	0	0	0	0	0	0	0
Clydesdale W	Bill	14 Sep 1935	Fallin		1960		Aberdeen		14	0	1	0	0	0	0	0
Coates WA	Walter		Burnhope		1928		Newport County		2	0	0	0	0	0	0	0
Cochrane GT	Terry	23 Jan 1953	Killyleagh		1986		Millwall	Billingham Synthonia	2	0	0	0	0	0	0	0
Common J	John	1895	Sunderland		1923		South Shields		32	0	0	0	4	0	0	0
Conlon B	Bryan	14 Jan 1943	Shildon		1972	1973	Cambridge United	Shildon	41	0	1	0	3	0	0	0
Conlon PR	Paul	05 Jan 1978	Sunderland		1995		Trainee	Sunderland	15	0	0	0	4	0	0	0
Connell D	David				1922		Greenock Morton		15	2	0	0	0	0	0	0
Connor P	Paul	12 Jan 1979	Bishop Auckland		1997		Middlesbrough (loan)		5	0	0	0	0	0	0	0
Cook JA	Alec	1900	Trimdon Grange		1922	1924	Trimdon Grange	Spennymoor United	28	6	0	0	3	3	0	0
Cook MC	Mitch	15 Oct 1961	Scarborough		1994		Blackpool	Guiseley	24	0	0	0	0	0	0	0
Cooper D	Doug	18 Oct 1936	Middlesbrough		1960		Rotherham United		16	1	0	0	6	1	0	0
Cooper JT	Jim	28 Dec 1939	Glasgow		1965		Brighton & Hove Albion	Addington	19	1	2	0	1	0	1	0
Cooper MN	Mark	18 Dec 1968	Wakefield		1996		Exeter City	Leyton Orient	33	1	2	1	9	0	0	0
Copeland E	Teddy	19 May 1921	Hetton-le-Hole		1938		Easington Juniors	Blackhall CW	38	2	0	2	9	0	0	0
					1946	1947	Easington CW	Spennymoor United								
Copeman R	Bobby		Washington		1937		Washington Colliery	Washington CW	1	0	0	0	0	0	0	0
Corbett AM	Alex	20 Apr 1921	Saltcoats		1953		Weymouth	Llanelly	7	0	0	0	0	0	0	0
Coulthard FR	Frank	1909	Cockerton		1934		Evenwood Town		4	0	0	0	0	0	0	0
Cowan WD	Billy	09 Aug 1896	Edinburgh		1930		Peebles Rovers	Darlington	3	0	0	0	2	0	0	0
Cowell W	Billy	07 Dec 1902	Acomb		1924	1925	Huddersfield Town	Derby County	78	9	0	0	0	0	0	0
Cox BR	Brian	07 May 1961	Sheffield		1990		Mansfield Town		34	2	4	3	0	0	0	0
Coyne JD	John	18 Jul 1951	Liverpool		1972	1973	Tranmere Rovers	Dundalk	55	3	2	0	10	0	0	0

Name		Date of Birth	Place of Birth	Died	First Season	Last Season	Previous Club	Next Club	Appearances League	FAC	FLC	Oth.	Goals Leag	FAC	FLC	Oth.
Craig J	John				1925	1926	Dipton United	Crewe Alexandra	30	1	0	0	6	1	0	0
Creamer PA	Peter	20 Sep 1953	Hartlepool		1976	1977	Doncaster Rovers	Gateshead	63	3	0	0	3	0	0	0
Crilly T	Tommy	20 Jul 1895	Stockton-on-Tees	1960	1920	1921	Stockton	Derby County	37	11	0	0	0	0	0	0
Crook LR	Les	26 Jun 1949	Manchester		1970		Oxford United	Macclesfield Town	25	1	1	0	3	0	0	0
Cross P	Paul	31 Oct 1965	Barnsley		1991	1993	Barnsley	Darlington	74	4	8	5	1	0	0	0
Cross R	Ryan	11 Oct 1972	Plymouth		1992	1993	Plymouth Argyle	Bury	50	5	8	5	2	0	0	0
Crowther GL	George	1892	Bishop Middleham		1921	1922	Southern League football	Tranmere Rovers	25	1	0	0	10	0	0	0
Crowther SJ	Steve	16 Jan 1955	Romiley		1975		Stockport County	Stalybridge Celtic	3	0	2	0	0	0	0	0
Crumplin I	Ian	12 Sep 1954	Lemington		1978	1979	Blue Star	Bishop Auckland	29	3	3	0	5	1	0	0
Cullen DJ	Jon	10 Jan 1973	Durham		1997		Morpeth Town	Sheffield United	34	1	2	2	12	0	0	0
Cummings RD	Bobby	17 Nov 1935	Ashington		1967	1968	Darlington	Port Elizabeth	52	1	1	0	12	0	0	0
Cunningham D	Dave	10 Aug 1953	Kirkcaldy		1976		Southend United (loan)		12	0	0	0	1	0	0	0
Cunningham KH	Ken	26 Oct 1941	Glasgow		1963		Falkirk		2	0	1	0	0	0	0	0
Curry SP	Sean	13 Nov 1966	Liverpool		1989		Blackburn Rovers	Preston North End	1	0	0	0	0	0	0	0
Curtis ER	Ernie	01 Jun 1907	Cardiff	1992	1937		Coventry City	retired	16	0	0	0	1	0	0	0
Dalton P	Paul	25 Apr 1967	Middlesbrough		1988	1991	Manchester United	Plymouth Argyle	151	7	10	9	37	1	2	3
Danskin J	Jason	28 Dec 1967	Winsford		1987		Mansfield Town (loan)		3	0	0	0	0	0	0	0
Darling M	Malcolm	04 Jul 1947	Arbroath		1977		Sheffield Wednesday	Morecambe	4	0	0	0	0	0	0	0
Daughtry PW	Paul	14 Feb 1973	Oldham		1994		Droylsden	Moron Bollklubbe	15	0	0	0	0	0	0	0
Davidson DL	Dave	04 Jun 1905	Aberdeen	1969	1937		Newcastle United	Gateshead	6	0	0	0	0	0	0	0
Davies AJ	Andy	06 Jun 1972	Wolverhampton		1990	1991	Torquay United	Torquay United	7	1	0	2	0	0	0	0
Davies G	Glen	20 Jul 1976	Brighton		1996	1997	Burnley	Worthing	52	1	3	1	1	0	0	0
Davies GP	Geoff	01 Jul 1947	Ellesmere Port		1976		Port Vale (loan)		5	0	0	0	1	0	0	0
Davies KF	Kenny	22 Dec 1970	Stockton-on-Tees		1989	1990	Trainee	Gateshead	6	0	3	1	0	0	0	0
Davis KG	Kelvin	29 Sep 1976	Bedford		1997		Luton Town (loan)		2	0	1	0	0	0	0	0
Davison E	Ted	15 Apr 1933	Seaham		1953		Seaham Juniors		1	0	0	0	0	0	0	0
Dawes M	Malcolm	03 Mar 1944	Trimdon		1970	1975	Aldershot	Workington	195	6	12	0	12	0	0	0
Dearden KC	Kevin	08 Mar 1970	Luton		1989		Tottenham Hotspur (loan)		10	0	0	0	0	0	0	0
Debont AC	Andy	07 Feb 1974	Wolverhampton		1995		Wolverhampton W (loan)		1	0	0	0	0	0	0	0
Denham CH	Charlie	28 Apr 1937	Hartlepool		1958		West Amateurs		5	0	0	0	3	0	0	0
Denham JW	John	06 Nov 1925	Middleton		1949		Hull City		1	0	0	0	0	0	0	0
Derbyshire T	Tommy	10 Dec 1930	Manchester		1950		Army football	Army football	1	0	0	0	0	0	0	0
Desmond P	Peter	23 Nov 1926	Cork	1990	1953		Stockton	Blackhall CW	1	0	0	0	0	0	0	0
Di Lella GM	Gustavo	06 Oct 1973	Buenos Aires		1997		Blyth Spartans		5	0	0	0	2	0	0	0
Diamond JJ	Jack	30 Oct 1910	Middlesbrough	1961	1938		Oldham Athletic	Hyde United	9	0	0	1	1	0	0	4
Dickenson J	Jimmy	1908	Pittington		1930		Easington Colliery	Blackpool	23	1	0	0	1	1	0	0
Dixon AP	Andrew	05 Aug 1968	Hartlepool		1986	1987	Seaton Holy Trinity		17	0	2	0	1	0	0	0
					1995		RAEC Mons	Bishop Auckland								
Dixon C	Charlie	1891	Sacriston		1922	1925	Middlesbrough		66	5	0	0	0	0	0	0
Dixon, Colin	Colin	24 Sep 1963	Newcastle upon Tyne		1983		Southampton		1	0	0	0	0	0	0	0
Dixon JW	Johnny	12 Mar 1934	Hartlepool		1958	1960	Throston Wanderers	Horden CW	35	5	0	0	2	0	0	0
Dixon KL	Kevin	27 Jul 1960	Blackhill		1983		Carlisle United (loan)		127	4	8	4	33	1	1	0
					1984	1986	Carlisle United	Scunthorpe United								
					1988		Scunthorpe United	York City								
Dixon RH	Bobby	08 Feb 1908	Pelton	1993	1928	1932	Birtley	Rhyl Athletic	114	3	0	0	27	1	0	0
Dobbing R	Bobby	27 Jun 1949	Sunderland		1969		Coventry City	Australian football	34	2	2	0	1	0	0	0
Dobell D	Danny	1906	Stoke		1926	1929	Chilton Colliery	Spennymoor United	62	0	0	0	5	0	0	0
Dobson P	Paul	17 Dec 1962	Hartlepool		1981	1982	Newcastle United	Horden CW	111	6	3	2	32	1	0	1
					1983	1985	Horden CW	Torquay United								
Dobson WE	Warren	05 Nov 1978	North Shields		1997		Scarborough	Spennymoor United	1	1	1	0	0	0	0	0
Doig R	Russell	17 Jan 1964	Millport		1987	1989	Leeds United	Nuneaton Borough	33	1	2	2	2	0	0	0
Don RP	Robert	1915	Glasgow		1938		Galston SA	South Shields	4	0	0	0	0	0	0	0
Donald RS	Bob		Durham		1921		South Shields	Wallsend	8	1	0	0	0	0	0	0
Donaldson RS	Bobby	26 Feb 1921	South Shields		1947	1951	Newcastle United		131	7	0	0	4	0	0	0
Dougherty J	Joe	1892	Darlington		1921		Shildon	Lincoln City	32	0	0	0	0	0	0	0
Douglas JS	John	01 Dec 1917	Hartlepool		1938		Trimdon Grange	Middlesbrough	32	0	0	0	1	0	0	0
					1948	1949	Middlesbrough	Halifax Town								
Douglas JS (2)	Jimmy	16 Sep 1941	Sunderland		1962		Willington	Bishop Auckland	13	0	0	0	4	0	0	0
Downing DG	Derrick	03 Nov 1945	Doncaster		1977		York City	Scarborough	40	5	2	0	4	1	0	0
Dowson F	Francis	1897	North Ormesby		1922		Middlesbrough		18	2	0	0	0	1	0	0
Dreyer G	Gordon	1914	Sunderland		1934		Washington Colliery	Hull City	41	4	0	3	0	0	0	0
					1936		Hull City	Luton Town								
Drysdale B	Brian	24 Feb 1943	Wingate		1965	1968	Lincoln City	Bristol City	170	7	5	0	2	0	0	0
Duggan AJ	Andy	19 Sep 1967	Bradford		1990		Huddersfield Town (loan)		2	0	1	0	0	0	0	0
Dunbar I	Ian	06 Jun 1971	Newcastle upon Tyne		1989	1990	Trainee		3	0	0	0	0	0	0	0
Dunn BJ	Brian	04 Oct 1940	Boston		1958	1960	Grimsby Town		27	1	0	0	1	0	0	0
Dunn R	Dick	23 Dec 1919	Easington	1986	1949		West Ham United	Wingate Welfare	13	0	0	0	2	0	0	0
Duthie JF	John	07 Jan 1903	Fraserburgh	1969	1923		Fraserburgh	Norwich City	3	1	0	0	0	1	0	0
Dyson J	Jim	16 Dec 1935	Ryhope		1954	1958	Seaham CW	Murton CW	63	5	0	0	0	0	0	0
Edgar E	Eddie	31 Oct 1956	Bristol		1976	1978	Newcastle United	Canadian football	75	6	2	0	0	0	0	0
Edgar J	Johnny	09 Apr 1936	Barnsley		1961	1962	York City	Exeter City	72	1	3	0	31	0	0	0
Edwards E	Ted	13 Feb 1936	Seaham		1957		Dawdon Juniors	Horden CW	1	0	0	0	0	0	0	0
Edwards R	Richie	09 Nov 1964	Hartlepool		1986				1	0	0	0	0	0	0	0
Elder AYP	Alex	11 Sep 1923	Perth		1951	1952	Dundee United	Forfar Athletic	65	4	0	0	20	2	0	0
Elliott A	Andy	02 May 1974	Newcastle upon Tyne		1996	1997	Spennymoor United		8	1	0	0	0	0	0	0
Elliott K	Kevin	05 Sep 1958	Chilton		1975	1976	Juniors	Willington	27	1	2	0	1	0	0	0
Ellis K	Ken	29 May 1948	Sunderland	1992	1971		Scarborough	Racing Jet	34	1	2	0	4	1	0	0
Ellison AL	Lee	13 Jan 1973	Bishop Auckland		1992		Darlington (loan)		4	0	0	0	1	0	0	0
Ellison WR	Roy	05 Jul 1948	Newbiggin		1970		Barrow (loan)		5	0	0	0	0	0	0	0

Name		Date of Birth	Place of Birth	Died	First Season	Last Season	Previous Club	Next Club	Appearances League	Appearances FAC	Appearances FLC	Appearances Oth.	Goals Leag	Goals FAC	Goals FLC	Goals Oth.
Embleton D	David	14 Sep 1952	Newcastle upon Tyne		1973	1975	Bury	Gateshead United	26	0	1	0	0	0	0	0
Embleton E	Eddie	1916	South Moor		1937		Bradford City	Gateshead	22	2	0	2	6	1	0	1
Emerson D	Dean	27 Dec 1962	Salford		1992	1993	Coventry City	Stockport County	45	4	7	4	1	0	0	0
Endean B	Barry	22 Mar 1946	Chester-le-Street		1975	1976	Huddersfield Town	Workington	25	0	2	0	5	0	0	0
English S	Sam	1910	Coleraine	1967	1936	1937	Queen of the South	Duntocher Hibs	69	3	0	3	27	3	0	1
Entwistle RP	Bobby	06 Oct 1938	Bury		1964		Llandudno	Chesterfield	14	2	0	0	3	2	0	0
Entwistle WP	Wayne	06 Aug 1958	Bury		1989		Altrincham	Curzon Ashton	2	0	0	0	0	0	0	0
Errington A	Darkie		Low Walker		1926	1930	Scotswood	Spennymoor United	81	1	0	0	0	0	0	0
Evans DT	Dave	06 Apr 1959	Peterlee		1978	1979	Juniors	Horden CW	4	0	0	0	0	0	0	0
Fagan MJ	Mike	22 Feb 1960	Gosforth		1979	1982	Carlisle United	Blyth Spartans	37	0	4	2	1	0	0	0
Fairhurst R	Dick	05 Sep 1911	St Helens		1934		Burnley	Tranmere Rovers	11	0	0	1	0	0	0	0
Fairhurst WS	Billy	01 Oct 1902	Blyth	1979	1933	1934	Northampton Town		58	6	0	1	0	0	0	0
Farnaby C	Craig	08 Aug 1967	Hartlepool		1984		Trainee	Easington Colliery	5	0	0	0	0	0	0	0
Fell JW	Jackie	14 May 1902	Quebec	1979	1928		Southend United	Connah's Quay & Shotton	21	1	0	0	0	0	0	0
Fenton I	Isaac	1910	Birtley		1937		Brentford	Consett	1	0	0	0	0	0	0	0
Ferguson GC	Cliff	1909	Langley Moor		1930		Durham City	Crook	1	0	0	0	0	0	0	0
Finch M	Mike	30 Jun 1965	Stockton-on-Tees		1983	1984	Juniors	Billingham Town	3	0	1	0	0	0	0	0
Finnigan J	Joseph				1933		Blackhill	Blackhill	3	0	0	0	0	0	0	0
Firman JR	John	1915	Evenwood		1935	1936	Evenwood Town	South Shields	2	0	0	1	0	0	0	1
Flanders F	Fred	01 Jan 1894	Derby	1967	1922		Newport County	Nuneaton Town	3	0	0	0	0	0	0	0
Fletcher SM	Steve	26 Jul 1972	Hartlepool		1990	1991	Trainee	Bournemouth	32	3	2	4	4	0	1	1
Fogarty AG	Amby	11 Sep 1933	Dublin		1963	1966	Sunderland	Cork Hibernian	127	7	4	0	22	3	0	0
Foggon A	Alan	23 Feb 1950	West Pelton		1977		Southend United (loan)		18	0	0	0	2	0	0	0
Folland R	Bobby	03 Dec 1940	Hartlepool		1959	1962	Newcastle United	Blackhall Club	58	4	2	0	24	4	0	0
Ford G	Gary	08 Feb 1961	York		1995		Harstad IL		3	0	1	0	0	0	0	0
Forrest K	Keith	18 Feb 1951	Hartlepool		1969	1970	St James	Bishop Auckland	6	0	0	0	0	0	0	0
Forster GP	Geoff	03 Aug 1954	Middlesbrough		1980		Whitby Town	South Bank	14	0	2	0	4	0	1	0
Foster JH	Jack	1894	Wombwell		1924	1926	Luton Town		54	3	0	0	2	0	0	0
Foster L	Lee	21 Oct 1977	Bishop Auckland		1995		Trainee	Tow Law Town	1	0	0	0	0	0	0	0
Foster WP	Wayne	11 Sep 1963	Leigh		1994		Heart of Midlothian (loan)		4	0	0	2	1	0	0	0
Fowler M	Martin	17 Jan 1957	York		1979		Blackburn Rovers (loan)		6	0	0	0	0	0	0	0
Fox A	Alan	10 Jul 1936	Holywell		1964	1965	Wrexham	Bradford City	58	3	3	0	0	0	0	0
Francis T	Terry	18 Jun 1943	Hartlepool		1963	1964	Billingham Synthonia	Consett	18	0	1	0	4	0	0	0
Franks A	Tony		Hartlepool		1919	1922	Spennymoor United		45	5	0	0	0	0	0	0
Fraser AM	Andy	29 Aug 1940	Newtongrange		1961	1963	Toronto City		82	2	1	0	2	0	0	0
Gabbiadini R	Riccardo	11 Mar 1970	Newport		1990	1991	Sunderland	Scarborough	14	0	4	1	2	0	1	0
Gadsby MD	Mick	01 Aug 1947	Oswestry		1971		York City	Dover	21	2	2	0	0	0	0	0
Gadston JE	Joe	13 Sep 1945	Hanwell		1972		Aldershot (loan)		1	0	0	0	0	0	0	0
Gaffney T	Terry	15 Feb 1952	Hartlepool		1977		Billingham Synthonia	Billingham Synthonia	13	0	2	0	1	0	0	0
Gallacher J	John	26 Jan 1969	Glasgow		1992	1993	Newcastle United	Falkirk	23	0	3	2	2	0	0	0
Gallagher I	Ian	30 May 1978	Hartlepool		1995	1996	Trainee	Seaham Red Star	1	0	0	1	0	0	0	0
Garrett S	Scott	09 Jan 1974	Gateshead		1993	1994	Trainee	Bishop Auckland	15	0	0	0	0	0	0	0
Gate KB	Ken	26 Oct 1948	Hartlepool		1969		St Josephs	Shildon	1	0	0	0	0	0	0	0
Gauden A	Allan	20 Nov 1944	Ashington		1973	1974	Grimsby Town	Gillingham	63	4	10	0	15	0	5	0
Gavin MW	Mark	10 Dec 1963	Baillieston		1984		Leeds United (loan)		10	0	0	0	1	0	0	0
					1997		Scunthorpe United									
Gibb DA	Dean	26 Oct 1966	Newcastle upon Tyne		1986	1987	Brandon United	Brandon United	48	2	2	4	3	1	0	0
Gibb T	Tommy	13 Dec 1944	Bathgate		1977		Sunderland		40	5	2	0	4	0	0	0
Gibbon AT	Arthur	24 May 1937	Durham		1958		Local amateur	Horden CW	13	0	0	0	0	0	0	0
Gilchrist PA	Phil	25 Aug 1973	Middlesbrough		1992	1994	Middlesbrough	Oxford United	82	4	5	5	0	0	0	0
Gill GA	George	1894	Heaton		1913	1923	Newcastle City		65	17	0	0	0	0	0	0
Gill J	Joe	10 Nov 1945	Sunderland		1968		Ashington	Bishop Auckland	4	0	0	0	0	0	0	0
Gill JBA	John	03 Feb 1941	Wednesbury		1965	1970	Mansfield Town	Nuneaton Borough	204	7	6	0	1	0	0	0
Goad AM	Alan	08 Aug 1948	Hailsham		1967	1977	Exeter City	retired	375	20	23	0	11	0	0	0
Godbold H	Harry	31 Jan 1939	Springwell		1960	1962	Sunderland	Boston United	65	3	2	0	8	0	0	0
Goldthorpe W	Wayne	19 Sep 1957	Staincross		1976		Huddersfield Town (loan)		54	3	1	0	9	1	1	0
					1978	1979	Huddersfield Town	Crewe Alexandra								
Gollogly J	John	04 Jul 1962	Bridlington		1982		Juniors	Guisborough Town	31	1	2	1	5	0	0	0
					1984	1986	Whitby Town									
Gorry MC	Martin	29 Dec 1954	Derby		1978	1979	Newcastle United	Shildon	59	4	4	0	0	0	0	0
Gourlay AM	Archie	29 Jun 1969	Greenock		1994		Preston North End	Whitley Bay	1	0	0	0	0	0	0	0
Graham J	Jack	1911	Newcastle upon Tyne		1934		Shelbourne		5	0	0	0	0	0	0	0
Graham JA	Jimmy	13 Jan 1911	Rothwell		1935		York City	Southend United	18	2	0	0	3	0	0	0
Graham SJ	Sam				1936		Walker Celtic	Bristol Rovers	12	0	0	0	0	0	0	0
Grant BP	Brian	10 May 1943	Coatbridge		1965	1966	Nottingham Forest	Bradford City	35	1	2	0	0	0	0	0
Granycome N	Neal	23 Oct 1958	Middlesbrough		1980		South Bank	South Bank	1	0	0	0	0	0	0	0
Gray T	Tom		Ashington		1924		Huddersfield Town		11	0	0	0	0	0	0	0
Grayson SD	Simon	21 Oct 1968	Sheffield		1987	1989	Sheffield United	Sheffield	44	5	3	2	13	0	2	0
Green L	Les	17 Oct 1941	Atherstone		1965	1966	Burton Albion	Rochdale	34	0	0	0	0	0	0	0
Green W	Bill	22 Dec 1950	Newcastle upon Tyne		1969	1972	Juniors	Carlisle United	131	2	4	0	9	0	0	0
Gregory CF	Fred	24 Oct 1911	Doncaster		1946		Crystal Palace	Rotherham United	21	2	0	0	0	0	0	0
Gregson WCS	Bill		Stockton-on-Tees		1921				1	0	0	0	0	0	0	0
Gribbin BT	Brian	02 Jun 1954	Newcastle upon Tyne		1972		Juniors	Whitley Bay	1	0	0	0	0	0	0	0
Griffiths S	Steve	28 Nov 1957	Billingham		1974		Apprentice	Billingham Synthonia	1	0	0	0	0	0	0	0
Guthrie R	Ralph	13 Sep 1932	Hartlepool	1996	1956	1957	Arsenal	Horden CW	78	3	0	0	0	0	0	0
Guy EF	Eddie	06 Feb 1956	Hartlepool		1974		Apprentice	Easington CW	1	0	0	0	0	0	0	0
Guy K	Keith	19 May 1959	Seaham		1978		Newcastle United	Seaham CW Red Star	10	0	2	0	0	0	0	0
Haigh P	Paul	04 May 1958	Scarborough		1987	1988	Carlisle United	Gretna	50	5	4	4	0	0	0	0
Hall AD	Tony	17 Jan 1969	Billingham		1987		Tranmere Rovers	East Fife	1	1	0	1	0	0	0	0

Name		Date of Birth	Place of Birth	Died	First Season	Last Season	Previous Club	Next Club	Appearances League	Appearances FAC	Appearances FLC	Appearances Oth.	Goals Leag	Goals FAC	Goals FLC	Goals Oth.
Hall B	Bertie	1903	Newburn		1926	1928	Lemington Glass Works	Peterborough & Fletton U	88	2	0	0	3	0	0	0
Halliday SW	Stephen	03 May 1976	Sunderland		1993	1997	Charlton Athletic	Motherwell	140	5	11	6	25	1	0	0
Halstead FD	Fred	1896	Crawshawbooth		1922		Southend United	Tranmere Rovers	8	0	0	0	0	0	0	0
Hamilton H	Hughie	16 Jun 1942	Glasgow		1963	1965	Falkirk	Scarborough	39	0	2	0	7	0	0	0
Hamilton J	Jimmy	1904	Hetton-le-Hole		1931	1932	Crystal Palace	City Of Durham	48	3	0	0	2	0	0	0
Hamilton J (2)	Jimmy	14 Jun 1955	Uddingston		1982		Gretna	Gretna	3	1	0	0	0	0	0	0
Hampson W	Walker	24 Jul 1889	Radcliffe	1959	1922		Charlton Athletic	Chesterfield	22	0	0	0	4	0	0	0
Hampton D	Derek	25 Apr 1952	Loftus		1979	1981	Whitby Town	Whitby Town	74	2	3	3	18	1	0	0
Harden LJ	Leo	07 May 1923	Hartlepool		1946	1955	Railway Athletic	Thornley CW	169	11	0	0	47	5	0	0
Harding A	Alan	14 May 1948	Sunderland		1978	1982	Lincoln City	Blue Star	84	1	3	2	8	0	1	0
Hardy C	Cecil	1898	Kimblesworth	1975	1920	1927	Blackhall Colliery	Horden CW	124	11	0	0	45	3	0	0
Hardy LR	Dick	1913	South Bank		1931	1936	South Bank East End	Bradford City	150	14	0	4	26	1	0	0
Hardy S	Sid	1902	Kimblesworth		1924	1927	Blackhall Colliery	Spennymoor United	62	10	0	0	19	2	0	0
Harland T	Tommy	1905	Wingate	1985	1928	1930	Sherburn Hill	Shotton CW	39	0	0	0	0	0	0	0
					1931	1933	Shotton CW	Gas & Water								
Harley JR	John	22 Apr 1949	March		1976		Wokingham Town	Wokingham Town	4	0	0	0	1	0	0	0
Harper SA	Steve	14 Mar 1975	Easington		1997		Newcastle United (loan)		15	0	0	0	0	0	0	0
Harrington P	Paul	26 Sep 1964	Hartlepool		1983		Juniors	Billingham Town	2	0	0	0	0	0	0	0
Harris G	George				1935		Hesleden Rising Star	Horden CW	1	0	0	0	1	0	0	0
Harris J	Jack	1901	Hesleden		1921	1922	Hesleden Celtic		4	0	0	0	0	0	0	0
Harris J(2)	John	19 Mar 1896	Redcar	1933	1927		Darlington		1	0	0	0	0	0	0	0
Harris M	Martin	22 Dec 1955	Doncaster		1977		Workington		1	0	0	0	0	0	0	0
Harrison EG	Eric	05 Feb 1938	Mytholmroyd		1964	1965	Halifax Town	Barrow	81	6	3	0	4	0	0	0
Harrison H	Harry	21 Nov 1893	Redcar		1926	1927	Durham City	Darlington	68	2	0	0	0	0	0	0
Harrison W	Walter		Langley Moor		1929	1930	Shildon	Darlington	10	0	0	0	2	0	0	0
Hartnett JB	Jimmy	21 Mar 1927	Dublin		1957		Barry Town	York City	7	0	0	0	1	0	0	0
Harvey D	David	15 Feb 1954	Hetton-le-Hole		1970		Coventry City		5	0	0	0	0	0	0	0
Hawkes B	Barry	21 Mar 1938	Shotton		1961		Darlington	Chelmsford City	9	0	0	0	0	0	0	0
Hawkins H	Harry	24 Nov 1915	Middlesbrough	1992	1947	1948	Gateshead	Blyth Spartans	30	1	0	0	4	0	0	0
Healey WR	Bill	22 May 1926	Liverpool		1955		Fulham		6	0	0	0	0	0	0	0
Heaney NA	Neil	03 Nov 1971	Middlesbrough		1990		Arsenal (loan)		3	0	0	0	0	0	0	0
Heath D	Don	26 Dec 1944	Stockton-on-Tees		1973	1974	Peterborough United	Crook Town	37	1	6	0	2	0	0	0
Hedley G	Graeme	01 Mar 1957	Easington		1984		Horden CW	Whitby Town	32	2	2	2	9	0	1	0
Henderson DM	Damian	12 May 1973	Leeds		1994	1995	Scunthorpe United	Blyth Spartans	48	1	4	2	6	0	0	0
Henderson G	George	07 Mar 1946	Hartlepool	1991	1970		Bishop Auckland	Horden CW	1	0	0	0	0	0	0	0
Henderson L	Lauchlan		Kilbarchan		1921		Paisley Juniors		2	0	0	0	0	0	0	0
Henderson T	Tommy		Lemington		1925		Lemington Glass Works		1	0	0	0	0	0	0	0
Hepple JA	John	12 Mar 1970	Middlesbrough		1988		Sunderland (loan)		2	0	0	0	0	0	0	0
Hepplewhite W	Wilson	11 Jun 1946	Washington		1967	1968	Carlisle United	Port Elizabeth	52	3	3	0	2	0	0	0
Herd G	George	06 May 1936	Gartcosh		1970		Sunderland	retired	15	0	1	0	0	0	0	0
Herring H	Harry	04 Jan 1939	Hartlepool		1958		Caledonians		2	0	0	0	0	0	0	0
Heward HA	Aubrey	31 Aug 1910	Hetton-le-Hole		1935		Bradford Park Avenue	Yeovil Town	28	2	0	0	0	0	0	0
Hewitt CW	Chuck	10 Apr 1884	Greatham	1966	1919	1921	Crystal Palace		6	11	0	0	0	3	0	0
Hewitt JJ	Josh	15 Jun 1911	Evenwood	1984	1930	1933	Everton	Norwich City	110	6	0	1	53	2	0	0
Hewitt MD	Marty	24 Jul 1965	Hartlepool		1985	1986	St James	Billingham Synthonia	14	1	0	1	2	0	0	0
Heywood AE	Napper	12 May 1913	Hartlepool	1989	1946		Sunderland	Horden CW	39	2	0	0	0	0	0	0
Hick WM	Billy	13 Feb 1903	Beamish	1972	1921		Consett Celtic	South Shields	1	0	0	0	0	0	0	0
Hickman J	Joe	1901	Durham	1980	1926	1927	Lintz Colliery	Aston Villa	27	0	0	0	0	0	0	0
					1928		Aston Villa	Scarborough								
Higgins AM	Andy	12 Feb 1960	Bolsover		1982		Kings Lynn	Kings Lynn	4	0	1	0	1	0	0	0
Higgins RJ	Rob	23 Dec 1958	Bolsover		1979		Burnley (loan)		2	1	0	0	0	0	0	0
Hill R	Reg	1907	Gibraltar		1932	1936	Tranmere Rovers	Darlington	139	13	0	5	6	0	0	0
Hillyard RW	Ron	31 Mar 1952	Rotherham		1971		York City (loan)		23	0	0	0	0	0	0	0
Hinchliffe J	Jackie	04 Jun 1938	Tillicoultry		1961	1963	Workington	Weymouth	88	4	3	0	8	0	1	0
Hinshelwood W	Willie	11 May 1935	Chapelhall		1963		Tonbridge	Hamilton Academical	17	1	1	0	3	0	0	0
Hird T	Tommy	31 Dec 1912	Crook	1989	1933	1934	West Stanley	Portsmouth	84	6	0	4	22	0	0	2
Hislop TK	Kona	21 Dec 1970	London		1996		Livingston	Blyth Spartans	27	2	0	1	0	0	0	0
Hodge MJ	Martin	04 Feb 1959	Southport		1991	1992	Leicester City	Rochdale	69	6	8	6	0	0	0	0
Hodgson M	Mike	06 Jul 1945	Newcastle upon Tyne		1964		Billingham Synthonia	Whitby Town	1	0	0	0	0	0	0	0
Hodgson W	Bill		Hartlepool		1928		Perseverance		4	1	0	0	1	0	0	0
Hogan RD	Roy	24 Sep 1960	Hartlepool		1977	1982	Peterlee Catholic Club	Crook Town	284	11	12	12	32	2	2	0
					1983	1986	Crook Town	Australian football								
Hogan T	Terry	03 Jun 1933	Hartlepool		1957		Local amateur	Shotton CW	9	0	0	0	1	0	0	0
Hollund M	Martin	11 Aug 1975	Stord		1997		SK Brann		28	0	0	2	0	0	0	0
Holmes S	Stan	27 Nov 1920	Easington		1949		Local amateur		1	0	0	0	0	0	0	0
Holmes SP	Steve	13 Jan 1972	Middlesbrough		1994		Preston North End (loan)		5	0	0	0	2	0	0	0
Homer C	Chris	16 Apr 1977	Stockton-on-Tees		1994	1996	Trainee		7	0	1	1	0	0	0	0
Honour B	Brian	16 Feb 1964	Horden		1984	1994	Peterlee Newtown	Spennymoor United	319	22	24	19	25	2	3	6
Honour J	John	01 Nov 1953	Horden		1972	1975	West Bromwich Albion	Workington	112	8	7	0	6	1	0	0
Hooper HR	Harry	16 Dec 1910	Burnley	1970	1947	1949	Sheffield United	retired	66	0	0	0	4	0	0	0
Hope JWM	John	30 Mar 1949	Shildon		1975		Sheffield United		23	4	1	0	0	0	0	0
Hopkins W	Pop	11 Nov 1888	Esh Winning	1938	1921	1922	South Shields	Durham City	53	3	0	0	1	0	0	0
Horace A	Alain	04 Dec 1971	Madagascar		1996		Mulhouse	Ayr United	1	0	0	0	0	0	0	0
Horne BS	Brian	05 Oct 1967	Billericay		1994	1995	Portsmouth	Dover Athletic	73	2	4	3	0	0	0	0
Houchen KM	Keith	25 Jul 1960	Middlesbrough		1977	1981	Chesterfield	Orient	279	7	18	6	92	0	2	0
					1993	1996	Port Vale	retired								
Howard DF	David	03 Jun 1962	Hartlepool		1980	1981	Newcastle United	Crook Town	9	0	0	3	4	0	0	0
Howard SJ	Steve	10 May 1976	Durham		1995	1997	Tow Law Town		114	3	6	5	21	0	1	2
Howe JR	Jack	07 Oct 1915	Hartlepool	1987	1934	1935	Wingate United	Derby County	24	0	0	2	0	0	0	0

Name		Date of Birth	Place of Birth	Died	First Season	Last Season	Previous Club	Next Club	Appearances League	FAC	FLC	Oth.	Goals Leag	FAC	FLC	Oth.
Howells P	Peter	23 Sep 1932	Middlesbrough		1956		Sheffield Wednesday		1	0	0	0	0	0	0	0
Hubery R	Bob		Kelloe		1921		Kelloe St Helens		1	0	0	0	0	0	0	0
Huggins A	Albert	1914	Grange Villa		1934	1935	Birtley Welfare	Spennymoor United	11	0	0	2	2	0	0	0
Hughes J	Jimmy	29 Aug 1909	Tudhoe	1966	1935		York City	York City	8	0	0	0	3	0	0	0
Hughes, Jack	Jack		Tanfield		1937		Aldershot	Consett	36	2	0	2	1	0	0	0
Hughes WH	Billy	21 Oct 1920	Cardiff		1946	1949	Local amateur	Annfield Plain	124	7	0	0	2	0	0	0
Humphreys DJB	Derek	05 Oct 1949	Belfast		1969		Sunderland (loan)		4	0	0	0	0	0	0	0
Hunt TR	Tom	1902	Shiney Row		1923		Seaham Harbour	Carlisle United	2	0	0	0	0	0	0	0
Hunter A	Albert		Hartlepool		1925		West Hartlepool St Oswald	Horden CW	1	2	0	0	0	1	0	0
Hunter P	Phil	28 Sep 1950	Hartlepool		1969		Local amateur	Bishop Auckland	1	0	0	0	0	0	0	0
Hunter R	Bob	25 Mar 1951	Gateshead		1970		Newcastle United		1	0	0	0	0	0	0	0
Hutchison D	Don	09 May 1971	Gateshead		1989	1990	Redheugh Boys	Liverpool	24	2	2	1	3	0	0	0
Hutt SG	Stephen	19 Feb 1979	Middlesbrough		1995	1997	Trainee		5	0	0	1	0	0	0	0
Hyson MA	Matty	02 May 1976	Stockton-on-Tees		1994		Trainee	Gateshead	5	0	1	0	0	0	0	0
Ingram SD	Denny	27 Jun 1976	Sunderland		1993	1997	Trainee		154	5	11	5	6	0	0	0
Irvine SC	Stuart	01 Mar 1979	Hartlepool		1996	1997	Trainee		13	1	0	1	1	0	0	0
Isaac J	Jimmy	23 Oct 1916	Cramlington	1993	1947	1948	Bradford City		56	4	0	0	9	2	0	0
Jacques J	Joe	12 Sep 1944	Consett	1981	1975		Dartford	Crook Town	5	0	0	0	0	0	0	0
Jarps J	Joe				1931		Perseverance	Blackhall CW	2	0	0	0	0	0	0	0
Jarrie F	Fred	02 Aug 1922	Hartlepool		1945	1947	Local amateur	Crook Town	1	2	0	0	0	0	0	0
Jobson JT	Jack	08 Aug 1903	Hebburn		1924	1926	Plymouth Argyle	Stockport County	102	10	0	0	2	0	0	0
Johnrose L	Lennie	29 Nov 1969	Preston		1991	1993	Blackburn Rovers	Bury	66	5	6	5	11	1	4	0
Johnson D	Dennis	20 May 1934	Seaham		1957		Seaham CW	South Shields	2	0	0	0	0	0	0	0
Johnson, David	David	19 Nov 1955	South Shields		1974		Bristol City	Gateshead	1	0	0	0	0	0	0	0
Johnson DA	David	29 Oct 1970	Dinnington		1991		Sheffield Wednesday (loan)		10	2	0	1	2	1	0	1
					1992		Sheffield Wednesday (loan)									
Johnson H	Harry	08 Aug 1913	Walker	1976	1938		Port Vale		24	2	0	1	0	0	0	0
Johnson JJ	Jack	1911	Gateshead		1933	1934	Davison Villa	Chesterfield	52	3	0	3	0	0	0	0
Johnson K	Ken	15 Feb 1931	Hartlepool		1949	1963	Seaton Holy Trinity	retired	384	26	3	0	98	6	2	0
Johnson KP	Kevin	29 Aug 1952	Doncaster		1974	1976	Workington	Huddersfield Town	148	7	12	5	11	1	2	0
					1980	1983	Halifax Town	Gateshead								
Johnson MH	Matt	26 Jul 1910	South Shields	1988	1933		Sheffield Wednesday	Northwich Victoria	6	0	0	0	0	0	0	0
Johnson TO	Tom	1917			1937				12	0	0	0	0	0	0	0
Jones H	Jerry	28 Sep 1918	Hartlepool		1946	1948	Belle Vue Congs		75	2	0	0	1	0	0	0
Jones K	Ken	01 Oct 1936	Easington		1960	1961	Sunderland	Kings Lynn	33	1	1	0	0	0	0	0
Jones S	Steven	31 Jan 1974	Stockton-on-Tees		1991	1995	Trainee	Billingham Town	48	2	4	1	0	0	0	0
Joyce J	John	06 Jan 1949	Easington		1966	1968	Peterlee Juniors	Shildon	4	0	0	0	0	0	0	0
Keenlyside G	George		Jarrow		1923		South Shields	Jarrow	24	3	0	0	1	1	0	0
Kell G	George		Gateshead		1925	1927	Brentford	Gainsborough Trinity	71	4	0	0	1	0	0	0
Kelly JP	Jimmy	22 Nov 1951	Sacriston		1971		Juniors	South Shields	5	0	0	0	0	0	0	0
Kelly TJ	Tom	28 Mar 1964	Bellshill		1985		Queen of the South	Torquay United	15	0	2	1	0	0	0	0
Kennedy AP	Alan	31 Aug 1954	Sunderland		1987		K Beerschot VAV	Grantham Town	5	0	0	1	0	0	0	1
Kennedy R	Ray	28 Jul 1951	Seaton Delaval		1983		Swansea City	Pezopolikos	23	0	0	1	3	0	0	0
Kerr P	Peter	03 Jan 1928	Glasgow		1949		Maryhill Hearts	Chesterfield	2	0	0	0	0	0	0	0
Kerr R	Bobby	16 Nov 1947	Alexandria		1980	1981	Blackpool	Whitby Town	49	2	3	3	2	0	0	0
Kessler LP	Laurie		Woolwich		1920	1921	Army football	Shildon	13	11	0	0	0	3	0	0
Key LW	Lance	13 May 1968	Kettering		1995		Sheffield Wednesday (loan)		1	0	0	0	0	0	0	0
King A	Alan	25 Nov 1947	Gateshead		1967		Horden CW	Shildon	1	0	0	0	0	0	0	0
Kirk HJ	Harry	25 Aug 1944	Saltcoats		1969	1970	Darlington	Scunthorpe United	45	2	0	0	5	1	0	0
Knowles DT	Darren	08 Oct 1970	Sheffield		1996	1997	Scarborough		53	1	2	2	1	0	0	0
Knox T	Tom	11 Nov 1905	Ushaw Moor		1933		Darlington	Notts County	25	3	0	1	0	0	0	0
Lackenby G	George	22 May 1931	Newcastle upon Tyne		1960	1962	Gateshead		86	3	1	0	1	0	0	0
Lamb A	Alan	30 Jan 1970	Gateshead		1989	1990	Nottingham Forest	Brandon United	14	1	0	2	0	0	0	0
Lambert EV	Eric	04 Aug 1920	Derby		1946		Derby County		16	2	0	0	0	0	0	0
Langland JR	Johnny	09 Nov 1929	Easington		1958	1959	Blyth Spartans	Blyth Spartans	38	3	0	0	11	0	0	0
Langridge J	John	14 Nov 1957	Newcastle upon Tyne		1982		Easington CW	Shotton Comrades	6	0	0	0	0	0	0	0
Larkin GT	Gordon	12 Oct 1958	Hartlepool		1977	1979	Billingham Synthonia	Blyth Spartans	14	0	1	0	1	0	0	0
Larsen SO	Stig Olav	26 Sep 1973	Bergen		1997		Fana IL	Norwegian football	4	0	0	1	0	0	0	0
Lawrence M	Mark	04 Dec 1958	Stockton-on-Tees		1977	1983	Nunthorpe Athletic	Whitby Town	168	8	8	3	24	0	1	1
Lealman F	Fred	1915	Hackworth		1938		Blackhall CW	Blackhall CW	7	0	0	1	2	0	0	0
Lee GB	Graeme	31 May 1978	Middlesbrough		1995	1997	Trainee		67	3	3	4	3	0	1	1
Lee JW	Jack	01 Feb 1902	Pegswood	1990	1924		Blackhall Wesleyans	Horden Athletic	2	0	0	0	0	0	0	0
Lee B	Bert				1921		Hesleden Celtic		3	0	0	0	1	0	0	
Lee TJ	Tommy	19 Dec 1949	Horden		1969		Sunderland College	Horden CW	6	0	1	0	0	0	0	0
Lees N	Norman	18 Nov 1948	Newcastle upon Tyne		1970		Hull City (loan)		20	0	0	0	1	0	0	0
Leonard H	Harry	19 May 1924	Jarrow		1948		Bradford Park Avenue		2	1	0	0	0	0	0	0
Lester MJ	Mike	04 Aug 1954	Manchester		1985		Scunthorpe United (loan)		11	0	0	2	1	0	0	0
Liddle B	Bryan	23 Jun 1961	Durham		1984		Brandon United	Chester-le-Street Town	13	0	0	0	0	0	0	1
Liddle I	Isaac		Sunderland		1927		South Hetton		12	0	0	0	2	0	0	0
Lilley T	Tom	1900	Newbottle	1964	1924	1925	Nelson	Sunderland	60	3	0	0	0	0	0	0
Linacre J	John	13 Dec 1955	Middlesbrough		1977	1981	Whitby Town	Whitby Town	211	12	7	1	12	1	0	0
					1983		Hamrun Spartans	Billingham Town								
Linacre P	Phil	17 May 1962	Middlesbrough		1980	1982	Coventry City	Whitby Town	82	6	2	3	17	3	0	0
					1983		Whitby Town	Bishop Auckland								
Linacre W	Billy	10 Aug 1924	Chesterfield		1953	1955	Middlesbrough	Mansfield Town	89	12	0	0	10	2	0	0
Lindsay DM	Duncan	01 Jan 1907	Cambuslang		1934		Northampton Town	Barrow	37	3	0	3	21	1	0	0
Linighan A	Andy	18 Jun 1962	Hartlepool		1980	1983	Henry Smith BC	Leeds United	110	8	8	5	4	0	1	4
Linighan D	David	09 Jan 1965	Hartlepool		1981	1985	Hartlepool Schools	Derby County	91	4	4	3	5	0	1	1
Lister J	Jimmy	1895	Glasgow		1920	1921	Bury	Llanelly	8	7	0	0	2	6	0	0

Name		Date of Birth	Place of Birth	Died	First Season	Last Season	Previous Club	Next Club	Appearances League	FAC	FLC	Oth.	Goals Leag	FAC	FLC	Oth.
Lithgo G	Gordon	14 Aug 1942	Hartlepool		1960	1963	Seaton Holy Trinity	Scarborough	37	0	2	0	8	0	1	0
Little A	Alan	05 Feb 1955	Horden		1985	1986	Halifax Town	retired	12	0	1	1	1	0	0	0
Little RA	Robert		Sunderland		1926		Lambton Star		4	0	0	0	0	0	0	0
Livingstone AM	Allan	02 Dec 1899	Alexandria	1970	1924		Scunthorpe United	Crewe Alexandra	3	0	0	0	1	0	0	0
Livingstone J	Joe	18 Jun 1942	Middlesbrough		1965	1966	Carlisle United	Stockton	15	0	2	0	5	0	1	0
Livsey GW	Gordon	24 Jan 1947	Keighley		1977		Workington	Nuneaton Borough	6	0	0	0	0	0	0	0
Loadwick D	Derek	04 Oct 1956	Middlesbrough		1978	1979	Stockport County	Whitby Town	51	4	2	0	1	0	0	0
Locker S	Stephen	05 Nov 1970	Ashington		1988		Nottingham Forest	Blyth Spartans	1	0	0	0	0	0	0	0
Lockhart KS	Keith	19 Jul 1964	Wallsend		1986		Wolverhampton W	Cambridge City	2	0	0	0	0	0	0	0
Longmore SJ	Jimmy		Hartlepool		1922			Derby County	12	0	0	0	0	0	0	0
Lonie A	Arthur		Wingate		1923		Trimdon Grange	Spennymoor United	10	3	0	0	0	2	0	0
Lonsdale JS	Stan	13 Apr 1931	Washington		1960		Halifax Town		9	0	0	0	0	0	0	0
Love RW	Bob	1914	Llaymain	1990	1938		Winsford United	Blackhall CW	13	0	0	2	2	0	0	1
Lowe K	Kenny	06 Nov 1961	Sedgefield		1981	1983	Apprentice	Billingham Town	67	2	4	3	6	0	0	0
					1995		Birmingham City (loan)									
Lowe SJ	Simon	26 Dec 1962	Westminster		1986		Halifax Town	Colchester United	14	0	2	2	1	0	0	0
Lucas R	Richard	22 Sep 1970	Chapeltown		1996	1997	Scarborough	Halifax Town	49	1	2	1	2	0	0	0
Luckett P	Paul	12 Jan 1957	Coventry		1975	1976	Halifax Town	Australian football	19	0	0	0	0	0	0	0
Luke GT	George	17 Dec 1933	Newcastle upon Tyne		1953	1959	Newcastle United	Newcastle United	186	19	0	0	60	8	0	0
Lumley R	Bobby	06 Jan 1933	Leadgate		1954	1957	Charlton Athletic	Chesterfield	145	7	1	0	25	1	0	0
					1960		Gateshead	Kings Lynn								
Lumley S	Sydney	1910	Lanchester		1931		Sunderland Omnibus	Newport County	25	1	0	0	18	0	0	0
Lynch CJ	Chris	18 Nov 1974	Middlesbrough		1992	1995	Halifax Town	Bishop Auckland	50	1	7	1	2	0	0	0
McAndrew A	Tony	11 Apr 1956	Glasgow		1988		Darlington	Darlington	4	0	0	0	0	0	0	0
McAuley S	Sean	23 Jun 1972	Sheffield		1995	1996	St Johnstone	Scunthorpe United	84	3	6	3	1	0	0	0
McBurney ML	Mike	12 Sep 1953	Wrexham		1974		Bolton Wanderers (loan)		6	0	0	0	1	0	0	0
McCaffery A	Aiden	30 Aug 1957	Newcastle upon Tyne		1986		Exeter City	Whitley Bay	6	0	0	0	0	0	0	0
MacCallum S	Stewart	09 May 1927	Dumbarton		1956		Coventry City	Southport	2	0	0	0	0	0	0	0
McCambridge J	Jim	1905	Larne		1936		Sheffield Wednesday	Cheltenham Town	16	0	0	1	4	0	0	0
McCarthy JD	Jon	18 Aug 1970	Middlesbrough		1987		Juniors	Shepshed Charterhouse	1	0	0	0	0	0	0	0
McClenn J	Jim	17 Jan 1903	Sedgefield	1986	1926		Stakeford United	Bedlington United	20	1	0	0	3	0	0	0
McClure W	Willie	16 May 1921	Shotts		1950	1952	Carlisle United		118	6	0	0	24	2	0	0
McCluskey A	Andy	29 Mar 1951	Manchester		1969		St Josephs	Yeovil Town	6	0	0	0	0	0	0	0
McCready TS	Tom	28 Sep 1923	Port Glasgow		1949		Cowdenbeath	Lincoln City	34	2	0	0	3	0	0	0
McCreery D	David	16 Sep 1957	Belfast		1991		Heart of Midlothian	Coleraine	39	4	3	0	0	0	0	0
					1994		Carlisle United	retired								
McCubbin R	Bert	13 Feb 1943	Kilmarnock		1963		Ayr United		2	0	0	0	0	0	0	0
McDonald C	Chris	14 Oct 1975	Edinburgh		1996	1997	Stoke City		15	0	2	0	0	0	0	0
Macdonald G	Garry	26 Mar 1962	Middlesbrough		1989	1990	Stockport County	South Bank	18	0	1	0	1	0	0	0
McEwan S	Stan	08 Jun 1957	Wishaw		1989		Wigan Athletic	Boston United	14	1	1	1	2	0	0	1
McGarry T	Tommy	28 Sep 1918	Heworth	1953	1938		Newcastle United	Bradford Park Avenue	20	2	0	2	12	0	0	2
McGeough J	Jim	14 Jul 1946	Waterford		1972		Lincoln City (loan)		2	0	0	0	0	0	0	0
McGinley J	John	11 Jun 1959	Rowlands Gill		1986		Rotherham United (loan)		2	0	0	0	1	0	0	0
McGovern JP	John	28 Oct 1949	Montrose		1965	1968	Central Park Juniors	Derby County	72	2	2	0	5	0	2	0
MacGregor JP	Peter	22 Dec 1931	Hartlepool	1994	1953	1954	Elwick Road Old Boys	Darlington	2	0	0	0	0	0	0	0
MacGregor TJ	Terry	24 May 1938	Hartlepool		1956	1962	Pools Juniors	Thornley CW	47	1	0	0	2	0	0	0
McGuckin TI	Ian	24 Apr 1973	Middlesbrough		1991	1996	Trainee	Fulham	152	6	14	6	8	0	1	0
McGuigan T	Tommy	22 Nov 1922	Whiterigg	1997	1950	1957	Ayr United	Spennymoor United	325	25	0	0	75	4	0	0
McKellar DN	David	22 May 1956	Irvine		1988		Dunfermline Athletic (loan)		5	0	2	0	0	0	0	0
McKenna F	Frank	08 Jan 1933	Blaydon		1959		Carlisle United	North Shields	32	1	0	0	5	0	0	0
McKeown J	Joe	09 Apr 1924	Bannockburn		1950		Stirling Albion		46	2	0	0	7	0	0	0
McKinnon R	Rob	31 Jul 1966	Glasgow		1986	1991	Newcastle United	Motherwell	247	15	15	15	7	0	0	0
McLaughlin J	Jimmy	10 Dec 1926	Stirling		1953		Alloa Athletic		13	0	0	0	2	0	0	0
McLean DJ	David	24 Nov 1957	Newcastle upon Tyne		1986		Scunthorpe United (loan)		6	0	0	0	0	0	0	0
McLean JD	Derek	21 Dec 1932	Brotton		1961	1963	Middlesbrough	Scarborough	89	5	2	0	16	1	0	0
McLean R	Robert	1917			1937		Seaham CW		1	0	0	0	0	0	0	0
McLeod RA	Bobby	24 Feb 1947	Inverness		1965	1968	Sunderland College	South Shields	28	1	0	0	0	0	0	0
McMahon FG	Frank	04 Jan 1950	Belfast		1973		Darlington (loan)		7	0	0	0	0	0	0	0
McMahon HJ	Hughie	24 Sep 1909	Grangetown	1986	1945	1947	Sunderland	Rotherham United	28	4	0	0	7	3	0	0
McMahon K	Kevin	01 Mar 1946	Tantobie		1973	1975	York City	Gateshead United	107	7	12	0	29	1	4	0
McMaster C	Chris	16 Jun 1959	Darlington		1976	1977	Apprentice	Tow Law Town	4	0	0	0	0	0	0	0
McMordie AA	Eric	12 Aug 1946	Belfast		1976	1977	York City	retired	47	2	2	0	2	0	0	0
McNamee G	Ged	16 Aug 1960	Consett		1979	1982	Juniors	Consett	4	0	0	0	1	0	0	0
McNamee J	John	11 Jun 1941	Coatbridge		1973		Morton	Lancaster City	2	0	0	0	0	0	0	0
McPartland D	Des	05 Oct 1947	Middlesbrough		1969	1970	Northampton Town	South Shields	56	1	1	0	0	0	0	0
MacPhail J	John	07 Dec 1955	Dundee		1990	1994	Sunderland	Brinkburn CA	163	11	11	11	4	0	1	0
McPheat W	Willie	04 Sep 1942	Caldercruix		1965		Sunderland	Airdrieonians	15	2	0	0	2	2	0	0
McStay WJ	Willie	26 Nov 1961	Hamilton		1989		Notts County (loan)		3	0	0	0	0	0	0	0
Mackey TS	Tom	22 Oct 1908	Cassop	1969	1928	1929	Ferryhill Athletic	Sheffield Wednesday	30	2	0	0	1	0	0	0
Mackie J	Jimmy	1916	Hebburn		1937	1938	Bolton Wanderers	Horden CW	6	0	0	1	2	0	0	0
Maddison WH	Hartley	06 Apr 1954	Sunderland		1973	1974	Juniors	Gateshead United	4	0	0	0	0	0	0	0
Maggiore A	Tony	28 Oct 1957	Sunderland		1975	1976	Sunderland	Gateshead	28	1	2	0	0	0	0	0
Makepeace R	Ralph	1910	Trimdon Grange		1932	1933	Sunderland	Blackhall CW	45	3	0	1	2	0	0	0
Malley P	Phil	01 Nov 1965	Felling		1983		Sunderland	Berwick Rangers	1	0	0	0	0	0	0	0
Malone RP	Dick	22 Aug 1947	Carfin		1977	1978	Sunderland	Blackpool	36	2	4	0	2	0	0	0
Marshall WF	Billy	11 Jul 1936	Belfast		1964	1965	Oldham Athletic	Horden CW	57	0	3	0	0	0	0	0
Mason A	Arthur	1895	Cornsay Colliery		1929	1931	Norwich City	Crook	18	1	0	0	0	0	0	0
Mason R	Bob		Whitburn	1981	1928		Bristol Rovers	West Stanley	13	1	0	0	1	0	0	0
Mason TWM	Sandy	21 Apr 1925	Hartlepool		1946		Railway Athletic		5	0	0	0	0	0	0	0

Name		Date of Birth	Place of Birth	Died	First Season	Last Season	Previous Club	Next Club	Appearances League	Appearances FAC	Appearances FLC	Appearances Oth.	Goals Leag	Goals FAC	Goals FLC	Goals Oth.
Melville AA	Alan	13 Mar 1941	Hartlepool		1960	1961	St Josephs	Horden CW	5	0	1	0	0	0	0	0
Middleton CW	Charlie	1914	West Stanley	1984	1936		West Stanley	Walker Celtic	1	0	0	0	0	0	0	0
Midgley CS	Craig	24 May 1976	Bradford		1997		Bradford City		9	0	0	0	3	0	0	0
Mike AR	Adie	16 Nov 1973	Manchester		1996		Stockport County (loan)		7	0	0	0	1	0	0	0
Millar JM	Jack	31 Dec 1906	Coatbridge		1929		Barnsley	Workington	18	1	0	0	5	0	0	0
Miller LR	Bob	03 Aug 1938	Blaydon		1962		Sheffield United		9	0	0	0	2	0	0	0
Miller TW	Tommy	08 Jan 1979	Easington		1997		Trainee		13	0	0	0	1	0	0	0
Miller W	Walter	11 Aug 1930	Cornforth		1949		Local amateur	Spennymoor United	1	0	0	0	0	0	0	0
Mills WE	William	1903			1923		Maple Star	Fatfield Albion	2	0	0	0	0	0	0	0
Mitchell JG	John	01 Aug 1919	Gateshead	1977	1946		Billingham Synthonia		3	0	0	0	2	0	0	0
Mitchell N	Norman	07 Nov 1931	Sunderland		1957	1958	Workington	Blyth Spartans	23	0	0	0	6	0	0	0
Mitchell T	Tommy	27 Jun 1905	Trimdon Grange	1970	1922	1923	Trimdon Grange	Stockport County	35	0	0	0	1	0	0	0
Mittel JL	Jimmy	28 Feb 1906	Merthyr Tydfil	1976	1935	1936	Derry City	Barrow	65	10	0	3	0	0	0	0
Moore M	Malcolm	18 Dec 1948	Silksworth		1973	1975	Tranmere Rovers	Workington	129	8	12	0	34	3	5	0
Moore WR	Bill	1903	Sunderland	1962	1936		Southend United		16	0	0	0	0	0	0	0
Moore W	Watty	30 Aug 1925	Hartlepool	1967	1948	1959	Oxford Street Old Boys	Horden CW	447	25	0	0	3	0	0	0
Mordue J	Jack	11 Sep 1906	Sacriston	1991	1927	1931	Langley Park	Annfield Plain	131	4	0	0	31	0	0	0
Mordue T	Tucker	22 Jul 1905	Horden	1975	1928	1930	Sheffield United	Shotton	101	3	0	0	26	1	0	0
Mordue WM	Billy	1903	Horden	1980	1922		Middlesbrough	Horden Athletic	111	5	0	0	18	0	0	0
					1927	1929	Blackpool	Crook								
Morrell RI	Bobby	04 Jun 1944	Hesleden		1963	1964	Blackhall Club	Thornley CW	34	3	1	0	0	0	0	0
Morris D	Doug	29 Jul 1925	Durham		1945	1950	Ushaw Moor	Kings Lynn	19	2	0	0	3	0	0	0
Morris H	Harry		Stoke		1923		Manchester United	Wigan Borough	7	0	0	0	2	0	0	0
Morrison GC	George	27 Nov 1924	Ayr		1951		St Johnstone	Horden CW	2	0	0	0	0	0	0	0
Moses G	George	11 Sep 1920	High Spen		1946		Newcastle United		19	2	0	0	4	0	0	0
Moses J	Jackie	1916	Tow Law		1934	1936	York Road Juniors	Scunthorpe United	21	0	0	3	3	0	0	0
Moverley R	Rob	18 Jan 1969	Batley		1988	1989	Bradford City		29	5	0	2	0	0	0	0
Muggleton CD	Carl	13 Sep 1968	Leicester		1988		Leicester City (loan)		8	0	0	2	0	0	0	0
Mulholland TS	Tom	1888	Belfast		1920		Belfast Celtic		5	6	0	0	1	2	0	0
Mulvaney J	Jimmy	13 May 1941	Sunderland	1982	1965	1967	Whitby Town	Barrow	69	3	2	0	31	1	1	0
Murray J	Joe	1916	Houghton-le-Spring		1934	1935	Shiney Row Swifts	Shotton CW	7	0	0	0	0	0	0	0
Musgrave JW	Joe	1912	Durham		1938		Swindon Town	Spennymoor United	20	0	0	1	3	0	0	0
Mutrie LA	Les	01 Apr 1952	Newcastle upon Tyne		1984		Colchester United	Gateshead	18	2	2	0	4	0	0	0
Myers EC	Colin	1894	Ecclesfield	1984	1926		Exeter City	Gainsborough Trinity	22	0	0	0	8	0	0	0
Naisbitt E	Eddie	12 Oct 1951	Boldon		1971		Longbenton Juniors	Ashington	1	0	0	0	0	0	0	0
Nash M	Marc	13 May 1978	Newcastle upon Tyne		1997		Benfield Park		1	0	0	0	0	0	0	0
Nesbitt MT	Mark	11 Jan 1972	Doncaster		1990	1991	Middlesbrough	Ferryhill Athletic	2	0	0	0	0	0	0	0
Nevin W	Billy		Burnopfield		1937		Ashington		4	0	0	1	2	0	0	0
Nevins L	Laurie	02 Jul 1920	Gateshead		1947	1948	Brighton & Hove Albion		18	1	0	0	8	0	0	0
Newton JL	Jackie	25 May 1925	Bishop Auckland		1946	1957	Newcastle United		332	29	0	0	15	4	0	0
Newton R	Bob	23 Nov 1956	Chesterfield		1977	1982	Huddersfield Town	Port Vale	161	11	8	4	50	10	2	0
					1985		Chesterfield	Bristol Rovers								
Nicholson BC	Ben	1898	Thornley		1921	1924	Thornley Wesleyans	Thornley Dunelm	17	2	0	0	0	0	0	0
Nicholson S	Stan	20 Aug 1931	Middlesbrough		1958		Horden CW		7	1	0	0	1	0	0	0
Nobbs AK	Keith	19 Sep 1961	Bishop Auckland		1985	1993	Bishop Auckland	Gateshead	280	13	17	16	1	0	0	0
Nobbs H	Harold	05 Jan 1903	Bishop Middleham	1971	1929	1931	South Bank		68	1	0	0	1	0	0	0
Nobbs W	Walter		Ferryhill		1935	1936	Ferryhill Athletic	Horden CW	21	0	0	1	1	0	0	0
Noble B	Barry	05 Jun 1951	Stockton-on-Tees		1971		Juniors		1	0	0	0	0	0	0	0
Normanton GS	Graham	13 Nov 1959	Hartlepool		1979	1980	Middlesbrough	Horden CW	18	0	0	0	0	0	0	0
Norton DJ	Dave	24 Jan 1957	Gateshead		1978	1979	Whickham	Gateshead	17	1	1	0	2	0	0	0
Norton P	Paul	17 Sep 1969	Mexborough		1988		Sheffield United	Bridlington Town	5	1	0	0	0	0	0	0
O'Connor PD	Paul	17 Aug 1971	Easington		1995	1996	Blyth Spartans	Bedlington Terriers	31	1	0	1	0	0	0	0
O'Connor VJ	Jackie	12 Mar 1929	Durham		1948		Middlesbrough	Spennymoor United	2	0	0	0	0	0	0	0
O'Donnell J	Jack	25 Mar 1897	Gateshead		1932		Blackpool	Wigan Athletic	28	2	0	0	2	0	0	0
O'Donnell JD	Jon	21 Mar 1954	Leeds	1997	1976		Cambridge United	Scunthorpe United	31	1	2	0	1	0	0	0
Oakley N	Norman	04 Jun 1939	Norton		1958	1963	Scunthorpe United	Swindon Town	182	8	3	0	0	0	0	0
Odhams JR	James	1913	Hartlepool		1933		Local amateur		1	0	0	0	0	0	0	0
Ogden P	Paul	16 Oct 1969	Salford		1988	1989	Oldham Athletic	Fleetwood Town	12	1	1	2	0	0	0	0
Oldham E	Eric	27 Jun 1933	Newcastle upon Tyne		1959		Kidderminster Harriers		12	0	0	0	0	0	0	0
Oliver HD	Derek	16 Apr 1950	Sunderland		1968		Sheffield Wednesday		1	0	0	0	0	0	0	0
Oliver HS	Harry	16 Feb 1921	Sunderland	1994	1937		Houghton CW	Brentford	9	0	0	0	0	0	0	0
Oliver K	Keith	15 Jan 1976	South Shields		1993	1995	Trainee	Bishop Auckland	32	1	8	3	0	0	0	0
Ollerenshaw J	John	03 Apr 1925	Stockport		1950		Arsenal	Oldham Athletic	2	0	0	0	0	0	0	0
Olsson P	Paul	24 Dec 1965	Hull		1989	1993	Scarborough	Darlington	171	11	13	10	13	0	0	2
Osmond JE	Joe	1897	Sunderland		1924		Clapton Orient		1	0	0	0	0	0	0	0
Owbridge CR	Charlie		Hartlepool		1931	1932	Belle Vue Congs	Trimdon Grange Colliery	19	0	0	0	0	0	0	0
Owens R	Richard	1915	Hartlepool		1935		Trimdon Grange	Southport	1	0	0	0	0	0	0	0
Owens TL	Les	17 Oct 1919	Sunderland	1974	1949		Southport	Norwich City	28	3	0	0	12	1	0	0
Owers P	Phil	28 Apr 1955	Bishop Auckland		1987		Brandon United	Bishop Auckland	2	0	2	0	0	0	0	0
Pape AA	Albert	13 Jun 1897	Bolton-on-Dearne	1955	1929		Darwen	Halifax Town	37	1	0	0	21	0	0	0
Park O	Ossie	07 Feb 1905	Darlington		1934	1936	Northampton Town	North Shields	104	15	0	4	1	1	0	0
					1937		North Shields	Consett								
Park RC	Bobby	03 Jul 1946	Edinburgh		1974		Northampton Town	Eppleton CW	17	0	2	0	0	0	0	0
Parkes BJ	Barry	21 Jan 1940	Hartlepool		1960	1962	Easington CW	Reading	29	2	0	0	7	1	0	0
Parkes S	Sid	20 Sep 1919	Hartlepool		1946	1947	Hetton United	Blackhall CW	6	2	0	0	0	0	0	0
Parkinson J	John	02 Jun 1953	Trimdon		1971		Trimdon Village Juniors	Shildon	1	0	0	0	0	0	0	0
Parkinson TO	Tot		Hartlepool		1921	1924	Local amateur	Shildon	60	1	0	0	19	0	0	0
Parry AJ	Tony	08 Sep 1945	Burton-upon-Trent		1965	1971	Burton Albion	Derby County	189	7	8	0	5	0	0	0
Parsons D	Davie		Redcar		1921		Eston United	Stockton	2	0	0	0	0	0	0	0

Name		Date of Birth	Place of Birth	Died	First Season	Last Season	Previous Club	Next Club	Appearances				Goals			
									League	FAC	FLC	Oth.	Leag	FAC	FLC	Oth.
Patterson GT	George	15 Sep 1934	Castleton		1960		York City	Gateshead	18	0	1	0	1	0	0	0
Peake J	Jason	29 Sep 1971	Leicester		1991		Leicester City (loan)		6	0	0	0	1	0	0	0
Pears S	Stephen	22 Jan 1962	Brandon		1996		Liverpool	retired	16	1	2	0	0	0	0	0
Pearson J	John	08 May 1951	Ferryhill		1968		Ferryhill Athletic	Ferryhill Athletic	1	0	0	0	0	0	0	0
Pearson JG	John	10 Apr 1931	Gateshead		1952		Reyrolles		1	0	0	0	0	0	0	0
Peart R	Ron	08 Mar 1920	Brandon		1938		Langley Moor	Derby County	8	0	0	3	0	0	0	0
Pedersen JO	Jan Ove	12 Nov 1968	Oslo		1997		SK Brann (loan)		17	1	0	2	1	1	0	1
Pedwell R	Ralph	1910	Durham		1929	1933	Durham West End	Barnsley	156	7	0	1	66	2	0	0
Peek J	Jim	07 Jul 1933	Hartlepool		1959		West View Albion		7	0	0	0	0	0	0	0
Peverell NJ	Nicky	28 Apr 1973	Middlesbrough		1992	1993	Middlesbrough	Kuitan Sports	36	1	1	2	3	1	0	0
					1994		Kuitan Sports	York City								
Phythian ER	Ernie	16 Jul 1942	Farnworth		1965	1967	Wrexham	Southern Suburbs	124	5	6	0	51	1	3	0
Pickard F	Frank	1912	Darlington		1935		City Of Durham	Blyth Spartans	3	0	0	0	1	0	0	0
Pickering A	Archie	26 Dec 1913	Murton	1961	1937		Murton CW	Murton CW	1	0	0	0	0	0	0	0
Pimblett FR	Frank	12 Mar 1957	Liverpool		1979		Brisbane City	Australian football	3	0	0	0	0	0	0	0
Plaskett SC	Stephen	24 Apr 1971	Newcastle upon Tyne		1988	1989	North Shields	Gateshead	20	0	0	2	0	0	0	0
Platt JA	Jim	26 Jan 1952	Ballymoney		1978		Middlesbrough (loan)		13	0	0	0	0	0	0	0
Pollard BE	Brian	22 May 1954	York		1984		Scarborough	North Ferriby United	2	0	0	2	0	0	0	0
Poole K	Kevin	21 Jul 1963	Bromsgrove		1990		Middlesbrough (loan)		12	0	0	0	0	0	0	0
Porter W	Bill	23 Nov 1923	Durham	1975	1945	1946	Horden CW		2	2	0	0	0	0	0	0
Poskett M	Malcolm	19 Jul 1953	Middlesbrough		1976	1977	Whitby Town	Brighton & Hove Albion	56	3	2	0	20	1	0	0
					1985		Stockport County (loan)									
Potter GR	George	07 Oct 1946	Arbroath		1971	1976	Torquay United	Gateshead United	213	13	16	0	4	1	1	0
Powton B	Brian	29 Aug 1929	Newcastle upon Tyne		1952		Preston North End		4	0	0	0	0	0	0	0
Poyntz WI	Billy	18 Mar 1894	Tylerstown	1966	1927		Crewe Alexandra		31	1	0	0	0	0	0	0
Price J	Jack	29 Aug 1918	Shotton		1938	1948	Portsmouth	York City	89	5	0	3	12	1	0	1
Price KE	Ken	25 Mar 1939	Ellesmere Port		1961		Tranmere Rovers	Peterborough United	8	0	0	0	3	0	0	0
Priestley JA	Jason	25 Oct 1970	Leeds		1989		Carlisle United (loan)		16	0	0	0	0	0	0	0
Pringle B	Brian	12 Mar 1949	Chathill		1972		Alnwick Town	Ashington	1	0	0	0	0	0	0	0
Proctor JR	Jack	1911	New Delaval		1934	1937	Bournemouth & BA	Blyth Spartans	149	13	0	9	20	2	0	1
Proctor MG	Mark	30 Jan 1961	Middlesbrough		1996		South Shields	retired	6	0	0	0	0	0	0	0
Proctor MH	Harry	07 Jul 1912	Ushaw Moor	1984	1932	1933	Washington Colliery	Norwich City	61	3	0	1	14	0	0	0
Proudlock P	Paul	25 Oct 1965	Hartlepool		1984	1985	Juniors	Middlesbrough	21	1	0	1	0	0	0	0
					1992		Carlisle United (loan)									
Prudham CE	Eddie	12 Apr 1952	Gateshead		1976		Carlisle United (loan)		3	0	0	0	0	0	0	0
Prudhoe M	Mark	11 Nov 1963	Washington		1983		Sunderland (loan)		16	0	0	0	0	0	0	0
					1987		Walsall (loan)									
Race H	Harry	07 Jan 1906	Evenwood	1941	1938		Shrewsbury Town		3	0	0	0	0	0	0	0
Race W	Billy	05 Feb 1896	Leeholme	1974	1929	1930	Spennymoor United	Horden CW	19	0	0	0	2	0	0	0
Ramsden B	Barney	08 Nov 1917	Sheffield		1949		Sunderland	USA football	13	0	0	0	0	0	0	0
Ray P	Phil	21 Nov 1964	Wallsend		1983		Burnley (loan)		5	2	0	0	1	0	0	0
Rayment J	Joe	1905			1927		Perseverance	Perseverance	19	1	0	0	2	0	0	0
Rayment JW	Joe	25 Sep 1934	Hartlepool		1955	1957	Middlesbrough	Darlington	63	2	0	0	17	0	0	0
Reddish S	Shane	05 May 1971	Bolsover		1994	1995	Carlisle United	Harstad IL	43	0	1	0	0	0	0	0
Reed HD	Hugh	23 Aug 1950	Alexandria	1992	1976		Huddersfield Town		6	0	0	0	1	0	0	0
Reid TS	Tom	1915	Newcastle upon Tyne		1937		North Shields	North Shields	7	0	0	2	0	0	0	0
Reilly P	Peter				1924		East Fife	East Fife	1	0	0	0	0	0	0	0
Reilly WJ	Billy	24 Dec 1902	Lanark		1933		Southend United	Ashington	7	0	0	0	0	0	0	0
Richardson F	Fred	18 Aug 1925	Middlestone		1947	1948	Chelsea	Barnsley	149	16	0	0	35	8	0	0
					1952	1955	Chester	Thornley CW								
Richardson GC	Graham	20 Mar 1958	Sedgefield		1975	1980	Darlington	Easington Colliery	89	3	5	0	0	0	0	0
Richardson GEH	George	04 Dec 1891	Seaham Harbour	1969	1927		Bradford City	Bradford City	3	0	0	0	0	0	0	0
Richardson GW	George	1901	East Rainton		1924	1927	Derby County	Newport County	106	6	0	0	13	0	0	0
Richardson W	Billy	29 May 1909	Framwellgate Moor	1959	1928		United Bus Company	West Bromwich Albion	29	0	0	0	19	0	0	0
Richley L	Len	02 Jul 1924	Gateshead		1951	1953	Tonbridge	Kings Lynn	72	4	0	0	0	0	0	0
Ridley J	Jimmy	19 Jan 1903	Tanfield Lea		1932		Tow Law Town	Annfield Plain	8	0	0	0	1	0	0	0
Rimmington N	Norman	29 Nov 1923	Barnsley		1947	1951	Barnsley	Wisbech Town	124	7	0	0	0	0	0	0
Rivers JE	Jimmy	1908	Kirk Merrington		1928	1932	Kirk Merrington		129	4	0	0	0	0	0	0
Robbins P	Paddy	1914	Birr		1938		Oldham Athletic	Accrington Stanley	24	1	0	4	5	0	0	1
Roberts BJ	Ben	22 Jun 1975	Bishop Auckland		1995		Middlesbrough (loan)		4	0	0	1	0	0	0	0
Roberts J	Jeremy	24 Nov 1966	Middlesbrough		1983		Trainee	Leicester City	1	2	0	0	0	0	0	0
Roberts W	Windy	05 Jul 1939	Hartlepool		1958		Caledonians	Horden CW	3	3	0	0	0	0	0	0
Robertson A	Alec	1911	Beith		1935	1937	Kilmarnock	Horden CW	79	11	0	6	16	3	0	1
Robertson P	Peter		Greenock		1921	1922	Greenock Morton	Doncaster Rovers	36	2	0	0	18	0	0	0
Robertson T	Tommy	1906	Trimdon		1927	1928	Trimdon Colliery	Bury	35	1	0	0	0	0	0	0
Robinson A	Arthur		Middlestone Moor		1931		Cockfield	Crook	1	0	0	0	0	0	0	0
Robinson A	Tony	05 Nov 1958	Hebburn		1986		Blue Star	North Shields	2	0	0	0	0	0	0	0
Robinson DA	David	14 Jan 1965	Haverton Hill		1983	1985	Billingham Town	Halifax Town	66	3	2	3	1	0	0	0
Robinson H	Henry		Chilton		1930		Nelson	Spennymoor United	6	0	0	0	1	0	0	0
Robinson J	Joe	04 Mar 1919	Morpeth	1991	1938		Hexham Hearts	Blackpool	11	0	0	0	0	0	0	0
Robinson JN	John	10 Feb 1934	Middlesbrough		1959		Horden CW		9	0	0	0	0	0	0	0
Robinson JW	Billy	13 Apr 1932	Chester-le-Street		1955	1957	West Stanley	Gateshead	43	4	0	0	11	1	0	0
Robinson MW	Mark	22 Oct 1961	Middlesbrough		1982	1983	Guisborough Town	Whitby Town	35	2	2	0	4	0	0	0
Robinson WA	Billy	20 Dec 1898	Pegswood Colliery	1975	1924	1927	Pegswood Colliery	Bradford Park Avenue	62	1	0	0	38	1	0	0
Robson C	Cud	19 Oct 1900	High Wheatley	1972	1927		Southend United	Connah's Quay & Shotton	20	0	0	0	5	0	0	0
Robson DM	David	05 Oct 1966	Castle Eden		1986				1	0	0	0	0	0	0	0
Robson FE	Fred		Sunderland		1925		Durham City	Durham City	12	3	0	0	0	0	0	0
Robson L	Lance	27 Dec 1939	Newcastle upon Tyne		1969		Darlington	Stockton	8	0	0	0	2	0	0	0
Robson PT	Percy		Scotswood		1930		Wolverhampton W	West Stanley	3	0	0	0	1	0	0	0

Name		Date of Birth	Place of Birth	Died	First Season	Last Season	Previous Club	Next Club	Appearances League	FAC	FLC	Oth.	Goals Leag	FAC	FLC	Oth.
Rodger JJ	Jimmy	1914	Sunderland		1937		Sunderland		12	0	0	1	0	0	0	0
Rose LER	Les	30 Nov 1914	Weston-super-Mare	1987	1938		Bristol Rovers		12	2	0	0	0	0	0	0
Ross WE	Eric	19 Sep 1944	Belfast		1971		Northampton Town (loan)		2	0	0	0	0	0	0	0
Rowe GW	George	1899	Saltburn	1966	1921	1922	Loftus Albion	Derby County	28	2	0	0	1	0	0	0
Rowlands JH	John	07 Feb 1945	Liverpool		1975		Seattle Sounders	San Jose Earthquakes	49	5	0	0	10	1	0	0
					1976		San Jose Earthquakes	San Jose Earthquakes								
Rush D	David	15 May 1971	Sunderland		1991		Sunderland (loan)		8	0	0	0	2	0	0	0
Russell WH	Bill	19 Oct 1919	Coatbridge		1946	1947		Stockton	13	0	0	0	1	0	0	0
Rutherford J	Jack	06 Nov 1908	Nenthead		1937		Dartford	Barrow	4	1	0	2	0	0	0	0
Rylands DR	Dave	07 Mar 1953	Liverpool		1975		Hereford United (loan)		11	0	0	0	0	0	0	0
Sales RD	Ronnie	19 Sep 1920	South Shields		1950		Leyton Orient	South Shields	3	0	0	0	0	0	0	0
Saville AV	Andy	12 Dec 1964	Hull		1991	1992	Barnsley	Birmingham City	37	4	4	3	14	5	1	1
Scaife RH	Bobby	12 Oct 1955	Northallerton		1975	1977	Middlesbrough	Rochdale	80	5	2	0	10	2	0	0
Scorgie J	John	1896			1921		Birmingham	Redditch Town	4	0	0	0	2	0	0	0
Scott J	Jack	05 Feb 1908	Sunderland		1936	1937	Exeter City	Blyth Spartans	70	6	0	2	20	2	0	0
Scott JC	Joe	09 Jan 1930	Fatfield		1958	1959	Middlesbrough	York City	62	1	0	0	8	0	0	0
Scott MR	Mike	04 Dec 1945	Gosforth		1964		Burnley	Dutch football	2	0	1	0	0	0	0	0
Scott RW	Bobby	22 Feb 1953	Liverpool		1976		Wrexham	Rochdale	37	1	2	0	0	0	0	0
Scott S	Sammy	14 Jun 1922	Ashington		1946	1947	Ashington	Ashington	49	2	0	0	17	2	0	0
Scott T	Tom	1917	Newcatle upon Tyne		1936		Easington CW		6	0	0	1	0	0	0	0
Scrimshaw S	Stan	07 Aug 1915	Hartlepool		1935	1936	Easington CW	Bradford City	18	0	0	2	1	0	0	0
Self ER	Eddie	1914	South Shields		1936	1938	Bury	Hull City	114	8	0	7	16	5	0	0
Sharkey D	Nick	04 May 1943	Helensburgh		1970	1971	Mansfield Town	South Shields	60	2	1	0	12	0	1	0
Shaw RA	Robert	1900	South Hylton		1923		Robert Thompsons		12	0	0	0	0	0	0	0
Sheridan J	John	25 May 1938	Ramsgate		1966	1969	Notts County	Derby County	120	2	7	0	1	0	0	0
Sherratt JA	Jimmy	24 Dec 1921	Warrington		1948		Arsenal	Leyton Orient	20	0	0	0	4	0	0	0
Short W	Billy		Gosforth		1920	1921	Leeds City		18	6	0	0	0	4	0	0
Shotton JM	John	17 Aug 1971	Hartlepool		1990		Manchester United		1	0	0	0	0	0	0	0
Shotton R	Bobby	27 Oct 1910	Witton Gilbert		1931		Leeds United	Barnsley	33	1	0	0	0	0	0	0
Shoulder A	Alan	04 Feb 1953	Bishop Auckland		1985	1987	Carlisle United	Ferryhill Athletic	66	3	4	3	24	2	0	0
Shoulder J	Jimmy	11 Sep 1946	Esh Winning		1973	1974	Scarborough	retired	63	4	9	0	[illegible]	0	0	0
Siddall B	Barry	12 Sep 1954	Ellesmere Port		1989		Stockport County	West Bromwich Albion	11	0	0	0	[illegible]	0	0	0
Simmons HR	Harry	1910	Sunderland		1930		Bankhead Albion	Preston North End	31	1	0	0	17	0	0	0
Simpkin CJ	Chris	24 Apr 1944	Hull		1976	1977	Huddersfield Town	Scarborough	47	0	2	0	0	0	0	0
Simpkins K	Ken	21 Dec 1943	Wrexham		1963	1967	Wrexham	Boston United	121	8	5	0	1	0	0	0
Simpson R	Bobby	15 Sep 1915	Bishop Auckland		1947		Darlington	Stockton	13	1	0	0	1	0	0	0
Sinclair J	Jade	06 Nov 1971	Saltburn		1989		Middlesbrough		4	1	0	0	0	0	0	0
Skedd AS	Antony	19 May 1975	Hartlepool		1992	1994	Southampton	Spennymoor United	46	2	2	0	1	0	0	0
Skillen K	Keith	26 May 1948	Cockermouth		1975		Workington		6	0	1	0	1	0	1	0
Slater D	Darren	04 Jan 1979	Bishop Auckland		1995		Trainee		1	0	0	0	0	0	0	0
Sloan J	Jimmy	22 Feb 1924	Newcastle upon Tyne		1946	1951	Newcastle United		83	5	0	0	28	4	0	0
Sloan SM	Scott	14 Dec 1967	Wallsend		1994	1995	Falkirk		35	2	3	2	2	1	0	0
Small JH	John	14 Jan 1945	Billingham		1965		Head Wrightson		2	0	0	0	0	0	0	0
Smith A (1)	Tony	31 Dec 1943	Sunderland		1967		Watford		2	0	0	0	1	0	0	0
Smith A	Tony	20 Feb 1957	Sunderland		1984	1988	Halifax Town	Blue Star	200	11	10	12	8	1	0	1
Smith A (3)	Anthony	21 Sep 1971	Sunderland		1991		Sunderland (loan)		5	0	0	2	0	0	0	0
Smith DB	Dave	11 Dec 1950	Sheffield		1974	1975	Cambridge United	Gateshead United	42	4	2	0	13	1	0	0
Smith E	Eddie	22 Oct 1902	Sunderland		1923	1924	Robert Thompsons	Newport County	56	7	0	0	0	0	0	0
Smith G (1)	George	1905	Sherburn		1928		Arsenal		4	0	0	0	0	0	0	0
Smith G	George	07 Oct 1945	Newcastle upon Tyne		1977	1979	Swansea City	retired	85	7	4	0	2	0	0	0
Smith GH	George	13 Apr 1936	Nottingham		1967	1969	Notts County	Arnold	112	5	5	0	0	0	0	0
Smith J	Jackie	24 Apr 1936	Hartlepool		1953	1959	Local amateur	Watford	119	5	0	0	49	1	0	0
Smith M	Mick	28 Oct 1958	Sunderland		1989	1991	Seaham Red Star	retired	55	0	2	2	6	0	0	0
Smith RMS	Rob	25 Apr 1950	Hull		1972	1975	Grimsby Town	Scarborough	152	11	13	0	4	0	0	0
Smith RW	Bobby	14 Mar 1944	Prestbury		1971	1972	Chester	Bury	69	5	2	0	7	0	1	0
Smith TM	Trevor	04 Apr 1959	Middlesbrough		1976	1978	Whitby Town	Dartford	65	7	4	1	4	1	1	0
					1982		Whitby Town	Whitby Town								
Smith TP	Potter	1901	Newcastle upon Tyne	1978	1924		Hull City	Merthyr Town	30	5	0	0	7	1	0	0
Smith W	Billie	1914	Kirkcaldy		1937		Doncaster Rovers	Queen of the South	28	2	0	3	1	0	0	0
Smith WE	Billy	19 Nov 1900	Sheffield		1923	1924	Southend United	Rochdale	44	3	0	0	21	9	0	0
Smithies MH	Mike	18 Sep 1962	Billingham		1982	1986	Local amateur	Easington Colliery	35	1	0	1	0	0	0	0
Solan K	Ken	13 Oct 1948	Middlesbrough	1971	1968		Middlesbrough (loan)		6	2	0	0	1	0	0	0
Somers MR	Mick	27 Feb 1945	Mapperley		1966	1968	Torquay United	retired	66	0	5	0	3	0	0	0
Southall LN	Nicky	28 Jan 1972	Stockton-on-Tees		1991	1994	Darlington	Grimsby Town	138	8	7	8	24	0	3	0
Speirs G	Gardner	14 Apr 1963	Airdrie		1989		St Mirren	Airdrieonians	1	0	1	0	0	0	0	0
Spelman I	Isaac	09 Mar 1914	Newcastle upon Tyne		1946		Tottenham Hotspur	retired	25	2	0	0	0	0	0	0
Spelman MT	Mick	08 Dec 1950	Newcastle upon Tyne		1971	1976	Watford	Newcastle Sunday football	121	8	12	0	4	0	0	0
Spencer JT	John	1898	Stockton-on-Tees		1922		Stoke City		1	0	0	0	0	0	0	0
Spraggon F	Frank	27 Oct 1945	Marley Hill		1976		Minnesota Kicks	retired	1	0	0	0	0	0	0	0
Spry WH	Billy	1905	West Cramlington		1928		Blackpool	Blyth Spartans	15	0	0	0	2	0	0	0
Staff P	Paul	30 Aug 1962	Hartlepool		1979	1983	Apprentice	Aldershot	98	4	4	4	14	0	1	0
Stalker JAH	John	12 Mar 1959	Musselburgh		1982		Darlington		4	0	0	0	0	0	0	0
Stamper FFT	Frank	22 Feb 1926	Hartlepool		1949	1957	Colchester United	Blyth Spartans	301	25	0	0	26	4	0	0
Stephenson JR	Jackie	01 Jun 1899	Ryton	1969	1929		Norwich City	Crawcrook Albion	11	0	0	0	0	0	0	0
Stephenson P	Paul	02 Jan 1968	Wallsend		1997		York City		3	0	0	0	0	0	0	0
Stevenson A	Alan	06 Nov 1950	Staveley		1984		Rotherham United	retired	35	2	1	1	0	0	0	0
Stewart DC	David	20 May 1958	Belfast		1982		Goole Town	Grantham	8	0	0	0	0	0	0	0
Stimpson BG	Barrie	08 Feb 1964	Billingham		1980	1983	Billingham Schools	Chesterfield	86	5	6	7	2	0	0	0
					1984		Chesterfield	Gateshead								

Name		Date of Birth	Place of Birth	Died	First Season	Last Season	Previous Club	Next Club	Appearances League	FAC	FLC	Oth.	Goals Leag	FAC	FLC	Oth.
Stokes WD	Wayne	16 Feb 1965	Wolverhampton		1987	1989	Stockport County	Gateshead	62	6	4	3	1	0	0	1
Stokle D	David	01 Dec 1969	Hartlepool		1986	1989	Trainee		9	0	1	1	0	0	0	0
Stokoe G	Graham	17 Dec 1975	Newcastle upon Tyne		1995		Stoke City (loan)		8	0	0	0	0	0	0	0
Stonehouse D	Derek	18 Nov 1932	Lingdale		1963	1964	Middlesbrough	retired	34	4	0	0	0	0	0	0
Storer C	Charlie	29 Mar 1891	Ibstock		1924	1925	Bradford City		31	5	0	0	0	1	0	0
Storey J	John	1901	Marley Hill		1923		Preston North End	Grimsby Town	13	0	0	0	0	0	0	0
Storton SE	Stan	05 Jan 1939	Keighley		1964	1965	Darlington	Tranmere Rovers	72	6	3	0	0	0	0	0
Strong GJ	Jimmy	07 Jun 1916	Morpeth	1989	1933		Pegswood United	Chesterfield	1	0	0	0	0	0	0	0
Summerfield WH	Harry	1896	Haverton Hill		1920	1924	Haverton Hill		59	9	0	0	0	0	0	0
Sunderland JP	Jon	02 Nov 1975	Newcastle upon Tyne		1996		Scarborough	Gateshead	13	0	0	0	1	0	0	0
Sunley M	Mark	13 Oct 1971	Stockton-on-Tees		1994		Stalybridge Celtic	Spennymoor United	2	0	0	0	0	0	0	0
Sutcliffe P	Percy	1889	Ramsbottom		1923		Darlington		19	3	0	0	0	0	0	0
Sweeney A	Alan	31 Oct 1956	Glasgow		1979	1981	Emley		97	4	3	2	2	0	0	0
Sweeney PMF	Paul	10 Jan 1965	Glasgow		1994		Gateshead	Gateshead	1	0	1	0	0	0	0	0
Swift A	Arnold	21 Apr 1910	Hartlepool	1966	1930		Steelworks	Trimdon Grange Colliery	3	0	0	0	0	0	0	0
Sword TW	Tommy	12 Nov 1957	Newcastle upon Tyne		1986		Stockport County	Stockport County	18	1	2	2	0	0	0	0
Sykes K	Ken	29 Jan 1926	Darlington		1949		Middlesbrough	Murton CW	1	0	0	0	0	0	0	0
Tait MP	Mick	30 Sep 1956	Wallsend		1992	1993	Darlington	Gretna	139	3	11	2	3	0	1	0
					1994	1996	Gretna	retired								
Talia F	Frank	20 Jul 1972	Melbourne		1992		Blackburn Rovers (loan)		14	0	0	1	0	0	0	0
Taylor A	Allan	01 Dec 1905	North Shields	1981	1937		Tottenham Hotspur		25	1	0	1	0	0	0	0
Taylor GL	George	11 May 1926	Edinburgh		1953	1954	Aldershot	Easington CW	34	3	0	0	0	0	0	0
Taylor M	Mark	05 Dec 1962	Hartlepool		1982		Henry Smith BC	Wingate	1	0	0	2	0	0	0	0
Taylor PMR	Mark	20 Nov 1964	Hartlepool		1983	1985	Brinkburn Juniors	Blackpool	47	2	1	3	4	1	0	0
Telford R	Bob		Invergarry		1926		Leith Athletic	Doncaster Rovers	3	0	0	0	0	0	0	0
Telling H	Bert	1913	Swindon		1937		Crystal Palace		2	0	0	0	0	0	0	0
Thayne W	Billy	13 Dec 1909	Hartlepool	1986	1930	1933	Crystal Palace	Luton Town	101	6	0	1	8	0	0	0
Theaker CA	Cam	08 Dec 1912	Spalding	1992	1947		Newcastle United		14	1	0	0	0	0	0	0
Thomas E	Ernie	1915	Rhos		1937	1938	Tottenham Hotspur		62	2	0	3	0	0	0	0
Thomas JW	John	05 Aug 1958	Wednesbury		1991		Preston North End	Halifax Town	7	0	0	0	1	0	0	0
Thompson AS	Stan		Durham		1935		Brighton & Hove Albion	Exeter City	34	4	0	1	11	0	0	1
Thompson JE	Jimmy		Thornaby-on-Tees		1929	1931	Whitby United	Falkirk	67	0	0	0	22	0	0	0
Thompson KJ	Kevan	08 Sep 1948	Middlesbrough		1969	1970	Threadhalls	Stockton	6	0	0	0	1	0	0	0
Thompson MG	Malcolm	19 Oct 1946	Beverley		1968	1969	Goole Town	Gillingham	46	1	2	0	9	0	0	0
Thompson N	Norman	1916	West Moor		1937		Sheffield United	Ashington	1	0	0	0	0	0	0	0
Thompson P	Peter	16 Feb 1936	Blackhall		1957	1958	Wrexham	Derby County	138	6	1	0	56	5	0	0
					1963	1965	Bournemouth & BA	Boston United								
Thompson PDZ	Paul	17 Apr 1973	Newcastle upon Tyne		1991	1994	Redheugh Boys	Gateshead	56	1	5	2	9	0	1	0
Thompson R (1)	Bob		Eldon		1926		Bury	Goole Town	4		0	0	3	0	0	0
Thompson R	Ray	21 Oct 1925	Leeholme	1996	1946	1957	Sunderland		396	27	0	0	2	0	0	0
Thompson TR	Tommy	1903	South Shields	1968	1921	1922	Local amateur		10	0	0	0	0	0	0	0
Thompson W	Billy	1886	Morpeth		1921		Newport County	Jarrow	1	0	0	0	0	0	0	0
Thoms H	Harry	19 Nov 1896	Greatham	1970	1920	1921	Greatham	Derby County	33	11	0	0	1	2	0	0
Thomson KG	Ken	25 Feb 1930	Aberdeen	1969	1962		Middlesbrough	retired	28	1	0	0	2	0	0	0
Thomson R	Bobby	21 Mar 1955	Glasgow		1987		Blackpool	Hamilton Academical	3	0	1	0	0	0	0	0
Thornton P	Percy		Wigton		1929	1932	West Stanley	Workington	97	4	0	0	10	2	0	0
Tinkler J	John	24 Aug 1968	Trimdon		1986	1991	Juniors	Preston North End	170	11	10	12	7	1	1	2
Tither J	Jack		South Shields		1929	1932	South Shields Corinthians	Spennymoor United	15	0	0	0	1	0	0	0
Todd A	Alex	07 Nov 1929	South Shields		1952	1953	South Shields Butchers	South Shields	4	0	0	0	0	0	0	0
Toman JA	Andy	07 Mar 1962	Northallerton		1986	1988	Bishop Auckland	Darlington	112	9	4	7	28	4	0	0
Tootill GA	George	20 Oct 1913	Walkden		1947		Sheffield United		18	0	0	0	0	0	0	0
Towse T	Tom	1894	Lazenby	1961	1921	1922	South Bank		13	1	0	0	5	0	0	0
Trail DJF	Derek	02 Jan 1946	Edinburgh		1969		Workington	South Sydney	39	2	0	0	2	0	0	0
Tremain S	Syd	1912	Lingdale		1932		Pease & Partners	Preston North End	16	0	0	0	0	0	0	0
Trewick J	John	03 Jun 1957	Bedlington		1989		Bromsgrove Rovers		8	0	0	1	0	0	0	0
Tunks RW	Roy	21 Jan 1951	Wuppertal, Germany		1988		Wigan Athletic	Preston North End	5	0	0	0	0	0	0	0
Tunstall EW	Eric	21 Nov 1950	Hartlepool		1968		St Patricks Juniors	Newcastle United	1	0	0	0	0	0	0	0
Tupling S	Steve	11 Jul 1964	Wensleydale		1989	1991	Cardiff City	Darlington	89	4	6	7	3	0	0	0
Turnbull TM	Terry	18 Oct 1945	Stockton-on-Tees		1976		Crook Town	Gateshead	13	0	1	0	3	0	1	0
Turner R	Richard	1918	Whitburn Colliery		1937		Hetton United		1	1	0	0	0	0	0	0
Turner RP	Rob	18 Sep 1966	Easington		1986		Cardiff City (loan)		7	0	0	0	1	0	0	0
Underwood WK	Bill	28 Dec 1921	Brigg		1947		South Bank	Shildon	1	0	0	0	0	0	0	0
Vass S	Steve	10 Jan 1954	Leicester		1979	1980	Wycombe Wanderers	Huddersfield Town	4	0	1	0	0	0	0	0
Veart R	Bobby	11 Aug 1944	Hartlepool		1970	1972	Whitby Town	South Shields	71	5	2	0	12	4	0	0
Veitch T	Tommy	16 Oct 1949	Edinburgh		1976		Halifax Town	Morton	10	0	0	0	0	0	0	0
Venus M	Mark	06 Apr 1967	Hartlepool		1984		Trainee	Leicester City	4	0	0	1	0	0	0	0
Vitty R	Ron	18 Apr 1927	Chilton		1949		Charlton Athletic	Bradford City	7	0	0	0	0	0	0	0
Waddell W	Willie	16 Apr 1950	Denny		1971	1973	Barnsley	Dundalk	48	4	2	0	9	0	0	0
Waddle AR	Alan	09 Jun 1954	Wallsend		1983		Hong Kong football	Peterborough United	16	0	1	2	2	0	0	1
					1984		Peterborough United	Swansea City								
Waite GH	George	01 Mar 1894	Bradford	1972	1926		Clapton Orient	York City	26	0	0	0	7	0	0	0
Walker JM	Jim	10 Jun 1947	Northwich		1969		Derby County (loan)		10	0	0	0	0	0	0	0
Walker JR	John	1901	Wheatley Hill		1922	1923	Wheatley Hill	Spennymoor United	24	2	0	0	0	0	0	0
Walker NS	Nigel	07 Apr 1959	Gateshead		1985	1986	Chester City	Blyth Spartans	82	3	4	3	8	0	0	0
Wallace J	Jack	20 Jun 1910	Blantyre	1992	1938		Derry City	Belfast Celtic	31	2	0	4	0	0	0	0
Waller H	Horace				1930	1931	Perseverance	Blackhall CW	10	1	0	0	7	1	0	0
Wallis DR	Derek	06 Oct 1937	Hartlepool		1963		Durham City	West Auckland Town	2	0	0	0	0	0	0	0
Walsh A	Alan	09 Dec 1956	Hartlepool		1994		Taunton Town	Bath City	4	1	2	2	1	0	0	0
Walsh W	Billy		Littletown		1923	1924	Horden Athletic		28	5	0	0	0	0	0	0

Name		Date of Birth	Place of Birth	Died	First Season	Last Season	Previous Club	Next Club	Appearances League	FAC	FLC	Oth.	Goals Leag	FAC	FLC	Oth.
Walton J	Jimmy	03 Dec 1904	Sacriston	1952	1926		Brentford		2	0	0	0	0	0	0	0
Walton PA	Paul	02 Jul 1979	Sunderland		1995	1996	Trainee	Bishop Auckland	10	0	0	0	0	0	0	0
Wann JD	Dennis	17 Nov 1950	Blackpool		1975		York City (loan)		2	0	0	0	0	0	0	0
Ward W	Billy	30 Jun 1949	Chester-le-Street		1971	1972	Spennymoor United	Seaham CW	95	3	3	0	10	0	1	0
					1972	1974	Shildon	Gateshead United								
Wardrobe B	Barrie	03 Jul 1963	Newcastle upon Tyne		1984		Sunderland	Gateshead	27	0	0	0	2	0	0	0
Warnock N	Neil	01 Dec 1948	Sheffield		1971	1972	Rotherham United	Scunthorpe United	60	2	4	0	5	1	0	0
Warren ET	Ernie	14 Sep 1910	Sunderland		1934		Northampton Town	South Shields	15	0	0	0	0	0	0	0
Watling BJ	Barry	16 Jul 1946	Walthamstow		1972	1975	Notts County	Sheffield Wednesday	139	7	12	0	0	0	0	0
Watson J	John	10 Apr 1959	Dewsbury		1978	1982	Huddersfield Town		44	3	6	2	0	0	0	0
Waugh K	Ken	06 Aug 1933	Newcastle upon Tyne		1956	1961	Newcastle United	Australian football	195	9	2	0	0	0	0	0
Wayman BO	Brian	1902	Nottingham		1924		Aberdare Athletic		5	0	0	0	0	0	0	0
Weatherspoon C	Charlie	03 Oct 1929	Newcastle upon Tyne		1952		Sheffield United	Hexham Hearts	3	0	0	0	2	0	0	0
Weir A	Alan	01 Sep 1959	South Shields		1983		Rochdale	Eppleton CW	10	0	1	0	0	0	0	0
Welford W	Bill	14 Apr 1934	Newcastle upon Tyne		1958		Crook Town	Kings Lynn	8	4	0	0	0	0	0	0
Welsh E	Eric	01 May 1942	Belfast		1971		Torquay United	Port Elizabeth	15	2	2	0	2	0	0	0
Welsh W	Billy	02 May 1904	Douglas Water	1978	1933		Gateshead	Jarrow	3	0	0	0	0	0	0	0
Wensley H	Harry		Eldon		1925	1926	Shildon	Shildon	76	4	0	0	37	1	0	0
West CW	Colin	19 Sep 1967	Middlesbrough		1993		Dundee	Bishop Auckland	36	1	4	2	5	0	1	0
West N	Norman	1918	Walker		1937	1945	Walker Celtic		19	2	0	1	7	0	0	0
Westmoreland W	Bill	1911	New Herrington		1934		Army football	Herrington CW	7	0	0	0	0	0	0	0
Whellans R	Robbie	14 Feb 1969	Harrogate		1987		Bradford C (loan, 2 spells)		11	1	0	1	1	0	0	0
White D	Dennis	10 Nov 1948	Hartlepool		1967	1972	Local amateur	South Shields	58	1	4	0	0	0	0	0
Whitelock A	Arthur	31 Jul 1931	Stockton-on-Tees		1950		South Bank		6	0	0	0	0	0	0	0
Whitfield M	Mick	17 Oct 1962	Sunderland		1983		Sunderland	Horden CW	16	2	2	0	0	0	0	0
Whyte C	Crawford	04 Dec 1907	Wallsend	1984	1937		Tranmere Rovers	Clapton Orient	5	1	0	3	0	0	0	0
Wiggett DJ	Dave	25 May 1957	Sheffield	1978	1976	1977	Lincoln City	deceased	54	4	2	0	1	0	0	0
Wigham J	Johnny	1911	Hebburn	1959	1931	1938	Hebburn Colliery	retired	264	23	0	4	95	7	0	4
Wildon LE	Eric	05 Apr 1924	Middlesbrough		1947	1954	Price's	Stockton	200	15	0	0	87	2	0	0
Wilkie D	Derrick	27 Jul 1939	Browney		1961	1963	Middlesbrough		74	3	1	0	0	0	0	0
Wilkinson J	Joe	08 Dec 1934	Seaham		1959	1961	Bradford City		74	3	2	0	0	0	0	0
Wilkinson K	Ken	09 May 1924	Gateshead		1946	1948	Huddersfield Town	Stockton	53	3	0	0	5	0	0	0
Wilkinson T	Tommy	08 May 1931	Blackhall		1953	1957	Blackhall Dynamoes	Horden CW	22	1	0	0	0	0	0	0
Wilks F	Fred		Haverton Hill		1932		Sheffield Wednesday	Billingham Synthonia	15	2	0	0	0	0	0	0
Willetts J	Joe	12 Jul 1924	Shotton		1946	1955	Newcastle United	Horden CW	239	19	0	0	20	2	0	0
Williams JT	Johnny		Hartlepool		1927	1928	Local amateur	Grimsby Town	41	2	0	0	1	0	0	0
Williams PA	Paul	08 Sep 1963	Sheffield		1989		Scunthorpe United	Stockport County	8	1	0	1	0	0	0	0
Willis JG	George	25 Jul 1933	Shotton		1954	1958	Leeds United	Blyth Spartans	25	0	0	0	7	0	0	0
Willox A	Sandy	05 Nov 1923	Lossiemouth		1951		Cowdenbeath		6	0	0	0	0	0	0	0
Wilson H	Harry	29 Nov 1953	Hetton-le-Hole		1983		Darlington	Crook Town	16	2	2	0	0	0	0	0
Wilson J	John	1909	Trimdon		1930		Horden CW		1	0	0	0	0	0	0	0
Wilson JB	Jack	1917	New Washington		1938		Margate		25	2	0	4	0	0	0	0
Wilson PM	Phil	05 Feb 1972	Billingham		1989		Trainee		1	0	0	0	0	0	0	0
Winn S	Steve	16 Sep 1959	Thornaby-on-Tees		1982		Scunthorpe United	South Bank	1	0	0	0	0	0	0	0
Winstanley CJ	Craig	23 Aug 1978	Hartlepool		1996		Trainee	Bishop Auckland	1	0	0	0	0	0	0	0
Woffinden RS	Richard	20 Feb 1917	Rotherham	1987	1938		Barnsley	Barnsley	15	0	0	0	1	0	0	0
Woods C	Cyril	1915	Tinsley		1938		Swindon Town	Hull City	25	1	0	0	6	1	0	0
Worthington PR	Bob	22 Apr 1947	Halifax		1974		Southend United (loan)		6	0	0	0	0	0	0	0
Wratten P	Paul	28 Nov 1970	Middlesbrough		1992	1993	Manchester United	Bishop Auckland	57	3	5	2	1	0	0	0
Wright GC	Cliff	18 Oct 1944	Lingdale		1964	1969	Middlesbrough	Darlington	184	8	9	0	31	2	1	0
Wright GJ	Gary	15 Sep 1964	Sunderland		1982		Oldham Athletic	Chester-le-Street Town	12	0	0	1	0	0	0	0
Wright J	Jim	11 Sep 1910	Okehampton		1938		Swansea Town		34	0	0	4	0	0	0	0
Wright RL	Ralph	03 Aug 1947	Newcastle upon Tyne		1970		Bradford Park Avenue	Stockport County	24	0	1	0	3	0	0	0
Wrightson JM	John	1901	Sunderland		1923		Robert Thompsons	Willington	1	0	0	0	0	0	0	0
Yews TP	Tom	28 Feb 1902	Wingate	1966	1920	1922	Local amateur	West Ham United	39	8	0	0	3	0	0	0
Young A	Alf	27 Nov 1900	Wingate	1975	1923	1927	Wingate	Gillingham	123	8	0	0	1	0	0	0
Young J	John	1906	Whitburn		1927	1928	Leeds United	Spennymoor United	19	0	0	0	4	0	0	0
Young JD	John	09 Nov 1951	Hartlepool		1968		Newcastle United		3	0	0	0	0	0	0	0
Young MS	Matty	1901	Cambois		1923		Preston Colliery	Reading	29	3	0	0	3	0	0	0
Young R	Ron	31 Aug 1945	Dunston		1968	1972	Hull City	South Shields	186	8	5	0	40	3	3	0
Younger W	Billy	22 Mar 1940	Whitley Bay		1962		Doncaster Rovers	Ramsgate Athletic	37	1	2	0	4	0	1	0

Name		Date of Birth	Place of Birth	Died	First Season	Last Season	Previous Club	Next Club	Appearances League	FAC	FLC	Oth.	Goals Leag	FAC	FLC	Oth.

Played in FA Cup only (other than 1945/46)

Woof W	Billy	16 Aug 1956	Gateshead		1983		Gateshead		0	2	0	0	0	0	0	0
Hold R	Ronnie	1949			1968		Local amateur	Hartlepool BWOB	0	1	0	0	0	0	0	0
Potter CB	Cecil	14 Nov 1888	West Hoathly	1975	1920	1921	Hull City	retired	0	11	0	0	0	1	0	0

Played in 1945/46 FA Cup Only

Brown					1945				0	1	0	0	0	0	0	0
Cliff A					1945		Local amateur		0	1	0	0	0	0	0	0
Gorman J	Jimmy	03 Mar 1910	Liverpool	1991	1945		Sunderland		0	2	0	0	0	0	0	0
Holland J					1945		Local amateur		0	1	0	0	0	1	0	0
Keeys F	Fred				1945		Thornville	Murton CW	0	1	0	0	0	0	0	0
Lewis L					1945		Army football		0	1	0	0	0	0	0	0
Robertson LV	Len	01 Mar 1916	Middlesbrough	1979	1945		Local amateur	Watford	0	2	0	0	0	0	0	0
Troman JV					1945		Local amateur		0	2	0	0	0	0	0	0
Woods PB	Paddy				1945				0	1	0	0	0	0	0	0

Played in FL Cup only

Harbron A	Andy	14 Dec 1955	Middlesbrough		1990		Billingham Synthonia	Billingham Synthonia	0	0	1	0	0	0	0	0
Albeson B	Brian	14 Dec 1946	Oldham		1975		Stockport County	Gateshead United	0	0	1	0	0	0	0	0
Young, Roy	Roy	1949			1969		Eastbourne United	Eastbourne United	0	0	1	0	0	0	0	0

Played in Miscellaneous games only

Wilson S	Stuart				1985				0	0	0	1	0	0	0	0
Halliday R	Robert				1938		Brandon SC		0	0	0	2	0	0	0	0
Spencer T	Tim	1920			1938		Brandon SC	Blackhall CW	0	0	0	3	0	0	0	1
Mathison G	George	24 Nov 1909	Walker	1989	1937		Burnley		0	0	0	1	0	0	0	0
Oxley G	George	1918			1936		Hetton Juniors	Usworth Colliery	0	0	0	1	0	0	0	0
Colquhoun DM	Duncan	24 Jul 1915	Glenfruin		1934		Sheffield Wednesday	Kings Park	0	0	0	1	0	0	0	1

Played in abandoned 1939/40 season only

Daniels G	George	1913	Winsford		1939		Crystal Palace	
Deacon J	Jimmy	23 Jan 1906	Glasgow		1939		Southend United	
Dodds LS	Les	20 Sep 1912	Patishead	1967	1939		Clapton Orient	
Earl AT	Stan	10 Feb 1915	Gateshead		1939		York City	Stockport County
Foreman JJ	Jack	1913	Tanfield		1939		Workington	
Mantle J	Joe	09 May 1908	Hetton-le-Hole	1977	1939		Heart of Midlothian	
Turner CJ	Charlie	1911	Athlone		1939		West Ham United	

Nearly Men

The following players have been named as substitute on one or more occasions to the end of season 1997/98, but never made a first team appearance:

Paddy Conway
Graham Cooper
Kenny Cramman
Jason Cuthbertson
Peter Davies
Steve Graham
Colin Hutchinson
Neil Maughan
Paul Lowery
Paul Linyard

Ernie Phythian

Rob McKinnon

Ambrose Fogarty

John McGovern

Keith Houchen

Bobby Moncur

Cyril Knowles

Alan Murray